Legal Reform in the Contemporary Socialist World

Legal Reform in the Contemporary Socialist World

NGOC SON BUI
Professor of Asian Laws, University of Oxford, UK

OXFORD
UNIVERSITY PRESS

OXFORD
UNIVERSITY PRESS

Great Clarendon Street, Oxford, OX2 6DP,
United Kingdom

Oxford University Press is a department of the University of Oxford.
It furthers the University's objective of excellence in research, scholarship,
and education by publishing worldwide. Oxford is a registered trade mark of
Oxford University Press in the UK and in certain other countries

Published in the United States of America by Oxford University Press
198 Madison Avenue, New York, NY 10016, United States of America

British Library Cataloguing in Publication Data

Data available

Library of Congress Control Number: 2023951620

ISBN 9780192857255

DOI: 10.1093/9780191948053.001.0001

Printed and bound by
CPI Group (UK) Ltd, Croydon, CR0 4YY

Acknowledgements

I especially thank Deans Mindy Chen-Wishart and John Armour at the Oxford Law Faculty and Principal Elish Angiolini at St Hugh's College for their continued support and encouragement. I also thank my colleagues Nicholas Barber, Matthew Erie, Tarun Khaitan, Van Anh Le, Natalie Mrockova, Fernanda Pirie, and Ewan Smith for their support and academic conversations.

Colleagues and friends have provided continued support, advice, and useful comments on my writings. I particularly thank Albert Chen, Hualing Fu, Tom Ginsburg, Andrew Harding, Jyh-An Lee, Pip Nicholson, Dan W Puchniak, Cheryl Saunders, Maartje De Visser, and Han Zhu. I thank Angela Huyue Zhang and HKU's Philip KH Wong Centre for Chinese Law for supporting my visiting fellowship here.

The Oxford Law Faculty Research Support Fund, which made the field trips to Laos and Vietnam possible, is acknowledged. Colleagues and friends have assisted my field trips to these two countries. I especially thank Kham Phaeng, Kazuo Fukuda, Vũ Văn Huân, Phùng Thị Hoàn, and Nguyễn Văn Tùng. I thank my Lao and Vietnamese correspondents for sharing useful knowledge.

Some portions of this book have been based on my three earlier articles: 'Vertical Law and Development' (2021) 54 Cornell International Law Journal; 'The Socialist Precedent' (2019) 52 Cornell International Law Journal; 'The Law of China and Vietnam in Comparative Law' (2017) 41 Fordham International Law Journal.

I am extremely grateful to my family for their love and support. I dedicate this book to my virtuous wife Nguyễn Thị Phượng (Jolie) and my lovely children Bùi Tố Nguyên (Fifi) and Bùi Ngọc Long (Fifa).

Contents

Table of Legislation

NATIONAL LEGISLATION

China

CONSTITUTION

STATUTES

France

Hong Kong

Japan

Laos

CONSTITUTION

STATUTES

North Korea

CONSTITUTION

STATUTES

Russia

Vietnam

CONSTITUTION

STATUTES

Soviet Union

CONSTITUTION

STATUTES

INTERNATIONAL INSTRUMENTS

Agreements, Treaties and Conventions

Free Trade Agreements

PART I

FOUNDATIONS

1
Introduction
The Socialist World in Comparative Law

I. WHAT IS THIS BOOK ABOUT?

From a comparative perspective, this book explores legal reform in five current socialist states—China, Vietnam, Laos, North Korea, and Cuba—over the last four decades. Since the fall of the Soviet Union and with the rise of globalization, these states have retained but significantly reformed socialist legal systems rooted in Marxist theory and Soviet law.

China, officially the People's Republic of China, the populous country of over 1.4 billion people, has built a sophisticated legal system since the introduction of the *Gǎigé kāifàng* (Reform and Opening-up) in 1978. The national legislature has enacted nearly 300 laws covering all aspects of the society. China has also built a sophisticated bureaucracy and judiciary. The development of the legal profession is also remarkable: over 522,000 lawyers currently work in over 34,000 law firms.

Like China, Vietnam (officially the Socialist Republic of Vietnam), a country of around 100 million residents, has comprehensively reformed their legal system since the introduction of the reform programme *Đổi mới* (Renovation) in 1986. The national legislature enacted over 200 laws covering all aspects of society. The courts handle thousands of legal cases annually. Over 16,000 lawyers provide legal services in 4,000 law firms.

In 1986—the same year Vietnam launched the *Renovation* programme—Laos (officially the Lao People's Democratic Republic), a landlocked country of over 7 million people, introduced a similar market reform programme called *Chintanakhan Mai* (New Thinking). Since then, Laos has comprehensively reformed its legal system. In 2009, the country adopted a master plan for rule of law reform. The implementation of the plan has significantly improved the legal system. Laos also enacted over 100 laws. The functional court system decides thousands of cases annually. Over 300 lawyers work in over 60 law firms.

North Korea (officially the Democratic People's Republic of Korea), a country of over 25 million people, does not have a comprehensive programme of legal reform but has introduced sporadic adjustments to the legal system. In this hermit kingdom, which has often been regarded as lacking legality, over 200 laws have been enacted, over 100 courts operate, and around 500 lawyers provide legal services.

Legal Reform in the Contemporary Socialist World. Ngoc Son Bui, Oxford University Press. © Ngoc Son Bui 2024.
DOI: 10.1093/9780191948053.003.0001

Cuba (officially the Republic of Cuba), an island country of over 10 million people, has undertaken extensive legal reforms. In the late 1980s and early 1990s, the country undertook sporadic legal reforms to respond to economic depression due to the demise of the Soviet bloc and the dissolution of the Soviet Union. Since the introduction of the reform policy Updating Socialism in 2011, Cuba has engaged in extensive legal reforms, including the adoption of the new Constitution in 2019 and a plan to enact over seventy laws. The court system has been strengthened, including the adoption of judicial review of violations of constitutional rights. Around 2,000 lawyers provide legal services in the island.

This book explores how and why these socialist countries have reformed their legal systems. It is the sequel to my preceding book *Constitutional Change in the Contemporary Socialist World*, which explores the change to the constitutions in the five socialist countries.[1] Having explored constitutional change, I think it is important to move further to explore the change to the national legal systems at the sub-constitutional level in these socialist countries. This book, however, focuses on the macro level of legal reforms. It explores general patterns of legislative reform and institutional legal reform.[2] The book examines:

- *Legislative reform*, including legislative process, achievements of legislative enactments, and the continuity of socialist law.
- *Administrative reform*, including achievements in public administration, reforms of administrative law, and the continuity of socialist administrative law.
- *Judicial reform*, including structural, functional, and personnel changes in the court system and the continuity of the socialist courts.
- *Legal profession reform*, including changes in the quantity and quality of lawyers, lawyers' role in the legal system, and the continuity of the socialist lawyers.

The macro-institutional focus of this book is due to two reasons. First, given the scope of a book dealing with five countries, it is not realistic to extensively explore legal reforms in specific areas of law (criminal law, business law, land law, labour law, and environmental law, etc.). Of course, this book refers to specific areas of law to illustrate legislative reforms. Second, the focus on the institutional aspects of the legal system allows us to understand legal reforms in the socialist world in a broader and systematic way. The achievements (except in the case of North Korea), challenges to socialist legal reforms, and the continuity of socialist law are systemic, not merely specific.

[1] Bui Ngoc Son, *Constitutional Change in the Contemporary Socialist World* (OUP 2020).

[2] For a similar institutional focus on China's legal reform, see Randall Peerenboom, *China's Long March toward Rule of Law* (CUP 2002).

II. Comparative Context

Legal reforms in the current socialist countries (perhaps except China) have been underexplored in comparative law scholarship. Scholars have explored legal reform and legal change in various contexts, such as Western democracies, post-communist states in Eastern Europe and the former Soviet Union, and other developing and transitional countries.[3] However, the socialist experiences of legal reforms have been understudied. To be sure, a rich body of scholarship has explored legal reforms in China.[4] But this literature tends to be nation focused and has not yet significantly compared legal reforms in China with other socialist countries. Some works have explored and compared important aspects of legal reforms in China and Vietnam.[5] These works have not yet considerably engaged with legal reforms in three other socialist countries: Laos, North Korea, and Cuba.[6] There is not yet a comprehensive and comparative treatment of legal reforms in the five socialist countries. This monograph seeks to fill in this gap.

The book also seeks to relocate socialist law and its reform dynamics in mainstream comparative law. During the Soviet era, socialist law was the main topic of comparative law scholarship.[7] After the collapse of the Soviet Union, socialist law was considered dead and has nearly disappeared from comparative law scholarship.[8] In fact, socialist law is still alive vividly in various aspects of the legal systems in China, Vietnam, Laos, North Korea, and Cuba. The current legal systems in these countries are the continued legal embodiments of Marxist-Leninist arguments for socialism. Four decades of legal reforms present the resilience, rather than dissolution, of socialist law. Socialist law in both traditional and reformative forms should be relocated to a main place in comparative law. The incorporation of

[3] M Schwartzberg, *Democracy and Legal Change* (CUP 2007); Peter H Solomon, Jr and Kaja Gadowska, *Legal Change in Post-Communist State: Progress, Reversions, Explanations* (Columbia University Press 2019); Tim Lindsey (ed), *Law Reform in Developing and Transitional States* (Routledge 2005).

[4] Y Zhao and M Ng (eds), *Chinese Legal Reform and the Global Legal Order: Adoption and Adaptation* (CUP 2017); Stanley B Lubman (ed), *The Evolution of Law Reform in China: An Uncertain Path* (Edward Elgar 2012); Randall Peerenboom, *China Modernizes: Threat to the West or Model for the Rest?* (OUP 2008); Stanley B Lubman, *Bird in a Cage: Legal Reform in China after Mao* (Stanford University Press 1999).

[5] John Gillespie and Albert HY Chen (eds), *Legal Reforms in China and Vietnam: A Comparison of Asian Communist Regimes* (Routledge 2010); John Gillespie and Pip Nicholson (eds), *Asian Socialism and Legal Change: The Dynamics of Vietnamese and Chinese Reform* (ANU 2005).

[6] There are some country-focused writings on these countries. See Matias F Travieso-Diaz, *The Laws and Legal System of a Free-Market Cuba: A Prospectus for Business* (Quorum Books 1997); Marjorie Zatz, *Producing Legality: Law and Socialism in Cuba* (Routledge 1994); Greyson Bryan, Scott Horton, and Robin Radin, 'Foreign Investment Laws and Regulations of the Democratic People's Republic of Korea' (1998) 21 Fordham Int'l LJ 1677; Darren C Zook, 'Reforming North Korea: Law, Politics, and the Market Economy' (2012) 48 Stan J Int'l L 131; Martin Stuart-Fox, 'Politics and Reform in the Lao People's Democratic Republic' Working Paper No 126 (University of Queensland, November 2005).

[7] Rene David and John EC Brierley, *Major Legal Systems in the World Today: An Introduction to the Comparative Study of Law* (Stevens 1968).

[8] William Partlett and Eric C Ip, 'Is Socialist Law Really Dead?' (2016) 48 NYU JILP 473.

socialist law and its reforms can enrich traditional comparative law, post-modern comparative law, and global comparative law.[9]

To begin with, the study of socialist law and its reforms can enrich traditional comparative law. The project of taxonomizing the world's legal systems in traditional comparative law can be enriched by the re-addition of the socialist legal tradition. The current legal systems in China, Vietnam, Laos, North Korea, and Cuba belong to the socialist legal tradition. This study demonstrates the continuity of socialist legal tradition in these countries at a macro and institutional level. It is possible to explore at the micro level the embodiment of socialist concepts and principles in specific substantive areas of law (such as economic statism in civil law and economic law; right statism in social law) in these countries. Moreover, the diversity of socialist law and its reform models cast doubt on the functionalist approach in traditional comparative law, which tends to overemphasize the common legal features.[10]

The study of socialist law and its reform can also contribute to post-modern comparative law, which focuses on the way similar legal words and concepts have different meanings in different legal systems.[11] Socialist law is not autonomous. It is not merely controlled by professional lawyers but is understood and practiced by a complex network of various actors. Socialist law and its reforms provide rich data for post-modernist comparative studies of law and ideology, law and politics, law and society, and legal pluralism.

Finally, the incorporation of socialist law and its reform dynamics can enrich global comparative law. The five countries provide rich data for the study of legal transplants and global legal diffusion. The transplants of socialist law in the five countries provide a laboratory for comparative examination of legal transplants. Moreover, reforms of socialist law (particularly in China, Vietnam, and Laos) provide significant data for study of legal global diffusion. Last but not least, the global revival of the 'law and development' movement has resonated in the socialist countries (except North Korea) whose legal reforms have been supported by external donors.[12] Socialist law and its reforms provide a significant venue for comparative study of law and development.

Socialist law and its reforms can also be located within the emerging body of scholarship on comparative authoritarian law. The global expansion of authoritarianism[13] has resulted in great academic interest in authoritarian law in general

[9] I adopt these three dimensions of comparative law from Mathias Siems, *Comparative Law* (3rd edn, CUP 2022).

[10] For functionalism, see Konrad Zweigert and Hein Kotz, *An Introduction to Comparative Law* (OUP 1998) 34.

[11] Siems (n 9) 142.

[12] For the evolution of law and development movement, see Michael Trebilcock, 'Law and Development: Forty Years after "Scholars in Self-Estrangement"' (2016) 66 Univ Tor LJ 301.

[13] Sarah Repucci and Amy Slipowitz, *The Global Expansion of Authoritarian Rule* (Freedom in the World 2022).

comparative law and comparative constitutional law.[14] Comparative authoritarian law is mainly the comparative study of how and why law and legal institutions operate under the authoritarian regimes, although this emerging area of inquiry also considers authoritarian legal practices in liberal democracies.[15] Law and legal institutions of socialist countries (particularly China and to some extent Vietnam) are often discussed in comparative study of authoritarian law.[16] The inclusion of socialist law and its reforms in other socialist countries (Laos, North Korea, and Cuba) can enrich comparative authoritarian law. The question to consider is how law in the socialist one-party regimes is similar to and different from law in other forms of authoritarianism (eg personal and military).

III. Approach and Methodology

The book adopts a comparative approach. It is comparative in internal and external senses. First, in the internal sense, the book compares legal reforms among the five socialist states. The 'controlled comparison' follows the 'most similar cases' principle in small-N comparative legal studies.[17] The five countries in consideration, namely China, Cuba, Laos, North Korea, and Vietnam, share many common features. They all have a communist history, survived the communist fall, and operate a socialist legal system. During the post-Soviet era, all the five socialist countries have adapted their legal systems. However, the scale, and pace, and influential factors of their legal reform present considerable variations. This book therefore not only explores the common features but also seeks to identify different models of socialist legal reforms. Second, in the external sense, the book situates socialist legal reforms within the global debates in comparative law, particularly comparative legal traditions, legal diffusion or transplant, and law and development.

The book mainly adopts qualitative methodology, although it also uses and creates quantitative data. It relies on local materials, including legal codes, statutes, reports, and political documents guiding law reforms. The book also involves empirical work, although this work was limited by the Covid 19 pandemic. Between 2022 and 2023, I conducted two field research trips to Laos and two field research trips to Vietnam to interview local officials, scholars, lawyers, and citizens and to collect materials. The writings on China are informed by my extensive conversations with Chinese scholars and students in Mainland China (before the

[14] T Ginsburg and A Simpser (eds), *Constitutions in Authoritarian Regimes* (CUP 2013); T Ginsburg and T Moustafa (eds), *Rule by Law: The Politics of Courts in Authoritarian Regimes* (CUP 2008); Mark Tushnet, 'Authoritarian Constitutionalism' (2015) 100 Cornell L Rev 391

[15] Cass R Sunstein (edited), *Can it Happen Here?: Authoritarianism in America* (Dey Street Books 2018).

[16] W Chen and H Fu (eds), *Authoritarian Legality in Asia: Formation, Development and Transition* (CUP 2020).

[17] Ran Hirschl, *Comparative Matters* (OUP 2014) 244–45.

pandemic), Hong Kong, Singapore, and Oxford. The writings on North Korea are informed by conversations with two South Korean experts on North Korean law. The writings on Cuba were informed by my trip to Cuba in 2019. Finally, the book relies on secondary English literature: scholarly and popular writings on legal reforms in the relevant countries.

IV. Theory, Argument, Contributions, and Book Structure

This book develops a general theoretical framework for understanding legal reform. Accordingly, legal reform is defined as intentional change to improve an existing legal order normally through legislation to bridge the gaps between existing law and foundational commitments, law and social change, and domestic law and transnational legal norms.

On that theoretical basis, the book argues that legal reform in the five socialist countries is the top-down project of political elites to improve the legal system while retaining its core socialist principles. Both substantive legal reforms and institutional legal reforms are carried out through legislative enactments, amendments, and replacements. The party-state adopts incremental strategies to sporadically or/and systematically reform the socialist legal system. The implementation of legal reform measures significantly improves the socialist legal system: the system is erected more on legislation than party policies and government decrees, more institutionalized, and staffed by more professional personnels. Socialist legal reform is animated by the gap between the aspirational commitments to socialism and the socialist rule of law and the reality of the socialist legal system, the gap between the legal system and societal change, and the gap between socialist law and transnational and comparative law. Despite significant reforms, the socialist principles of the legal system basically remain the same. Law in the socialist countries remains an instrument for the party-state to pursue socialist development. The Communist Party continues to play a leading, vanguard role in the legal process. Democratic centralism continues to inform the structure and operation of the legal institutions. Consequently, courts are externally subordinate to political institutions, and local courts are internally subordinate to the centralized control of the powerful supreme court. Individual rights are legally regulated and controlled by the state. Finally, the national economy remains under the centralized control of the state.

Legal reforms in the five socialist countries, however, presents considerable variations. This book identifies five different projects of socialist legal reform. China's exceptional project seeks to reform the legal system comprehensively so as to develop a distinctive Chinese legal model divergent from liberal legal models. Vietnam's universal project also aims at comprehensive legal reform but attempts to converge the domestic legal system with global legal standards. Laos's cooperative project seeks to court external supports for comprehensive legal reform, although it does not rely on global legal standards. In contrast, North Korea's self-reliant project aims to introduce some sporadic adjustments to the legal system by relying on domestic resources. Finally, Cuba's preservative project seeks to change the legal system extensively while committing to the Revolution.

This book makes both empirical and theoretical contributions. First, the book generates relatively comprehensive empirical knowledge on legal reforms in the five current socialist states in the last four decades. Such legal knowledge is important for understanding not only legal reforms but also socio-economic reforms in the socialist countries due to the interrelation of various reform projects. Second, the book has theoretical implications for comparative law generally. The book introduces a theoretical framework for understanding the intentional nature, the legislative method, the incremental strategy, the positive content, the gap factors, and the limitations of legal reform generally. The book conceptualizes the socialist legal tradition as a living legal tradition, the transformation of the socialist legality, the possibility of partial rule of law under socialist regimes, the dynamic instrumentality of authoritarian law, and vertical law and development.

The book is divided into three parts. Part I includes this Introduction, Chapter 1which develops the theoretical framework of legal reform, and Chapter 2, which conceptualizes the socialist legal tradition and its diffusion in the five socialist countries before the reform era. Part II includes five chapters on legal reforms in the five countries. These chapters basically follow the same structure. They (1) generalize features in the project of legal reform, (2) examine the achievements of legal reforms and the continuity of socialist legal features in four areas (legislative reform, administrative reform, judicial reform, and legal professional reform), and (3) provide concluding analysis. The concluding chapter in Part III compares similarities and differences of the five socialist projects of legal reform and addresses more general conceptual questions on the continuity of the socialist legal tradition, the transformation of socialist legality, socialist rule of law, authoritarian law, and law and development.

2

Theorizing Legal Reform

I. INTRODUCTION

Legal reform, a type of legal change, is common in global legal development. Legal reform has been a part of the transformation of Western modern legal systems such as those in the United States and the United Kingdom.[1] Legal reform is prevailing particularly in the developing countries. Developing countries deliberately reform their legal systems for various reasons, including to foster socio-economic development, support building of state institutions, and resolve ethnic conflicts. Following the collapse of the Soviet Union, former socialist countries in Central Europe have reformed their legal system to facilitate the transition to market economy and liberal democracy.[2] The remaining socialist countries (namely China, Vietnam, Laos, North Korea, and Cuba) have also reformed their legal systems in the last decades to foster social-economic reform and institutional adjustment. Legal reform is also dynamic in many other Asian countries such as South Korea, Indonesia, and Myanmar.[3]

Although legal reform particularly in developing countries has received great attention from academics and international donors of law and development,[4] positivist theorization of legal reform has been underdeveloped. Existing studies of legal reform tend to be evaluative and normative: these studies assess and provide techniques for assisting legal reform proposals. Integrating legal theory with social science theory, this chapter seeks to develop a positivist theoretical framework to understand the intentional nature, the legislative method, the incremental strategy, the positive content, the gap factors, and the limitations of legal reform.

[1] M Schwartzberg, *Democracy and Legal Change* (CUP 2007).

[2] Peter H Solomon, Jr and Kaja Gadowska (ed), *Legal Change in Post-Communist States Progress, Reversions, Explanations* (Columbia University Press 2019).

[3] Tom Ginsburg (ed), *Legal Reform in Korea* (Routledge 2004); Crouch M (ed), *The Politics of Court Reform: Judicial Change and Legal Culture in Indonesia* (CUP 2019); Andrew Harding (ed), *Constitutionalism and Legal Change in Myanmar* (Hart 2019).

[4] See Maciej Chmieliński and Michał Rupniewski, *The Philosophy of Legal Change: Theoretical Perspectives and Practical Processes* (Routledge 2020); Julio Faundez, *Good Government and Law: Legal and Institutional Reform in Developing Countries* (Macmillan Press 1994); Tim Lindsey (eds), *Law Reform in Developing and Transitional States* (Routledge 2007).

Legal Reform in the Contemporary Socialist World. Ngoc Son Bui, Oxford University Press. © Ngoc Son Bui 2024.
DOI: 10.1093/9780191948053.003.0002

II. LEGAL CHANGE IN COMPARATIVE LAW

A. Theories of Legal Change

The study of legal change is not new in comparative law. Legal comparativist and legal historian Alan Watson has written voluminously about legal change, and particularly emphasizes that legal change does not depend on social needs and legal transplants are the main mechanism of legal change.[5] However, *legal change* has not yet been well established as a category in the general field of comparative law. For example, there are no chapters on legal change in the *Oxford Handbook of Comparative Law* or the *Cambridge Companion to Comparative Law*.[6] To be sure, legal change has been contextualized in the existing concepts of comparative law such as legal transplants and law and development. However, legal change has its own meaning and logic and deserves a separate treatment. Key questions of legal change subject to comparative law's debate may include: What is the nature of legal change? How does legal change occur? Why does legal change happen?

Legal change has been undertheorized. Around two decades ago, Donald L Horowitz stated that 'Although doctrinal changes are staples of legal analysis, the concept of change itself is not a well-established category of legal theory.'[7] This statement seems true nowadays. Horowitz, however, identifies four strains of theories of legal change. Evolutionists, with Darwinian connections, explain legal change as a natural process determined by the stage of economic development beyond human intervention. Utilitarians see legal change as the consequence of social need. The theory of social change considers law the reflection of social structures, and legal change is determined by the change of social structures. Intentionalists attribute legal change to the will of the legal elite (eg lawyers).[8]

There may not be a single universal theory of legal change. Legal change through judicial precedents might be an evolutional process unmendable to human intervention, but legal change through legislative enactment is a volitional undertaking deriving from human will. Sometimes legal change is the consequence of social need. But the difficulty with the need-based explanation of legal change is that due to external influences countries may adopt foreign law out of internal demands. In some cases, law is reflective of social change, but in other cases, law is constructive to social change.

[5] Alan Watson, *Legal Transplants: An Approach to Comparative Law: An Approach to Comparative Law* (2nd edn, University of Georgia Press 1993); Alan Watson, *Society and Legal Change* (2nd edn, Temple University Press 2001); Alan Watson, *Sources of Law, Legal Change, and Ambiguity* (University of Pennsylvania Press 1997); Alan Watson, *Law Out of Context* (University of Georgia Press 1999).

[6] Reinhard Zimmermann (eds), *Oxford Handbook of Comparative Law* (2nd edn, OUP 2019); M Bussani and U Mattei (eds), *The Cambridge Companion to Comparative Law* (CUP 2012)

[7] Donald L Horowitz, 'The Qur'an and the Common Law: Islamic Law Reform and the Theory of Legal Change' (1994) 42 Am J Comp L 233, 238.

[8] ibid 244–52.

B. Legal Revolution, Legal Evolution, and Legal Reform

Legal change takes different modes. For the purpose of this study, I will focus on three modes: legal revolution, legal evolution, and legal reform.

Legal revolution is fundamental change of jurisprudential foundations leading to the replacement of a legal tradition. Watson anticipates four circumstances in which legal revolution occurs: laws remoting to social reality, which need profound change; legal transplants in large measure; social revolution; and political elites willing to revolutionize society and use law for this purpose.[9] Watson concludes:

> A revolution may occur in law or in society. With revolution in law, the legal tradition continues but with appropriate modifications: the basis of the law has been changed. With revolution in society the aim must also be to revolutionize law. The legal tradition is then replaced by another legal tradition in whole or in part.[10]

In other words, according to this view, legal revolution includes both modification and replacement of a legal tradition.

For Olúfẹ́mi Táíwò, only fundamental change leading to replacement of legal tradition deserves to be called legal revolution. According to him, legal revolution is 'epochal changes' or changes that breach the foundational elements of an epoch or the social structure.[11] Legal revolution 'can only be a part of a revolution in social formation that encompasses law in its ambit'.[12] Legal change within the boundary of the existing social structure is not legal revolution. As Olúfẹ́mi Táíwò said, 'the idea of breaching existing boundaries is essential to the idea of revolution'.[13] In Táíwò's conception, however, the distinction of legal revolution and social revolution is blurred. His view tends to suggest that legal revolution is essentially about fundamental change of social structure, not legal tradition.

Legal revolution, as an independent concept, should be distinguished from social revolution. Legal revolution is better understood as fundamental alteration of the normative foundations of a legal tradition. The normative foundations of a legal tradition are core principles (or arguments) justifying that legal tradition. Legal revolution occurs when core legal principles are comprehensively replaced. The comprehensive replacement of legal principles lead to the replacement of a legal tradition. Therefore, legal revolution is equal to the replacement of one legal tradition by another.

So understood, legal revolution only occurs in the last two circumstances mentioned in Watson's framework: social revolution and political elites being willing

9 Alan Watson, *The Evolution of Law* (The Johns Hopkins University Press 1985) 118.
10 ibid.
11 Olúfẹ́mi Táíwò, *Legal Naturalism: A Marxist Theory of Law* (Cornell University Press 1996) 157.
12 ibid 157.
13 ibid 157.

to radically change the society. Comprehensive change of legal rules and institutions through domestic innovations for legal transplant without comprehensive replacement of fundamental principles justifying the legal system is not revolutionary. Legal change is limited within the parameter of the existing legal tradition, and hence the normative foundations of the legal tradition basically remain intact.

Legal evolution is a less radical form of legal change. Legal evolution refers to incremental, natural change within an existing legal order. Legal evolution is tantamount to what Táíwò calls 'changes within epochs' or changes that do not alter the fundamental characters of the epochs.[14] Legal evolution is a natural process of legal change beyond human intention and intervention. The evolution of common law is the example of legal evolution.

Legal reform is intentional change within an existing legal order. Like legal evolution, legal reform is legal change within an epoch. Legal reform does not alter the essential features of the existing legal order. However, different from legal evolution, legal reform is not a natural process but an intentional human undertaking. Legal reform is designed to prevent legal evolution and legal revolution. Political elites would deliberately design legal reform projects to allow for legal innovation under their control while reserving the identity of the existing legal system. Section III will elaborate on elements of legal reform.

III. LEGAL REFORM: A THEORETICAL FRAMEWORK

Legal reform is intentional change to improve an existing legal order normally through legislation to bridge the gaps between existing law and foundational commitments, law and social change, and domestic law and transnational legal norms. Elements of legal reform include intentional nature, legislative method, incremental strategy, positive change, gap factors, and continuity.

A. Intentional Nature

Legal reform is, by nature, intentional. Legal reform derives from human will, beliefs, and aspiration, and concrete activities. Legal reform is not legal evolution independent from human intervention. Legal reform is a deliberate undertaking of a project. Paul W Kahn's conception of a 'project' is useful to understand the intentional nature of legal reform.[15] Kahn indicates that 'a project is always an

[14] ibid 153.
[15] Paul W Kahn, *Origins of Order: Project and System in the American Legal Imagination* (Yale University Press 2021).

effort to realize an idea that precedes it'.[16] He specifies that a project includes a pattern of ends, plans, and ownership.[17] A project is directed by goals, carried by plans, and possessed by someone.[18] A project of legal reform includes human ideas expressed in particular forms about goals and plans to improve an existing legal order. To adapt and extend Kahn's conception of a project, a project of legal reform can be specified as including these elements: ownership, forms, goals, plans, and principles.

Ownership: a project of legal reform expresses the intention of certain individuals. In both democracies and authoritarian regimes, a wide range of actors may be involved in legal reform, including domestic political elite, legal elites, citizens, and international donors and advisors. However, a project of legal reform is adopted by an authority who is the owner of the project. The ownership of a legal reform project can vary in three contexts: democracy, authoritarianism, and external imposition. In democracies, a legal reform project can be adopted by the citizens or their representatives (particularly the legislature). In this context, the project expresses the intention of the broad public, although it may reflect the interests of political elites. In authoritarian regimes, a legal reform project may be adopted by a narrow political elite. To be sure, authoritarian leaders may adopt legal reform projects in response to public pressures and discourse, although the public does not have the power to adopt the project. In the circumstance of legal imposition, a project of domestic legal reform is adopted by the external authority such as a colonial authority or sectors of the international community.

Forms: a project of legal reform is expressed in particular forms where the intention of reformers can be identified. These forms can be legal and political. First, a legal reform project can be embodied in legal instruments such as a constitution or a legislation. As the constitution is the foundation of a legal system, it may anticipate goals and principles for future legal development. A statute may include some general objectives that could direct its future development. Second, the project of legal reform may be expressed in political discourse and political instruments. Political speeches might express their intention of legal reform. An authority may adopt political instruments to lay down the goals, principles, and plans of legal reforms.

Goals: legal reform is directed by goals. The goals of legal reform are objectives that the reformers seek to realize by future actions of legal reform. The goals of legal reform can be internal or external to the legal order. The internal goals of legal reforms can be substantive ideals such as justice and equality. They can be functional goals such as efficiency and effectiveness in the operation of legal institutions. They

16 ibid 13.
17 ibid 16.
18 ibid.

can be individual goals such as professionalism of judges and lawyers. They can also be formal goals such as generality, consistency, and publicity of legal rules. Reformers may also seek to achieve goals external to the legal order such as domestic social cohesion, economic development, and transnational integration.

Plans: legal reform is undertaken through plans. Plans indicate the intention to actuate legal reform. Legal reform plans can be short, medium, or long term. A government may adopt a plan for legal reform within one year, several years, or a few decades. A legal reform plan includes particular measures to improve the existing legal order and dictates specific actions. and It also specifies functions of the various actors involved to allow them to work together to achieve the common goals of legal reform.

Principles: a project of legal reform is controlled by some principles or the reformer's aspirational commitments. Principles express the intention to limit legal reform. Legal reform involves change within the existing legal order, and principles set boundaries to ensure that certain cores in the existing legal order cannot be changed. A project of legal reform therefore is both forward- and backward-looking. It intends to improve the condition of the legal order while preserving its foundations.

B. Legislative Method

The methods of legal reform are normally legislative. They can be the repeal of a law, creation of new law, consolidation (changing an existing law), and codification (collection and systematic arrangement of the laws into legal codes).[19] The main method to repeal, create, consolidate, and codify legal rules is deliberative legislative enactment. As Táíwò observes, legislation, the establishment of legal rules by 'direct action of lawmaking organs of a given society', 'is the principal means by which changes are made in most modern legal systems'.[20] Particularly, legal reform normally involves legislative alteration of legal rules. 'Proposals for reform when they are accepted are normally executed by means of legislation'.[21] This is true for legal reform not only in civil law and socialist law jurisdictions where statutes are the main sources of law but also in common law jurisdictions. Legal reform measures in common law jurisdictions are mainly undertaken through legislation. Legislative enactment is the main target of both domestic (eg the UK Law Commission) and international (eg the World Bank) legal reform promoters.

The legislative methods of legal reform are closely connected to the intentional nature of legal reform. Jeremy Waldron states that 'legislation is intentional

[19] Legal and Economic Empowerment Global Network (LEEG-net), SDG-enabling Law Reform Drive. <https://www.leeg-net.org/sdgs-enabling-law-reform-drive> accessed 31 May 2024.
[20] Táíwò (n 11), 158.
[21] ibid 159

action.'[22] As legal reform is a deliberative human activity, it is carried out by the legislative decisions of institutional (eg the parliaments) or personal (eg kings and dictators) actors. In addition, as legal reform is change by design, it entails systematic, comprehensive methods of legislation rather than spontaneous adjudication. Alan Watson indicates that, differing from judicial case law, legislation 'can be very systematic, general in its purposes, and removed from individual particular cases. It can make drastic speedy reforms. Development by legislation can have a very satisfactory explicit or implicit theoretical base: and can thus point the way to further reform.'[23]

The legislative methods of legal reform are also connected to what Waldron calls 'the dignity of legislation.'[24] He considers the process of legislation as being when 'the representatives of the community come together to settle solemnly and explicitly on common schemes and measures that can stand in the name of them all, and they do so in a way that openly acknowledges and respects (rather than conceals) the inevitable differences of opinion and principle among them.'[25] The diversity of legislative platform, the openness of legislative activity, and the popular base of the legislature in most modern legal systems render legislative enactment a legitimate and common means of legal reform.

C. Positive Content

The content of legal reform is *positive.* Not all intentional change to the existing legal system is legal reform. Legal change can undergird and undermine the existing legal order. A negative change undermining an existing legal order is a legal regress, not legal reform. Legal reform refers to positive change that facilitates the development of law toward a better condition. The positive content is the realization of the goals of legal reform. A positive legal change can be substantive, functional, and personnel. A positive legal change improves the quality of substantive legal rules, the quality in the operation of legal institutions, and the quality of legal personnels.

The test for the positivity of a change can be assessing whether a legal reform achieves some rule of law ideals. In fact, many developing countries have introduced measures of legal reform to achieve some criteria of the rule of law.[26]

[22] Waldron J, *The Dignity of Legislation* (CUP 1999) 26.
[23] Alan Watson, 'Comparative Law and Legal Change' (1978) 37 Cam LJ 324.
[24] Waldron (n 22).
[25] ibid 2.
[26] Thomas Carothers, 'The Rule of Law Revival' (1998) 77 Foreign Aff 95; Linn Hammergren, 'Latin American Experience with Rule of Law Reforms and Applicability of Nation Building Efforts' (2006) 38 Case W Res J Int'l L 63; Ronald J Daniels and Michael Trebilcock, 'The Political Economy of Rule of Law Reform in Developing Countries' (2004) 26 Mich J Int'l L 99.

International agencies and developed countries also often rely on the standards of the rule of law to promote legal reform in the developing world, particularly in Russia, China, Latin America, Central and Eastern Europe, the Middle East, and Africa.[27] The common practice of rule of law-based legal reform and the global promotion of rule of law-based legal reform suggest that the rule of law ideals can be the test for the positivity of legal reform.

A legal change qualifies as a legal reform if it accommodates some elements of the rule of law ideals. As Richard H Fallon argues, 'The Rule of Law is an ideal that can be used to evaluate laws, judicial decisions, or legal systems.'[28] The rule of law is an ideal that humankind has tried to achieve in its broader course of pursuing just, decent, and organized society. The realization of the rule of law is 'a matter of degree'.[29] No legal system can realize the ideal of rule of law perfectly. 'A legal system that on the whole comports with the Rule of Law may nevertheless include regulations or decisions that do not.'[30]

The rule of law is normally conceived of as a component of the transition from authoritarian regime to democracy.[31] The implication is that the rule of law and authoritarianism cannot co-exist in a single polity. This is misleading. Even under well-established rule of law systems, legal authoritarianism can also be partially executed. In this case, the rule of law is still the hegemonic spirit of the polity, but authoritarian laws can be implemented in some aspects of the society under certain circumstances.[32] To illustrate, Robert Diab investigates in the United States

> law and policy defining four basic features of authoritarian legality, including the repudiation of absolute or 'non-derogable' human rights in torture, indefinite detention, and targeted killing; the expansion of state secrecy and surveillance; judicial deference to executive discretion; and a reluctance to remedy serious rights violations, or be held accountable for them.[33]

Conversely, even under well-established authoritarian systems, the rule of law can also be partially accommodated through legal reform. In this case,

[27] Thomas Carothers (ed) *Promoting the Rule of Law Abroad: In Search of Knowledge* (Carnegie Endowment for International Peace, 2006); Michael Zurn, Andre Nollkaemper, and Randy Peerenboom (eds), *Rule of Law Dynamics: In an Era of International and Transnational Governance* (CUP 2012)

[28] Richard H Fallon Jr, 'The Rule of Law as a Concept in Constitutional Discourse' (1997) 97 Colum L Rev 9.

[29] ibid.

[30] ibid.

[31] Ruti Teitel, 'Transitional Jurisprudence: The Role of Law in Political Transformation' (1997) 106 Yale LJ 2016.

[32] Lynne Henderson, 'Authoritarianism and the Rule of Law' (1991) 66 Ind LJ 382.

[33] Robert Diab, *The Harbinger Theory: How the Post-9/11 Emergency Became Permanent and the Case for Reform* (OUP 2015) 23.

authoritarianism remains the hegemonic spirit of the polity, but the rule of law can also be implemented in some aspects of the society under certain circumstances.

The rule of law is a multidimensional concept. Fallon's typology of the rule of law ideal is useful in this regard. Accordingly, although the rule of law is a contested ideal, virtually all contested arguments about the rule of law ideal can be modelled by a historicist, formalist, legal process, or substantive ideal type.[34] These types of the rule of law can be bases on which to test the positivity of legal change.

First, 'a historicist ideal type of the Rule of Law, in order to be coherent, must be conceived as internal to a legal culture, form of life, hermeneutic circle, or interpretive community; meaning cannot be conceived as independent of culture, context, or shared understandings'.[35] So, in a historic rule of law ideal, legal actors are bound by a pre-established legal legacy, legal culture, and shared underlining principles of an interpretive community. A legal change that subjects legal actors to the constraints of the broader interpretive community can be considered a legal reform. Legal change in the historical type of rule of law normally involves the change of judicial precedents. However, legislative reform can also support historical rule of law. A legislative change that empowers courts to interpret the law or to develop precedents can be considered a legal reform to support the historical rule of law.

Second, under the formalist ideal type, to borrow Justice Antonin Scalia's utterance, *the rule of law* means *a law of rules*.[36] Rules are conceived of as 'a clear prescription that exist prior to its application and that determine appropriate conduct or legal outcomes'.[37] The formalist rule of law is underpinned by the assumption of the 'human being as rational planners and maximizers, who reasonably demand to know in advance the legal consequences of alternative courses of action'.[38] Proponents of legal formalism include AV Dicey, Friedrich Hayek, John Rawls, Joseph Raz, and Lon L Fuller.[39] In particular, Fuller identifies eight requirements of formal rule of law or 'legality', including generality, clarity, public promulgation, stability, prospectivity, freedom from contradiction, possibility to obey, and consistency between promulgated laws and their actual administration.[40] These eight standards of formal rule of law can be used as a test for the positivity of legal reform. A legal change does not need to satisfy all these eight standards to be qualified as a legal reform. A legal change that partially accommodates the requirements of the formal rule of law is qualified as a legal reform. For example, the public enactment of a statute that basically includes general,

[34] Fallon (n 28), 10.
[35] ibid 14.
[36] Antonin Scalia, 'The Rule of Law as a Law of Rules' (1989) 56 U Chi L Rev 1175.
[37] Fallon (n 28), 14.
[38] ibid 15.
[39] ibid 16.
[40] L Fuller, *The Morality of Law* (Yale University Press 1963) 39.

prospective, and practicable rules is a legal reform, although the law has some vague and contradictory provisions.

Third, the legal process type focuses on procedural requirements in the development and application of legal norms.[41] These include, for example, fairness, due process, and judicial review of legislative, executive, and administrative actions.[42] Legal reforms are positive legal changes that seek to materialize the procedural requirements in the legal order. These include requirements for procedures of lawmaking such as representation, public participation, and transparency; and procedures of law-applying such as assumption of innocence, the right to counsel, functional judicial independence, public hearing, and equality under the law. For example, a legal change facilitating public participation in the lawmaking process is a legal reform. The adoption of a new rule in criminal procedure law recognizing the assumption of innocence is a legal reform.

Finally, the substantive ideal type of rule of law insists that 'the forms of law—which may encompass rules, conventions of legal reasoning, and process of legal deliberation—are unintelligible as legal norms in the absence of rationally cognizable purposes that possess reasonable claims to moral allegiances'.[43] Ronald Dworkin, for example, insists on individual rights as a substantive requirement of the rule of law.[44] Frank Michelman's 'Law's Republic' treats freedom under law as the substance of the rule of law.[45] Legal reforms are positive legal changes that seek to materialize the substantive values of justice and freedom in the legal order. For example, a change in family law prohibiting corporal punishment of children at home is a legal reform as this better protects the freedom and well-being of children. A change in criminal law abolishing or reducing capital punishment is a legal reform as this improves a government's treatment of its citizens.

The rule of law strands do not exist independently in a legal system. Rather, they are complexly interwoven and competing with each other.[46] There may be relative priority of different rule of law strands in different legal systems. And within a legal system, there may be relative priority of a certain strand of the rule of law in different periods. Therefore, an account of legal reform in different contexts must take into account the complex manifestation, interaction, and competition of different rule of law ideal types. In authoritarian regimes, legal reforms to promote formal and procedural rule of law may be more prominent than those to advance substantive rule of law. Public participation in lawmaking depends on the extent to which substantive political freedom (particularly freedom of speech and freedom of the press) is guaranteed. International donors may seek to promote substantive

41 Fallon (n 28), 18.
42 ibid 18.
43 ibid 21.
44 Ronald Dworkin, *Taking Rights Seriously* (Harvard University Press 1978).
45 Frank I Michelman, 'Law's Republic' (1988) 97 Yale LJ 1493
46 Fallon (n 28), 42.

human rights law reform, while the recipient countries may be more concerned with the assistance of technical, formal reforms, like consolidating a law website, to improve the publicity and accessibility of the law.

D. Incremental Strategy

The strategy for legal reform is incrementalist. Legal reform is an incremental process of legal change, which is different from wholesale legal replacement of a legal system. In this sense, incremental change is the observable pattern of legal reform. Incremental change, however, can be a deliberate strategy. Political elites may deliberately change the legal system incrementally. In this sense, incrementalism is a strategy to implement changes to improve the existing legal order over time.

Political scientist Charles E Lindblom developed the theory of incrementalism in the 1950s, which sees policy change as the result of small adjustments. He contrasts incrementalism with 'rational comprehensive method', which involves the formulation of an overall plan for policy change.[47] Lindblom believes that comprehensive policy decisions are unattainable due to disagreement on the objectives and insufficient knowledge to predict the consequences. He observes that 'democracies change their policies almost entirely through incremental adjustment'.[48]

Lindblom's incrementalism is a normative theory, but incrementalism can be a strategy of policy decision makers and a strategy of legal reform particularly. A range of factors influence the political elites' choices of incremental moves in legal reform: political elites do not have inadequate knowledge about existing laws, measures for legal reform are not specified, the consequences of legal reform are unpredictable, the reaction of citizens to legal reform is not apparent, and political elites' interests and references are conflicting.[49]

Incrementalism as a strategy does not necessarily contradict comprehensive plans for legal reform. The political elite may formulate a long-term, overall plan for legal reform but implement the measures of legal reform incrementally over a long time. Drawing on comparative political studies of policy change,[50] I identify two incrementalist strategies of legal reform, depending on the scale and pace of legal reform.

First, *classical incrementalism*, or incrementalism in Lindblom's sense, is a strategy to undertake small-scale legal reform with slow or speedy steps. The scale

[47] Charles E Lindblom, 'The Science of "Muddling Through"' (1959) 19 Pub Admin Rev 81.

[48] ibid 84.

[49] For the reasons of incrementalism generally, see Charles E Lindblom and Edward J Woodhouse, *The Policy-Making Process* (Prentice Hall 1993).

[50] Carolyn J Tuohy, *Remaking Policy: Scale, Pace, and Political Strategy in Health Care Reform* (University of Toronto Press 2018); Michael Howlett and Benjamin Cashore, 'The Dependent Variable Problem in the Study of Policy Change: Understanding Policy Change as a Methodological Problem' (2009) 11 J Comp Policy Anal: Res Prac 40.

of classical incremental legal reform is small. The reforms are sporadic adjustments to some substantive or institutional aspects of the legal system. They normally do not modify fundamental ideas or principles underlying the legal system. The pace of classical incremental legal reform can be slow or speedy. Reformers may adopt sporadic adjustments over a long or short period of time. There are three possible contexts in which classical incrementalism is adopted as a strategy of legal reform. The first is a transitional, developing country seeking to reform the legal system in the early stage. When a developing country engages in legal reform early on, the political elite may be cautious in their trial and error, and therefore they may initially try some small reforms to test their effects and social reactions. Another context is a non-transitional, developing country seeking to improve some aspects of the legal system. The third context is a developed country with an advanced modern legal system seeking to improve some aspects of it.

Second, *neo-incrementalism* is a strategy to implement a comprehensive plan for legal reform over an extensive period of time. With this strategy, the political elite designs a comprehensive plan for legal reform. The plan anticipates measures of reform to many aspects of the legal system. However, the measures will be implemented with series of steps over an extensive period of time. The scope of neo-incremental legal reforms is big, involving substantive, institutional, and ideational changes to the legal system. Neo-incremental legal reforms may involve extensive changes to the substantive and institutional aspects of the legal system such as the systematic adoption of many laws and systematic reconstruction of the courts. Neo-incremental legal reforms may also introduce new ideas or principles or modify the existing ideas or principles of the legal system. In general, the pace of the whole project of systematic legal reform is slow: the whole project will be implemented over an extensive period of time (eg five years, ten years, or several decades). However, some specific measures of systematic legal reforms may be implemented quickly, while others may be implemented slowly. Neo-incremental legal reforms are normally adopted when a country has already achieved some legal reforms. The use of a neo-incremental strategy is determined by the institutional settings where there is strong centralization of power and strong political consensus on legal reforms.

E. Gap Factors

Why does a country reform its legal system? Legal reform is carried out to bridge the gap between existing positive law and commitments, between law and societal change, and between domestic legal order and transnational legal order.

First, the gap between the fundamental commitment of the legal order and the reality of the existing law is the ideational factor of legal reform. Political elites seek to reform the legal system to bring positive law closer to fundamental ideas of the legal system. For example, the gap between the commitment to the legal idea of individual freedom and the reality of slavery law may induce legal reforms abolishing slavery. In addition, political elites might adopt new ideas, and this may drive legal reforms. For instance, for instrumental reasons, authoritarian leaders may aspire to develop the rule of law, and this aspiration could drive legal reforms to bridge the gap between the reality of authoritarian law and the rule of law ideal.

Second, the gap between law and societal change is the social factor of legal reform. Social and economic changes create new social relations and social tasks, which may require legal responses. New laws are enacted to regulate new social relations. Courts are improved to better handle new legal disputes. More law firms and lawyers are produced to meet the social demands of legal services. Political elites reform the legal system to both reflect and facilitate societal change. Legal reform institutionalizes and stabilizes existing societal change and creates new rules to facilitate further societal change.

Third, domestic legal reform is instigated by the divergence between domestic law and transnational legal order. Legal diffusion/transplant is a major mechanism of legal reform.[51] Countries, through legal transplants, adopt transnational legal ideas, institutions, and rules to bridge the gap between domestic law and transnational legal order. Legal transplants to narrow the divergence of domestic and transnational law are animated by the forces of *need* and *norm*. Countries adopt foreign law because of the external outcomes (need) and internal values (norm) of the transplanted law. On the need factor, countries adopt foreign law for external outcomes of legal transplant—such as to facilitate social-economic development, to create a convergent legal framework to attract foreign investment, to signal the political intention of the country's openness to the outside world, and to gain international legitimacy. On the norm factor, countries adopt foreign law because of the internal normative values of the translated law. The transplanted law is adopted not merely because it meets the need of the society but also because it is connected to normative values of the law associated with human freedom.

Instrumentalism (need) and rationalism (norm) also explain legal transplants for legal reform promoted by law and development actors. External actors promote legal transplants to support legal reform for their instrumental concerns such as to facilitate the global flow of capital or to create a common legal framework for foreign investment. International actors promote legal transplants to spread the normative values attached to the transplanted law.

Diffusion scholars have discussed various mechanisms of legal diffusions, including inducement (or coercion), competition, learning, and socialization.[52]

[51] On legal transplant scholarship, see Toby S Goldbach, 'Why Legal Transplants?' (2019) 15 Annu Rev Law Soc Sci 583.

[52] On diffusion literature, see Christoph Engel and Keren Weinshall, 'Diffusion of Legal Innovations' (2022) 18 Annu Rev Law Soc Sci 139.

Inducement, competition, and socialization are largely associated with the need for legal transplants. Countries reform their law by adopting foreign law or international law because they need gain material (foreign aids and investments) and social (international legitimacy) benefits. The learning mechanism is more associated with the normative forces of legal transplants. Countries learn from transnational legal experience because they are convinced by the normative values of the recipient law.

F. Continuity

The scope of legal reform is limited within an existing legal order. Legal reform is change within an epoch. Legal reform within the existing legal order entails two aspects: change and continuity.

Within the existing legal order, there is room for change surrounding legal identity—the aspirational legal commitments foundational to a legal order. The legal commitments are normally broad enough for change surrounding them. For example, the commitment of the socialist legal system to public ownership does not exclude the adoption of private ownership to the extent that public ownership remains dominant in the ownership regime. The accommodation of private ownership allows for private law reform in the socialist legal system.

Change during legal reform can be innovative and renovative. Legal innovations introduce new elements to improve the existing legal order. New elements supplement, rather than substitute, the old elements that constitute the identity of the legal order. In addition, legal innovations are marginal, not central to the legal system. The old elements remain dominant in the legal system. Legal renovations renew the regressive elements of the legal system so that they are once again in good condition. Legal renovations involve activities such as restoring abolished legal concepts and institutions, reconstructing legal institutions, consolidating the function of legal institutions, and reactivating dormant legal institutions.

Legal reform involves continuity: the identity of the existing legal order remains the same. Fundamental legal commitments that define the nature of the existing legal order are not changed. The continuity of legal identity is shaped by both material and intentional factors. First, the continuity of legal identity is shaped by the continuity of social formation. When there is no fundamental change to the deep structure of society or the mode of production, there is no fundamental change to the basic principles of the legal system.

However, the continuity of legal identity is not naturally reserved but is deliberately designed by intentional human intervention. The continuity of legal identity is intentionally designed to preserve the existing legal order and to prevent legal evolution and legal revolution. Political elites deliberately design legal reform to allow for legal innovations and renovations under their control. Political elites design legal reform to prevent systematic changes beyond their intention. They also design legal reform to ensure that legal changes will not incrementally culminate in radical transformation of the legal order.

When legal reform leads to more substantive changes to social structure, the deliberate control of legal change and the resistance to legal change become more intense. Legal reform may generate substantive changes to social formation, such as the emergence of new social class and the alteration in social relations of productions. Such substantive social changes may threaten fundamental principles of the legal order: new social relations require new arguments justifying the legal order; new social groups acquire new legitimacy ideas. The change of social relations and legal principles may challenge the power of the ruling class. Consequently, the ruling class will deliberately reserve the existing legal principles and resist legal reform. They may even reverse legal reforms or introduce legal measures to keep the existing social structure at bay.

To ensure the continuity in legal reform, legal identity is deliberately entrenched. The entrenchment of unchangeable legal identity can be formal and informal. Positive law may formally include provisions anchoring the essential features of the existing legal order. Such provisions can both consolidate the foundation of the legal system and prevent its change. The essential features of the legal system can be informally entrenched in the legal reform project. The function of a legal reform project is both facilitative and preventive. It anticipates measures for legal reform, but at the same time it prevents change outside the projected measures. A law reform project therefore limits the change within the existing legal order.

In short, legal continuity can be explained by a combination of materialism and intentionalism. Principles of the legal order are reserved by the continuity of the social formation and by the design of political elites.

3

The Socialist Legal Tradition

I. INTRODUCTION: THE SOCIALIST LEGAL TRADITION IN COMPARATIVE LAW

During the Soviet era, comparative law scholars added socialist law to the two other familiar legal traditions (ie common law and civil law).[1] After the collapse of the Soviet Union, socialist law has virtually disappeared from comparative law literature.[2] The socialist (or Soviet) legal tradition has been ignored as it is conceived of as having little or no relevance today.[3] Another reason for the lack of literature is that socialist law is considered a part of civil law. John Quigley, in his article published during the Soviet era, concluded that socialist law 'contains features' but 'those points of difference have not removed socialist law from the civil law tradition' because of 'the historical connection of socialist law to civil law and the continuing relevance in socialist law of civil law rules, methods, institutions, and procedures'.[4] Finally, the socialist legal tradition is neglected because some believe that it does not exist. Writing after the Soviet era, Inga Markovits argued that socialist law was not dead simply because it did not exist: the alleged features of socialist law are not confined to the law of the former socialist countries.[5]

Recently, some scholars have revitalized the debate on the existence and legacy of the socialist legal tradition. William Partlett and Eric C Ip argue that socialist law has distinctive features and that it is not dead but still influences the current Chinese public law.[6] A recent edited book 'argues that the scholarly focus on the emergence of liberal legalism has marginalized the ongoing normative and structural legacy of Asian socialism found in various guises in contemporary Vietnam and China'.[7] Some scholars even explore the legacies of socialist law in former socialist countries such as Russia and Poland.[8]

[1] Rene David and John EC Brierley, *Major Legal Systems in the World Today: An Introduction to the Comparative Study of Law* (Stevens 1968).

[2] William Partlett and Eric C Ip, 'Is Socialist Law Really Dead?' (2016) 48 NYU J Int'l L & Pol 473.

[3] Mathias Siems, *Comparative Law* (3rd edn, CUP 2022) 110.

[4] John Quigley, 'Socialist Law and the Civil Law Tradition' (1989) 37 Am J Comp L 781, 808.

[5] Inga Markovits, 'The Death of Socialist Law?' (2007) 3 Ann Rev Law Soc Sci 233.

[6] Partlett and Ip (n 2) 465.

[7] Hualing Fu and others, 'Socialist Law in Socialist East Asia' in Hualing Fu and others (eds), *Socialist Law in Socialist East Asia* (CUP 2018) 3.

[8] Ekaterina Mishina, 'The Re-birth of Soviet Criminal Law in Post-Soviet Russia' (2017) 5 Russian LJ 57; Rafał Mańko, 'Demons of the Past? Legal Survivals of the Socialist Legal Tradition in Contemporary Polish Private Law' in Rafał Mańko, Cosmin Sebastian, and Cercel Adam Sulikowski (eds), *Law and Critique in Central Europe* (Counterpress 2016) 66.

Legal Reform in the Contemporary Socialist World. Ngoc Son Bui, Oxford University Press. © Ngoc Son Bui 2024.
DOI: 10.1093/9780191948053.003.0003

This chapter explores the nature of the socialist legal tradition and its diffusion in five countries: China, Vietnam, Laos, North Korea, and Cuba. It argues that socialist law is a distinctive, living legal tradition. Macintyre defines a living tradition as a 'historically extended, socially embodied argument, and an argument precisely in part about the goods which constitute that tradition'.[9] Adapting from Macintyre's concept of tradition, this chapter defines the socialist legal tradition as a historically extended, legally embodied form of Marxism-Leninism.

Section II of this chapter provides an overview of Marxist-Leninist political-economic concepts. Section III considers the key features of the socialist legal traditions as legal embodiments of Marxist-Leninist arguments for socialism. Section IV deals with the transnational diffusion of the socialist legal tradition into the five countries. Section V concludes by generalizing features of socialist legal revolution in the five countries.

II. FOUNDATIONS OF THE SOCIALIST LEGAL TRADITION

The socialist legal tradition is rested on Marxism-Leninism. The Marxist concept of history views human progress as being determined by material conditions, not ideals. Marx and Engels write in *The German Ideology* that 'what individuals are depends on the material conditions of their production'.[10] The way individuals produce, or the 'mode of production', is a combination of 'productive forces' and 'productive relations'.[11] Productive forces refer to the means individuals use to produce everything—such as lands, machines, buildings, labour, knowledge, and skills. Productive relations are the relations or interactions between individuals in production, which include property rights.[12]

Marxist historical materialism holds that the 'economic base' (or simply 'base') as the manifestation of 'productive relations' is the foundation for intellectual life, and social and political structures. Marxist theory distinguishes 'infrastructure' from 'superstructure'.[13] Infrastructure refers to economic structure of the society. Superstructure involves the ideational, social, and institutional structure of the society. Superstructure includes things such as ideology, family, and political institutions. Marxist historical materialism believes that infrastructure determines superstructure. Intellectual life, and social and political institutions are the reflection of economic structure.

Marxist historical materialism sees class struggle as the cause of human development. There are no classes in 'primitive communist society'. Social class appears

[9] Alasdair Macintyre, *After Virtue* (Bloomsbury Publishing 2013) 195.
[10] K Marx and F Engels, *The German Ideology* (Progress Publishers 1976) 37.
[11] Michael Freeman, *Lloyd's Introduction to Jurisprudence* (Sweet & Maxwell 2008) 1132–33.
[12] Brian Leiter, 'Marx, Law, Ideology, Legal Positivism' (2015) 101 Virginia L Rev 1179, 1180.
[13] Freeman (n 11) 1134.

as the consequence of the advent of private ownership and hence economic differentiation between the haves and the have-nots. Class struggle is generated by the change in productive forces. Productive forces are not constantly stable as people acquire more knowledge, discover new technology, and invent new ways to make products. Change in productive forces may conflict with the existing productive relations. To resolve the contradiction, new social groups and social classes seek to use new productive forces to struggle against the hegemony of the existing ruling class. The consequence is a social revolution, which leads to a higher level of human development with the radical formation of new productive relations. Human history is therefore the series of class struggles between free persons and slaves, between feudal lords and peasants, and between capitalists and workers. Marxism anticipates that the struggle between the working class (or the proletariat) and the capitalists (or the bourgeoisie) will lead to a proletarian revolution, which will result in the working class's political domination (or a proletarian dictatorship). The working class will create the socialist society as a transitional phase in the ultimate creation of a 'scientific communist society' in which, as private property and economic differentiation disappear there is no class.

III. FEATURES OF THE SOCIALIST LEGAL TRADITION

A. Instrumentalism

Marxist historical materialism conceptualizes law as the 'superstructure' or the expression of economic relationships, in which the exploiting class uses law as an instrument to maintain the existing economic conditions and control the exploited class.[14] So, unlike Dworkinism, a Marxist version of legal positivism conceives of law not as something morally justifiable but as something the officials consider constituting and instrumental to the existing economic relations, whether the relations are just or harmful.[15] Socialist law therefore boils down to 'a set of commands to be religiously observed'.[16]

The instrumental nature and function of law is manifested in two aspects: expressive and oppressive. First, law expresses the will and interests of the ruling class. Second, law serves as a tool for the rulers to oppress the ruled. In this Marxist view, law in the slave state is an instrument for the free person to oppress the slaves,

[14] Inga Markovits, 'Civil Law in East Germany—Its Development and Relation to Soviet Legal History and Ideology' (1968) 78 Yale LJ 4.

[15] Leiter (n 12) 1179, 1192; see also Zdenek Kuhn, 'Worlds Apart: Western and Central European Judicial Culture at the Onset of the European Enlargement' (2004) 52 Am J Comp L 540 (citing Central European jurists' view that 'in socialism, according to its official ideology, jurisprudence was still dominated by rule-positivism').

[16] Inga Markovits, 'Socialist vs. Bourgeois Rights—An East–West German Comparison' (1978) 45 U Chi L Rev 629.

law in the federal state is a tool for the lords to dominate the peasants, and law in the capitalist state is an instrument for the bourgeoisie to exploit the workers. Socialist law has similar instrumental nature and function. It is the expression of the working class's aspirations to socialist development. Socialist law also serves as a tool for the working class to oppress the bourgeoisie and other social groups hostile to socialist revolution and the socialist state. The expressive and oppressive functions of law vary in different historical periods due to different material conditions. However, under the Marxist lens, the general course of global legal history reveals a common pattern: law is the tool of the ruling class conditioned by material circumstances.

The consequence of the instrumental, material concept of law is the concept of 'socialist legality'. The Soviet concept of socialist legality (*sotsialisticheskaia zakonnost*) 'is defined as a strict observation of law by all agencies of the state, social organizations, institutions, government officials, and citizens'.[17] It is different from the Western concept of the rule of law in several significant aspects. First, socialist legality focuses mainly on the strict observation of law by citizens and government offices and 'is not a meta-legal principle binding the legislative power'.[18] Second, the emphasis on the observation of law by citizens and government offices 'indicates that socialist legality is not primarily intended to limit administrative power in relation to citizens'.[19] Instead, socialist legality underlines the implementation of law as a tool for realizing the communist party's policy and for 'social engineering'.[20] In this regard, socialist legality is the socialist form of rule *by* law rather than the rule *of* law. Third, according to the concept of socialist legality, law derives from the state and therefore law means written law or positive law.[21] As law is the tool of the ruling class, it must derive from the state—the political organization of the ruling class. Law means legal rules enacted by state institutions, and the state institutions here mean the legislative and administrative institutions, not courts. The sources of law are therefore legislative statutes and governmental regulations, not judicial precedents.

The instrumental nature of law presents a Marxist version of law and development. As law is determined by economic conditions, when there is a change in the economic system, there will be a change in the legal system. In the Marxist view, law seems reflective rather than constructive of economic development. However, Marxist writings suggest that legal development, albeit based on economic

[17] Samuel Kucherov, 'Socialist Legality' in FJM Feldbrugge and others (eds), *Encyclopedia of Soviet Law* (M Nijhoff Publishers 1985) 706.

[18] ibid.

[19] ibid.

[20] ibid.

[21] Nguyễn Xuân Tùng, 'Bàn về "nguyên tắc pháp quyền Xã hội chủ nghĩa"' ['Commenting on the "Principle of Socialist Rule of Law"'] (Bộ Tư Pháp [Ministry of Justice], 13 October 2011) <https://moj.gov.vn/qt/tintuc/Pages/nghien-cuu-trao-doi.aspx?ItemID=1463> [<https://perma.cc/MX3F-ZKFZ>] accessed 5 June 2024.

development, interacts with other elements of superstructure such as philosophy, politics, and religion.[22]

Instrumentalism shapes the functions of socialist legal institutions. In the Marxist-Leninist view, 'the court is but the tool which administers the law. As such the court is a class tool, an implement used by the state machine to further the interests of the ruling groups.'[23] As a political tool, socialist courts do not merely have adjudicative function. They also have political, educative function. To illustrate, Article 3 of the Fundamental Principles of Court Organization of the USSR and the Union Republics states:

> By all its activity a court shall educate citizens in the spirit of loyalty to the Motherland and to the cause of communism, and in the spirit of exact and undeviating execution of Soviet laws, of a protective attitude toward socialist property, of observance of labor discipline, of an honorable attitude toward state and social duty, and of respect for the rights, honor, and dignity of citizens and for the rules of socialist community life.[24]

Thus, Soviet courts have a political, instrumental function: to educate citizens on their duties to be loyal to the nation and communism, and to respect Soviet laws and socialist property.

Socialist lawyers are also instrumental agents of the state. 'In the Soviet Union the role of the lawyer like that of any other "worker in the legal field", e.g., judge or prosecutor, is the promotion of "socialist legality".'[25] In other words, socialist lawyers are an instrument for the state to promote the strict observation of the law by citizens. In addition, socialist lawyers do not just defend their clients; they must protect the state interests.

> The Soviet defense lawyer cannot convert himself into the servant of his client, blindly following him in the defense of his interests, even though those interests are not legal and detract from, rather than contribute to, the interests of Socialist justice. In defending the rights and legal interests of his client, the Soviet defense lawyer must stop short at the brink where truth ends and falsehood begins, where the interests of the State and society are damaged by the counterposing to them of the illegal interests of client.[26]

[22] Freeman (n 11) 1136.
[23] John N Hazard, 'Soviet Law: An Introduction' (1936) 36 Colum L Rev 1236, 1242–43.
[24] Cited in Harold J Berman, 'What Makes Socialist Law Socialist' (1971) 20 Probs Communism 24, 30.
[25] GM Razi, 'Legal Education and the Role of the Lawyer in the Soviet Union and the Countries of Eastern Europe' (1960) 48 Calif L Rev 776, 793.
[26] ibid 797.

B. The Vanguard Party

The leadership of a communist party is the key feature of socialist law. John N Hazard states that '"Guidance of the working mass by the working class, the core of which is the Marxist-Leninist party" become the primary basic law to be observed by any country embarking upon a Marxian socialist course.'[27] To be sure, one-party rule is not distinctive to socialist law but common in other forms of authoritarian law. However, the distinctiveness of party leadership lies in the idea of vanguardism, which holds that the working class is intellectually more advanced than the working masses, and therefore leads the latter in the course of social progress towards socialism and ultimately communism. The most advanced members of the working class are organized into a communist party. The party is therefore a vanguard party leading the state and society to achieve socialist goals. As the party aims to achieve socialism, it takes Marxism-Leninism as the guiding ideology.

The party's vanguard leadership is the identity of socialist law. John N Hazard writes that 'the role of the Communist party is so fundamental to the inspiration, drafting, and application of law in Marxist socialist states that its inclusion among other criteria of classification is obligatory'.[28] More specifically, socialist law is the legal embodiment of the party policy. Legal institutions such as courts and lawyers are under party leadership. Leaders of the legal institutions are normally senior party members. Therefore, legal institutions operate under the party's vanguard leadership.

C. Democratic Centralism

The Leninist doctrine of 'democratic centralism' aims to combine 'democratic' discussion and centralized decision and action. After 'democratic' discussion, superiors will issue a decision that requires unquestioning obedience from their inferiors.[29] Democratic centralism was originally developed as a principle of the party but was then extended to state institutions. Applied in state institutions, this principle rejects the separation of powers, subordinates the judiciary to the legislature and the government, and subjects local courts to the control of a powerful centralized super court.[30] The consequence is that courts are not allowed to make laws and must apply legislative and administrative regulations.

[27] John N Hazard, *Communists and Their Law* (University of Chicago Press 1969) 19.
[28] ibid 33.
[29] A Nove, 'Some Aspects of Soviet Constitutional Theory' (1949) 12 Mod L Rev 19.
[30] Partlett and Ip (n 2) 502.

D. Statist Rights

Individual rights in socialist law are statist in three senses: derivative, collective, and regulative.

First, socialist rights derive from the state, not from individuals as human beings. Rights are gifts the state confers on individuals. The practice of rights therefore depends on the state's positive duties, including implementing relevant policies, investigating violations of rights, and educating citizens about their rights.[31]

Second, socialist rights are collective. Individuals are allowed to practice their rights, not merely for their personal interests but for collective interests, particularly for legal, political, economic, and social development towards socialism. The collective interests are the state interests, and other interests of society determined by the state. In socialist law:

> emphasis is placed on collective action since collectively the citizens can better provide for the interests of the individual. The real elevation of the individual depends upon the coalescing of his interests with the interests of the state, and as a result it is the duty of every citizen to submit his personal interests to the collective interests of the state.[32]

Third, to ensure that rights are practiced for state interests, rights are under the state's regulation. Regulation means 'intentional intervention in the activities of a target population, where the intervention is typically direct—involving binding standard-setting, monitoring, and sanctioning—and exercised by public-sector actors on the economic activities of private-sector actors'.[33] Regulation of rights refers to the state's intentional intervention into the practice of rights of individuals for state interests. To regulate rights, the state sets up legal rules for rights practice, supervises rights practice, and punishes individuals the state considers to be abusing their individual rights to undermine collective interests. The punishment includes the withdrawal of the rights. Thus, socialist rights are under the state's regulative control. The consequence is that rights do not limit the state but are limited by the state.

[31] Thomas E Towe, 'Fundamental Rights in the Soviet Union: A Comparative Approach' (1967) 115 U Pa L Rev 1251, 1265–66.

[32] ibid 1264.

[33] Christel Koop and Martin Lodge, 'What is Regulation? An Interdisciplinary Concept Analysis' (2015) 11 Regul Gov 95, 105.

E. Statist Economy

Another Marxist-Leninist idea underpinning the socialist legal tradition is economic statism, which holds that the state should take the lead in the economy to ensure economic development towards socialism. One way for the state to lead the economy is through planning. Economic planning

> is an essential feature of socialism. It expresses the fact that socialist economy does not develop in an elemental way but that its development is guided and directed by the conscious will of organized society. Planning is the means of subjecting the operation of economic laws and the economic development of society to the direction of human will.[34]

The Marxist-Leninist theory of planning believes that:

> the way to ensure that a socialist economy exhibits superior rationality to the anarchy of production prevalent under capitalism is for a national economic plan to be drawn up and subsequently implemented. Each person, guided by the internalized desire to achieve social rationality, will strive to carry it out in an efficient way. The forces of production will be organized rationally.[35]

The centrally planned economy was adopted in USSR in 1930–34, and after World War II widely extended to the socialist world, 'first in Eastern Europe in 1949–53, then in China in 1953–7, and then in countries such as Vietnam and Cuba'.[36]

Apart from economic planning, the socialist state can also control the economy through the entrenchment of the leading role of the state economic sectors in the economy, the prominent role of state ownership, and the state's regulation of the economy by law. In the socialist legal tradition, the statist economy is embedded in law. The classical socialist constitutions established the principle of a planned economy, state ownership, the leading role of the state economic sectors, and the state's management of the economy by law. The statist economy was established by ordinary law, particularly economic law. Economic law is a body of legal rules that the socialist states use to manage the economy to ensure its development towards socialism.

IV. DIFFUSION OF THE SOCIALIST LEGAL TRADITION

Socialist law or Soviet law was formulated in Russia after the communist revolution of 1917 and historically extended throughout the Soviet Union in the 1920s, and

[34] Oskar Lange, 'The Role of Planning in Socialist Economy' (1958) 4 Indian Econ Rev 1.
[35] Michael Ellman, 'The Fundamental Problem of Socialist Planning' (1978) 2 Ox Econ Pap 249.
[36] Michael Ellman, *Socialist Planning* (3rd edn, CUP 2014) 11.

to Eastern and Central Europe after World War II.[37] After World War II, the Soviet Union supported socialist revolutions in China, Vietnam, Laos, North Korea, and Cuba. Consequently, the new socialist states created following the revolutions relied heavily on Soviet law to construct their socialist legal systems, usually with the support of the Soviet Union.[38] The diffusion of socialist law is evident in three aspects: ideational, institutional, and substantive. The five states adopt socialist ideas, institutions, and substantive rules.

A. Diffusion of Socialist Law in China

Before the advent of the socialist legal tradition, Chinese law was shaped by the Confucian and civil legal traditions. The Confucian legal tradition dominated traditional legal systems for a thousand years from the Han dynasty (202 BCE–9 CE, 25–220 CE) to the fall of the Qing dynasty (1636–1912).[39] The Xinhai Revolution in 1911 overturned the Qing dynasty and created the Republic of China. The republican government enacted the 'Code of Six Laws' (*Liu Fa Quan Shu*), which relied heavily on civil law tradition.[40]

The civil law system of the Republic of China was not applied to the entire Chinese territory due to the domestic conflict between the Nationalist Party of China and the Communist Party of China (CPC). The CPC was created in 1921. In 1931, it founded the Chinese Soviet Republic (CSR) within the territory of China's Jiangxi province, which existed until 1937. The CSR attempted to create a socialist legal system, modelled on Soviet law. The CSR enacted several laws for the protection of the ruling working class from landlords, rich peasants, and 'national bourgeoisie'. These include an outline of a draft constitution, a land law, a labour law, a family law, a resolution on economic policy, and regulations on the punishment of counterrevolutionaries. The CSR also established a system of people's courts.[41]

After defeating the Nationalist Party of China, the CPC founded the People's Republic of China (PRC) in 1949. The CPC abolished the Six Codes and other laws of the republican government. This abolition aimed to eradicate capitalist influences and to create a national system of socialist law in China.[42] To create a

[37] Peter B Maggs, 'Soviet Law', Britannica <https://www.britannica.com/topic/Soviet-law> accessed 5 June 2024.

[38] Partlett and Ip (n 2) 463.

[39] See generally Geoffrey MacCormack, *The Spirit of Traditional Chinese Law* (University of Georgia Press 1996).

[40] See generally Michael Ng, *Legal Transplantation in Early Twentieth-Century China Practicing Law in Republican Beijing (1910s–1930s)* (Routledge 2014).

[41] Albert Chen, *An Introduction to the Legal System of the People's Republic of China* (5th edn, LexisNexis 2018) 27–28. See also William Elliott Butler, *The Legal System of the Chinese Soviet Republic, 1931–1934* (Transnational Publishers 1983).

[42] Mo Zhang, 'The Socialist Legal System with Chinese Characteristics: China's Discourse for the Rule of Law and a Bitter Experience' (2010) 24 Temp Int'l & Comp LJ 32.

national system of socialist law, between 1949 and 1953, the communist government in China enacted several laws, including the Land Reform Law, the Regulations on the Punishment of Counterrevolutionaries, the Regulations on the Punishment of Corruption, the Marriage Law, the Trade Union Law, and the Outline for Regional National Autonomy. The PRC's socialist legal system is not completely new, however, as it is based on the laws of the CSR.[43]

Similarly to the way socialist law was introduced in the CSR, the diffusion of Soviet law played an important role in the creation of PRC's socialist legal system.[44] 'Almost all laws and regulations promulgated in the country in early 1950s, including the 1954 Constitution, evidenced a clear Soviet influence.'[45] During the period 1949–57:

> A massive project of Soviet assistance was launched, involving 'roughly ten thousand' Soviet advisors who came to teach in China. The concept of a universal socialist legal system for new communist states was a major area of collaboration in this 'golden age' of Sino-Soviet cooperation. During this period, Chinese legal education 'was totally under the guidance of Soviet experts'. A survey of Russian-language Soviet literature on Chinese legal development showed that Soviet and Chinese models were converging at this point.[46]

The Cultural Revolution (1966–1976) was initiated by Mao Zedong to purge counterrevolutionaries, including traditional and capitalist elements within the Party. This socio-political movement induced the regression of socialist law in China. In the Party's official newspaper, lawlessness was lauded, and law was condemned as a bourgeois impediment to revolutionary masses. Courts were merged into the public security bodies, which were both placed under military control, law schools were closed, and the procuratorates were abolished in 1969.[47]

In 1974, a small group of young intellectuals, the Li Yizhe group, circulated a document condemning the Cultural Revolution as the cause of 'lawlessness' (*wufa wutian*) in China.[48] Mo Zhang notes that 'Many Chinese commentators describe the Cultural Revolution as a time of legal anarchy.'[49] In contrast, some commenters argue about the continuation of the socialist legal system under the Cultural

[43] Chen (n 41) 30.

[44] Partlett and Ip (n 2) 475–76. George Ginsburgs, 'Soviet Sources on the Law of the Chinese People's Republic' (1968) 18 Uni Tor LJ 179–97.

[45] Partlett and Ip (n 2) 33.

[46] ibid 475–76. See also Deborah Kaple, 'Agents of Change: Soviet Advisers and High Stalinist Management in China, 1949–1960' (2016) 18 J Cold War Stud 5.

[47] Chen (n 41) 36–37.

[48] Pierre Brunel, Stanley Rosen, and Jonathan Unger (eds), *On Socialist Democracy and the Chinese Legal System: The Li Yizhe Debates* (Routledge 2016).

[49] Zhang (n 42) 34.

Revolution.[50] These include the continuation of socialist legal principles such as the guiding role of socialist ideologies (Marxism-Leninism and Mao Zedong Thought), proletariat dictatorship, and the leadership of the CPC. Formal law was not completely absent. The National People's Congress passed a new Constitution, and the State Council enacted some new administrative regulations. The continuation was arguably also evident in legal institutions. Courts still existed and heard civil and criminal cases.[51]

Legal change in China under the Cultural Revolution is the regression of socialist law. The Cultural Revolution did not completely destroy socialist law in China. The identity of socialist law remained, particularly the ideological nature of socialist law as the tool to realize socialism. The ideological nature of socialist law was exceedingly amplified and personalized under the Cultural Revolution. At the same time, legal change occurred. But legal change under the Cultural Revolution was regressive in that it undermined the normal operation of legal institutions (such as courts) of the socialist legal system.

B. Diffusion of Socialist Law in Vietnam

Before the adoption of socialist law, the Vietnamese legal systems were dominated by the Confucian and civil legal traditions. The Confucian legal tradition diffused from China to Vietnam and shaped the legal systems of various Vietnamese dynasties from the fifteenth century. French colonialism resulted in the coercive diffusion of the civil legal tradition in Vietnam in the early twentieth century. The French colonists enacted three separate civil codes in three Vietnamese regions: the Abbreviated Civil Code 1883 in Cochinchina (south), the Civil Code Implements in the Vietnamese Courts in Tokin (north) *1983*, and the Central Vietnam Civil Code 1936 in Annam (centre).[52] In addition, the colonists also enacted the Vietnamese Commercial Code in 1942 and numerous regulations concerning civil and commercial law issues.[53] Moreover, the colonists 'seconded French legal personnel including judges, court officials, and lawyers to administer the system'.[54]

[50] Shao-Chuan Leng, 'The Role of Law in the People's Republic of China as Reflecting Mao Tse-Tung's Influence' (1977) 68 J Crim L & Criminology 356; Xu Lizhi, 'Beyond "Destruction" and "Lawlessness": The Legal System during the Cultural Revolution' in Daniel Leese and Puck Engman (eds), *Victims, Perpetrators, and the Role of Law in Maoist China: A Case-Study Approach* (De Gruyter Oldenbourg 2018) 28–40.

[51] Lizhi (n 50) 28–40.

[52] Bui Xuan Hai, 'Vietnamese Company Law: The Development and Corporate Governance Issues' (2006) 18 Bond L Rev 22, 23.

[53] Pham Duy Nghia, *Vietnamese Business Law in Transition* (The Gioi Publishers 2002) 32.

[54] John Gillespie, 'Understanding Legality in Vietnam' in Stéphanie Balme and Mark Sidel (eds), *Vietnam's New Order: International Perspectives on the State and Reform in Vietnam* (Springer 2007) 140–41.

The Indochinese Communist Party, created by Ho Chi Minh in 1930, led a revolution in 1945, which overturned French colonial rule in Vietnam and founded the Democratic Republic of Vietnam (DRV). The DRV, however, selectively reserved some elements of colonial law and adopted some Western liberal-democratic legal institutions, as evident in the 1946 Constitution. The diffusion of socialist law from the Soviet Union took place in North Vietnam around the 1950s and expanded to the whole country after the 1975 unification.[55]

The Soviet concept of 'socialist legality' was first adopted by the Party Congress in 1960. Socialist legality emphasizes the use of law as an instrument of proletariat dictatorship.[56] As the embodiment of instrumentalism, socialist law developed in Vietnam before the reform period was mainly public law with Soviet influence. The court and procuracy systems were transplanted from the Soviet Union, as evident in the enactment of the 1959 Constitution, the 1960 Law on the Organization of the People's Courts, and the 1960 Law on the Organization of the People's Procuracy.[57]

Particularly the Law on the Organization of the People's Courts defines that the goals of the courts' adjudication are, among others, to contribute to building socialism in North Vietnam (Article 1). Thus, the courts are considered an instrument for the state to pursue socialist transformation. The Law creates a hierarchical court system along the line of the Soviet model, including: the Supreme People's Court; the local people's courts at provincial and district levels and at autonomous regions; and the military courts (Article 2). The Law provides that 'The Supreme People's Court guides lower-level People's Courts to apply laws, guidelines, policies and procedures in adjudication' (Article 21). This demonstrates the centralized nature of the socialist court system according to which local courts are under the control and supervision of the highest court.

The Constitution of the Socialist Republic of Vietnam, promulgated in December 1980, strictly adhered to the 1977 Constitution of the USSR, evident by the confirmations of the principle of dictatorship of the proletariat, the exclusive leadership of the Communist Party, the centrally planned economy, citizen's duties and statist rights, and the Leninist constitutional structure consisting of the supreme National Assembly, the collective presidency called Council of State, the subordinate government called Council of Ministers, the procuracies, and the courts.[58]

Economic statism was embodied in the law and legal institutions establishing the state ownership and the centrally planned economy. The 1953 Land Reform

[55] Penelope Nicholson, *Borrowing Court Systems: The Experience of Socialist Vietnam* (Brill 2007); P Nicholson and PL Phuong, 'Roots and Routes: Adapting the Soviet-Inspired Vietnamese Court and Procuracy System' in Hualing Fu and others (eds), *Socialist Law in Socialist East Asia* (CUP 2018) 224; PD Nghia and DH Ha, 'The Soviet Legacy and Its Impact on Contemporary Vietnam' in Hualing Fu and others (eds), *Socialist Law in Socialist East Asia* (CUP 2018) 97.

[56] Nicholson and Phuong (n 55) 229–30.

[57] ibid 227–28.

[58] Bui Ngoc Son, *Constitutional Change in the Contemporary Socialist World* (OUP 2020) 118.

Law, influenced by Chinese and Soviet experiences, created the legal base for an agrarian reform between 1953 and 1956, which led to a large-scale collectivization of agriculture and redistribution of lands from landlords and rich peasants to poor and middle-class peasants.[59] The Soviet model of the centrally planned economy was prevailing in North Vietnam in the mid-1960s and expanded to the whole county after the 1975 unification.[60] The 1980 Constitution provides the foundational legal base for public ownership of means of productions and the state's centralized management of the economy (Articles 19 and 20).

C. Diffusion of Socialist Law in Laos

When Laos was a part of French Indochina, its law was shaped by the civil law tradition, like the case of Vietnam. In 1975, the Lao socialist state, formally named Lao People's Democratic Republic (Lao PDR), was created after a revolution led by Lao People's Revolutionary Party (LPRP), a communist party that overthrew the royalist government and ended three decades of civil war. The LPRP quickly adopted the socialist legal model with the assistance of East German legal experts, among others.[61] Consequently, in the first decade after the communist revolution, some elements of socialist law were diffused in Laos.

The LPRP, which adopted Marxism-Leninism as its official ideology, functioned as a ruling, vanguard party leading socialist transformation in Laos.[62]

> The instructions and decisions made within the Party were considered binding for all citizens and thus formed an integral part of the country's legal system. The Party rule was also strong at the level of the 17 provinces (one of them being the Prefecture of Vientiane) and at the level of districts and villages.[63]

This means the Party was not merely a political institution, separate from the state. Rather, it was a legal institution, an essential part of the legal system, with its resolutions and policy having legal binding effects.

Law and legal institutions were instruments for the party-state to pursue socialist transformation, including suppressing counterrevolutionaries. The new communist government abolished the former French-inspired constitution and

[59] Nghia and Ha (n 55) 99.

[60] ibid 99.

[61] Michael Bogdan, 'Legal Aspects of the Re-Introduction of a Market. Economy in Laos' (1991) 17 Rev Social L 108.

[62] See generally Martin Rathie, 'The History and Evolution of the Lao People's Revolutionary' in Vanina Boute and Vatthana Pholsena (eds), *Changing Lives in Laos: Society, Politics, and Culture in a Post-Socialist State* (NUS Press 2017) 19.

[63] Bogdan (n 61) 108.

laws and ruled without a constitution until 1991 and with few laws.[64] The government issued several resolutions, orders, and decrees to regulate social-economic administration.[65] Due to the dearth of legislation, the government managed society with the Party's guidelines, policies, and administrative regulation.[66] The official justification was that the law was deficient in Laos as the country needed to focus on restoration of the economy and national unity, which had been undermined by the civil war.[67]

In its Congress in 1973, the LPRP stipulated that democratic centralism must be adopted as the principle for the new state.[68] The Supreme People's Assembly, however, was not an elected body until 1989. It was appointed with forty-six members in 1975 by the National Congress of People's Representatives, a creation of the Pathet Lao movement under the control of the LPRP. The Supreme People's Assembly, in theory, was a legislature, but it met for short sessions once or twice a year only to approve the decisions and appointments already made by the LPRP.[69] Some pieces of legislation were enacted to support building administrative institutions, including the Law on the Establishment of the Council of Ministers of Lao PDR (1978); the Law on the Establishment of the People's Assembly and Local Administration (1978); and the Law on the Council of Ministers of Lao PDR (1982).[70]

Between 1975 and 1990, Laos lacked a separate court system and the Ministry of Justice performed judicial functions.[71] The subordination of judicial activities to the executive government reflects the centralist aspect of democratic centralism. From 1975 to 1982, the Judgment Department under the Ministry of Justice functioned as a central court. At the local level, by 1979, the provincial justice divisions functioned as the local courts under the control of the local administrative authorities. In 1982, on the base of the Judgment Department of the Ministry of Justice, the Supreme People's Court was created, consisting of civil and criminal chambers and five supportive divisions.[72] The judicial institutions were mainly

[64] Marcus Radetzki, 'From Communism to Capitalism in Laos: The Legal Dimension' (1994) 34 Asian Surv 799.

[65] Laos' Ministry of Justice, Office of the Supreme People's Prosecutor, People's Supreme Court, and Ministry of Security, *Master Plan on Development of the Rule of Law in the Lao P. D. R toward the Year 2020* (2009) (hereinafter, Master Plan).

[66] Chalơn Nhiapaohơ, 'Sự Hình Thành Và Phát Triển Chế Định Lập Pháp Nước CHDCND Lào' ['The Formation and Development of the Legislative Institution of Lao PDR'] (Tạp Chí Nghiên Cứu Lập Pháp, 1 December 2004), Sự hình thành và phát triển chế định lập pháp nước CHDCND Lào, <http://www.lapphap.vn> accessed 05 June 2024.

[67] Master Plan (n 65).

[68] Sẻng Vi Lay Phon Kẹo Pạ Sợt, *Một số Giải pháp Xây dựng Nhà nước Pháp Quyền ở Cộng Hòa Dân chủ Nhân dân Lào hiện nay [Some Solutions for Building the Rule of Law State in the Lao People's Republic Nowadays]* (PhD Dissertation, Ho Chi Minh Academy of National Politics 2005) 38.

[69] Bogdan (n 61) 107.

[70] Master Plan (n 65).

[71] ibid.

[72] ibid.

an instrument for the new government to punish counterrevolutionaries. The Institute of Legal Education was closed 'although a number of Laotians were sent to take law degrees in the USSR, Vietnam and other states sharing the ideology of the Vientiane regime'.[73]

In the early years after the communist revolution, the Lao new government adopted the Soviet model of centralized economy to quickly transform Laos into a socialist country. 'Means of production were collectivized: industry and trade by nationalization and agriculture by forcing the peasants into cooperatives'.[74] The centralized economy under state management did not require legislative laws but operated under governmental regulations such as the Decree on State Enterprises of 1985 and the Decree on Agricultural Cooperatives of 1978.[75] Fundamental rights were curtailed. The communists sent 'the officials of the previous regime and other persons suspected of being political adversaries' to 're-education camps' without trials.[76] Those who were put on trial 'were tried summarily and without the benefit of a defense counsel or any right to appeal'.[77]

In short, in the first decade after the communist revolution, the new government in Laos adopted major elements of socialist law. The incipient socialist legal system in Laos was under the vanguard leadership of a communist party. Law and institutions were instruments for the party-state to transform Laos into a socialist society. The public ownership of means of production and the centralized economy were established by governmental regulation. Political freedom was under the state's strict control.

D. Diffusion of Socialist Law in North Korea

Korea's traditional law was shaped by the Confucian legal tradition and its modern law was influenced by the civil legal tradition under Japanese colonization (1910–45).[78] After liberation from Japan in 1945, Korea was divided into two zones: the north was occupied by the Soviet Union and the south was occupied by the United States. The Soviet Union's occupation of North Korea led to the diffusion of Soviet law in the territory. In 1946, the North Korean Workers' Party was formed on the basis of merging the North Korean Communist Party with the New Democratic Party. This created the foundation for the emergence of the Party's vanguardism as the fundamental norm of legal formation.

[73] Bogdan (n 61) 109.
[74] ibid 108.
[75] ibid.
[76] ibid.
[77] ibid
[78] William Shaw, *Legal Norms in a Confucian State* (Institute of East Asian Studies Publications Series, Korea Research Monographs, No 5, University of California, Berkeley 1981); Kim MS-H, *Law and Custom in Korea: Comparative Legal History* (CUP 2012).

The pro-Soviet body called the North Korean Provisional People's Committee (NKPPC) created in 1946 enacted several laws of socialist nature. In June 1946, it passed a labour law protecting the eight-hour workday and worker's basic rights.[79] In August 1946, it enacted a law nationalizing industry, transport, communication, and banks.[80] 'The general framework contained in these Korean laws followed the general pattern laid down in similar Soviet legislation.'[81] These laws institutionalized Kim II Sung's Twenty-Point Platform, a programme for social-economic revolution in North Korea.[82] Christopher Hale states:

> most of the Platform's points (with the exception of the anti-Japanese facets) merely summarized the political, economic, and social measures found in the 1936 Soviet Constitution. Whatever the case, the Platform fulfilled its role well, serving as a guide for future legislation and, more importantly, adding to the sense of legitimacy of the government during this crucial formative period.[83]

Thus, the laws during the formative time were an instrument to implement a political programme. They translated some aspects of the statist economy rooted in the Soviet Constitution into legal forms.

The North Korean socialist state, or Democratic People's Republic of Korea (DPRK), was established in 1948 under the support of the Soviet Union. In the early years after its establishment, the North Korean state abolished the Japanese colonial law and adopted socialist law with the Soviet Union's assistance.[84] Pyong Choon Hahm states:

> as a product of Marxism-Leninism, the North Korean legal theory had followed the Soviet model very closely until the Soviet mentor began to change course subsequent to Khrushchev's attack on Stalin at the 20th Congress of the Communist Party of the Soviet Union in February 1956. Until this time the North Korean legal system was almost an exact replica of the Soviet system[85]

The North Korean state adopted the instrumentalist, vanguardist conceptions of socialist law and legal institutions. To illustrate, in a national conference for legal workers in 1958, Kim II Sung stated:

[79] Christopher Hale, 'North Korea in Evolution: The Correlation Between the Legal Framework and the Changing Dynamic of Politics and the Economy' (2002) 33 Korea Obs 368.
[80] ibid 367.
[81] Ilpyong J Kim, 'The Judicial and Administrative Structure in North Korea' (1963) 14 China Q 96.
[82] Hale (n 79) 368.
[83] ibid 382–83.
[84] Patricia Goedde, 'Law "Of Our Own Style": The Evolution and Challenges of the North Korean Legal System' (2003) 27 Fordham Int'l LJ 1269.
[85] Hahm Pyong Choon, 'Ideology and Criminal Law in North Korea' (1969) 17 Am J Comp L 77.

> The law of our country is an important weapon for implementing the policies of our state. The policies of our state are the policies of our Party. It is impossible to enforce the law without knowledge of the political line and policies of our Party . . . Our judicial functionaries are political workers who implement the policies of our Party and all the policies of our state. Law cannot exist by itself without definite basis. Being a reflection of policies, law must be subordinated to policies and must not be divorced from them.[86]

This exemplifies the ideological diffusion of socialist law in North Korea. Following socialist jurisprudence, the North Korean leader understood law as an instrument to implement state policy. Law is also conceived as being the expression of the Party's policy, which means law is the embodiment of Party's vanguard leadership. Legal institutions are also an instrument to implement state policy under the Party's vanguard leadership. The instrumental and vanguardist conceptions of legal institutions are further elaborated in this statement by Kim II Sung during the same conference:

> It is all right to call for obeying the law alone. Since judges and public procurators exercise their duties on the strength of the law, there is nothing wrong with their adhering to the law alone. But obeying the law by no means implies rejecting the leadership of the Party. As a matter of fact, those who obey the law are those who obey the Party. Those who obey the law alone and do not obey the Party are, in fact, those who do not obey the law either.[87]

Apart from ideological diffusion, institutional diffusion of socialist law in North Korea is also evident. North Korea adopted Soviet legal institutions. Patricia Goedde points out that:

> Soviet advisors in North Korea had a heavy role in drafting the 1948 DPRK Constitution along with numerous reform laws and ordinances . . . Although the advisors did not implant pure Soviet law in North Korea, North Korean judicial practice started to follow a Soviet pattern in terms of court structure and the procuracy.[88]

The 1948 Constitution of North Korea and the Court Organization Law of 1950 established a court system modelled after the Soviet model. Like other socialist courts, according to the Court Organization Law, North Korean courts do not merely have adjudicative function; they also have political function to educate

[86] Cited in Cho Sung Yoon, 'The Judicial System of North Korea' (1971) 12 Asian Surv 1180.
[87] Cited in ibid 1179.
[88] Goedde (n 84) 1270.

'both the criminal and the public in the strict observance of the law and in loyalty to the country'.[89] Thus, courts are political instruments for protecting the state interests. The court system is centralized, including the Supreme Court, provincial courts, district people's courts, and special courts in military units.[90] The Supreme Court is vested with the power to supervise the judicial work of all courts.[91] It supervises inferior courts by issuing 'guiding directives', which are summaries of judicial cases formulated by the Supreme Court or by its plenary sessions.[92]

As in the Soviet Union and other socialist states, ordinary citizens were allowed to participate in the first trial as people's assessors who had equal rights with judges.[93] According to Sung Yoon Cho:

> this system was instituted in North Korea by the Communists during the early days of the Soviet occupation ... The assessors are elected in the same manner as judges by the people's assemblies at various levels, after having been nominated by workers' and people's organizations. In practice the Workers' Party exercises tight control over the selection of assessors.[94]

Thus, judicial practices are not merely legal professional practices; they are also political work involving mass participation under the Party's leadership.

North Korea also adopted the Soviet style of lawyers as state workers. The state issued two regulations on lawyers and lawyers' associations in 1947 and 1948 respectively.[95] The lawyer system is the embodiment of instrumentalism and the Party's vanguardism.

> The fundamental duties of the lawyer, a North Korean lawyer said, are to cooperate with the court in discovering the objective truth and promoting administrative justice as well as to safeguard the interests of the state and the people from criminals and various criminal acts, thereby defending and implementing the policy of the Workers' Party.[96]

In other words, lawyers are the instrumental agents for protecting the state interests and under the Party's leadership.

The 1948 Constitution created the Leninist-style procuracy as an institution for protecting socialist legality, which was authorized to supervise the observation of the law by all ministries, officials, and citizens (Article 90). It also established

[89] Yoon (n 86) 1181.
[90] ibid 1168.
[91] Constitution of the Democratic People's Republic of Korea (1948), art 89.
[92] Yoon (n 86) 1169.
[93] Constitution of the Democratic People's Republic of Korea (1948), art 84.
[94] Yoon (n 86) 1171.
[95] ibid 1176.
[96] ibid 1178 (internal citation omitted).

a statist (albeit not purely socialist) economy. The Constitution confirmed the state ownership of means of production, although private ownership is tolerated (Article 5). It provides for the state's planning economy, although private economy is allowed (Article 10). The state controls foreign trade. The Constitution stipulates that 'foreign trade is conducted by the state or under its supervision' (Article 5).

North Korea also adopted the Soviet model of criminal law and criminal procedural law. North Korea's Criminal Code and Code of Criminal Procedure enacted in 1950 are considered 'the Korean language translations of the Soviet codes'.[97] Like the Soviet model, these laws particularly functioned as an instrument for the state to educate the people (eg demonstration trials) and to legalize collective moral duties (eg criminal sanctions imposed on a parent who failed to look after their child).[98]

North Korea also sought to mirror the Soviet model of civil law. North Korea declared:

> On February 1, 1958, the Government of the Republic made a decision on writing and preparation of civil law and civil procedure law. Drafting participants are putting wisdom and endeavor in, and are committed to reflect the base results that we have achieved under the wise leadership of our party after the liberation, based on the Marxist and Leninist legal theory and the advanced legislative experience of the Soviet Union.[99]

This statement explicitly acknowledges the Marxist and Soviet bases of North Korean civil law. The statement also suggests that legislative civil lawmaking embodies party vanguardism.

Elements of socialist law are fully embodied in the 1972 Socialist Constitution of the DPRK. The Constitution states that 'the law of the Democratic People's Republic of Korea reflects the wishes and interests of the working people and is a basic instrument for state administration, and all institutions, enterprises, organizations and citizens shall conscientiously observe it' (Article 17). Thus, the instrumental conception of socialist legality is firmly entrenched at the constitutional level. The Constitution also confirmed the Juche idea of the Workers' Party of Korea as the guiding ideology of the state, the principle of democratic centralism, the means of production owned by the state and social cooperative organizations, a planned economy, and citizen rights consistent with the socialist system (Articles, 4, 9, 31, and 50).

Following the enactment of the 1972 Constitution, North Korea enacted several laws in late 1970s and early 1980s. The Criminal Code and Code of Criminal Procedure were amended in 1974. The first Code of Civil Procedure was adopted in 1976 to institutionalize party policy, regulate socialist ownership, and facilitate

[97] Choon (n 85) 77.
[98] ibid 85, 86.
[99] Cited in Lee Hyowon, 'Review on the Form and System of North Korean Law' (2018) 27 IJKUS 87.

economic plans. A new Land Law was adopted in 1977 to consolidate the state's ownership of land. The new Socialist Labor Law was promulgated in 1978, which focused on labour administration rather than workers' rights as in the previous labour law.[100] Thus, these laws continue to embody various aspects of socialist law, particularly instrumentalism, party vanguardism, and the statist economy.

E. Diffusion of Socialist Law in Cuba

Cuba gained independence from Spain in 1898, followed by the rule of the US military government until 1902. 'As a result, Cuba's legal system has dual origins. Its primary parentage is Spanish law and European civil legal tradition, but it reflects some aspects of U.S. law as well.'[101] After the Cuban Revolution in 1959 overturned the Government of Fulgencio Batista, socialist law diffused in Cuba.

In 1961, the revolution was recognized as being socialist and Fidel Castro displayed his commitment to Marxism-Leninism.[102] The revolutionary leaders began to control political and legal institutions.[103] Between 1956 and 1963, the new revolutionary government enacted over a hundred laws, including the first Agrarian Reform Law (1959), the Urban Reform Law (1960), the Nationalization of Law (1960) nationalizing private enterprises, the Nationalization of Education Law (1961), and the second Agrarian Reform Law (1963).[104] The revolutionary laws dismantled the pre-existing laws of the old regime and sought to radically transform the social and economic order.[105] As these laws were enacted by socialist revolutionaries, they have some features of socialist law. They were an instrument for the revolutionary government to pursue socialist transformation. The nationalization of private enterprises reflects the socialist principle of statist economy.

Particularly, the creation of popular courts in 1961 was the consequence of the diffusion of Soviet law. These courts 'were patterned after comrades' courts in the Soviet Union and charged with educating the rural poor in correct behavioral patterns'.[106] Fidel Castro explained that the function of these courts was 'to recognize and resolve these problems, not with sanctions, as in the traditional style, but rather with measures that would have a profound educational spirit'.[107] Thus, like Soviet courts, Cuban popular courts are an instrument for the new regime to transform behaviours so as to create the *socialist person*.

[100] Hale (n 79) 382–83.
[101] Debra Evenson, *Law and Society in Contemporary Cuba* (2nd edn, Kluwer Law International 2003) 3.
[102] Max Azicri, 'An Introduction to Cuban Socialist Law' (1980) 6 Rev Social L 153; Evenson (n 101) 3.
[103] Evenson (n 101) 6.
[104] ibid 7.
[105] ibid.
[106] Luis Salas, 'The Judicial System of Postrevolutionary Cuba' (1983) 8 Nova LJ 48.
[107] Cited in ibid.

In the 1970s, Soviet-socialist law was systemically diffused in Cuba when the new government sought to institutionalize the state. In the late 1960s, the Central Committee of the Communist Party of Cuba created the Commission on Judicial Studies to formulate new laws. Members of the Commission included jurists trained in capitalism but committed to socialist doctrine. Cubans studied Soviet legislation closely, although they did not simply copy it.[108] Consequently, major institutional, procedural, and substantive laws were adopted, including: the Law of the Organization of the Judicial System (1973); the Law of Criminal Procedure (1973); the Law of Civil and Administrative Procedure (1974); the Maternity Law (1974); the Family Code (1975); the Constitution (1976); the Law of the Political-Administrative Division of the Republic (1976); the Electoral Law (1976); the Law of the Organization of the Central Administration of the State (1976); the New Law of the Organization of the Judicial System; and the Criminal Code (1979).[109] With the enactments of these legal instruments, the socialist state and legal Marxist-Leninist principles and institutions were established in Cuba. The 1976 socialist Constitution in particular and the 1973 and 1977 reorganization of the judicial system created the institutional framework for the socialist legal system.[110]

The 1976 Constitution (Article 9) confirms the instrumental nature of socialist legality:

> The Constitution and the laws of the socialist State are the juridical expression of the socialist relations of production and of the interests and the will of the working people. All the organs of the State, their leaders, functionaries, and employees, act within the limits of their respective competences and are under the obligation to strictly observe the socialist legality and to see to the respect for it in the life of the entire society.

This provision indicates the Marxist materialist conception of law as the superstructure determined by economic relations. It also articulates the class nature of socialist law as the expression of the will of the working class. Consequently, socialist law is the instrument for the working class to control the strict compliance of the entire population.

The Constitution (Article 5) also embodies party vanguardism:

> The Communist Party of Cuba, the organized Marxist-Leninist vanguard of the working class, is the superior leading force of the society and of the State, which

108 Evenson (n 101) 9. See also Erik Luna, 'Cuban Criminal Justice and the Ideal of Good Governance' (2004) 14(2) Transnat'l L & Contemp Probs 539.

109 Marjorie S Zatz, *Producing Legality: Law and Socialism in Cuba* (Routledge 1994) 54–55.

110 Azicri (n 102) 156.

organizes and orients the common efforts toward the high objectives of the construction of socialism and the progress toward the communist society.

Thus, the Constitution establishes the vanguard role of the Communist Party, its Marxist-Leninist ideology, and its aspirations to achieve socialism and ultimately communism.

The Constitution confirms the principle of democratic centralism and even moves further to articulate in detail its forms such as: 'the provisions of superior State organs are obligatory for the inferior organs'; 'the inferior State organs respond to the superior organs and render account of their management'; and 'the freedom of discussion, the exercise of criticism and self-criticism and the subordination of the minority to the majority, govern in all collegiate State organs' (Article 6).

The Constitution also commits the state to protect many rights. It particularly emphasizes the state's protection of the social rights of workers such as the right to work, the right to rest, the protection of workers with disability, the right to safety and hygiene at work, the right to medical care, and the right to compensation or retirement (Articles 44, 45, 46, and 48). Given that the socialist state is ruled by the working class, it is understandable that the Constitution underlines the statist rights of the workers: the rights that the state grants to the workers, which entail the state's positive duties.

The Constitution establishes key features of the statist economy, including the socialist state ownership of means of production, the state's organization and control of the national economic activity in accordance with the Sole Plan of Socioeconomic Development, the state's organization of enterprises, and foreign trade as an exclusive function of the state (Articles 15, 16, 17, and 18). Thus, the Constitution mandates the dominant role of the state in the national economy.

The 1973 Laws on the Reorganization of the Judicial System established a hierarchical court system including four tiers, namely: the People's Supreme Court; the People's Provincial Courts; the People's Regional Courts; and the People's Courts at the Base. The law stipulates the instrumental role of the courts to protect 'socialist legality'. The law ensures 'democratic centralism' as a principle of judicial administration. The People's Supreme Court is under the supervision of the National Assembly of People's Power.[111]

The 1975 Cuban Family Code was influenced by both Soviet legal experience and pre-revolutionary Cuban civil law.[112] Particularly, the law requires parents to educate and guide their children 'according to the principles of socialist

[111] Max Azicri, 'Change and Institutionalization in the Revolutionary Process: The Cuban Legal System in the 1970s' (1980) 6 Rev Social L 175–76.

[112] Max Azicri, 'The Cuban Family Code: Some Observations on Its Innovations and Continuities' (1980) 6 Rev Social L 183.

morality'.[113] Thus, the family is the institution for preparing the next generations of the socialist person. The Family Code is an instrument for transforming the family structure to pursue socialist objectives.

In short, in the two decades after the Revolution, Cuba adopted principles of socialist law to radically transform its social, political, and economic structure. The diffusion of the socialist law of the Soviet Union and other socialist European countries played an important role in the creation of the socialist legal system in Cuba.

V. CONCLUDING ANALYSIS: TRADITION AND REVOLUTION

Socialist revolution and the diffusion of the socialist legal tradition have resulted in legal revolutions in China, Vietnam, Laos, North Korea, and Cuba. Before the introduction of the socialist legal tradition, the normative foundations of modern legal systems of these five countries had been shaped by principles of the civil law tradition. Socialist legal revolution transforms the normative foundations of the legal order. Marxism-Leninism has become the justification for the new legal order. Legal revolution leads to the replacement of the pre-existing civil legal tradition by the socialist legal tradition.

The socialist legal revolutions in the five countries share a common *context*: social revolutions led by communist leaders and largetransplants of Soviet law. The communist revolutions fundamentally changed the social structure and communist elites use law as an instrument to revolutionize society. Law is used to transform the social structure or the 'mode of production' in Marxist terminology. It is also used as a powerful instrument to create the socialist political, social, and economic relations: the dominant role of the working class over other classes, the state ownership of means of production, the centralized power of the working class, and the state's planned economy.

A socialist legal revolution is accompanied by a large transplantation of Soviet law into the five socialist countries. The communist elites turn to Soviet law because it has already been used to revolutionize the Russian society, it meets the revolutionary purposes of the five countries, and is amenable to the political and legal elites in these countries either through the assistance of Soviet experts or domestic experts' studying Soviet law. The mechanism of Soviet legal transplant is material inducement. The five countries are independent states but they were allies of the Soviet Union. The Soviet Union supported the socialist revolution in these countries and provided them with financial support. The political-economic connections encouraged the five socialist states to adopt Soviet law to secure continued political alliance and economic support.

[113] ibid 186.

Socialist legal revolutions do not occur suddenly but through three common processes: institutionalization, actualization, and legitimatization. These processes are not necessarily sequential but intricately intertwined.

Institutionalization refers to the enactment of formal law along the lines of the socialist legal tradition. The law establishes fundamental principles for socialist relations in power, production, and social life. These principles include socialist legality, the vanguard role of the Communist Party, democratic centralism, the state's ownership of the means of production, the planned economy, the state's protection of social rights, and citizens' duties to the state. Constitution-making plays an important role in this aspect. Formal institutionalization also involves the enactment of legal rules for the establishment of socialist legal institutions (such as the legislature, the bureaucracy, the courts, and the procuracy). This institutionalization is carried out through both constitution-making and legislative enactment of institutional law. Another part of formal institutionalization is the enactment of substantive and procedural legal rules to facilitate the dismissal of old social relations and creation of new social relations. This institutionalization is undertaken by the formal enactments of laws such as land law, criminal law, criminal law procedure, and family law.

Institutionalization involves both the negation of old elements of the previous legal order and the creation of new elements of the socialist legal order. Legal negation radically dismantles elements of the previous legal order. The common feature of legal negation is land reform law. Negation, however, does not mean a clean break with the past. The natural persistence of past legal traditions and socialist revolutionaries' intentional concerns of stability renders the continuity of some old elements in the early process of socialist legal revolution. Creation involves the enactment of new laws (mainly public laws) to set up new institutions and a new system of punishment.

Actualization refers to the real creation and operation of socialist institutions and the use of socialist law to transform the social structure. For example, the communist party takes control over state institutions; courts are set up and punish forces of the former regimes; land is collectivized; private enterprises are abolished; state enterprises are created; and the planned economy is introduced.

Legitimatization involves political efforts to inculcate the new normative principles justifying socialist law among political elites, officials, and the masses so that they will accept these principles. Political elites employ political discourse to inform their fellows, officials, and the public about and indoctrinate new socialist values. The populist courts (the people's courts) trial cases in public to educate the people about the new values of the socialist system. Lawyers, as agents of the state, justify and persuade the public to accept new principles of socialist law.

As the consequence of institutionalization, actualization, and legitimatization, new socialist normative foundations of the emerging legal order are established and inform legal practices. Legal revolution occurs: the socialist legal tradition replaces the civil legal tradition in the five countries.

PART II

SOCIALIST PROJECTS OF LEGAL REFORM

4

China: Legal Reform and Legal Divergence

I. INTRODUCTION

This chapter explores legislative, administrative, judicial, and legal professional reform in China since the country introduced the reform policy in 1978. After four decades of reforms, China has created a sophisticated legal system. This chapter argues that Chinese legal reform is a top-down process of the party-state. Legal exceptionalism incrementally emerges as the dominant intention shaping Chinese legal reform. Chinese legal reform embodies the party-state's aspiration to develop a Chinese socialist legal model divergent from alternative liberal models. Despite significant reforms, the Chinese legal system remains essentially socialist. The current Chinese legal system is a socialist legal system, the extended legal embodiment of the Marxist-Leninist arguments for socialism. Chinese legal reform has nearly reached to its zenith. Room for China's substantive legal reform in the future is narrow due to the limitations of the socialist legal principles.

Chinese legal reform has attracted great academic attention from both Chinese and international scholars.[1] This chapter engages with this body of scholarship. It is also based on my extensive conversations in Mainland China, Hong Kong, Singapore, and Oxford (United Kingdom) on various aspects of Chinese law with Chinese scholars and students.

II. THE EXCEPTIONAL PROJECT OF LEGAL REFORM

After Mao's death, legal reform was introduced as a top-down project of the Chinese Communist Party (hereinafter, the Party or CCP). The legal reform project derives from Party leaders' exceptional intention to create a distinctive Chinese socialist legal model. Legal exceptionalism emerges as the Party leaders' dominant intention shaping legal reform. The Party leaders conduct legal reform to develop a distinctive Chinese socialist legal model.

[1] Xiaobing Li and Qiang Fang (eds), *Modern Chinese Legal Reform: New Perspectives* (University Press of Kentucky 2013); Stanley B Lubman, *Bird in a Cage: Legal Reform in China after Mao* (Stanford University Press 1999); Yan Wang, *Chinese Legal Reform* (Routledge 2003); Y Zhao and M Ng (eds), *Chinese Legal Reform and the Global Legal Order: Adoption and Adaptation* (CUP 2017); R Peerenboom, *China's Long March toward Rule of Law* (CUP 2002).

Legal Reform in the Contemporary Socialist World. Ngoc Son Bui, Oxford University Press. © Ngoc Son Bui 2024.
DOI: 10.1093/9780191948053.003.0004

A. The Socialist Legal System

The programme for socialist modernization was adopted in late 1978, at the Third Plenum of the Eleventh Central Committee of the Communist Party of China. The Plenum marked the beginning of China's 'Reform and Opening-up' (*gaige kaifang*) initiated by Deng Xiaoping. Deng considered law necessary for socialist modernization. Therefore, law reform was initiated as a part of a broader programme for socialist modernization.[2] The Communique recognized the importance of law for political stability and adumbrated directions for law reform, including legislative, judicial, and administrative reforms. It states:

> In order to safeguard people's democracy, it is imperative to strengthen the socialist legal system so that democracy is systematized and written into law in such a way as to ensure the stability, continuity and full authority of this democratic system and these laws; there must be laws for people to follow, these laws must be observed, their enforcement must be strict and law breakers must be dealt with. From now on, legislative work should have an important place on the agenda of the National People's Congress (NPC) and its Standing Committee. Procuratorial and judicial organizations must maintain their independence as is appropriate; they must faithfully abide by the laws, rules, and regulations, serve the people's interests, keep to the facts; guarantee the equality of all people before the people's laws and deny anyone the privilege of being above the law.[3]

The project of legal reform as embodied in the Communique is not clearly exceptionalist, although the Party intended to develop a socialist legal system as a part of Chinese socialism. The expected outcomes of legal reform are social and political stability and economic development, the necessary conditions for socialist modernization in China. Albert Chen identifies three factors shaping the Party's choice of legal reform. First, the lack of acceptance of the authority of law induced the usurpation of political power during the Cultural Revolution. Second, the new leadership believed law and legality are necessary for political and social stability. Third, the new leadership's pragmatic approach to Chinese socialism requires legal reform to facilitate economic development.[4] The new leadership's

[2] PB Potter, 'Legal Reform in China: Institutions, Culture, and Selective Adaptation' (2004) 29 L & Soc Inquiry 465; Carlos Wing-Hung Lo, 'Socialist Legal Theory in Deng Xiaoping's China' (1997) 11 Colum J Asian L 469; Richard Baum, 'Modernization and Legal Reform in Post-Mao China: The Rebirth of Socialist Legality' (1986) 19 Stud Comp Communism 69–103; Carlos WH Lo 'Deng Xiaoping's Ideas on Law: China on the Threshold of a Legal Order' (1992) 32 Asian Surv 649.

[3] Communique of the Third Plenary Session of the 11th Central Committee of the Communist Party of China <https://www.bjreview.com/Special_Reports/2018/40th_Anniversary_of_Reform_and_Opening_up/Timeline/201806/t20180626_800133641.html>accessed 5 June 2024.

[4] Albert Chen, *An Introduction to the Legal System of the People's Republic of China* (5th edn, LexisNexis 2018) 39–40.

concerns of how law can prevent the personal seizure of political power, maintain political stability, and facilitate economic development explain why their direction for legal reform focuses on institutional questions. Lawmaking agendas, judicial independence, and law enforcement became necessary to ensure that the state institutions are under the authority of law, to maintain social stability, and to foster economic development.

Between the 1970s and the 1980s, the strategy for legal reform was classical incrementalism. In 1978, Deng Xiaoping proposed sporadic incremental legal reform, stating that:

> There is a lot of legislative work to do, and we don't have enough trained people. Therefore, legal provisions will have to be less than perfect to start with, then be gradually improved upon. Some laws and statutes can be tried out in particular localities and later enacted nationally after the experience has been evaluated and improvements have been made. Individual legal provisions can be revised or supplemented one at a time, as necessary; there is no need to wait for a comprehensive revision of an entire body of law. In short, it is better to have some laws than none, and better to have them sooner than later.[5]

Deng's classical incrementalism seeks to introduce some small legal changes such as sporadic enactments and revisions of some pieces of legislation. Deng invoked the lack of human resources as the basis for his incrementalism. Yet, several other factors shaped his sporadic incrementalist strategy. Legal reform seeks to facilitate economic reform, but economic reform has no clear direction, and hence legal reform must be carried out in a sporadic incremental manner.[6] In addition, in the 1970s and 1980s China was at the early stage of legal reform; the direction and measures for legal reform were not clear. Although Deng underlines the importance of law, it is not clear what kinds of laws are necessary for long-term economic development and social-political stability. Therefore, sporadic legislative enactments and adjustments to deal with immediate economic, social, and political issues became strategies for legal reform.

B. The Socialist Legal System with Chinese Characteristics

The achievements of legal reform over two decades made China confident to develop its own legal model. In its 15th National Congress in 1997, the Party decided

[5] Deng Xiaoping, 'Emancipate the Mind, Seek Truth from Facts and Unite as One in Looking to the Future' (*Marxists* 1978) <https://www.marxists.org/reference/archive/deng-xiaoping/1978/110.htm> accessed 5 June 2024.

[6] Jianfu Chen, *Chinese Law: Context and Transformation* (Brill 2015) 57.

to establish a 'socialist legal system with Chinese characteristics' by 2010.[7] This marks the start of Chinese legal exceptionalism: the Party's intention to create a distinctive Chinese socialist legal model. The Report delivered by Jiang Zemin at the Congress articulates a project for building socialism with Chinese characteristics, part of which is building the socialist legal system with Chinese characteristics.[8] Therefore, the Report includes a plan for legal reform until 2010.

Notably, the Report considered 'the rule of law' a basic strategy of law reform.[9] It defines the meaning of the rule of law in the Chinese socialist legal system, justifies its normative goals, and anticipates directions for law reform in line with the rule of law ideal. The Report states:

> ruling the country by law means that the broad masses of the people, under the leadership of the Party and in accordance with the Constitution and other laws, participate in one way or another and through all possible channels in managing state affairs, economic and cultural undertakings and social affairs.[10]

The Report underlines that 'To safeguard the dignity of the Constitution and other laws, we must see to it that all people are equal before the law and no individuals or organizations shall have the privilege to overstep it.'[11] Thus, the rule of law does not carry Western legal meanings but is reconstructed with distinctive Chinese features. The Chinese model of the rule of law essentially means that the Communist Party of China rules the Chinese people by the Constitution and other laws.

The Report regards the rule of law as 'the basic strategy employed by the Party in leading the people in running the country'.[12] In this sense, the rule of law is not considered a theory or a principle but a strategic way to develop the socialist legal system to achieve political and economic goals. Socialist law reform in line with the rule of law aims to achieve institutional stability, which means 'laws will not change with changes in the leadership or changes in the views or focus of attention of any leader'.[13] The rule of law is also considered necessary for economic development or 'the objective demand of a socialist market economy'.[14] Thus, the Party's

[7] Jiang Zemin, Report at the 15th National Congress of the Communist Party of China: 'Hold High the Great Banner of Deng Xiaoping Theory for an All-round Advancement of the Cause of Building Socialism with Chinese Characteristics to the 21st Century' *Beijing Review* (12 September 1997) <https://www.bjreview.com/document/txt/2011-03/25/content_363499_11.htm> accessed 5 June 2024.

[8] ibid.

[9] For the development of the Party's doctrine of rule of law, see Ewan Smith, 'The Rule of Law in Party Documents' (2019) 4 CLSR 41; Tiffert G, 'Socialist Rule of Law with Chinese Characteristics: A New Genealogy' in Hualing Fu and others (eds), *Socialist Law in Socialist East Asia* (CUP 2018).

[10] Jiang (n 7).

[11] ibid.

[12] ibid.

[13] ibid.

[14] ibid.

perception is that the rule of law is instrumental to external social, political, and economic outcomes.

The Report then speculates directions for legal reform in line with the rule of law. The directions include strengthening legislation, improving its quality, and establishing a socialist legal system with Chinese characteristics by the year 2010; ensuring all government organs' performance of their duties according to the law; promoting judicial independence and fairness; and educating citizens about the law.[15] The commitment to creating 'a socialist country under the rule of law' was added to China's Constitution through the 1999 amendment.[16]

C. The Socialist Rule of Law with Chinese Characteristics

The arrival of Xi Jinping as a Chinese top leader in 2012 deepened Chinese legal exceptionalism. The 18th National Congress of the Chinese Communist Party began on 8 November 2012. Xi was selected as the General Secretary, and new policy was adopted, including 'ruling the country according to the law'. In 2014, Xi articulated a set of political goals called Four Comprehensives, which includes comprehensively ruling the country according to law.[17] To carry out Xi's view on comprehensive rule of law, in 2014, the CCP Central Committee adopted a Decision exclusively devoted to the rule of law reform, entitled the Decision concerning Some Major Questions in Comprehensively Moving Governing the Country According to the law Forward (hereinafter, Rule of Law Decision).[18] It articulates a comprehensive plan for legal reform towards the 'socialist rule of law with Chinese characteristics'. It sets down five principles for rule of law reform: party leadership, the dominant role of the people, the equality of rights and duties under the law, integrating the rule of law with the rule of socialist and Chinese traditional virtue, and Chinese reality as the basis for the rule of law construction. The Rule of Law Decision then anticipates directions for comprehensive legal reforms, including legislative, administrative, and judicial reforms, and legal education reform.[19]

[15] ibid.
[16] ibid.
[17] The three others are comprehensively building a moderately prosperous society, deepening reform, strictly governing the Party. For scholarly discussion of rule of law reform under Xi, see Jacques Delisle, 'The Rule of Law with Xi-Era Characteristics: Law for Economic Reform, Anticorruption, and Illiberal Politics' (2015) 20 Asia Policy 23–29; John Garrick and Yan Chang Bennett (eds), *China's Socialist Rule of Law Reforms Under Xi Jinping* (Routledge 2016).
[18] CCP Central Committee Decision Concerning Some Major Questions in Comprehensively Moving Governing the Country According to the Law Forward (China Copyright and Media 28 October 2014) <https://chinacopyrightandmedia.wordpress.com/2014/10/28/ccp-central-committee-decision-concerning-some-major-questions-in-comprehensively-moving-governing-the-country-according-to-the-law-forward/> accessed 5 June 2024.
[19] Sanzhu Zhu, 'Socialist Rule of Law in the 21th [sic] Century China', (2015) 7 Hague J Rule Law 75–81; Eva Pils, 'China, the Rule of Law, and the Question of Obedience: a Comment on Professor Peerenboom's Analysis of the CCP 4th Plenary Decision on Law Reform, Reply to Professor Peerenboom's Reply' (2015) 7 Hague J Rule Law 97–98.

Commentators offer different views about the Rule of Law Decision. Carl Minzner contends that the Rule of Law Decision's invocation of the concept of the rule of law is to institutionalize Party rule, to signal a 'limited range of legal and judicial reforms', and 'to reshape the legal landscape with Xi's signature rhetoric—specifically, the Chinese Dream'.[20] From this perspective, the Decision's invocation of the concept of the rule of law is for instrumental purposes, rather than an indicator of the real commitment to the rule of law. Differently, Randall Peerenboom opines that the Decision sought 'to reconfirm for domestic and international audiences that China is pursuing its own path of development aimed at establishing socialist rule of law with Chinese characteristics', to provide a central-level comprehensive plan for legal reform, and to promote the norms and practices of a rule of law culture.[21] This view tends to consider rule of law as China's commitment, rather than political rhetoric to achieve political goals.

The Rule of Law Decision is the embodiment of mature Chinese legal exceptionalism. While China attempted to construct its distinctive legal system prior to the Decision, the achievements of legal reforms in three decades provide the empirical foundation for the Chinese party-state to be confident about its own methods of legal development. Legal exceptionalism is well expressed in the following statements in the Rule of Law Decision:

> We must start from our country's basic circumstances, adapt to the incessant deepening of reform and opening-up, summarize and use the successful experience of the Party leading the people in carrying out rule of law, focus on major theoretical and practical questions in the construction of Socialist rule of law, move rule of law theory innovation forward, develop Socialist rule of law theory that is adapted to China's realities, has Chinese characteristics, and reflects social development laws, to provide theoretical guidance and academic support for ruling the country according to the law. Draw from the quintessence of Chinese legal culture, learn from beneficial experiences in rule of law abroad, but we can absolutely not indiscriminately copy foreign rule of law concepts and models.[22]

The Rule of Law Decision presents a consolidated version of Chinese legal exceptionalism, or an enhanced attempt and a strong perception to construct a Chinese distinctive, socialist model of rule of law. The Rule of Law Decision's five principles of socialist law reform essentially underline 'Chinese characteristics' of the socialist rule of law. The sources of Chinese legal exceptionalism come

[20] Carl Minzner, 'How China's Leaders Will Rule on the Law' ChinaFile (15 October 2014), <https://www.chinafile.com/reporting-opinion/viewpoint/how-chinas-leaders-will-rule-law> accessed 5 June 2024.

[21] Randall Peerenboom, 'Fly High the Banner of Socialist Rule of Law with Chinese Characteristics!' (2015) 7 Hague J Rule Law 49, 50.

[22] Rule of Law Decision.

from both Chinese traditional values (such as the rule of virtue stemming from Confucian tradition) and Chinese modern socialist experiences (such as the Party's leadership and equality of rights and duties under the law). While the Rule of Law Decision does not deny learning from external legal lessons (foreign laws), it stresses internal conditions (Chinese social development and its essential legal culture) as the basis for the Chinese model of socialist rule of law. The Decision even proposes the creation of a 'socialist rule of law theory', drawing on Chinese reality, to guide rule of law reform in the country. This expresses Chinese legal exceptionalism, an aspiration to develop a Chinese version of rule of law theory and practice as an alternative to Western versions.

Chinese legal exceptionalism is also embodied in the Plan on Building the Rule of Law in China (2020–25) (hereinafter, Rule of Law Plan) issued by the Party's Central Committee in 2021.[23] The Plan expresses the Party's and Xi's intentions to develop a distinctive Chinese model of socialist rule of law. The Party's aspiration as embodied in the Plan is that by 2025 China will have 'a more complete socialist legal system with Chinese characteristics', and that by 2035 'a socialist rule of law system with Chinese characteristics will basically have taken shape' in China.[24] This language indicates the Party's exceptional intention. Echoing the Decision, the Plan particularly proposes that rule of law reform should develop from the realities in China and

> consider as a whole the comprehensive factors such as economic and social development, the overall process of the construction of the rule of law, and changes in the needs of the people based on the basic national conditions of our country, absorb the essence of Chinese legal culture, learn from the useful experience of foreign rule of law.[25]

Thus, while the Party does not deny learning from foreign rule of law experiences, it emphasizes Chinese realties, national conditions, and Chinese legal culture as the bases for socialist rule of law with Chinese identity.

D. Chinese Legal Exceptionalism

Chinese legal reform projects (such as the Report of the Party's 15th National Congress and the Rule of Law Decision and Plan) embody a kind of exceptionalism,

[23] 'Plan on Building the Rule of Law in China (2020–25)' (China Law Translate 10 January 2021) <https://www.chinalawtranslate.com/en/%E6%B3%95%E6%B2%BB%E4%B8%AD%E5%9B%BD%E5%BB%BA%E8%AE%BE%E8%A7%84%E5%88%92%EF%BC%882020-2025%E5%B9%B4%EF%BC%89> accessed 5 June 2024.

[24] ibid.

[25] ibid.

an intention to develop a distinctive Chinese legal model. The achievements of legal reform in four decades led to the exceptionalist intention to develop a distinctive Chinese legal model. In addition, the domestic economic development during that time created the material condition for confidence in the development of a socialist legal system with Chinese features. Moreover, China's rise as a global power consolidates the Party's confidence to develop a distinctive Chinese socialist legal model as a competing alternative to Western liberal legal models.

Legal exceptionalism does not mean China completely rejects external legal norms. In fact, transplantations of foreign and international law are common in Chinese legal reform. However, the Party does not intend to use external legal norms as the convergent point for Chinese legal reform. Rather, the Party stresses Chinese reality and attempts to develop a unique legal model rooted in Chinese reality. The exceptional view allows for the selective adoption and adaption of international and comparative law in the Chinese legal system.

The exceptionalist legal reform projects shape Chinese legal reform in four ways. First, they *coordinate* Chinese legal reform. They allow different state and party agencies to work together to undertake legal reform to achieve the common goals of developing a distinctive Chinese legal model and Chinese socialism.

Second, the exceptionalist legal reform projects *express* the political elite's socialist commitments. A survey of various legal reform projects introduced by the Party in the last four decades indicates that the Party does not intend to change the socialist cores of the Chinese legal system. From Deng to Xi, from 'socialist legal system' to 'socialist rule of law', the Party leaders insist on legal reform surrounding the socialist legal identity. The exceptionalist projects for legal reform are expressive of the Party's commitments to the construction of socialism and socialist law in China. This explains why Chinese legal reform projects normally include the principles of legal reform. These principles are essentially socialist commitments—such as the persistence of Party leadership and the adherence to socialist ideologies (from Marxism-Leninism to Mao Zedong Thought, Deng Xiaoping Theory, and Xi Jinping Thought). Socialist commitments shape legal reform. Legal reforms are carried out to incrementally realize aspirational commitments to socialist law, socialist rule of law, and socialism generally.

Third, exceptionalist legal reform projects *signal* the Party's confidence in and perception of developing a distinctive Chinese socialist legal model. Additionally, they send a transformative message that the socialist legal system works in China and the country is confident to follow their own socialist path of legal development. Projects to develop a distinctive Chinese socialist legal model also signal that China is resistant to fundamental principles of Western liberal legal models (such as separation of powers and judicial independence). China may borrow some legal institutions, not fundamental principles, of Western liberal legal systems. The exceptionalist legal reform projects are resistant to domestic and international actors' attempts to change the Chinese legal system towards Western liberal directions.

Fourth, the exceptionalist legal reform projects seek to *limit* legal reform. They aim to disable or prevent changes that alter the fundamental features of the Chinese socialist legal system. Although principles and measures of legal reform facilitate legal reform, they at the same time exclude certain directions and measures that may lead to fundamental legal change. The intention of the principle of persistence on Party leadership, for example, is to exclude legal change that might challenge the Party power. In the same vein, the principle of adherence to socialist ideologies aims to limit the spread of liberal-democratic ideas in China and their influences on Chinese legal reform. The list of measures of legal reform also seeks to contain legal reform. Measures outside the list are not adopted for legal reform because they may provoke changes to the core features of the Chinese socialist legal system.

III. LEGISLATIVE REFORM

A. The Legislature

The enactment of laws by Chinese legislature (the NPC and its Standing Committee) has played a key role in legal reform in China. Reform in substantive areas of law and legal institutions normally involves legislative enactments.

Statutes are the primary sources of law in China. According to China's 1982 Constitution, the NPC and its Standing Committee both exercise the legislative power (Article 58). The NPC exercises legislative power by enacting and amending 'basic laws' governing criminal offences, civil affairs, the state organs, and other matters (Article 62). The Standing Committee is allowed to enact and amend 'laws', with the exception of those enacted by the NPC (Article 67).

In reality, however, the sources of law in China are sophisticated. They include not only the laws by the NPC and its Standing Committee but also numerous regulations by different central and local state institutions. This generates a need for a legal framework to govern lawmaking power. In addition, incremental enactments of legal instruments by various agencies induce the concerns of consistency and coherence of the legal system. Therefore, a legal framework governing the making of legal rules becomes necessary. Consequently, China enacted the Legislation Law in 2000 to govern the power, methods, and processes of lawmaking. The Law was revised in 2005.[26] The sources of Chinese law, as stipulated in the Legislation Law, include:

> the law (*Falu*) enacted by the NPC; administrative regulations (*Tiaoli*, *Guiding* or *Banfa*) enacted by the State Council (central government); administrative rules

[26] Chen (n 6) 234–39.

(*Guizhang*) enacted by the State Council organs; local regulation enacted by the local People's Congress (*Di Fang Tiaoli*); and local rules (*Guizhang*) enacted by local governments.[27]

Despite various sources, the enactment of laws by the NPC and its Standing Committee is the main method of legal reform. Therefore, I will focus on the laws enacted by these institutions.

The Legislation Law further clarifies the scope of legislative power. It provides that the following affairs shall only be governed by statutory laws:

(1) state sovereignty;
(2) the establishment, organization and authority of various people's congresses, people's governments, people's courts and people's procuratorates;
(3) the system of ethnic region autonomy, the system of special administrative regions, and the system of autonomy of the public at the basic level;
(4) crimes and criminal punishment;
(5) compulsory measures and punishments that deprive citizens' political rights or restrict their physical liberty;
(6) basic systems for taxation such as the establishment of taxes, determination of tax rates, and the collection and management of taxes;
(7) expropriation and requisition of non-state-owned assets;
(8) basic civil systems;
(9) basic economic systems, and basic fiscal, customs, financial, and foreign trade systems;
(10) systems for litigation and arbitration;
(11) other matters (Article 8).

This list has implications for the method of legal reform. Legal reform in substantive areas of law (such as criminal, civil, and economic law) and in legal institutions (such as courts) must be carried out through legislative enactments.

The legislative process in China, according to Murray Scot Tanner, includes five different stages: agenda setting; inter-agency review; top leadership approval; legislative debate and passage; and implementation by both explication of the law through administrative regulations and adjudication of the law.[28] An important point is that the Party dominates the legislative process.[29] A Party document called Several Opinions on Strengthening Party Leadership in State Legislative

[27] Qianlan Wu, 'How has China Formed Its Conception of The Rule of Law? A Contextual Analysis of Legal Instrumentalism in ROC and PRC Law-Making' (2017) Int JLC 5.

[28] Murray Scot Tanner, 'How a Bill Becomes a Law in China: Stages and Processes in Lawmaking' (1995) 141 China Q 43–44.

[29] Jiangyu Wang, 'Party in the Legislature and the Judiciary' in Zheng Yongnian and Lance LP Gore (eds), *The Chinese Communist Party in Action: Consolidating Party Rule* (Routledge 2020) 181, 185.

Work (1991) requires that 'Legislative bills concerning constitutional amendments, important political issues, or very important economic or administrative issues, must be reviewed and approved by both the Politburo and the Central Committee, before they are presented to the NPC.'[30] Statutes are the institutionalization of the Party's policy in relevant areas. A statute is normally adopted after the Party adopts a relevant policy. The Party can also provide instruction on the state's making of a particular statute. The Party controls the legislative process to ensure that the Party's legal reform projects will be implemented through legislation.

B. Legislative Development

1. Overview

By the end of the 1970s, China had enacted seven laws. Four of these laws dealt with major state institutions, including the Law on the Election of the NPC and Local People's Congress, the Law on Organization of the Local People's Congress and Local People's Government, the Law on the Organization of the People's Court, and the Law on the Organization of the People's Procuratorate. To establish criminal justice, China enacted the Criminal Law and the Criminal Procedure Law. To facilitate economic construction, the country promulgated the Sino–Foreign Equity Joint Venture Law.[31]

In two decades (between the 1980s and the 1990s), the Chinese socialist legal system was incrementally reconstructed thanks to legislative, administrative, judicial, and legal profession reforms. On legislative reform, substantive legal rules were created by legislation. China promulgated a new Constitution in 1982 to facilitate the reconstruction of state institutions and economic development. Particularly, the Constitution includes provisions to facilitate the marketization of the economy, including the recognition of private economic sectors.[32] On the constitutional base, the Chinese legislature enacted several laws to provide a legal framework for market development. These laws include the Company Law (1994), the General Principles of Civil Law (1987), the Contract Law (1999), and the Labor Law (1995).[33]

In 2011, the Chinese government published an official report to demonstrate that the Socialist System of Laws with Chinese Characteristics had been established. The report states that 'by the end of August 2011, the Chinese legislature had enacted 240 effective laws including the current Constitution, 706 administrative

[30] Cited in ibid 185.
[31] Vai Lo Lo, *Law and Society in China* (Edward Elgar 2020) 146.
[32] Constitution of People's Republic of China (amended 2019), arts 11 and 12.
[33] Stanley Lubman, 'Bird in a Cage: Chinese Law Reform after Twenty Years' (1999–2000) 20 NW J Int Law Bus 383, 386.

regulations, and over 8,600 local regulations'.[34] It documents the enactments of a tone of formal law regulating virtually all aspects of society. The report demonstrates that Chinese formal laws were enacted to promote the development of the socialist market economy, to facilitate China's joining the World Trade Organization (WTO), to deal with social issues, to support state building, to implement the policy called 'one country, two systems' applied to Hong Kong and Macau, and to handle crimes, among other things.

After four decades of reform, China has created a socialist legal system, and legislature has played a key role in this reform through its enactment of numerous statutes. At the time of writing (2023), the Chinese legislature has enacted 293 laws divided into 7 'branches' of law: constitution-related, administrative, criminal, civil and commercial, economic, social, and litigation and non-litigation procedural.[35] As constitutional law has been explored in my previous book,[36] this section describes the statutes in four branches and saves administrative law for the section IV.

2. *Criminal Law*

Criminal law in China has witnessed important reforms. Major reforms include the enactment and amendments of the Criminal Code; the abolition of the system of re-education through labour; and the reduction of the application of the death penalty.

Shortly after the introduction of the reform policy, the Chinese legislature enacted the Criminal Code in 1979. The Code is the first of its kind in Chinese socialist legal history. It was drafted with Soviet influence.[37] The 1979 Criminal Code dealt with common crimes, but the legacies of the Mao era remained, particularly evidenced in the 'counterrevolutionary crimes' or acts intended to overturn the proletarian dictatorship, undermine the socialist system, and harm the Chinese socialist state.[38] By 2022, the 1979 Criminal Code was amended eleven times. Some important amendments are described below.

The Criminal Code was comprehensively amended in 1997 in response to China's significant social, political, and economic changes after two decades of reform. The 1997 amendments sought to dismantle some legacies of the Mao era. For example, the amendments replaced 'counterrevolutionary' with 'harming national security' as a criminal category. In response to the rise of corruption, the amendments increased the threshold of punishment for corruption cases. The

[34] Information Office of The State Council, People's Republic of China, 'The Socialist System of Laws with Chinese Characteristics' (2011), <The Socialist System of Laws with Chinese Characteristics (www.gov.cn) >] accessed 5 June 2024.

[35] ibid.

[36] Bui Ngoc Son, *Constitutional Change in the Contemporary Socialist World* (OUP 2020).

[37] Albert Chen, *The Changing Legal Orders in Hong Kong and Mainland China: Essays on 'One Country, Two Systems'* (City University of Hong Kong Press 2021) 218–19.

[38] Xiaoqun Xu, *Heaven Has Eyes: Law and Justice in Chinese History* (OUP 2020) 234–36.

amendments also added new crimes such as money laundering, drug trafficking, using digital technology to commit crimes, securities fraud, insider trading, and illegally collecting and supplying blood.[39] These new crimes emerged as the consequence of China's transition to a socialist market economy. Criminal law reform is therefore a response to social and economic reform.

The Criminal Code was further amended in 2015. The amendments removed the application of the death penalty to nine offences. The amendments also added several acts constituting the crime of terrorism such as financing terrorist training and spreading terrorist books or media. The amendments also deal with cybercrime, the obstruction of justice, and the offence of organizing and forcing others to engage in prostitution.[40]

More amendments were introduced to the Criminal Code in 2020, which increased the sentencing levels for non-state functionaries. These amendments added new crimes such as commercial espionage and implanting gene-edited or cloned human embryos into human or animal bodies, or implanting gene-edited or cloned animal embryos into human bodies.[41]

An important achievement in the reformation of the criminal justice system in China is *the abolition of the re-education through labour (laojiao)* in 2013. Laojiao, created in China in 1955, 'is an administrative punishment imposed by the police according to laws, regulations or policies, under which the police can bypass the criminal process and summarily subject a person guilty of "minor offences" to a maximum of three years' incarceration'.[42] The Chinese legislature issued a legal instrument in 1981 to provide the legal base for the laojiao system.[43] Fu Hualing argues that the system functioned as an instrument for crime control, drug rehabilitation, investigative detention, and political control.[44]

During the revision of the Criminal Code in 1997, it was argued that the laojiao system should be reformed or abolished.[45] In the twenty-first century, debates on the system by domestic scholars, activists, and government officials were intensified.[46] The system was questioned on international, constitutional, and legal bases. It has been argued that 'since the system deprived citizens' freedom without due process and a court decision', it is inconsistent with international human rights norms, China's Constitution, and China's Law on Legislation.[47] In November 2013, the Central Committee of the Chinese Communist Party adopted measures

[39] ibid 161–62.
[40] Xu (n 38) 267–68.
[41] 'China: Multiple Areas of Criminal Law Changing under New Amendment', China: Multiple Areas of Criminal Law Changing under New Amendment | Library of Congress (loc.gov).
[42] Hualing F, 'Re-Education through Labour in Historical Perspective' (2005) 184 China Q 811.
[43] Xu (38) 266.
[44] Hualing (n 42) 823–29.
[45] Chen (n 6) 396.
[46] Xu (n 38) 266.
[47] ibid 266.

for judicial reforms, including abolishing laojiao.[48] In December 2013, the Chinese legislature adopted a resolution to formally abolish the laojiao system.[49] No official reasons for the abolition of the system were provided. The Judicial Office of Central Committee of the CCP contended that 'all previous penalty decisions on Laojiao were legal and valid'.[50] Jianfu Chen argued that:

> the abolition of Laojiao was not a result of concerns for human rights violation or illegality or unconstitutionality, but a result of its being less useful. Perhaps, the Judicial Office here was trying to close the door to any future compensation for imprisonment under Laojiao by emphasizing the legality of Laojiao practice.[51]

Regardless of normative or necessity reasons, the abolition of laojiao is an important development in the criminal justice system in China. The abolition was celebrated as being progress towards better protection of human rights.[52]

Death penalty reform is another important aspect of Chinese criminal justice. During the Reform era, reduction in the application of the death penalty is an important reform. The amendments to the Criminal Code in 2011 removed the application of the death penalty to the following non-violent offences: smuggling cultural relics; smuggling precious metals; smuggling precious and rare animals; smuggling goods and objects subject to high tax; fraud with financial bills, certificates, and other financial instruments; fraud in credit certificates; fraud in special value-added tax invoices or other invoices fraudulently claiming export refunds or offsetting taxes; forging or selling forged special invoices for value-added tax; stealing public or private property or money; teaching methods of committing crimes; digging up and robbing ancient cultural ruins or tombs with historical, artistic, or scientific value; and digging up and stealing ancient human fossils and ancient vertebrate fossils with historical, artistic, or scientific value.[53]

The Chinese government's attitude towards the death penalty is reformist (such as reducing the application of the death penalty and civilizing execution machinery) rather than abolitionist. Michelle Miao's empirical study indicates that Chinese death penalty reform is the consequence of 'the dissemination of international human rights values in China, the diverging interests and priorities between central-level and lower-level legal authorities, and the vulnerability of penal decision-making bodies to bodies to populist pressures'.[54] In other words, the

[48] ibid 266–67.
[49] ibid 267.
[50] Chen (n 6) 398.
[51] ibid 398.
[52] Xu (n 48) 267.
[53] Chen (n 6) 405–06.
[54] Michelle Miao, 'The Politics of China's Death Penalty Reform in The Context of Global Abolitionism' (2013) 53 Br J Criminol 500, 501.

combination of the external diffusion of international human rights norms and the internal interests and pressures has engendered death penalty reform in China.

3. *Economic Law*

Since China carried out economic reform in 1979, economic law has emerged as an area of law. Chinese economic law 'regulates the economic relationships generated by state actions at "macro"-level in the coordination and regulation of economic activities and the state's interventions in the market economy, including intervention for the purpose of promoting and maintaining a competitive market order'.[55] The justification for the regulatory nature of economic law in China is that the interventions are considered 'necessary because of market failures'.[56] In addition, it is argued that economic law is an instrument for the state to pursue macroeconomic policy measures.[57] Chinese economic law regulates macroeconomy, competition, foreign trade and commerce, key industries, natural resources, and the standardization of economic activities.[58] Recent legislative enactments in economic law are, for example, the Foreign Investment Law (2019), the Resource Tax Law (2019), the Urban Maintenance and Construction Tax Law (2020), the Deed Tax Law (2020), the Export Control Law (2020), the Yangtze River Protection Law (2020), the Rural Revitalization Promotion Law (2021), the Data Security Law (2021), the Hainan Free Trade Port Law (2021), and the Stamp Tax Law (2021).[59]

Economic law embodies the *socialist* nature of the 'socialist market economy' in China. The Chinese state has used economic law as an instrument to regulate the economy to pursue socialist goals. The function of economic law is to control the enterprises and the market.[60] Although economic reform has enabled the transformation of the Chinese centralized planned economy into a market economy, the Chinese state's main concern is to make sure that the development of market economy would not lead to China's transition into a capitalist society. Therefore, the state must ensure socialist direction of the market development. This has been achieved through legislation: the state has employed economic law to direct the development of the market economy towards the socialist direction. Particularly, the state's regulation of macroeconomic policies, prices, key industries, natural resources, and behaviours of economic activities illustrates that the state retains the dominant control of the economy, although market development has been allowed. Despite being adapted by the transition from a centralized planned economy into a

[55] Chen (n 4) 289.
[56] ibid 289.
[57] ibid 289.
[58] 'Legislation: China's National Laws', NPC Observer, <https://npcobserver.com/legislation/statutes> accessed 5 June 2024; 'Legislation: China's Current Statutes', NPC Observer (Last updated 28 April 2024),
[59] ibid.
[60] Donald C Clarke, 'Regulation and Its Discontents: Understanding Economic Law in China' (1992) 28 Stanford JIL 283, 288.

socialist market economy, economic statism, the essence of socialist legal tradition, remains.

4. *Civil Law and Commercial Law*

In 2020, the Chinese legislature enacted a Civil Code, the first of its kind in Chinese socialist legal history.[61] The Civil Code comprehensively codifies general principles of civil law and specific civilian legal institutions in China. The enactment of this Code is the culmination of decades of civil law reform in the country. During the Reform era, the emergence of private property, market economy, and private economic sectors induced the need for a legal framework for civilian relations. Economic and social transition generated various civil disputes, including 'land-use rights, property ownership, breach of contracts, violation of trademarks, debts, marriage and divorce, inheritance, and newly emerging matters such as torts and intellectual property rights'.[62] A civil law regime has incrementally emerged to deal with civil transactions and disputes, culminating in the enactment of the 2020 Civil Code.

Before the enactment of the Code, the socialist state in China had four abortive attempts to codify civil law. The first attempt was in 1954 when the legislature created a working group responsible for drafting a civil code. The group produced a draft civil code in 1956, which was largely based on the 1922 Soviet Civil Code. The second attempt to codify civil law occurred between 1962 and1964, resulting in a draft civil code that sought to depart from the Soviet model and 'represented an extreme example of pursuing Chinese characteristics and rejecting virtually all things foreign'.[63] The first and second attempts failed due to the 'nihilism of law' school of thought—which was the consequence of political campaigns such as the 1957 Anti-Rightists Movement, the 1958 Great Leap Forward, and the Cultural Revolution.[64]

The third attempt was in 1979, when the reform policy was introduced. The Chinese legislature, however, halted the codification project, describing it as 'a piecemeal approach towards legislation advocated by Deng Xiaoping [that] quickly began to take hold'.[65] Consequently, rather than enacting a comprehensive civil code, the Chinese legislature enacted the General Principles of Civil Law (GPCL)

[61] For timely academic writings on the Civil Code, see Hao Jiang, 'The Making of a Civil Code in China: Promises and Perils of a New Civil Law' (2021) 95 Tul L Rev 777; Papers in 'Special Section: The Chinese Civil Code' (2021) 29 APLR 287; Jian Qu, 'Trusts and the Chinese Civil Code: toward a New Era of Codification' (2021) 27 T&T 82; Bing Ling, 'The New Contract Law in the Chinese Civil Code' (2020) 8 CJCL 558.

[62] Xu (n 38) 285.

[63] Chen (n 6) 460–61.

[64] Zhang Lihong, 'The Latest Developments in the Codification of Chinese Civil Law' (2009) 83 Tul L Rev 999, 1001.

[65] Chen (n 6) 61.

in 1986.[66] Article 2 of this legislation provides that 'The Civil Law of the People's Republic of China shall adjust property relationships and personal relationships between civil subjects with equal status, that is, between citizens, between legal persons and between citizens and legal persons.'[67] The GPCL includes principles such as protecting private property, intellectual property rights, personal rights, and freedom of contract.[68] As the GPCL only dealt with general principles, the Chinese legislature enacted many statutes governing specific civil law institutions, including the Contract Law (1981), the Foreign-related Economic Contract Law (1986), the Marriage Law (1981), and the Succession Law (1986).[69]

The fourth attempt was in the 2000s; but again the plan changed as the Chinese legislature adopted a 'step-by-step'—rather than comprehensive—approach to civil law reform. Consequently, the legislature enacted more statutes on concrete civil law matters, including the Property Law (2007), the Tort Liability Law (2009), and the Law on the Application of Law in Foreign-related Relations (2010).[70]

The fifth attempt led to the successful enactment of a comprehensive civil code. The CCP Central Committee's Decision on the rule of law reform in 2014 called for compiling a civil code. The legislature then proceeded with two steps. First, in 2017, it adopted the GPCL, which constitutes the general part of the Civil Code. Then, in August 2018, six Separate Parts of the Code were submitted to the Standing Committee of the NPC. In May 2020, the NPC voted to adopt the Civil Code.[71] The Civil Code became effective on 1 January 2021. Article 1260 of the Civil Code abolishes the Marriage Law, the Succession Law, the GPCL, the Adoption Law, the Security Law, the Contract Law, the Property Law, the Tort Liability Law, and the General Provisions of Civil Law.[72]

China's Civil Code includes 1,260 articles, divided into 7 books. Book 1, *General Part*, is basically converted from the GPCL. It includes rules on the three types of civil entities (natural persons, legal persons, and unincorporated organizations), agency relationships, civil liabilities, and limitations periods. Book 2, *Property Rights*, is based on the Property Law and Security Law, and introduces new rules such as those on the right of habitation, homeowners' rights, and renewal of the right to use land for residential construction. Book 3, *Contracts*, is based on the Contracts Law and introduced many new rules such as those on quasi-contracts and unjust enrichment. Book 4, *Personality Rights*, stands alone but is based on some provisions in the 1986 GPCL. This book protects the rights to life, body, and

[66] On the process leading to the enactment of this law and its features, see Tong Rou and Jonathan K Ocko, 'The 'General Principles of Civil Law of the PRC': Its Birth, Characteristics, and Role' (1989) LCP 151.

[67] General Principles of the Civil Law of the People's Republic of China (1986), art 2.

[68] General Principles of the Civil Law of the People's Republic of China, ch V (ss 1, 2, 3, 4).

[69] Chen (n 6) 462; Chen (n 4) 288.

[70] Chen (n 6) 465.

[71] Zhang Mingqi, 'The Compilation of Specific Laws of the Civil Code' (2020) 8 China Legal Sci 3, 5.

[72] China's Civil Code (2020), art 1260.

health; rights of name and title; likeness right; rights of reputation and honour; and right to privacy. Book 5, *Marriage and Family*, integrates the Marriage and Adoption Laws, and includes new features such as a cooling-off period for divorces and community debt. Book 6, *Inheritance*, is based on the Inheritance Law, and includes new changes such as new forms of wills (printed wills and wills in the form of video recordings) and the role of estate administrators. Book 7, *Tort Liability* is based on the Tort Liability Law and includes new features such as the 'assumption of risk' doctrine, the 'self-help' doctrine, and liability for injury caused by objects falling out of buildings.[73] In short, the Civil Code codifies existing rules and introduces new rules on civil law matters.

Lei Chen argues that China's codification of civil law is animated by the party-state's interests and willing to respond to the demand of the growing middle class towards legal protection of their private property and contractual rights.[74] Chen adds that the need to create a systemic and coherent civil law regime drives China's codification of civil law. He states that 'many provisions in various laws and regulations before the Civil Code are abstract and hortatory. Sometimes they appear tautological. Therefore, there is a pressing need to tackle the discrepancy among different rules. Indeed, systemization has the benefit of making it easier to locate and interpret the rules.'[75]

The contents of the Civil Code present a mixture of Western, socialist, and Chinese traditional values. Hao Jiang observes that:

> French, German, and Anglo-American influences are seen throughout the Code. The German concept of *Rechtsgeschaft* (civil juristic act) is the bedrock of the general theory of Chinese civil law, and the renowned French Civil Code articles 1240–1241 (formerly articles 1382–1383) form the basis of fault liability. Surprisingly, common law doctrines that seemingly would not grow on civil law soil also made their way into the Chinese Civil Code.[76]

Jiang, however, points out that the Marxist theory of public land ownership remains dominant in the Civil Code, although the Code allows citizens to enjoy private land use rights.[77] In addition, Chinese Confucianism informs several contents of the Civil Code such as the provision on liability without fault.[78]

The enactment of the 2020 Civil Law is a significant achievement in civil law reform in China. Formally, it lays down a comprehensive legal framework for civil

[73] 2020 NPC Session: A Guide to China's Civil Code (Updated) (NPC Observer May 2020), <https://npcobserver.com/2020/05/2020-npc-session-a-guide-to-chinas-civil-code>accessed 5 June 2024.

[74] Lei Chen, 'Continuity and change: some reflections on the Chinese Civil Code' (2021) 29 APLR, 287, 297.

[75] ibid 298.

[76] Jiang (n 61) 794–95 (citation omitted).

[77] ibid 792.

[78] ibid 812.

transactions and disputes in China. Substantively, it protects private property rights, which were rejected in the tradition of socialist law. In addition, legal diffusion results in the adoption of norms of Western civil codes in China's Civil Code.

Despite the influence of legal diffusion, China's Civil Code is not a liberal civil code but a socialist one. The socialist nature of the Code is presented in procedural, substantive, and teleological aspects. The lawmaking process is shaped by a unique socialist feature: party leadership. The legislative process of making codes was only initiated after the CCP agreed to codify civil law. The codification process was therefore under the leadership of the Party. The enactment of the Civil Code expresses the Party's power. Consequently, the Civil Code— creating a comprehensive legal framework for civil law— is consistent with the Party's policy to comprehensively create a socialist rule of law state and more generally to realize socialism in China. This is in turn a part of Xi Jinping's Four Comprehensives. Therefore, the Civil Code retains the core of the socialist property regime: state ownership of the means of production, including all land, which is hegemonic in the property regime. Finally, although the Civil Code adopts some civil law norms of Western liberal countries, it serves socialist goals. Article 1 of the Code states that the Code meets 'the needs for developing socialism with Chinese characteristics and carrying forward the core socialist values'. In other words, China's Civil Code is enacted to implement socialism in China. Liberal institutions of civil law are employed not to transform China into a liberal polity underpinned by a capitalist economy. Rather, like the way institutions of market economy are used as an instrument for creating a socialist market economy, China pragmatically used liberal institutions of civil law to create a socialist civil code.

Apart from the civil law, commercial law has emerged as a new area of law in China in response to the development of the socialist market economy, which has attracted great academic attention.[79] Unlike Vietnam, China does not have a commercial code. Rather, 'China practices fusion of commercial law and civil law'.[80] The logic of the fusion is that 'the general principles and rules of civil law provide the foundation for commercial law, which develops on the base of the civil law more specific principles and rules applicable to the relationships between and activities of profit-making business entities or equal legal status'.[81] Commercial law includes specific areas of law such as company law, securities law, and bankruptcy law.

[79] For review of the scholarship on Chinese commercial law, see Wei Shen and Casey G Watters, 'Do All Roads Lead to China? Chinese Commercial Law Scholarship in The Past Decade (Part 1)' (2016) 16 China Rev (2016) 165; Wei Shen and Casey G Watters, 'Do All Roads Lead to China? Chinese Commercial Law Scholarship in The Past Decade (Part 2)' (2016) 16 China Rev 213. See also Tianshu Zhou and Mathias Siems, 'Contentious Modes of Understanding Chinese Commercial Law' (2015) 6 Geo Mason J Int'l Com L 177.

[80] Chen (n 4) 289.

[81] ibid 290.

In addition to the Civil Code, legislative enactments on Chinese commercial law include the following laws:

Trademark Law (1982)
Patent Law (1984)
Law on Industrial Enterprises Owned by the Whole People (1988)
Copyright Law (1990)
Maritime Law (1992)
Law on the Protection of Consumers' Rights and Interests (1993)
Company Law (1993)
Commercial Banks Law (1995)
Negotiable Instruments Law (1995)
Insurance Law (1995)
Auction Law (1996)
Partnerships Law (1997)
Securities Law (1998)
Sole Proprietorships Law (1999)
Bid Invitation and Bidding Law (1999)
Trust Law (2001)
Rural Land Contracting Law (2002)
Securities Investment Funds Law (2003)
Electronic Signature Law (2004)
Enterprise Bankruptcy Law (2006)
Farmers' Specialized Cooperatives Law (2006)
Law on the Application of Law to Foreign-Related Civil Relations (2010).[82]

Reform of commercial law in China presents both alteration and continuity of the socialist law. On one hand, commercial law reform considerably departs from the socialist legal tradition. Particularly, the adoption of private enterprises in Chinese company law deviates from the socialist tradition of economic statism. Diffusion of Western commercial legal norms into China is also evident. Scholars have observed that 'A number of reforms of the 2000s can be seen as transplants from the US, namely the requirement that listed companies have independent directors, the availability of shareholder-appraisal rights and derivative actions, and the introduction of cumulative voting, which enhances minority shareholders' voting power in public companies.'[83] One the other hand, Chinese commercial

[82] NPC Observer (n 58).

[83] Zhou and Siems (n 79), 182 (internal citations omitted). See also Tang X, 'Independent Directors in China: Facts and Reform Proposals' in Dan W Puchniak, Harald Baum, and Luke Nottage (eds), *Independent Directors in Asia: A Historical, Contextual and Comparative Approach* (CUP 2017); Clarke DC and Howson NC, 'Pathway to Minority Shareholder Protection: Derivative Actions in the People's Republic of China' in Dan W Puchniak, Harald Baum, and Michael Ewing-Chow (eds), *The Derivative Action in Asia: A Comparative and Functional Approach* (CUP 2012).

law embodies core features of socialist law. For example, in China's Company Law, there are 'provisions about the overall purpose of this legislation, the government supervision of companies, and the requirements that companies have a party organization and that a socialist trade union is active in practice'.[84] These provisions express core socialist legal features. The legal base for the state supervision of companies presents the continuity of economic statism. Although private enterprises are allowed, the state retains control over them to achieve the state's socialist goals. The requirements on the Party cells within companies express vanguardism: the leading role of the Communist Party in all aspects of society, including the economy.

5. *Social Law*

Legislative reforms in China not only involve law for the market but also law for society. Social law in China deals with 'labor relations, social security, social welfare and protection of the rights and interests of special groups'.[85] Recent enactments of social law in China include the Anti-Domestic Violence Law (2015), the Charity Law (2016), the Law on the Management of the Activities of Overseas Non-Governmental Organizations in Mainland China (2016), the Veterans Protection Law (2020), the Legal Aid Law (2021), and the Family Education Promotion Law (2021).[86]

The development of social law in China is in part shaped by economic development. Economic reforms have generated new social issues (such as the labour market, health, and social security) that require legislative responses. At the same time, social law reflects the socialist policies of the Chinese state. The Chinese state believes that:

> [its social law] follows the principle of justice, harmony and appropriate state intervention. By performing their duties, the state and society provide necessary protection for the rights and interests of laborers, the unemployed, the incapacitated for work, as well as other special groups in need of help so as to safeguard social equity and promote social harmony.[87]

This ideological discourse suggests that social law is a tool to promote socialism in China.

To illustrate consider labour law reform in China. China's 1994 Labor Law is an important achievement in labour law reform. As Mary E Gallagher and Baohua Dong demonstrate:

> [this law] made a radical break with the past by regulating employment relations across ownership sectors that previously had been treated separately and

[84] Zhou and Siems (n 79) 185–86.
[85] Information Office of The State Council (n 34).
[86] NPC Observer (n 58).
[87] Information Office of The State Council (n 34).

> differently. We could say that state-sector employees saw their workplace rights reduced through the law, whereas employees in the foreign and private sectors saw their rights clarified and expanded.[88]

This change responds to the demand for equal treatment of different ownership sectors in the market economy. At the same time, Cynthia Estlund and Aaron Halegua argue that China's labour law regime retains socialist features.[89] For example, the All-China Federation of Trade Unions (ACFTU) is an instrument for the CCP to control the collective representation of workers.[90] The Trade Union Law (enacted in 1992, amended in 2001) requires trade unions to 'uphold the socialist road, the people's democratic dictatorship, leadership by the Communist Party of China' (Article 4). The ACFTU embodies party vanguardism in the Chinese labour law regime. It is a means for the Party to play a leading role in labour legal relations to implement socialist policy.

6. *Procedural Law*

A body of Chinese legislation deals with legal procedure for litigation and alternative dispute resolutions such as arbitration and mediation. Legislative enactments of procedural law include:

Criminal Procedure Law (1979)
NPCSC Decision on the Exercise of Criminal Jurisdiction over the Crimes Prescribed by the International Treaties to which the People's Republic of China is a Party or has Acceded (1987)
Administrative Litigation Law (1989)
Civil Procedure Law (1991)
Arbitration Law (1994)
Special Maritime Procedure Law (1999)
Extradition Law (2000)
Law on the Mediation and Arbitration of Labor Disputes (2007)
Law on the Mediation and Arbitration of Disputes over Contracted Management of Rural Land (2009)
People's Mediation Law (2010)
International Criminal Justice Assistance Law (2018)[91]

[88] Mary E Gallagher and Baohua Dong, 'Legislating Harmony: Labor Law Reform in Contemporary China', in Sarosh Kuruvilla, Ching Kwan Lee, and Mary E Gallagher (eds), *From Iron Rice Bowl to Informalization: Markets, Workers, and the State in a Changing China* (Cornell University Press 2011) 36, 39.
[89] Estlund C and Halegua A, 'What Is Socialist about Labour Law in China?' in Hualing Fu and others (eds), *Socialist Law in Socialist East Asia* (CUP 2018), 257.
[90] ibid.
[91] NPC Observer (n 58).

To illustrate, consider important reforms in procedural criminal law.[92] The Chinese legislature enacted the Criminal Procedure Law in 1979, the same year the Criminal Code was enacted. The Criminal Procedure Law laid down principles and rules for procedural criminal justice. Particularly, the Law provided that all cases shall be decided based on evidence. Formally, this is an important departure from the previous judicial rules of the dynastic and socialist government, although functionally torture and physical abuse would still happen.[93]

The Criminal Procedure Law was amended several times. The amendments to the Law in 1996 removed some of the 1979 version's ideological language—such as 'under the guidance of Marxism-Leninism-Maoism' and 'exercise proletarian dictatorship'. The amendments underlined independence in adjudication, provided for the right to an attorney, allowed lawyers to conduct their own legal investigations, and protected the witness and their close relatives.[94] The Criminal Procedure Law was further amended in 2012. The amendments include the commitment to respect human rights. They consolidate the right of the accused to have an attorney when being questioned by an investigating agency for the first time. The amendments also enlarge the right of defence lawyers and prohibit torture and obtaining evidence illegally. With these legal reforms, standard criminal procedures in Western countries were incrementally introduced into China.[95] Despite significant reforms, the Criminal Procedure Law retains features of socialist law. Bo Yin and Peter Duff argue that 'modern Chinese criminal procedure should be categorized as socialist'.[96] For example, the Criminal Procedure Law aims to maintain 'socialist public order' (Article 1) and 'ensure the smooth progress of the socialist cause' (Article 2). The Criminal Procedure Law is a tool for the party-state to pursue socialism in China. This embodies the instrumental nature of socialist legality.

IV. ADMINISTRATIVE REFORM

A. Public Administrative Reform

Imperial China had a long tradition of a centralized and hierarchical administrative system that had many features of a Weberian modern bureaucracy.[97] The

[92] See generally Ahl B (ed), *Chinese Courts and Criminal Procedure: Post-2013 Reforms* (CUP 2021).
[93] Xu (n 38) 237.
[94] ibid 262.
[95] ibid 264–65.
[96] Yin B and Duff P, 'Criminal Procedure in Contemporary China: Socialist, Civilian or Traditional?' (2010) 59 ICLQ 1099.
[97] Francis Fukuyama, *Political Order and Political Decay: From the Industrial Revolution to the Globalization of Democracy* (Farrar, Straus and Giroux 2014) 370.

imperial bureaucracy in China was sophisticatedly organized, which included the famous six ministries (Ministry of Personnel, Ministry of Revenue, Ministry of Rites, Ministry of Defense, Ministry of Justice, and Ministry of Works) responsible for administrating different national affairs, in addition to specific institutions concerning imperial education, imperial history, and administrative supervision.[98] The imperial administrative system was staffed with well-educated personnel recruited mainly through the civil examination system. The bureaucracy could perform functions that serve the public good like legal drafting and enforcement, public security, national defence, and especially controlling floods to ensure agricultural activities. Yet, corruption was a serious problem in the imperial bureaucracy.[99]

After the bureaucratic dysfunction in China during the Mao era, China revitalized a capable bureaucracy in the last three decades when the country implemented socio-economic reform programmes. Francis Fukuyama argues that the new bureaucracy that emerged in China since the beginning of the reforms in 1978 corresponded to 'the massive shift from the centrally planned economy to a more open and marketized one'.[100] In a comprehensive report, Yukai Wang traces three phases of administrative reform in China corresponding to the congresses of the CCP where the Party decided policies on administrative reform.[101] The first phase (1978–92) aimed to 'put an end to the highly centralized planned economy and model of administrative management'.[102] This involved reforms such as dismantling the people's commune system, strengthening grassroots power at the township levels, expanding the autonomy of enterprises and production units, and delegating more management power to local authorities.[103] The second phase (1992–2002) aimed to reform the administrative system to support the development of the market economy.[104] This included reform efforts such as decentralizing authority, minimizing administrative processes, and reducing the government's direct intervention in the economy.[105] The third phase (from 2002 to present) seeks 'to build a service-oriented government and a government that abides by the rule of law' and involves all aspects of administrative reform.[106] After three decades of reform, the administrative system in today's China 'is centralized, massive, and extraordinarily complex'.[107]

[98] See generally Qian Mu, *Traditional Government in Imperial China* (Chinese University Press 1982).
[99] Chong-chor Lau and Rance PL Lee, 'Bureaucratic Corruption in Nineteenth-Century China: Its Causes, Control, and Impact' (1979) 7 Southeast Asian J Soc Sci 114.
[100] Fukuyama (n 97) 371.
[101] Yukai Wang, *A Report on China's Administration Reform* (Springer 2021) 4.
[102] ibid 4.
[103] ibid 4.
[104] ibid 4.
[105] ibid 5.
[106] ibid 5.
[107] Fukuyama (n 97) 374.

B. Administrative Law Reform

To promote administrative reform in China, many pieces of legislation were enacted, including:

Law of Administrative Litigation (1989)
State Compensation Law (1994, amended 2010 and 2012)
Law on Administrative Punishment (1996)
Law of Administrative Supervision (1997, amended 2010)
Law of Administrative Review (1999)
Law of Administrative Licensing (2003)
Law on Civil Servants (2005)[108]

In the formal aspect, legislative enactments in administrative law demonstrate attempts to legalize the administrative system in China. To subject the administrative structure and actions to law is an important departure from the administrative management by personal fiats during the Mao era. However, to use law to regulate the administrative system is not new in socialist law. Another aspect of administrative reform is substantive. Several pieces of administrative legislation seek to impose legal constraints on the administrative power to protect individual rights. This departs from the conventional function of administrative law in the socialist legal tradition and resonates with the function of administrative law in liberal democracies. At the same time, the reform retains the core of administrative law in socialist law. To illustrate, consider some legislative enactments to facilitate administrative reform.

1. Law on Administrative Litigation

The Law on Administrative Litigation enacted in 1989 (amended through 2017) provides a legal tool for citizens to sue administrative agencies. The Law provides that:

> if a citizen, a legal person or any other organization considers that his or its lawful rights and interests have been infringed upon by a specific administrative act of an administrative organ or its personnel, he or it shall have the right to bring a suit before a people's court in accordance with this Law.[109]

Thus, 'a specific administrative act' can be subject to litigation. The scope of specific administrative acts includes:

[108] Chen (n 4) 304.
[109] Administrative Litigation Law of the People's Republic of China (amended through 2017), art 1.

(1) an administrative sanction such as detention, fine, rescission of a licence or permit, or an order to suspend production, business, or confiscation of property;
(2) a compulsory administrative measure such as restricting the freedom of a person or the sealing up, seizing, or freezing of property;
(3) infringement upon one's managerial decision-making powers;
(4) refusal by an administrative organ to issue a permit or licence;
(5) refusal by an administrative organ to perform its statutory duty of protecting one's rights of the person and of property;
(6) cases where an administrative organ is considered to have failed to issue a pension according to law;
(7) cases where an administrative organ is considered to have illegally demanded the performance of duties; and
(8) cases where an administrative organ is considered to have infringed upon other rights of the person and of property.[110]

The Law on Administrative Litigation is an important reform. The idea that citizens can sue government agencies in court is unconventional within the context of the previous history of socialist law in China, when law (including administrative law) was considered a tool for the state to control citizens, not vice versa.[111] The Law of Administrative Litigation, however, presents a cautious reform.[112] Citizens can only issue specific administrative actions, not normative documents (administrative regulations that have general legal effect). In practice, arguably there are difficulties in the implementation of the Law of Administrative Litigation—such as the difficulty of getting an administrative lawsuit registered, the low winning rate of citizens, and the difficulty of implementing court decisions.[113] Ordinary citizens therefore considered administrative litigation to be 'hurling an egg against a rock'.[114] The Law of Administrative Litigation is a reform but does not depart from the instrumental nature of administrative law in socialist law: administrative law is a tool to consolidate, not to constrain, the administrative power.

2. *State Compensation Law*

The State Compensation Law enacted in 1994 enables citizens to claim state compensation when their rights are infringed upon by administrative agencies and

[110] Administrative Litigation Law of the People's Republic of China (amended through 2017), art 11.
[111] Chen (n 4) 268.
[112] He Haibo, 'How Much Progress Can Legislation Bring? The 2014 Amendment of the Administrative Litigation Law of PRC' (2018) 13 ALR.
[113] ibid 143–47.
[114] ibid 142.

their personnel.[115] Citizens can claim state compensation when their personal and property rights are violated by administrative agencies or their officers when exercising their administrative powers.

The State Compensation Law specifies the conditions under which personal rights are infringed upon by the exercise of administrative power, including:

(1) detaining a citizen in violation of the law or unlawfully taking compulsory administrative measures in restraint of their personal freedom;
(2) unlawfully taking a citizen into custody or depriving them of their right of the person by other unlawful means;
(3) using, instigating, or indulging violence such as beating someone up and abuse, thereby causing bodily injury or death to a citizen;
(4) unlawfully using weapons or police restraint implements, thereby causing bodily injury or death to a citizen; and
(5) other unlawful acts causing bodily injury or death to a citizen.[116]

The State Compensation Law establishes the conditions under which property rights are violated by the exercise of administrative power, including:

(1) illegally inflicting administrative sanctions such as imposing fines, revoking certificates and licences, ordering suspension of production and business, or confiscating property;
(2) illegally implementing compulsory administrative measures such as sealing up, distraining, or freezing property;
(3) illegally requisitioning or expropriating properties; and
(4) other illegal acts causing damage to property.[117]

The State Compensation Law, however, establishes conditions under which the state shall not be liable for compensation, including:

(1) individual acts of a functionary of an administrative organ, which have nothing to do with the exercise of their functions and powers;
(2) damage arisen from acts done by citizens, legal persons, or other organizations themselves; and
(3) other circumstances provided by law.[118]

[115] The State Compensation Law also provides for criminal compensation, which allows the citizens to claim state compensation when their personal and property rights are violated by the exercise of the judicial power (arts 15 and 16). This section focuses on administrative compensation.

[116] State Compensation Law of the People's Republic of China (amended in 2010), art 3.

[117] ibid art 4.

[118] ibid, art 5.

On compensatory procedure, a claimant shall first apply to the organ liable for compensation.[119] Then, the organ liable for compensation shall pay the compensation within two months from the date of receiving the application. If payment has not been made within this period, or if the claimant is not satisfied with the amount of compensation, he or she may bring a lawsuit in a court.[120]

Albert Chen comments that the enactment of State Compensation Law in China 'is a liberal enactment that confers on the Chinese citizen a set of rights against the state which are in some respects even more extensive than those available under corresponding circumstances in legal systems belonging to the Common Law family, since there is no well-established concept of "state compensation" in these legal systems'.[121] Xixin Wang contends that the State Compensation Law is a significant achievement of legal reform but points out its limitations:

> The establishment and improvement of state compensation system revealed the desire and efforts of the government to adapt itself to the changing social and political situations and to reinforce the legitimacy of its governance. At the same time, the current state compensation system also reveals the hesitation and anxiety of the government, as evident in the substantial limits of individuals' right to state compensation, including the scope of state compensation, unreasonably low standards for compensation, the problem of judicial independence, and the like.[122]

Some of these limitations were addressed in amendments to the State Compensation Law in 2010 and 2012. For example, the amendments expanded the scope of compensation, increased compensation standards, and simplified the compensation procedures.[123]

The State Compensation Law presents a significant administrative reform and the continuity of socialist law and embodies the statist nature of socialist rights. The state establishes the conditions for the right to compensation. These rights are more like the state's benevolent granting to citizens than legal entitlements for citizens to challenge the state. Particularly, the requirement that the administrative procedure must be exhausted before the initiation of judicial litigation enables the administrative agencies to control the compensation procedure and to prevent citizens' challenging administrative power in courts.

[119] ibid art 9.
[120] ibid art 13.
[121] Chen (n 4) 308.
[122] Xixin Wang, 'Suing the Sovereign Observed from the Chinese Perspective: The Idea and Practice of State Compensation in China' (2003) 35 Geo Wash Int'l L Rev 681, 689.
[123] Huaide Ma and Jingbo Wang, *State Compensation and Government Accountability* (Springer 2018) 198–200.

3. *Supervision Law*

The Supervision Law adopted in 2018 details the constitutional amendments that provide for supervisory institutions. It repealed the Administrative Supervision Law and established a comprehensive system of supervision. The Law was enacted 'for the purposes of furthering the reform of the national supervision system, strengthening the supervision of all public officials exercising public power, realizing the full coverage of national supervision, conducting the anti-corruption work in an in-depth manner, and promoting the modernization of the national governance system and governance capacity'.[124]

According to the Law, the supervisory system includes the National Supervisory Commission (NSC)—the highest supervisory organ—and supervisory commissions created in provinces, autonomous regions, municipalities, autonomous prefectures, counties, autonomous counties, cities, and municipal districts.[125]

The Supervision Law is an important reform. It seeks to discipline the use of public power. The Law, however, continues vanguardism in socialist legal tradition. The Law mandates 'The leadership of the Communist Party of China over the national supervision work.'[126] It also requires that the creation of the supervision system must be guided by Marxism-Leninism, Mao Zedong Thought, Deng Xiaoping Theory, the Theory of Three Represents, the Scientific Outlook on Development, and Xi Jinping Thought on Socialism with Chinese Characteristics for a New Era.[127] The new unified and hierarchical system of supervision merges the Party's Discipline Inspection Commission with the State Supervision Commissions to centralize the Party's control over anti-corruption agencies.[128] The supervisory system is the institutional embodiment of the socialist tradition of party vanguardism in the legal system of contemporary China.

Fu Hualing comments that:

> While the centralization of power in the NSC and the direct role of the Party breaks some new ground and represents a significant departure from the tripartite design, it is more a demonstration of institutional flexibility and resilience than institutional decay or destruction. After all, there is little in the NSC that is truly innovative and provocative in its actual anti-corruption design.[129]

[124] Supervision Law of the People's Republic of China (2018), art 1.
[125] ibid art 7.
[126] ibid art 2.
[127] ibid art 2.
[128] Jinting Deng, 'The National Supervision Commission: A New Anti-Corruption Model in China' (2018) 52 Int J Law Crime Just 58, 66.
[129] Fu Hualing, 'Understanding the Evolving Relationship between the Party and the Law: The Case of China's National Supervision Commission' (2020) University of Hong Kong Faculty of Law Research Paper No 2020/072, 11 <https://ssrn.com/abstract=3743636> or <http://dx.doi.org/10.2139/ssrn.3743636>accessed 5 June 2024.

If there is no substantive institutional change, why was the Supervision Law adopted? One possible explanation is party vanguardism. The supervisory system is the legal expression of the socialist commitment to the Party leading the state and society, including anti-corruption activities. The previous system of supervision did not express party vanguardism in legal form, although party leadership was embedded in the supervisory system. The enactment of the Supervision Law allows for vanguardism to be explicitly and legally expressed.[130] As the legal embodiment of party vanguardism, the Supervision Law establishes party leaders' ideologies as the foundation for the creation of the supervisory system, places the function of the system under the Party's leadership, and merges party and state institutions into a unified system of supervision.

V. JUDICIAL REFORM

In the post-Mao era, China has carried out many measures of judicial reforms, leading to the creation of a sophisticated, functional court system.[131] Ji Li observes that 'few institutions in China have undergone a more dramatic transformation than the judiciary. From bare existence in the Cultural Revolution, Chinese courts have evolved into multifunctional institutions resembling their peers in advanced civil law countries.'[132] This section explores a political project for judicial reform, the enactment of several formal laws on the judicial institutions and actors, and notable trends in judicial reforms.

A. Overview

Judicial reform is a part of China's broader legal reform. Judicial reform is a component in the Party's legal reform policy articulated in the Party's Third Plenum in 1978. Since 1997, when the Party decided to establish a socialist rule of law state, judicial reform has been discussed in each Party congress. China's Supreme People's Court (SPC) issued five-year plans for judicial reforms in 1999, 2009, 2015, and 2019.[133] For example, the plan for the years 2019–23 consists of sixty-five measures

[130] A critic believes that the legalization of the supervisory system means that anything done the by Supervisory Commission system is legal, but the Supervision Law says little about the limitation of the Supervisory Commission's power and its accountability. Donald Clarke, 'Order and Law in China' (2022) 2022 U Ill L Rev 541, 566–67.

[131] See generally Yuwen Li, *The Judicial System and Reform in Post-Mao China: Stumbling towards Justice* (Ashgate 2014).

[132] Li Ji, 'The Power Logic of Justice in China' (2017) 65 AJCL 95.

[133] Albert HY Chen, 'China's Long March towards Rule of Law or China's Turn against Law?' (2016) 4 CJCL 21; 'Supreme Court Issues Five-Year Plan on Judicial Reform', Xinhua (27 February 2019), English.news.cn (xinhuanet.com) accessed 5 June 2024.

for judicial reforms, including better use of big data and artificial intelligence in judicial work.[134]

The party-state also created institutions responsible for implementing the judicial reform policy. The Central Leading Group for Comprehensively Deepening Reform was created in early 2014, headed by Xi Jinping. This group created six subgroups, including the Central Leading Group for Reform of the Judicial System. Apart from this party institution, the SPC also established a leading group for judicial reform.[135]

China's judicial reform is a project. That means judicial reform has been deliberately designed by the party-state in a top-down manner. The designed nature of the Chinese judicial reform is manifested in the Party's policy for judicial reform and the SPC's five-year plan for judicial reform. The policy and plan for judicial reform also demonstrate the political commitment and institutional capacity to systematic reform of the court system. The party-state considers judicial reform a long-term project, which will require continued efforts and programming. The creation of groups responsible for judicial reform, which would require financial and personnel investment, demonstrates the institutional capacity to carry out measures of judicial reform.

B. Legislation for Judicial Reform

The enactment of China's 1982 Constitution and the subsequent enactments and amendments of several judicial statutes concretizing constitutional provisions on the judiciary present the achievement of judicial reform at a formal level.

China's 1982 Constitution establishes the legal foundation for judicial reform during the post-Mao area. The Constitution provides that the people's courts are the judicial organs of China.[136] The people's courts include the SPC, people's courts at various local levels, and special people's courts.[137] The Constitution also establishes fundamental principles of judicial activities, including public hearing, the right to defence, and judicial independence.[138] The Constitution additionally stipulates the internal relationship between the courts. Accordingly, the SPC, the highest judicial organ, 'supervises the administration of justice by the people's courts at various local levels and by the special people's courts', while 'People's courts at higher levels supervise the administration of justice by those at lower

[134] 'Supreme Court Issues Five-Year Plan on Judicial Reform', ibid.

[135] China's Supreme People's Court, *White Paper on Judicial reform of Chinese court from 2013 to 2018* (2018) 71–73 <https://english.court.gov.cn/specials/ChineseCourtJudicialReform2013-2018.pdf>accessed 5 June 2024.

[136] Constitution of the People's Republic of China, art 123.

[137] ibid art 124.

[138] ibid arts 125 and 126.

levels.'[139] In addition, the Constitution stipulates the external relationship between the courts and the representative institutions. It states that: 'The Supreme People's Court is responsible to the National People's Congress and its Standing Committee. Local people's courts at various levels are responsible to the organs of state power which created them.'[140] The Constitution mandates that a law will prescribe the organization of the people's courts.[141]

The People's Courts Organic Law of the People's Republic of China (hereinafter, Courts Law) was adopted in 1979 and amended in 1983, 2006, 2018, and 2019, contributing to the institutionalization of the court system.[142] According to the Courts Law, the Chinese court system includes the SPC, local people's courts, and specialized people's courts.[143] The local courts are divided into three levels: higher people's courts, intermediate people's courts, and basic-level people's courts.[144] The specialized courts include military courts, maritime courts, intellectual property courts, financial courts, and so on.[145] The Courts Law establishes a two-tier jurisdiction of the courts. The basic-level people's courts try first-instance criminal and civil cases. The intermediate people's courts hear appeals from the basic-level courts and try first-instance cases. The high people's courts hear appeals from the intermediate courts and try first-instance cases of provincial significance. The SPC hears appeals from the high people's courts and tries first-instance cases at national level.[146]

The Judges Law of the People's Republic of China (hereinafter, Judges Law) was adopted in 1995 and amended in 2001, 2007, and 2019. The enactment of the Judges Law is considered 'a major step taken towards the institutionalization and professionalization of the Chinese judiciary'.[147] Chapter I of the Judges Law lays down legal and ethical principles guiding the judges' works—such as observing the Constitution and laws, safeguarding social fairness and justice, treating the parties and other participants in the proceedings fairly, staying diligent, honest, and clean, and living by professional ethics.[148] Chapter II of the Judges Law provides for the judges' duties and rights. For example, judges are required to handle cases impartially, promote the rule of law awareness, and enjoy professional guarantee, personal safety, and safety of property and residence.[149]

[139] ibid art 127.
[140] ibid art 128.
[141] ibid art 124.
[142] 'People's Courts Organic Law of the People's Republic of China' (NPC Observer), https://npco bserver.com/legislation/peoples-courts-organic-law> accessed 5 June 2024.
[143] People's Courts Organic Law of the People's Republic of China, art 12.
[144] ibid art 13.
[145] ibid art 15.
[146] ibid arts 16, 21, 23, and 25. See also Weixia Gu, 'Courts in China: Judiciary in the Economic and Societal Transitions' in Jiunn-rong Yeh and Wen-Chen Chang (eds), *Asian Courts in Context* (CUP 2014) 491.
[147] Chen (n 4) 161.
[148] Judges Law of the People's Republic of China, arts 3, 4, and 5.
[149] ibid arts 10 and 11.

Chapter III of the Judges Law establishes political, legal, and ethical requirements for selecting judges. These requirements include being a national of the People's Republic of China; upholding the Constitution, the Party leadership, and the socialist system; having political integrity, professional competence, and decent ethics; being physically fit to perform their duties; having an undergraduate diploma in law and a Bachelor of Laws or a higher degree in law from a college or university; and having five years of legal experience.[150] The requirement of a law degree and legal experience is an important reform to facilitate judicial professionalism. Before the 1983 amendment to the Judges Law, legal knowledge was not compulsory for prospective judges.[151] To facilitate judicial professionalism, the Judges Law requires that 'judges serving for their first post shall obtain legal professional credentials through the National Unified Legal Professional Qualification Examination'.[152] The National Unified Legal Professional Qualification Examination was introduced in 2018 to replace the National Judicial Examination created by the 2001 amendments to the Judges Law.[153]

Chapter IV of the Judges Law deals with appointment and removal. Accordingly, the president of the SPC shall be elected or removed by the NPC, while its vice-presidents, adjudication committee members, division heads, deputy division heads, and other adjudicators are appointed or removed by request of the president to the Standing Committee of the NPC.[154] The appointment and removal of local judges follow the same procedure.[155] The remaining chapters of the Judges Law are about judge management, appraisal, awards, disciplinary actions of judges, and professional guarantees.

The People's Assessors Law of the People's Republic of China (hereinafter, Assessors Law) was adopted in 2018. The Assessors Law aims to 'ensure citizens' lawful participation in trial activities, to promote judicial fairness, and to enhance public trust in the judiciary'.[156] Citizens serving as people's assessors must be least twenty-eight years old and shall usually have a high school education or higher.[157] The people's assessors are randomly selected among the population and appointed by the standing committees of the people's congresses for a non-consecutive five-year term.[158]

[150] ibid art 12.
[151] Björn Ahl, 'The Politicization of the Chinese National Judicial Examination, 2007–2012' (2018) 44 Mod China 215.
[152] Judges Law of the People's Republic of China, art 12.
[153] Jing Li, 'The Legal Profession of China in a Globalized World: Innovations and New Challenges' (2019) 26 IJLP 231.
[154] Judges Law of the People's Republic of China, art 18.
[155] ibid.
[156] People's Assessors Law of the People's Republic of China, art 1.
[157] ibid art 5.
[158] Chen (n 4) 333.

The Assessors Law distinguishes between two types of collegial panels: a three-member panel and a seven-member panel.[159] The second type (including three judges and four people's assessors) is applied in people's courts' trials of first-instance cases that have major social impact—such as criminal cases where a sentence of ten years or more imprisonment, indefinite detention, or the death penalty might be given; public interest litigation cases; cases involving land requisition and demolitions, ecological and environmental protection, or food and drug safety.[160] The functions of the people's assessors in the three- and seven-member panels are different. In the three-member panel, people's assessors can vote on both fact-finding and the application of law, while in the seven-member panel, the assessors can only vote on fact-finding, not on questions of the application of law.[161]

The enactment and amendments of judicial acts (the Courts, Judges, and Assessors Laws) have contributed to the institutionalization and professionalization of the Chinese court system. These legal instruments lay down the formal framework with which judicial institutions will be established and operate, and judicial actors will be selected and act.

C. Trends in Judicial Reform

After four decades of judicial reforms, China has created a sophisticated court system. I focus on three aspects of major trends in judicial reform: structural, personnel, and functional.

Notable structural trends in Chinese judicial reform are characterized here as establishment, departmentalization, and specialization. *Establishment* is to set up a stable court system. Based on the Constitution and the Courts Law, China has established thousands of district-level basic people's courts staffed by 46,000 judges, hundreds of prefecture-level intermediate people's courts staffed by 36,000 judges, 31 provincial-level high people's courts staffed by 7,000 judges, and the SPC at the central level staffed by more than 500 judges.[162] Chinese local courts have been established corresponding to administrative units. This arrangement seeks to ensure local governments' supervision of local courts.

Departmentalization refers to grouping judicial activities into divisions or tribunals within Chinese courts. Chen observes that in China 'since the 1980s, courts divisions have proliferated. At first there were only criminal and civil divisions; then economic and administrative divisions were created. Subsequent creations

[159] Qiu Qunran and Yan Chen, 'The People's Assessors in China's Legal System: Current Legal Structure for Their Duty and Its Justification' (2019) 12 Tsinghua China L Rev 171, 175.
[160] People's Assessors Law of the People's Republic of China, art 16.
[161] Qunran and Chen (n 159) 175.
[162] Gu (n 146) 489–92.

include divisions for the enforcement of judgments, and divisions for handling petitions and initiating cases.'[163] Social-economic development and growing litigations have generated the need to create different divisions within Chinese courts to focus on particular judicial tasks.

Specialization is the trend of creating specialized courts. Specialized courts are 'courts with limited jurisdiction over one or more specific fields of law'.[164] China has created specialized people's courts outside the generalist people's courts. During the Mao era, early specialized courts included military courts, railway transport courts, and water transport courts. In the Reform era, China has increasingly created specialized courts. In the 1980s, the country created specialized courts in forest affairs, petroleum, mining, and farmland. In the Xi era, new specialized courts emerged, including the creation of the Intellectual Property (IP) Courts in Beijing, Shanghai, and Guangzhou in 2014; the Internet Courts in Hangzhou, Guangzhou, and Beijing in 2017 and 2018; the Shanghai Financial Court and the China International Commercial Court in 2018; the SPC's IP Court in 2019; the Hainan IP Court in 2020; and the Beijing Financial Court in 2021.[165]

Mark Jia explains that China's speedy construction of specialized courts is due to the political benefits of judicial specialization. These benefits include signalling the regime's law reforms in areas of strategic importance (such as IP, finance, internet, and global commerce); demonstrating the regime's adherence to legality in some areas of law (such as traffic torts and e-commerce claims) but not in other politically and socioeconomically sensitive areas of law (such as corruption and labour disputes); and preventing courts from local protectionism.[166]

A notable personnel trend in Chinese judicial reform is *professionalization*. Professionalization involves giving judges professional qualities such as expertise, efficiency, and consistency.[167] As mentioned earlier, the enactment of the Judges Law presents an effort to professionalize the personnel of the judiciary. In practice, to promote judicial professionalism, China has implemented judicial examinations since 2002.[168] Chen commented that 'as a result of this reform and other related efforts, the average educational standards of Chinese judges have improved considerably in the course of decade'.[169] To improve judges' professional ethics,

[163] Chen (n 4) 165.

[164] Mark Jia, 'Special Courts, Global China' (2022) 62 Virginia JIL 8.

[165] ibid 16–29; Weixia Gu, 'China's Law and Development: A Case Study of the China International Commercial Court' (2021) 62 Harvard Int'l LJ 67; Wei Cai and Andrew Godwin, 'Challenges and Opportunities for The China International Commercial Court' (2019) 68 ICLQ 869; Ya-Feng Zhang, Li-Ming Li, and Ke Xu, 'Do Specialized Intellectual Property Courts Show a Pro-patent Propensity? Evidence from China' (2022) 70 Int'l Rev Law Econ 106065; Yang Lin, 'China's Three Internet Courts' (2021) 2 AC: J of SALS 531.

[166] Jia (n 164) 51–54.

[167] ibid 10; Taisu Zhang, 'The Pragmatic Court: Reinterpreting the Supreme People's Court of China' (2012) 25 Colum J Asian Law 1.

[168] Ahl (n 151) 208.

[169] Chen (n 133) 22.

in 2010 the SPC issued the revised Basic Norms of Professional Ethics of Judges and Code of Conduct for Judges.[170] In addition, China has recently implemented measures of judicial reforms to 'reward high performers with substantially higher salaries and greater responsibilities while retaining other personnel in less prestigious positions' in order to 'attract more qualified individuals into the judiciary, thereby expanding its legal expertise and adjudicatory capacity'.[171]

A functional trend is that Chinese courts have the judicial *capacity* to resolve a vast number of legal disputes. Between 1978 and 2008, Chinese courts' caseload increased twenty times. Between 2009 and 2014, the total number of cases accepted by courts continued to increase, with 11.37 million cases in 2009, 11.7 million cases in 2010, 12.2 million cases in 2011, 14.2 million cases in 2013, and 15.65 million cases in 2014.[172] Although these numbers may not tell us how courts actually work, the fact that the courts handled such numerous cases demonstrates the judicial capacity to deal with legal disputes.

Another functional trend is the *legal* function of Chinese courts. Different from the Mao era, Chinese courts in the Reform era are not merely a political instrument of proletarian dictatorship mainly punishing criminals but have also played the role of arbiters of social-economic disputes among citizens and administrative disputes between citizens and government agencies.[173] Particularly, Weixia Gu observes that among different types of cases, 'civil and commercial cases far outnumbered', 'because in the course of deepening marketization, Chinese courts have more and more been expected to serve as impartial arbiters of civil and commercial disputes among citizens and market entities'.[174]

Another notable functional trend in Chinese judicial reform is a precedent-like system called 'guiding cases', created in 2010.[175] China's guiding cases refer to 'rulings and judgments that have already come into legal effect' released by the SPC of China, which 'People's courts at all levels should refer to . . . when adjudicating similar cases'.[176] By 3 January 2017, the Court issued seventy-seven guiding cases in fifteen sets.[177] The introduction of something akin to common law into the

[170] China: Code of Ethics for Judges Revised (Library of Congress, 28 December 2010) 5 June 2024 <https://www.loc.gov/item/global-legal-monitor/2010-12-28/china-code-of-ethics-for-judges-revised>.

[171] Taisu Zhang and Tom Ginsburg, 'China's Turn toward Law' (2019) 59 Virginia JIL 306, 328.

[172] Chen (n 133) 24.

[173] Chen (n 4) 181.

[174] Gu (n 146) 495.

[175] Jia Mark, 'China Common Law? Guiding Cases and Judicial Reform' (2016) 129 Harvard L Rev 2213, 2213.

[176] 《最高人民法院关于案例指导工作的规定》 [Provisions of the Supreme People's Court Concerning Work on Case Guidance] (passed by the Adjudication Committee of the Supreme People's Court, 15 November 2010, effective 26 November 2010) China Guiding Cases Project, English Guiding Cases Rules (12 June 2015 edn) <http://cgc.law.stanford.edu/guiding-cases-rules/20101126-english>. [<https://perma.cc/J9XS-VL5L>] accessed 1 January 2020.

[177] Mo Zhang, 'Pushing the Envelope: Application of Guiding Cases in Chinese Courts and Development of Case Law in China' (2017) 26 Washington ILJ 269, 271.

socialist world is unusual, which explains why this move 'has captured the attention of the world outside of China'.[178] The Stanford Law School launched the China Guiding Cases Project.[179] 'Universities such as Yale, Stanford, and the City University of Hong Kong as well as institutions such as the European Union have held training programs with [Chinese] Court staff on the case method.'[180]

D. Chinese Socialist Courts

Scholars hold divergent views about Chinese judicial reform. Carl F Minzner argues that after several decades of judicial reform, in the early twenty-first century China turned against courts and resorted to meditation and alternative resolutions in response to 'increasing social unrest generated by civil conflicts between citizens, and between citizens and the state'.[181] Conversely, Taisu Zhang and Tom Ginsburg argue that, in the Xi era, measures of judicial reform have been undertaken to empower courts, including 'increased financial independence from local governments, expanded jurisdiction over administrative disputes, the creation of circuit courts, greater authority to interpret statutes, substantially stronger enforcement powers, and heightened levels of legal proficiency and professionalism among judges'.[182] They state that 'the courts have never in PRC [People's Republic of China] history been as independent, professional, and powerful as they currently are'.[183]

Chen offers a balanced view. He explores the achievements of Chinese judicial reform—such as funding the courts, national judicial examinations, efforts to promote public trials and transparency in the work of the courts, and regulating behaviours and professional ethics of judges.[184] At the same time, Chen identifies structural problems of the Chinese judiciary such as the limits of judicial independence due to Party's interference in judicial activity and local judiciaries' dependence on local government. In addition, Chen points out personnel problems of Chinese courts such as the quality of judges, corruption among judges, and judges' occupational insecurity. Moreover, according to Chen, Chinese courts

[178] Susan Finder, 'How the Supreme People's Court Uses Case Law & Other Sources When It Guides the Lower Courts' (Supreme People's Ct Monitor, 8 March 2017) <https://supremepeoplescourtmonitor.com/tag/guiding-cases> [<https://perma.cc/KR3F-CK9M>] accessed 5 June 2024.

[179] Stanford Law School, 'China Guiding Case Project' <https://cgc.law.stanford.edu> [https://perma.cc/Q4GS-93C4] accessed 31 December 2019.

[180] Susan Finder, 'Case law Chinese Style—Where Is It Going?' (Supreme People's Ct Monitor, 18 January 2015) <https://supremepeoplescourtmonitor.com/2015/01/18/case-law-chinese-style-where-is-it-going> [<https://perma.cc/ZN47-LFN5>] accessed 5 June 2024.

[181] Carl F Minzner, 'China's Turn Against Law' (2011) 59 AJCL 938.

[182] Zhang and Ginsburg (n 171) 311.

[183] ibid.

[184] Chen (n 133) 21–22.

have been confronted with functional problems such as huge workload and the poor enforcement of their decisions.[185]

Particularly, scholars express conflicting views about judicial independence in China.[186] Some scholars emphasize that Chinese courts have been under the Party's control.[187] Ling Li explains that the Party exercises control over courts through both the Party's macro-instructions of courts on judicial policies and its micro-instructions of courts on judicial outcomes of particular cases.[188] Wang Yuhua argues that courts have been under the party's control in the political realm but judicial fairness has been promoted in the commercial realm.[189] The logic of the Chinese government's dualist approach to courts is that:

> a fair and efficient court will not only protect investors whose assets are crucial for local officials' political advancement but also provide openings for discontented citizens and social groups to challenge the state, which undermines the officials' careers. Therefore, the best strategy for the government is to curb corruption in the commercial realm while imposing constraints on citizens' rights to sue the authoritarian state through legal channels.[190]

The issue of judicial independence is just a part of a broader academic debate on the institutional context in which Chinese courts operate. In a recent book, drawing on sociological literature on institutions, Hang Ng and Xin He argue that Chinese courts are embedded institutions.[191] By that, they mean the institutional context shapes the various operations of Chinese courts. Ng and He distinguish four types of Chinese courts' institutional embeddedness. First is administrative embeddedness, which denotes the idea that the decisions of Chinese courts are internally supervised by superior judges and externally shaped by the interests of local party organs and government bureaus. The second type of embeddedness is political, which means Chinese courts are a means for political ends such as maintaining social and political stability. The third is social embeddedness, meaning that the various operations of Chinese courts are shaped by judges' social connections (eg the judges' friends and relatives, and the friends and relatives of the judges' superiors and colleagues). Finally, there is economic embeddedness or court finance reflective of the local economy. Based on the bottom-up account

[185] Chen (n 4) 183–92.

[186] See generally Peerenboom R (ed), *Judicial Independence in China: Lessons for Global Rule of Law Promotion* (CUP 2009).

[187] Qiang Fang and Li Xiaobing, *Power versus Law in Modern China: Cities, Courts, and the Communist Party* (University Press of Kentucky 2017).

[188] Ling Li, 'The Chinese Communist Party and People's Courts: Judicial Dependence in China' (2016) 64 AJCL 64, 59.

[189] Yuhua Wang, *Tying the Autocrat's Hands: The Rise of the Rule of Law in China* (CUP 2014) 44, 48.

[190] ibid 7.

[191] Ng KH and He X, *Embedded Courts: Judicial Decision-Making in China* (CUP 2017).

of Chinese courts' institutional embeddedness, Ng and He doubt the effects of the SPC's ongoing top-down measures of judicial reforms to render Chinese courts increasingly professional and independent legal institutions.[192]

Another interdisciplinary account of Chinese courts is given by Ji Li. Drawing on sociological, economic, and political theories, Li develops a unified theory that the broader power structure determines the operation of Chinese courts in three phases: case filing, adjudication, and enforcement of court decisions. More specifically, Li contends that the operation of Chinese courts is shaped by both the structure of de jure power (formal political power distributed among state institutions under the Party leadership) and de facto power (the capacity to organize collective action by actors such as leaders of crime syndicates, respected local professionals, and clan elders).[193] This view echoes in some way Ng and He's account of the institutional context shaping Chinese courts. Li's theory, however, seems to suggest a more positive prediction about Chinese judicial reform. Li believes that measures of judicial reforms, such as consolidating the personnel and financial decisions of provincial courts and the creation of new cross-jurisdictional courts, 'will certainly enhance the courts' power status relative to local and regional litigants, and hence will greatly improve judicial fairness'.[194]

I contend that four decades of judicial reform in China have resulted in important achievements, including the establishment of a functional court system, departmentalization of the court's internal structure, the creation of specialized courts, professionalization of judges, courts' capacity to handle a vast number of cases, the courts' role as legal institutions for resolving social disputes, and the creation of the guiding case system. Many changes to the Chinese court system are unconventional to the socialist legal tradition—such as the legal role of courts in rights protection and the creation of specialized courts like the internet court and the commercial courts.

However, I argue that the Chinese court system remains essentially socialist despite significant reforms. Chinese courts are socialist courts. The structure, functions, and personnel of Chinese socialist courts are shaped by five properties of the socialist legal tradition.

First, the political function of Chinese courts presents the continuity of the socialist model of legal instrumentalism. Chinese courts are both legal and political institutions. In response to the emergence of new social disputes as the consequence of market development, Chinese courts have played the legal role of resolving social disputes. At the same time, the socialist nature and function of the courts remain the same: the courts are an instrument for the party-state to

[192] ibid 14–30. The sceptical view of Chinese courts as legal institutions is echoed in Clarke, (n 130), 541.
[193] Li (n 132) 108–09.
[194] ibid 139.

implement political policies, to consolidate political power, and to maintain the existing socialist regime.

Second, vanguardism continues to shape Chinese courts. The Party's influences on the court's structure, operation, and personnel are the functional embodiment of party vanguardism in the Chinese judiciary. From a critical perspective, one may perceive these influences as the limitations of the judicial independence in China. From a macro-legal tradition perspective, the Party's influences on Chinese courts demonstrate the continuity of vanguardism, a core of the socialist legal tradition.

Third, democratic centralism continues to shape Chinese courts' external and internal institutional relationships. Externally, due to democratic centralism, Chinese courts are under the supervision of the people's assemblies. Internally, Chinese local courts are under the centralized control of the SPC. Although Chinese courts can be functionally and partially independent (particularly in commercial cases), they are structurally dependent on other state institutions as the consequence of centralized power.

Fourth, rights statism is embodied in the operation of Chinese courts. Chinese courts are both the forum for local citizens to pursue rights and the instrument for the state to control rights practices. The fact that Chinese courts can handle numerous cases and that citizens file cases to courts demonstrates that the courts are the legal forum for citizens to pursue their rights. At the same time, Chinese courts are political institutions and they operate as a tool for the state to regulate rights. In this aspect, Chinese courts legitimate the restriction of rights practice and direct the rights practice in certain directions referred by the party-state. This demonstrates the politics of statist rights in Chinese judiciary.

Finally, economic statism is manifested in Chinese courts' consolidation of state ownership. An empirical study of 3,323 commercial lawsuits involving listed companies in China suggests that 'Chinese courts favor state firms and private firms with personal political ties'.[195] Particularly, the study demonstrates that 'state-owned enterprises (SOEs) fare significantly better than non-SOEs in [Chinese] court'.[196] The explanation is that 'given that Chinese courts are not independent from the Party and government, decisions against these firms incur political risk, which most judges tend to avoid'.[197] Chinese courts' favouring state firms and private firms with personal political connections 'likely reflects the fact that the state uses its nonindependent judiciary to redistribute wealth from parties that are not politically favored to those that are'.[198] The effect of state ownership on Chinese court outcomes is the functional embodiment of economic statism in the judicial

[195] Haitian Lu, Hongbo Pan, and Chenying Zhang, 'Political Connectedness and Court Outcomes: Evidence from Chinese Corporate Lawsuits' (2015) 58 J Law Econ 829.
[196] ibid 830.
[197] ibid 835.
[198] ibid 857.

field. This is connected to two previous features: vanguardism and democratic centralism. As Chinese courts are under the party's leadership and structurally dependent on other state institutions, they consolidate the state ownership, which is regarded by the party-state as the core of Chinese socialism. The courts favour state firms in commercial lawsuits in order to consolidate state ownership and the state's hegemonic role in the economy.

VI. LEGAL PROFESSIONAL REFORM

A. Achievements of Lawyer System Reform

The lawyer system in China has experienced significant reforms since the reform era, which has drawn extensive academic attention.[199] I underline major structural, personnel, and functional trends in the reform of the lawyer system in China as below.

A notable trend in the structural-personnel reform of the legal profession in China is the rapid growth in the number of lawyers and law firms. While in 1979–80 there were fewer than 300 lawyers working in a dozen law firms,[200] by the end of 2020 there were more than 522,000 lawyers working in over 34,000 law firms.[201] There are over 424,400 full-time lawyers (81.23%), over 13,500 part-time lawyers (2.59%), over 59,100 public lawyers (11.32%), over 16,100 corporate lawyers (3.09%), and 1,500 military lawyers (0.29%).[202] The law firms include over 20,600 partnership firms (60.59%), over 870 state-owned firms (2.56%), and over 9,400 individual firms (27.65%).[203] In addition, by the end of 2020, 234 law firms from 23 countries and regions had established 300 representative offices in mainland China.[204] These figures demonstrate the structural pluralization of the Chinese lawyer system, which includes various types of lawyers and law firms. The lawyer

[199] Li (n 153); Elizabeth M Lynch, 'China's Rule of Law Mirage: The Regression of the Legal Profession since the Adoption of the 2007 Lawyer's Law' (2010) 42 Geo Wash Int'l L Rev 535; William P Alford, '"Second Lawyers, First Principles": Lawyers, Rice-roots Legal Workers, and the Battle Over Legal Professionalism', in William P Alford, William Kirby, and Kenneth Winston (ed), *China Prospects for the Professions in China* (Routledge 2011); Carlos Wing-Hung Lo and Ed Snape, 'Lawyers in the People's Republic of China: A Study of Commitment and Professionalization' (2005) 53 AJCL 433. This section focusses on the reform of the lawyer system in China. For reform of legal education in China, see Weidong JI, 'Legal Education in China: Reforms and Requirements' (2016) 3 Asian J Law Soc 237; Carl F Minzner, 'The Rise and Fall of Chinese Legal Education' (2013) 36 Fordham Int'l LJ 334.

[200] Chen (n 6) 198–99.

[201] Ministry of Justice of China, 'Statistical analysis of lawyers and grassroots legal services in 2020' (Ministry of Justice of China, 11 June 2021) <http://www.moj.gov.cn/pub/sfbgw/zwxxgk/fdzdgknr/fdzdgknrtjxx/202106/t20210611_427394.html>accessed 5 June 2024.

[202] ibid.

[203] ibid.

[204] ibid.

system has not been dominated by the state-owned law firms as there are numerous private law firms and representative offices of foreign law firms.[205]

A functional trend is that Chinese lawyers have been transformed from the Soviet style of state workers to professional persons.[206] The 1980 Provisional Regulation on Lawyers defined lawyers as 'state legal workers', which designated lawyers as government officials subject to the government's control.[207] A major reform approved by the State Council in 1986 allowed for the establishment of financially independent law firms.[208] Another reform in 1994 transformed law firms from administrative organs controlled by the Ministry of Justice into professional organs regulated by lawyers' associations.[209] The Lawyers Law enacted in 1996 consolidated previous reforms and significantly changed the nature of the Chinese lawyer system.[210] The Law defined a lawyer as a provider of legal services to society.[211] The 2007 amendment to the Lawyers Law redefined a lawyer as a 'professional who has acquired a lawyer's practice certificate pursuant to law, and is authorized or designated to provide the parties with legal services'.[212] Lawyers are therefore considered professional persons rather than government officials.

Another notable functional trend is the partial independence of lawyers in China. Jianfu Chen comments that 'Although lawyering in China is not deemed to be a "free profession", today's lawyers are increasingly independent and willing to take on the state.'[213] Criminal lawyers are more aggressive in using their rights provided by the Criminal Procedure Law to defend their clients. Lawyers also rely on administrative laws to sue the government or challenge government decisions; and they play more important roles in commercial cases.[214]

Thus, the Chinese lawyer system has experienced significant structural-personnel and functional change. The proliferation of private lawyers and law firms, the transformation of lawyers from state workers to professional persons, and the relative independence of lawyers during the Reform era are the important alterations to the status of lawyers during the Mao era. Several internal and external factors account for this change. Internally, Chinese market development has generated the need for legal services, leading to the increase in lawyers and law firms, and the changing role of lawyers from state workers to professional persons. In addition, the emergence of social disputes as the consequence of social and economic reform induced the need for professional lawyers to represent clients

205 Chen (n 6) 201.
206 Chen (n 4) 201.
207 ibid 202.
208 Chen (n 5) 199.
209 Chen (n 6) 200.
210 ibid.
211 ibid.
212 Law of the People's Republic of China on Lawyers (amendment through 2007), art 2.
213 Chen (n 6) 203.
214 ibid 203–04.

in courtrooms. Moreover, the rise of rights conscience has contributed to citizens relying on lawyers to protect their rights. Externally, China's integration into the global market facilitates the development of international law firms in China. Particularly, by allowing foreign law firms to operate in China, the Chinese government signalled 'to foreign investors that China also had a legal profession that was autonomous to the state and the Communist Party, thus convincing them to stay and invest in China'.[215]

B. Chinese Socialist Lawyers

Despite significant reforms, the identity of socialist lawyers remains intact in China. First, socialist lawyers are under the control of the state, which is the embodiment of legal instrumentalism. Legal instrumentalism perpetuates the marginal status of lawyers in the Chinese socialist legal milieu.[216] Law and legal institutions like lawyer systems are placed under political control to ensure that they serve the state's interests and socialist goals. Therefore, the Lawyers Law seeks 'to enable lawyers to play their role in the development of the socialist legal system'.[217] Thus, although Chinese lawyers are no longer conceived of as state workers, they are still under the state's control and serve the state's goals of social and economic development.[218]

Structurally, the All China Lawyers' Association (ACLA) is under the control of the Ministry of Justice (MOJ), while local lawyers' associations are under the control of local bureaus.[219] Although in theory the ACLA is intended to be the self-regulatory organization for Chinese lawyers, it 'barely has any substantive independence from the MOJ or the state regulatory power in general'.[220] According to Jianfu Chen, 'lawyering is a tightly controlled profession in China, and the Ministry of Justice and/or its local bureaus exercises extensive powers over this profession and its practice'.[221]

In addition, the Chinese lawyer system embodies party vanguardism. That means Chinese lawyers are placed under Party leadership. The foremost mission of the ACLA is 'upholding the leadership of the Chinese Communist Party'

[215] Li (n 153) 234.
[216] Ethan Michelson, 'Lawyers, Political Embeddedness, and Institutional Continuity in China's Transition from Socialism' (2007) 113 Am J Sociol 362.
[217] Law of the People's Republic of China on Lawyers (amended 2007), art 1.
[218] Dongjin Lee, 'Infrastructural Developmental Citizenship: Chinese Lawyers and State-Framed Marketization' (2020) 24 Citizenship Stud 904; Sida Liu, 'The Changing Roles of Lawyers in China: State Bureaucrats, Market Brokers, and Political Activists' in Heinz Klug and Sally Engle Merry (eds), *The New Legal Realism: Studying Law Globally, vol 2* (CUP 2016) 180.
[219] Chen (n 6) 205.
[220] Li (n 153) 2342.
[221] Chen (n 6) 205.

according to its charter.[222] In a speech in 2021, President Xi Jinping states that: '[We should] educate and guide lawyers to consciously abide by the basic requirements of supporting the leadership of the Communist Party and the socialist rule of law in China and strive to be good lawyers satisfied by the party and the people.'[223] The regulatory framework and political discourse on Chinese lawyers illustrate that the Party's vanguard role extends to the legal profession.

Moreover, socialist lawyers embody rights statism: the way lawyers invocate rights is regulated by the state. Although Chinese lawyers may be independent to some extent in commercial cases, they are controlled by the state in politically sensitive cases such as human rights cases.[224] Particularly, the Chinese party-state crackdown on human rights lawyers in 2015 illustrates that 'the Party-state has developed tight control, through fear and enhanced management, over the profession, which is now structured in such a way that the political role of lawyers is now negligible.'[225] The political control of human rights lawyers in China indicates the continuity of rights statism. As rights are regulated by the state, lawyers are not merely the device for citizens to protect their rights against the state. The state controls human rights lawyers to prevent citizens from using rights and lawyers to challenge the state.

VII. CONCLUDING ANALYSIS

A. Exceptional Intention

Chinese legal reform is a top-down project initiated and led by the Party. Legal reform is shaped by the Party's *exceptional intention* to create a distinctive Chinese model of a socialist legal system. Although Chinese legal reform involves various internal and external actors (legal scholars, lawyers, activists, foreign governments, and international agencies), the Party plays a dominant role in legal reform. The Party initiates legal reform projects, anticipates measures for legal reforms, supervises the implementation of these measures, and puts limitations on the scope of legal reforms. Bottom-up dynamics may put some pressures on legal reform, but the Party retains the power to adopt policies for legal reform and to decide on the scope of legal reform.

[222] Li (n 153) 232.

[223] Guo Rui, 'Xi Jinping Wants Lawyers in China to "Follow and Embrace" the Communist Party's Leadership' South China Morning Post (9 December 2021) <https://www.scmp.com/news/china/politics/article/3158969/xi-jinping-wants-lawyers-china-follow-and-embrace-communist>accessed 5 June 2024.

[224] Chen (n 6) 205; Eva Pils, *China's Human Rights Lawyers: Advocacy and Resistance* (Routledge 2015).

[225] Hualing Fu, 'The July 9th (709) Crackdown on Human Rights Lawyers: Legal Advocacy in an Authoritarian State' (2018) 27 J Contemp China 565.

B. Legislative Method

Legal reform in China is carried out through *legislative method*. Substantive legal rules are newly adopted, revised, and removed through the legislative process. The Chinese legislature also enacts or revises organic laws to facilitate institutional legal reforms. Although the Chinese legislature is normally criticized for its symbolic role, it is the only national institution formally created by the people, which makes it a legitimate platform for legal reform.

C. Incremental Strategies

The Party adopts *incremental strategies* for legal reform. During the period between the 1970s and 1980s, classical incrementalism was the strategy for legal reform. The Party did not formulate a coherent, overall plan for legal reform but carried out some sporadic legal changes. Since 1997, the Party turned to neo-incrementalism. Accordingly, the Party adopted overall plans for legal reform, which will be gradually implemented over a long time. The 1997 plan to establish a 'socialist legal system with Chinese characteristics', the 2014 Rule of Law Decision, and the 2021 Rule of Law Plan are overall plans for legal reform. They will be implemented incrementally over many years. To illustrate, the 2014 Rule of Law Decision states that 'comprehensively moving ruling the country according to the law forward is a systemic project, it . . . requires long-term, arduous efforts'.[226] In the same vein, the 2021 Rule of Law Plan states that rule of law reform should 'make progress in a gradual and long-term basis to ensure that the design of various systems is feasible and effective'.[227]

The turn to neo-incrementalism as a strategy for Chinese legal reform is because, after several decades of reform, the Party has a specified direction for economic and legal development, namely a socialist market economy and socialist rule of law. After Deng Xiaoping's Southern Tour in early 1992, the 14th Party Congress in October 1992 adopted the concept of the 'socialist market economy' as the direction for Chinese economic development. The concept was then written into Article 15 of China's Constitution through the 1993 amendment. As the direction towards the socialist market economy is specified, the direction for legal reform became clearer. The socialist market economy is a rule-based system and requires the legalization of private property. It is clear that the legal reform would involve legislative enactments to create market legal institutions, particularly the enactment of private law.[228] In addition, the 15th Party Congress in 1997 adopted

[226] Rule of Law Decision (n 18).
[227] Rule of Law Plan (n 23).
[228] Donald C Clarke, 'Legislating for a Market Economy in China' (2007) 191 China Q 571.

the concept of socialist rule of law as the direction for Chinese legal development. As the socialist market economy and socialist rule of law are adopted as the dominant ideas directing economic and legal development, the Party can formulate overall plans for legal reform to facilitate legal development in that direction. Apart from the specified socialist direction, the political consensus under the centralized single-party-rule system in China makes it convenient for the Party to formulate overall plans for legal reform. Party members may disagree on specific policy issues but they agree on the socialist direction for Chinese development generally and legal development particularly.

The overall plans for legal reform require incremental, long-term implementation due to the limited capacity. The legal reform plans involve numerous interrelated works, which require tremendous human, institutional, and financial resources. The limited capacity makes it difficult to implement legal reform measures immediately and comprehensively in a big-bang manner, requiring step-by-step practices over many years. The incremental implementation of the legal reform plans is also due to concerns of stability. Gradual legal adjustments render the legal system stable, which is necessary for the development of the predictable rules-based socialist market economy.

D. Positive Change

Efforts of legal reform generate *positive change* to the Chinese legal system. After four decades of legal reform, China has created a sophisticated legal system. The legal system acquires some formal features of the rule of law. It also adopts substantive legal norms such as the partial independence of the courts, the professionalization of lawyers, the legal protection of individual rights, private ownership, and private economic sectors.

E. Factors

Chinese legal reform is driven by three *gap factors*: the internal gap between the party-state's commitments to socialism and the existing law; the external gap between social change and the existing law; and the normative gap between Chinese law and transnational legal norms. China needs to carry out legal reform to narrow the gaps to enhance the legitimacy of both the socialist political regime and the socialist legal system.

The internal gap between socialist commitments and the existing law causes legal reform in China. When the existing law fails to serve as an instrument for realizing socialist commitments, legal reform becomes necessary. The Chinese party-state is committed to building socialism in China. Since China undertook reform in 1978, law has been considered an instrument for realizing socialist commitments. Consequently, legal reform is introduced not as an independent project but as a part of the broader project for the construction of Chinese socialism.

The fact that the Party initiated the reform policy in 1978 generates a gap between existing law and the reform commitments. The lack of laws and legal institutions as the consequence of the Cultural Revolution is at odds with the reform commitments. For example, the lack of a legal framework for foreign investment is dissonant with the Party's Open-Door commitment, which would open the door for foreign investment in China. Legal reform was therefore introduced to mitigate the gap. To facilitate socialist modernization, China needs a legal framework for the normal operation of state institutions and for economic development, which in turn would generate legal reform. The sporadic enactments of some public laws and economic laws during this early period are driven by the need to realize the commitment to socialist modernization.

The party-state's new commitment to the socialist market economy in 1992 has generated a further internal gap. The socialist market economy is not a reality but the aspirations that the Chinese party-state seek to realize in the long term. The existing laws, which lack private laws, are at odds with that commitment, which induces legal reform. Consequently, the legislative enactments of numerous private laws are driven by the need to realize the commitment to the development of a socialist market economy. In fact, the Chinese government has a clear vision for undertaking legal reform to realize the commitment to the socialist market economy.[229]

However, the development of private laws is not sufficient to realize the socialist market economy. To develop the socialist market economy, China needs effective governance, which in turn puts pressure on administrative reform. The commitment to socialist market economy also results in judicial and legal professional reform to deal with private legal disputes. In short, institutional legal reforms are driven by the need to realize the commitment to a socialist market economy.

The party-state's new commitments to the construction of a socialist rule of law state in 1997 create further internal gaps. For example, administrative corruption and the lack of professional judges and lawyers are inconsistent with a socialist rule of law commitment. Consequently, China undertakes legal reform (particularly legal institutional reform) to bring the legal system closer to a socialist rule of law commitment. To govern the country by law, China needs to carry out legal institutional reform to improve the enforcement of the law, the adjudication of legal disputes, and the dissemination of law among the public.

The external gap between existing law and socio-economic change is another cause of Chinese legal reform. Socio-economic change generates an external gap

[229] Information Office of The State Council (n 34).

between the existing laws and society, which leads to legal reform to bridge the gap. Narrowing the gap between the law and society is necessary for the social acceptance of the law.

Law and development theory conventionally attribute economic development to legal origins. However, scholars point out that economic development in China has little to do with law.[230] Franklin Allen, Jun Qian, and Meijun Qian argue that 'China is a significant counterexample to the findings of the existing literature on law, institutions, finance, and growth. Despite its poor legal and financial systems, China has one of the fastest growing economies in the world.'[231]

Chinese legal reform is not the cause but the effect of economic development. The relationship between law and economic development in China can be explained by this logic: economic development generates gaps between the existing law and new economic relations, which induces legal reform to deal with these relations. For example, China's 1999 Unified Contract Law was adopted twenty years after the introduction of economic reform. Economic development, as the consequence of the economic reform policy, creates new contractual private relations, while existing law is insufficient to regulate these relations. The enactment of contract law therefore becomes necessary to fill the external gap.[232]

Economic change in China results in social change: the emergence of new social groups (such as the middle class), new social relations (eg disputes and social security), new social problems (such as corruption and environmental pollution). Such social change creates an external gap: existing laws fail to deal with new social issues. Therefore, new statutes are enacted to regulate new social relations. Administrative reform is carried out to curb administrative corruption and protect citizens' rights from the arbitrary power of administrative agencies. Judicial reform is undertaken to deal with the rise of vast social disputes. The lawyer system is improved to provide more professional legal services to meet social needs.

China carries out legal reform to narrow the gap between domestic law and transnational legal norms. Scholars have documented the massive diffusion of comparative, transnational, and international law in China as a device for the country's legal reform.[233] Jianfu Chen points out the movement towards 'internationalization' of Chinese law since 1992 when the Party decided to establish a

[230] Shitong Qiao, 'Finance against Law: The Case of China' (2023) 64 Harvard Int'l LJ 431; Zhong Zhang, 'Law and Economic Growth in China: A Case-Study of the Stock Market' (2018) 5 Asian J Law Soc 333; Joseph Mazur and Anca-Elena Ursu, 'China's Disinterested Government and the Rule of Law' (2017) 4 Asia Pac Policy Stud 376.

[231] Franklin Allen, Jun Qian, and Meijun Qian, 'Law, Finance, and Economic Growth in China' (2005) 77 J Financ Econ 59.

[232] Ding Chen, 'Contract Law and Economic Reform in China', in TT Arvind and Jenny Steele (eds), *Contract Law and the Legislature: Autonomy, Expectations, and the Making of Legal Doctrine* (Hart Publishing 2020) 385.

[233] Chenguang Wang, 'Legal Transplantation and Legal Development in Transitional China' (2012) 4 World Bank Legal Rev 161.

socialist market economy.[234] Legal transplants are the mechanism for bridging the gap between Chinese law and transnational legal norms.

On legislative development, Chen states that:

> the leaders of the law-making authorities also explicitly endorsed bold adoption and the direct transplant of foreign laws. With such a legislative policy in place, the Maritime Code which had been in the making for over ten years and was primarily composed of borrowings from international conventions and practice, was not only adopted in 1992, but its adoption was heralded as an excellent example for harmonising Chinese law with international practice.[235]

Another example is the case of the 1999 Contract Law, in which 'the UNIDROIT Principles of International Commercial Contracts (1994) and the UN Convention on Contracts for the International Sale of Goods (1980) were the actual models, and in some places were copied article by article'.[236] International and comparative law not only affect private law but also public law. As Chen illustrates, 'the 1996–1997 (and again, the 2011–12) revisions to the Criminal Procedural Law and Criminal Law were aimed at absorbing commonly accepted international standards on justice and the rule of law, rather than following any particularly legal tradition'.[237]

On institutional reforms:

> [China] actively borrows and introduces foreign laws of legal supervision and control of governmental power, and sets up anticorruption bureaus in the procuratorial organs. In the process of judicial reform, China has pushed for adjudicative reform based on the adversarial model of common law while hesitating to adopt fully the principle of judicial independence; it introduced the reform of evidence rules based on foreign evidence structures; and it actively promoted China's guiding case system, based on the pattern of case law.[238]

Legal transplants in China are animated by the gap between Chinese law and transnational legal norms. The normative gap induces reformers to look outside to comparative, transnational, and international law, and to bring them home. China needs to bridge the normative gap between domestic and transnational law for instrumental reasons. Narrowing this gap can improve the Chinese legal system, ease transnational economic transactions, and facilitate China's integration into the global economy and the international political order.

234 Chen (n 6) 81.
235 ibid 82–83 (citations omitted).
236 ibid 85.
237 ibid 86.
238 Wang (n 233) 175.

Chenguang Wang discusses China's selective legal transplant, stating that:

> China's legal transplantation is by no means a blind or wholesale form of transplantation; to a great extent, it is a transplantation based on 'self-need.' It requires that recipients scrutinize the target laws to be transplanted, the problems to be solved by transplanted laws, the possible social effects of transplantation, and the differences and similarities of the social environments of exporting and importing countries in order to come up with an active, purposeful, and selective legal transplant.[239]

Chinese legal exceptionalism shapes the instrumental goals and selective manner of legal transplants. Transnational legal norms are adopted not because of their internal merits but because of their external outcomes: they can serve China's instrumental interests. For example, the transnational idea of the rule of law is not adopted as an end but as a means of facilitating social and economic development. Chinese legal exceptionalism leads to the selective adoption of transnational legal norms suitable to China's interests. Transnational legal norms (such as the separation of power, judicial constitutional review, and constitutionalism) inimical to the Party's monopoly of power would be rejected and even resisted.

F. Continuity of Socialist Law

Legal reform in China is *limited* by socialist legal and political principles. Despite significant reform over four decades, the legal system in contemporary China belongs to the socialist legal tradition. It is the historical extension of the legal embodiment of Marxist-Leninist arguments about socialism. Chinese law remains an instrument to pursue socialist objectives, particularly the stability of the socialist regime and socialist development. Chinese law is the embodiment of party vanguardism. It institutionalizes the party lines. Legal institutions, such as courts and lawyers, are under the Party's leadership and serve its political interests. Democratic centralism remains a principle of the legal system, which leads to the rejection of judicial review of legislative and executive actions and structural independence of the courts. Law both protects and regulates individual rights to ensure their balance with state interests. State ownership and the leading role of the state economic sectors remain dominant in civil and business law despite the adoption of private property and market elements.

[239] ibid 174–75.

G. Prospects

How far can legal reform go in China? Chinese legal reform has nearly reached its zenith: it has ideological and political limits. Chinese legal reform is constrained by socialist legal principles and the socialist political regime. Because of the socialist boundary, room for China's substantive legal reform in the future is narrow. Due to the instrumental nature of Chinese socialist law, it is difficult to carry out further legal reform to comprehensively subject the party-state to the rule of law. The rule of law can be partially, not comprehensively, achieved under the Chinese socialist legal system. Administrative and judicial agencies may be placed under the law, but it is difficult to comprehensively impose legal restraints on political leaders and political institutions (including state and party institutions). China's ongoing project of 'Comprehensively Moving Governing the Country According to the Law' does not equate to comprehensive rule of law. It is a project of comprehensive legal instrumentalism: to use the law as a tool to control every aspect of society. In addition, the vanguard leadership of the Party suggests that there is little room for institutional legal reform to subordinate the public power under legal restraints. In contrast, legal institutions are subject to political control. Due to economic statism, legislative enactments cannot go further to transform the Chinese economy into a free market economy. Right statism limits further enactment of laws protecting individual rights. Recent legal changes (such as the Party's further intervention into the legislative process, political control of courts and judges, and the crackdown of public interest lawyers) indicate legal regress rather than legal reform in China.[240] The future of Chinese legal reform will mainly be about the 'internal morality of law'—such as the consistency, transparency, clarity, stability, and practicability of the Chinese socialist legal system. These reforms are possible because they are about the formal features of the legal system and are less limited by socialist legal principles.

[240] Carl Minzner, *End of an Era: How China's Authoritarian Revival is Undermining Its Rise* (OUP 2018); Jianfu Chen, 'Chinese Law and Legal Reform: Where to from Here?' (2020) 50(1) HKLJ 243; Zhong Zhang, 'Ruling the Country without Law: The Insoluble Dilemma of Transforming China into a Law-Governed Country' (2022) 17 Asian J Comp Law 198.

5

Vietnam: Legal Reform and Legal Convergence

I. INTRODUCTION

Since the launch of the economic reform programme known as *Đổi mới* (Renovation) in 1986, Vietnam has comprehensively reformed its legal system. The Vietnamese legal system is now highly sophisticated in comparison to the Chinese legal system. Legal reform in Vietnam is a project initiated and led by the Communist Party of Vietnam (hereinafter, the Party). In contrast to Chinese legal exceptionalism, the law reform project in Vietnam indicates the political elites' universal intention to align the Vietnamese legal system with global legal standards.

In addition to various publications by domestic scholars,[1] Vietnamese law and legal reform have drawn some international attention. Some books on modern Vietnamese law and legal institutions have been published.[2] The international scholarship deals with various aspects of Vietnamese legal reform. Some writings focus on the legislative reform of substantive law, especially commercial law.[3]

[1] For some recent books, see Trần Quang Huy and others (eds), *Luật học Việt Nam—Những vấn đề đương đại [Vietnamese Legal Studies: Contemporary Issues]* (Judicial Publishing House 2019); Nguyễn Như Phát (eds), *Xây Dựng Hệ Thống Pháp Luật Thống Nhất, Đồng Bộ, Minh Bạch Và Hiệu Quả Trong Nhà Nước Pháp Quyền Việt Nam [Building a Unified, Synchronous, Transparent and Effective Legal System in the Rule of Law State of Vietnam]* (Social Science Publishing House 2014); Nguyễn Như Phát (eds), *Tổng Quan Tình Hình Nghiên Cứu Về Pháp Luật Ở Việt Nam Trong Hơn 30 Năm Qua [An Overview of Legal Studies in Vietnam in the Last Over 30 Years]* (Social Science Publishing House 2021).

[2] Tu Phuong Nguyen, *Law and Precarity: Legal Consciousness and Daily Survival in Vietnam* (CUP 2023); Tu Phuong Nguyen, *Workplace Justice: Rights and Labour Resistance in Vietnam* (Palgrave 2018); Penelope Nicholson, *Borrowing Court Systems the Experience of Socialist Vietnam* (Brill 2007); John Gillespie, *Transplanting Commercial Law Reform: Developing a 'Rule of Law' in Vietnam* (Routledge 2006); Mark Sidel, *Law and Society in Vietnam: The Transition from Socialism in Comparative Perspective* (CUP 2008); Jerome Alan Cohen and Ngọc Bích Nguyễn, *Investment Law and Practice in Vietnam: A Specially Commissioned Report* (Longman 1990); John Gillespie (ed), *Commercial Legal Development in Vietnam: Vietnamese and Foreign Commentaries* (Butterworths 1997).

[3] Phong Tran, 'Vietnam's Economic Liberalization and Outreach: Legal Reform' (2003) 9 Law & Bus Rev Am 139; Claude Rohwer, 'Progress and Problems in Vietnam's Development of Commercial Law' (1997) 15 Berkeley J Int'l L 275 ; Pham van Thuyet, 'Legal Framework and Private Sector Development in Transitional Economies: The Case of Viet-Nam' (1996) 27 Law & Pol'y Int'l Bus 541; Daniel Fitzpatrick and Alistair Wyvill, 'Business Bankruptcy Law Reform in Vietnam' (1996) 5 Asia Pac L Rev 37; Nghia D Pham, 'Commercial Legal Framework in Vietnam Since the Asian Crisis Development and Issues' (2004) 32 Int'l Bus Law 175.

Legal Reform in the Contemporary Socialist World. Ngoc Son Bui, Oxford University Press.
DOI: 10.1093/9780191948053.003.0005

Other writings explore administrative reforms.[4] Some deal with judicial reforms.[5] Others consider reforms of the legal profession.[6]

This chapter explores Vietnamese four aspects of legal reform: legislative, administrative, judicial, and legal professional reform. It is based on my extensive interviews in Vietnam with Vietnamese National Assembly (NA) delegates and officers, judges, court officers, and practicing lawyers. This chapter also employs original legal resources, including constitutions, statutes, administrative regulations, and judicial precedents. The study also uses primary resources in Vietnamese, including academic writings, reports, newspaper articles, discourse of political leaders, and the Party's political documents. Finally, this chapter is informed by my personal experiences in Vietnam as a law student and lecturer.

II. THE UNIVERSAL PROJECT OF LEGAL REFORM

Legal reform in Vietnam is a project initiated and led by the Party. As the Party is a single party dominating the state, it takes the lead in legal reform. The Party has introduced several legal reform plans since the 1986 Renovation. Law reform projects in Vietnam move from legal transition to converging the Vietnamese legal system with international and comparative legal norms.

A. Legal Transition

During its Sixth Congress in 1986, the Party adopted an economic reform policy known as *Đổi mới* (Renovation). Comparable to China's *gaige kaifang* policy,

[4] John Gillespie, 'Transplanting Legal Models: A Case Study of Administrative Reform in Vietnam' (1997) 33 Int'l Law News 23–34; Martin Painter, 'Public Administration Reform in Vietnam: Foreign Transplants or Local Hybrids?' in John Gillespie and Pip Nicholson (eds), *Asian Socialism and Legal Change* (Australian National University Press 2005) 267.

[5] Brian JM Quinn, 'Legal Reform and its Context in Vietnam' (2002) 15 Colum J Asian L 219; Brian JM Quinn, 'Vietnam's Continuing Legal Reform: Gaining Control over the Courts' (2003) 4 APLPJ 431; Pip Nicholson and Nguyen Hung Quang, 'The Vietnamese Judiciary: The Politics of Appointment and Promotion' (2005) 14 Pac Rim J L & Pol'y J001; Pip Nicholson, 'Judicial Independence and the Rule of Law: The Vietnam Court Experience' (2001) 3 AJAL37–58; John Gillespie, 'Rethinking the Role of Judicial Independence in Socialist-Transforming East Asia' (2007) 56 ICLQ 837–70; Pip Nicholson and S Pitt, 'Official Discourses and Court-Oriented Legal Reform in Vietnam' in John Gillespie and Pip Nicholson (eds), *Law and Development and the Global Discourses of Legal Transfers* (CUP 2012); Pip Nicholson, 'Renovating Courts: The Role of Courts in Contemporary Vietnam' in Jiunn-rong Yeh and Wen-Chen Chang (eds), *Asian Courts in Context* (CUP 2014).

[6] Mark Sidel, 'Law Reform in Vietnam: The Complex Transition from Socialism and Soviet Models in Legal Scholarship and Training' (1993) 11 UCLA Pac Basin LJ 221; Spencer Weber Waller and Lan Cao, 'Law Reform in Vietnam: The Uneven Legacy of Doi Moi' (1997) 29 NYU J Int'l L & Pol 555; Nguyen Hung Quang, 'Lawyers and Prosecutors under Legal Reform in Vietnam: The Problem of Equality' in Stephanie Balme and Mark Sidel (eds), *Vietnam's New Order* (Palgrave Macmillan 2007) 162–77.

Vietnam's *Đổi mới* policy aimed to transform the centrally planned economy into the 'socialist-oriented market economy'.[7] The *Đổi mới* policy allows and stipulates a certain degree of economic liberalization: de-collectivization of agriculture, private property, private companies, and foreign investments.[8] Although the *Đổi mới* policy focuses mainly on economic transition, it also includes a project for legal transition. The Party urged the state to:

> Improve the effectiveness of the state's management. Uphold the position and role of the National Assembly and People's Councils at all levels, and provide conditions for the elected bodies to perform their functions, duties and powers as prescribed by the Constitution. Strengthen socialist legality and manage the society by law. Clearly delineate the tasks, powers and responsibilities of state agencies at each level according to the principle of democratic centralism, clearly distinguish administrative-economic management functions from production and business management and combine management by sector with management by locality and territory. Adjust the state management apparatus in the direction of streamlining, lean, capable of institutionalizing the Party's guidelines into specific laws and policies, develop and organize the implementation of state plans, effectively manage and administrate social-economic activities, upholding law, discipline and social order and security.[9]

The Sixth Congress considered law an important instrument for effective governance. It anticipated some directions for administrative reforms, including the distribution of administrative functions and transparent governance. The reformist legal policy derives from economic reform policy. Economic reform requires the state to rule by law rather than by personal fiats. The goal of legal reform is largely to facilitate governing efficiency. At the same time, the Sixth Congress confirmed core features of socialist law, particularly the principles of socialist legality, democratic centralism, and party vanguardism. Law is an instrument for the state to regulate emerging social–economic relations. Power distribution must be within the framework of centralized power. Law is the institutionalization of Party lines.

The legal reform project adopted at the Sixth Congress was a project of domestic legal transition. The project focused mainly on some domestic institutional

[7] For comparison of economic reform in China and Vietnam, see Anita Chan and others (eds), *Transforming Asian Socialism: China and Vietnam Compared* (Rowman & Littlefield 1999).

[8] See generally Peter Boothroyd and Pham Xuam Nam (eds), *Socioeconomic Renovation in Viet Nam: The Origin, Evolution, and Impact of Doi Moi* (International Development Research Centre and Institute of Southeast Asian Studies 2000).

[9] Nghị quyết Đại hội đại biểu toàn quốc lần thứ VI của Đảng [Resolution of the VI National Congress of the Communist Party of Vietnam] (Báo điện tử Đảng Cộng sản Việt Nam) <https://tulieuvankien.dangcongsan.vn/ban-chap-hanh-trung-uong-dang/dai-hoi-dang/lan-thu-vi/nghi-quyet-dai-hoi-dai-bieu-toan-quoc-lan-thu-vi-cua-dang-1493>accessed 6 June 2024.

adjustments to improve the socialist legal system. It had not yet signified the universalist intention as Vietnam still limited its international relations to the Soviet Union, Laos, Cambodia, and other socialist countries.[10] The legal reform project embedded during the Sixth Congress adopts the classical incremental strategy. The Party sought to introduce some sporadic adjustments to the existing socialist legal system to respond to the immediate demands of social-economic transition, similar to the strategy adopted in China in 1978.

B. Legal Convergence

After nearly two decades of legal reform, the Party adopted a neo-incremental strategy to formulate a comprehensive plan for improving the legal system over the next decades. In 2005, the Politburo issued Resolution No 48-NQ/TW on the Strategy to Construct and Perfect the Vietnamese Legal System from Now to 2010 with a Vision to 2020 (hereinafter, Resolution 48).[11] This is the landmark policy for law reform in Vietnam. Resolution 48 confirmed the achievement of legal reform over nearly two decades, including legislative enactments in various areas and the incremental realization of the rule of law state. However, the Party recognized the shortcomings of the legal system, including inconsistency, low quality of legislation, slow enactment of laws, the lacking and weak institutions of legal enforcement, and deficiency in the internalization of international treaties to which Vietnam is a party. The Party attributes these shortcomings to the lack of a plan for comprehensive legal reform with a strategic vision.

Resolution 48 is an overall plan for neo-incremental reform of the Vietnamese legal system. The goals of the regal reform are:

> Building and perfecting a synchronous, consistent, feasible, open and transparent legal system, focusing on perfecting the socialist-oriented market economy institution, building a socialist rule of law state of Vietnam of the people, by the people and for the people; fundamentally renovate the mechanism of law making and implementation; promote the role and effectiveness of law to contribute to social management, maintaining political stability, economic development, international integration, building a clean and strong State, and realizing human rights, freedom and democracy of citizens, contributing to turning our country into a modern industrialized country by 2020.[12]

[10] The Constitution of The Socialist Republic of Vietnam (1980), art 14.
[11] Bộ Chính trị [Politburo], 48-NQ/TW, Nghị Quyết Về Chiến Lược Xây Dựng Và Hoàn Thiện Hệ Thống Pháp Luật Việt Nam Từ Nay Đến Năm 2010, Định Hướng Đến Năm 2020 [Resolution on the Strategy to Construct and Perfect the Vietnamese Legal System from Now to 2010 with a Vision to 2020].
[12] ibid.

The goals of legal reform as projected in Resolution 48 include formal and substantive aspects. First, the law reform aims to ensure that the Vietnamese legal system acquires universal formal standards of the rule of law such as consistency, feasibility, and transparency. Second, the law reform seeks to realize substantive values such as human rights protection, economic development, state-building, political stability, and international integration. To achieve these goals, Resolution 48 comprehensively proposes measures for legal reforms in six aspects.

The first is institutional legal reforms, including legislative, administrative, judicial, and legal profession reforms. On legislative reform, Resolution 48 urges speeding up the progress and improving the quality of legislative activities, better ensuring the democracy, legality, publicity, and transparency of the legal system. Resolution 48 particularly underlines that those statutes enacted by the NA should increasingly play a central role in the legal system, and hence regulations by central and local government must be limited. On administrative reform, Resolution 48 calls for simplification, openness, and transparency of administrative procedures, developing a legal framework for administrative litigation and supervision, and enacting laws on civil servants and anti-corruption. The document stresses that serious violations of public governance and law enforcement must be dealt with by judicial procedures. On judicial reform, it calls for courts' independence—particularly the structural independence of local courts from local government—and delimitation of the jurisdiction of the court of first instance and the court of appeals in accordance with the principle of two levels of trial. On legal profession reform, Resolution 48 proposes improving the law on judicial assistance (lawyers, notaries, assessors, judicial police, etc.) to meet the diverse needs of legal aids of people and businesses.[13]

The second is the reform of human rights law. Resolution 48 calls for implementing international treaties on human rights and citizens' political, economic, and socio-cultural rights to which Vietnam is a signatory. Particularly, it proposes the enactment of a law on state compensation and a law on referendum.[14]

The third is legal reform for the market economy. Resolution 48 proposes improving the laws on ownership and freedom of business; the laws for development of various markets (real estate, labour, science and technology, and stock markets); the laws on construction, electricity, post-telecommunications, food security, veterinary medicine, and fisheries; and the laws on public finance, environmental protection, and national resource.[15]

The fourth category involves reform of laws in the areas of education, science and technology, health, culture, information, sports, ethnicity, religion, population, family, children, and social policy.[16]

[13] ibid.
[14] ibid.
[15] ibid.
[16] ibid.

The fifth is the reform of laws regarding national defence and security, social order, and safety. Measures include developing laws on national borders, waters, and airspace; reforming criminal policy—such as limiting the death penalty, reducing the penalty of imprisonment, and expanding the imposition of monetary penalties; improving the law on the prevention of social evils such as prostitution, drugs, and HIV/AIDS; and enacting new laws on civil defence, defence education, protection of national security, and counterterrorism.[17]

Finally, Resolution 48 proposes legal reform to facilitate Vietnam's international integration. Measures include continuing to sign and accede to international treaties in the fields of economy, trade, investment, international credit, intellectual property (IP), tariffs, and environmental protection; enacting domestic laws consistent with the treaties Vietnam has signed; enacting laws to facilitate Vietnam's access to the World Trade Organization (WTO) and implementation of the country's Association of Southeast Asian Nations (ASEAN's) commitments; improving the law on settlement of economic disputes (arbitration and mediation) in accordance with international commercial customs; signing and acceding to international conventions on combating international terrorism, combating transnational organized crime, combating money laundering, anti-corruption, and mutual judicial assistance agreements.[18]

Resolution 48's measures for legal reform seek to improve the Vietnamese legal system comprehensively. The goals of these measures are not only to advance state efficiency but also to protect individuals' legal rights, support the development of the market economy, mitigate social problems, and facilitate Vietnam's integration into the global economic and legal order. These measures are largely a response to domestic transitions and Vietnam's increasing international integration over two decades. Therefore, Resolution 48 projects law reform to ensure that legislation will comprehensively cover emerging domestic social–economic relations and facilitate Vietnam's further international integration.

Resolution 48 embodies the emergence of legal universalism in Vietnam. Legal universalism is the attitude towards the convergence of the Vietnamese legal system with universal legal norms. Therefore, some universal legal standards (such as human rights, transparent governance, and judicial independence) are considered the basis for domestic law reform. Domestic law is perceived as a site for implementing international legal norms, as evident in the proposal to make law consistent with the international treaties Vietnam has signed. Resolution 48 also demonstrates Vietnam's willingness to further engage with international legal orders, for example, signing more treaties. This expresses the attitude towards convergence with international legal norms.

At the same time, Resolution 48 insists that the universal model of legal reform must be within the socialist boundary. It stipulates 'guiding opinions' for law reform,

[17] ibid.
[18] ibid.

including institutionalizing the Party's lines and ensuring the socialist direction of both the market economy and the Vietnamese state, and balancing international legal experience with Vietnamese reality and culture.[19] Thus, legal reform seeks to promote global legal convergence. But this convergence has a limit: it should not destroy the identity of socialist law. For example, judicial reform can facilitate structural independence of local courts from local government but not the separation of power—an antithesis to the socialist principle of democratic centralism.

After ten years implementing Resolution 48, on 4 April 2016, the Politburo issued Conclusion No 01-KL/TW (hereinafter, Conclusion 01) on the continuous implementation of the strategy with measures for legal reform from 2016 to 2020.[20] Conclusion 01 confirms the achievements of legal reform as consequences of implementing Resolution 48, including improvements in the quality of legislation and law enforcement, the expansion of international cooperation in lawmaking, and the increase in public legal awareness. At the same time, it recognizes many shortcomings of the legal system:

> The legal system has not yet been really perfect and synthetic; the effectiveness and the enforceability have not met with the actual demands. In some areas, laws have lacked stability; the predictability has not been high; the quality has not been guaranteed; the amendments and supplementations have been too frequent. The procedure of making the law has included too many stages, which made the process of enactment and enforcement slow. Legal enforcement is the weakest point in implementing the Resolution 48-NQ/TW. The delay in enacting regulations to detail and instruct [legal implementation] has been relatively popular. The review, systematization, and codification of law have not yet forcefully practiced; legal popularization, propaganda and education has lacked critical solutions and have not yet been highly effective; staffs in charge with law-making have not yet been consolidated to meet with the demands of the duties; the supervision and checking of legal documents have not been often; the dealing with errors and violations has not yet been thorough; and legal enforcement in some places and sometimes has been undisciplined and lacked the high effectiveness of deterrence and education.[21]

Conclusion 01 therefore proposes measures to continue implementation of legal reform according to the six categories anticipated in Resolution 48 in the period

[19] ibid.

[20] Bộ Chính trị [Politburo], Kết luận số 01-KL/TW, ngày 04/4/2016 của Bộ Chính trị về việc tiếp tục thực hiện Nghị quyết số 48-NQ/TW của Bộ Chính trị khóa IX về Chiến lược xây dựng và hoàn thiện hệ thống pháp luật Việt Nam đến năm 2010, định hướng đến năm 2020 [Conclusion No 01-KL/TW, dated 4 April 2016 on the Implementation of Resolution on the Strategy to Construct and Perfect the Vietnamese Legal System from Now to 2010 with a Vision to 2020].

[21] ibid.

2016–20. First, Conclusion 01 proposes improving the laws on state institutions to realize the new 2013 Constitution's commitments to building the socialist rule of law state in the context of international integration, controlling the state power, and horizontal and vertical distribution of power. Second, Conclusion 01 proposes improving human rights law to allow citizens to supervise state agencies and practice direct democracy. Third, it calls for continuing the reform of business laws to facilitate the development of various markets but stresses the need for economic laws (eg laws on tax, price, and property registration) for the state to regulate the economy. Fourth, Conclusion 01 suggests continuing the reform of social law, particularly improving the laws on religion, cultural heritage, and private health services. Fifth, it calls for strengthening laws on national security and independence, social security, and order. Finally, it proposes domesticizing the international treaties Vietnam has signed and signing more multilateral international treaties on judicial assistance and resolutions for commercial and investment disputes.[22]

Measures for Vietnamese legal reform in Conclusion 01 generally continue the universalist direction of legal reform projected in Resolution 08. Measures for domestic legal reforms seek to realize universal norms (such as human rights norms), internalize international law, and increase access to global legal order. However, Conclusion 01 tends to stress more on interventionist regulation of the economy by the state, as indicated in the measures to improve economic law. This demonstrates the state's attempt to control the rising market economy.

Resolution 48 only proposes measures for legal reform in fifteen years (from 2005 to 2020). In 2021, the Politburo issued Conclusion No 19-KL/TW on the Orientation of the Law-Making Programme for the XV Term of the National Assembly (hereinafter, Conclusion 19).[23] Conclusion 19 recognizes that the Vietnamese legal system has been basically complete, stable, and consistent, thanks to the implementation of Resolution 48. However, it also states that the legal system still includes elements that impede the country's development. Therefore, Conclusion 19 stresses continuing improvement of the legal system to facilitate the country's sustainable development and global integration.

Conclusion 19 mandates directions for the NA's lawmaking plan. Together with formal features of law such as consistency, stability, and transparency, Conclusion 19 underlines some new substantive issues. First, legislation should take the rights and interests of individuals and companies as the central concerns. Second, legislation should meet social needs. Conclusion 19 proposes that legislation 'set[s] high requirements for quality, does not run by quantity, must closely follow and promptly meet the requirements of reality'. Third, legislation should have high

[22] ibid.
[23] Kết luận 19-KL/TW 2021 định hướng Chương trình xây dựng pháp luật nhiệm kỳ Quốc hội khóa XV [Conclusion No 19-KL/TW on the Orientation of the Law-Making Programme for the XV Term of the National Assembly], issued by the Politburo of the Communist Party of Vietnam on 14 October 2021.

consensus. Conclusion 19 warns that urgent and new issues that generate different views should not be legislated. Fourth, law should not be generic. Conclusion 19 proposes that 'frame law, pipe law' (or generic law), should be avoided. Finally, legislation must not be influenced by 'group interests'. Conclusion 19 suggests legislation 'should not be dominated and affected by the unhealthy behaviors of any organization or individual, not letting the situation of integrating "group interests" and local interests of state management agencies in legal documents occur'.[24] Directions of Conclusion 19 respond to the shortcomings of lawmaking in Vietnam (the gap between law and social needs, generic law, and the influence of group interests), as will be discussed later.

In November 2022, the Party adopted Resolution No 27-NQ/TW (hereinafter, the Rule of Law Resolution) on the continued development of the Vietnamese socialist rule of law state.[25] This is the first time the Party in Vietnam adopted a resolution on the rule of law, comparable to the Rule of Law Decision adopted by the Chinese Communist Party in 2014. The Rule of Law Resolution recognizes the lack of effective mechanisms to control state power, the deficiency in protection of human rights, and administrative and judicial reform. It defines key features of the Vietnamese socialist rule of law state, including: the leadership of the Party over the state; the state of the people, for the people, and by the people; protection of human rights; the state's organization and operation according to the Constitution and the law; unity, distribution, and control of state powers; a legal system with substantive qualities (such as democracy and humanity) and formal qualities (such as coherence, transparency, feasibility, stability, and accessibility); functional dependence of the courts; respecting the international treaties Vietnam has signed.[26]

These are not descriptions of the existing features of the Vietnamese state but the aspirational features of a socialist model of the rule of law state that Vietnam is attempting to construct. These features are a mixture of both socialist (eg party leadership and centralized power) and rule of law elements (eg the internal morality of the rule of law and judicial independence, and human rights protection).

The Rule of Law Resolution then proposes comprehensive measures for socialist rule of law reforms to be carried out until 2030. These measures are grouped into ten categories:

(1) Propagandizing the aspirational features of the socialist rule of state.
(2) Respecting people's sovereignty, the Constitution and the law, human rights and citizens' rights.

[24] ibid.
[25] Nghị Quyết Hội Nghị Lần Thứ Sáu Ban Chấp Hành Trung Ương Đảng Khóa Xiii Về Tiếp Tục Xây Dựng Và Hoàn Thiện Nhà Nước Pháp Quyền Xã Hội Chủ Nghĩa Việt Nam Trong Giai Đoạn Mới [Resolution of the Sixth Conference of the XIII Party Central Committee on Continuing to Build and Perfect the Socialist Rule-of-Law State of Vietnam in the New Period], dated 9 November 2022.
[26] ibid.

(3) Improving the legal system and the mechanisms for law enforcement; improving the structure and activities of the legislature.
(4) Clarifying the function of the president of state.
(5) Building an effective, efficient, and professional state administration operating under the rule of law.
(6) Building a professional, fair, and honest judiciary.
(7) Improving the mechanism for controlling state powers and anti-corruption.
(8) Strengthening international integration.
(9) Strengthening the leadership of the Party.
(10) Promoting the role of the Vietnam Fatherland Front and the people in building the socialist rule of law state.[27]

The Rule of Law Resolution continues legal universalism. Global standards of the rule of law are invocated as the convergent point for domestic rule of law reform. These include formal standards of the rule of law (such as feasibility, stability, and accessibility) and substantive standards of the rule of law (such as judicial independence, transparent administration, and human rights protection). However, the Rule of Law Resolution is in fact a competing combination of measures to enhance socialist legality (eg consolidating legal propaganda and party leadership) and foster the rule of law. These measures exist in tension because the consolidation of socialist legal identity may constrain the rule of law reform. For example, measures for enhancing functional independence of courts are at odds with measures to consolidate vanguardism, including the party leadership over the courts. The cacophony of such measures indicates the dilemma of socialist rule of law reforms. On one hand, the party-state seeks to converge the legal system with the international standards of the rule of law to consolidate the adaptive resilience of the socialist legal system and the socialist political regime. On the other hand, convergence with the international rule of law would undermine and even present a threat to the survival of the socialist law and the socialist regime. To deal with this dilemma, the party-state ambiguously locates the rule of law reform project within the constraints of socialist legal-political principles.

C. Vietnamese Legal Universalism

The legal reform project in Vietnam, initiated and led by the Party, seeks to converge the Vietnamese legal system with global legal standards. While local

[27] ibid.

conditions are not ignored, the prevailing attitude is to reform the Vietnamese legal system while converging it with international and comparative legal norms. Universal legal norms are conceived of as standards for domestic legal reform in Vietnam. Legal universalism shapes the functions of Vietnamese legal reform projects. Due to the universalist intention, the Vietnamese projects of legal reform seek to coordinate not only relations of domestic actors but also Vietnam's international legal cooperation. They allow the Vietnamese government, foreign governments, and transnational and international agencies to work together to achieve the goals of legal reform. In addition, the project of legal reform expresses the party-state's commitments to both continuing legal reform and consolidating socialist legal principles. Finally, the project seeks to limit legal reforms within the boundary of socialist legal-political principles. The project for legal convergence explains the massive transplants of foreign law and international law into the Vietnamese legal system in the last two decades. It also explains the dysfunction of the legal system and the gap between formal law and social necessity. While formal convergence with universal legal norms becomes the dominant attitude, whether formal law meets social needs becomes less relevant.

Legal universalism in Vietnam is shaped by the country's international integration and the international movement of law and development. Vietnam's engagement with international legal regimes and the international engagement with Vietnamese development generate the need to reform domestic law according to global legal standards.

1. *International Integration*

Since the Cold War, Vietnam has widely diversified its international relations. The 1992 Constitution provided that the government 'carries out a policy of peace and friendship, seeks to expand its relations and cooperation with all countries in the world, regardless of their political and social regimes' (Article 13). This has created the constitutional foundation for the country's engagement with regional and international legal regimes such as those of the ASEAN and the WTO.[28]

On trade liberalization, Vietnam has officially participated in many free trade agreements (FTAs) including:

> ASEAN FTA (1996), ASEAN–China FTA (2003), ASEAN–Korea FTA (2007), ASEAN–Japan FTA (2008), Vietnam–Japan FTA (2009), ASEAN–India FTA (2010), ASEAN-Australia–New Zealand FTA (2010), Vietnam–Chile FTA (2011), Vietnam–Korea FTA (2015), Vietnam–Asia–Europe Economic Union FTA (2016), Comprehensive and Progressive Agreement for Trans-Pacific

[28] Hao Duy Phan, 'The Effects of ASEAN Treaties in Domestic Legal Orders: Evidence from Vietnam' (2019) 17 IJCL 205; Vu-Thanh Tu-Anh, 'Does WTO Accession Help Domestic Reform? The Political Economy of SOE Reform Backsliding in Vietnam' (2017) 16 World Trade Rev 85.

Partnership (2018), ASEAN–Hong Kong FTA (2019), and European Union–Vietnam FTA (EVFTA) (2019).[29]

Vietnam has engaged in negotiations for other FTAs, including the Regional Comprehensive Economic Partnership, the Vietnam FTA–European Free Trade Association, and the Vietnam–Israel FTA.[30] With these dynamics, a World Bank report considers Vietnam to be 'among the most open economies with a trade-to-GDP ratio of 190 percent in 2018'.[31] Trade liberalization necessitates legal reform according to international legal standards to facilitate foreign investments and transnational transactions.

Vietnam's international integration has generated the need to converge its national legal system with international legal standards. In an official document, the Party directed the state to:

> urgently review, supplement and perfect laws directly related to international economic integration, in accordance with the Constitution, and fully and properly complying with the rules of the market economy and commitments in international economic integration; internalize in domestic law, with an appropriate roadmap, international treaties to which Vietnam is a member, with a priority of laws on commerce, investment, IP, technology transfer, and labor–trade union.[32]

Thus, integration with international legal regimes induces the universalist intention to reform domestic law according to international legal standards.

2. *The Law and Development Movement*

Vietnamese legislative convergence is also shaped by the influence of the law and development movement. Foreign developed countries Australia (Australia and New Zealand), North America (US, Canada), Europe (UK, Denmark, Sweden, and France), and Asia (Japan and South Korea) and transnational (EU) and international agencies (UN Development Programme [UNDP], Work Bank,

[29] Lê Đình Tĩnh and Hàn Lam Giang, Hiệp định EVFTA Từ Góc Nhìn Chiến Lược [EVFTA Agreement from a Strategic Perspective] (Tạp Chí Cộng Sản, 13 March 2020) <http://www.tapchicongsan.org.vn/web/guest/media-story/-/asset_publisher/V8hhp4dK31Gf/content/hiep-dinh-evfta-tu-goc-nhin-chien-luoc> accessed 25 April 2020.

[30] ibid.

[31] Jung Eun Oh and others, *Vietnam Development Report 2019: Connecting Vietnam for Growth and Shared Prosperity* (World Bank 2019) 1.

[32] The Central Committee of the Communist Party of Vietnam, Nghị quyết Hội nghị lần thứ tư Ban Chấp hành Trung ương Đảng (khóa XII) Về Thực Hiện Có Hiệu Quả Tiến Trình Hội Nhập Kinh Tế Quốc Tế, Giữ Vững Ổn Định Chính Trị—Xã Hội Trong Bối Cảnh Nước Ta Tham Gia Các Hiệp Định Thương Mại Tự Do Thế Hệ Mới [Resolution of the Fourth Conference of the Party Central Committee (Session XII) on the Effective Implementation of the Process of International Economic Integration, Maintaining Socio-Political Stability in the Context of Our Country's Participation in the New Generation—Free Trade Agreements], dated 5 November 2016.

International Monetary Fund [IMF]) seek to promote legal reform to foster social-economic development in Vietnam.

The spread of the law and development movement in Vietnam stems from the developing status of the country. The *Đổi mới* (Renovation) launched in 1986 has transformed Vietnam from of one of the poorest countries in the world into a lower middle-income country.[33] According to the World Bank, in Vietnam, 'between 2002 and 2018, GDP per capita increased by 2.7 times, reaching over US$2,700 in 2019, and more than 45 million people were lifted out of poverty. Poverty rates declined sharply from over 70 percent to below 6 percent (US$3.2/day purchasing power parity [PPP]).'[34] The Politburo of the Communist Party of Vietnam envisaged a programme for the country to achieve the objectives of industrialization and modernization by 2030 and become an industrial developed country by 2045.[35] Vietnam's developing status and its vision to become a developed country provide the condition for external actors to be involved in its development, including its legal development.

In addition, Vietnam's experience and commitment to legal reform instigated the engagement of law and development agencies in the country. After the launch of the Renovation programme, Vietnam undertook law reforms to facilitate market reforms, including the enactment of numerous legislations dealing with market related issues such as the tax system, land property, foreign and domestic investment promotion, trade and commerce laws, banking, and company law.[36] This local experience attracted the attention of law and development agencies (including Japan and the European countries such as Denmark, Sweden, and France) to further facilitate the law reforms in the country.[37] Vietnam's continuing legal reform has created the condition for this engagement.

Due to the influence of law and development activities, Vietnam has been compelled to converge domestic law with universal legal norms. Scholars have indicated that small states 'are more vulnerable to the forces of globalization and thus

[33] On the 'Đổi mới' reform in Vietnam, see generally S Dean and others (eds), *Doi moi: Vietnam's Renovation, Policy, and Performance* (Australian National University 1991); Tran-Nam Pham and Chi Do Pham (eds), *The Vietnamese Economy: Awakening the Dormant Dragon* (Routledge 2003). For discussion on law and development in Vietnam in the context of middle-income countries, see John Gillespie, 'Growing Wealth in East Asian Middle-Income Countries with Transnational Production Regimes' in Randall Peerenboom and Tom Ginsburg (eds), *Law and Development of Middle-Income Countries: Avoiding the Middle-Income Trap* (CUP 2014) 108.

[34] The World Bank in Vietnam, The World Bank, <https://www.worldbank.org/en/country/vietnam/overview#1>accessed 6 June 2024.

[35] The Politburo of Communist Party of Vietnam, Nghị Quyết Của Bộ Chính Trị Về Định Hướng Xây Dựng Chính Sách Phát Triển Công Nghiệp Quốc Gia Đến Năm 2030, Tầm Nhìn Đến Năm 2045 [Resolution of the Politburo on the Orientation to Formulate National Industrial Development Policies to 2030, Vision to 2045], dated 22 March 2018.

[36] Brian JM Quinn, 'Legal Reform and its Context in Vietnam' (2002) 15 Colum J Asian L 223; 'Protection of Foreign Direct Investment in a New World Order: Vietnam—A Case Study' (1994) 107 Harv L Rev 1995.

[37] See generally Carol V Rose, 'The New Law and Development Movement in the Post-Cold War Era: A Vietnam Case Study' (1998) 32 Law & Soc'y Rev 111–13.

more susceptible to, and dependent upon, the international community, and their vulnerability incentivizes them to curry favor with the international community by adopting its norms'.[38] Vietnam intends to align domestic law with the globally spread legal norms adopted by powerful, successful countries and international bodies to gain international recognition and support.

The law and development movement in Vietnam takes two forms: horizontal and vertical. In horizontal law and development, external actors provide 'technical assistance'[39] to support domestic law reform. In vertical law and development, external actors use law reform as a tool to facilitate development vertically through international economic law. To illustrate, consider EU law and development in Vietnam.

3. *EU Law and Development*

The European Union has actively engaged in promoting law reforms to facilitate social and economic development in Vietnam.[40] According to an EU document, for the period 2014–2020, the EU Commission spent some EUR 50 million in Vietnam 'to promote democracy, strengthen governance and rule of law; and to enable the business environment by building accountable and transparent institutions that are responsive to citizens' rights, and that promote access to justice, participation and a conducive business environment'.[41] Particularly, through the European Instrument for Democracy and Human Rights (allocating EUR 3.5 million to Vietnam for the period 2014–2017) and the Civil Society Organizations and Local Authorities programme (allocating EUR 3.35 million to Vietnam for the period 2015–2017), 'the EU has been supporting civil society in Vietnam to promote and protect human rights and fundamental freedoms as well as reinforcing its capacity to be an actor of development'.[42] These programmes display horizontal law and development. Through legal aid, they have directly supported law reforms to foster social and economic development in Vietnam. The rule of law and justice are the norms for these law and development programmes.

The European Union does not merely directly involve itself in promotion of rule of law in the developing countries in the horizontal manner. It also integrates norms of international law into the trade deals with the developing countries, which may then be domesticized in the law of the EVFTA and exemplifies EU vertical law and development. The EVFTA, entered into force on 1 August 2020, is 'the most comprehensive trade agreement the [European Union] has concluded

[38] David S Law, 'Constitutional Archetypes' (2016) 95 Tex L Rev 209.

[39] Brent Doberstein, 'EIA Models and Capacity Building in Viet Nam: An Analysis of Development Aid Programs' (2004) 24 Environ Impact Assess Rev 283.

[40] See European Commission, 'Commission Staff Working Document: Human Rights and Sustainable Development in the EU–Vietnam Relations with Specific Regard to the EU–Vietnam Free Trade Agreement' (26 January 2016) 11 <http://trade.ec.europa.eu/doclib/docs/2016/january/tradoc_154189.pdf> (hereinafter, Commission Document).

[41] ibid 11.

[42] ibid 12.

with a developing country'.[43] The second FTA the European Union signed with an ASEAN country, and the fourth in Asia after Singapore, Japan, and South Korea,[44] the EVFTA will gradually eliminate almost all customs duties.[45] However, this trade deal does not merely deal with trade. It also includes provisions on human rights, labour rights, environmental protection, IP, institutional reforms, and cooperation. The trade deal's concerns are therefore not merely commercial but normative. It is a duct leading to the diffusion of norms of international law in the Vietnamese national legal system to foster domestic social and economic development.

The logic of EU vertical law and development through the EVFTA can be explained by (1) experimental compatibility; (2) institutional linking; (3) the content of international legal norms; (4) inducive mechanism; and (5) legislative convergence.

First, *experimental compatibility* constitutes the three conditions for EU vertical law and development through EVFTA. Vietnam's international integration, developing status, and existing experience of law reform provide the conditions for the European Union to promote, through the EVFTA, a vertical application of international law norms in Vietnamese law. EU law and development also stems from the fact that Vietnam's reforming law includes features compatible with civil law in continental Europe. Due to the colonial diffusion of French civil law and the convergent diffusion of socialist law that is in turn based on civil law, Vietnamese modern law shares the European civil law tradition's core elements, particularly the positivist conception on the nature of law as deriving from state and concomitantly legal codes and written statutes as the main sources of law.[46] The existing legal similarities at the deep ideational and structural level animate further efforts to diffuse European law or legal norms that the European Union supports into Vietnam through law and development projects. In addition, like civil law in Europe, Vietnamese modern law is more like a legal project developed through deliberate design than a legal system (like common law) developed through natural evolution. Consequently, Vietnamese legal development has been prominently animated through deliberate lawmaking and institutional design— areas easily targeted by deliberate law and development projects of external donors, including the European Union.

[43] European Commission, EU–Vietnam Trade Agreement Enters into Force (Press Release, 31 July 2020) <https://ec.europa.eu/commission/presscorner/detail/en/ip_20_1412>accessed 6 June 2024.

[44] On EU–Asia trade agreements, see Jappe Eckhardt and Arlo Poletti, 'The Politics of Global Value Chains: Import-Dependent Firms and EU–Asia Trade Agreements' (2016) 23 J Eur Pub Pol'y 1543; Daniela Sicurelli, 'Normative Trade Power Europe? The Case of EU Trade Agreements with Asian Countries' in Simone Raudino and Arlo Poletti (eds), *Global Economic Governance and Human Development* (Routledge 2018) 103.

[45] 'News European Parliament, Parliament Approves EU–Vietnam Free Trade and Investment Protection Deals' (Press Release, 12 February 2020) 6 June 2024 <https://www.europarl.europa.eu/news/en/press-room/20200206IPR72012/parliament-approves-eu-vietnam-free-trade-and-investment-protection-deals>.

[46] For elaboration of these features of civil law in Europe, see John Henry Merryman and Rogelio Pérez-Perdomo, *The Civil Law Tradition: An Introduction to the Legal Systems of Europe and Latin America* (Standford University Press 2018) 20–23.

Second, *institutional linking* defines the structural framework for connecting trade with law reform and development. The trade agreement is institutionally linked to a broader political EU–Vietnam agreement .[47] The political agreement creates the base for cooperation according to which the European Union will assist Vietnam in achieving development aims. The trade agreement, signed after the political agreement, is an instrument to implement broader development aims beyond trade and investment concerns.

Third, *international legal norms* are the contents promoted through the trade deal. Due to both instrumental and normative concerns, the deal seeks to promote in Vietnam the norms that the European Union shares with the broader international community, including norms of international human rights law, labour law, environment law, IP law, and the cosmopolitan ideal of the rule of law.

Fourth, the EVFTA mainly uses *inducive* mechanisms to diffuse international legal norms into the Vietnamese legal system. It includes legally binding obligations that compel Vietnam to comply with labour, environmental, and IP international standards in its domestic law and practices to foster law reforms in these areas and local socio-economic development.[48] The basis of influence is material interests—such as Vietnam's accession to the EU market, the attraction of EU investments in Vietnam, and development aid through cooperation. The forms of influence are material conditionality. The trade deal establishes the positive conditions to access the material benefits, including the accession to the EU market and possibly development assistance.[49] In addition, the non-execution human rights clause creates a negative conditionality or a threat of material sanction: the 'appropriate measures' in case of material breach of the essential element (human rights).[50] These measures potentially include suspension of market accession and limitations on development assistance.

Fifth, the diffusion generates *legislative convergence*. Vietnamese legislative laws in relevant areas (human rights, labour, environmental, and IP laws) formally incorporated norms of international legal regimes. Vertical law and development resulted in legislative convergence between Vietnamese law in relevant areas with international legal standards. To illustrate, the constitutional rights formally incorporate international human rights treaties that the country has signed, particularly the new labour and environmental rights. However, convergence also occurs at the sub-constitutional level, which is not necessarily associated with socialization. Vietnamese labour, environmental, and IP laws formally converge with the international standards in the signed international agreements in relevant areas.

[47] See Ha Hai Hoang, 'Understanding the EU–Vietnam Free Trade Agreement' (*East Asia Forum*, 21 May 2020) <https://www.eastasiaforum.org/2020/05/21/understanding-the-eu-vietnam-free-trade-agreement/> accessed 6 June 2024.

[48] See generally EVFTA.

[49] ibid.

[50] ibid.

The pressure to conform to international commitments drives the need to incorporate international legal standards into national law, leading to legislative convergence. The EVFTA is not the single factor of this formal convergence, but it has generated specific convergent effects. For example, due to the deal negotiation, Vietnam modified its Labor Code in compliance with international labour standards. More generally, during the trade negotiation, Vietnam was compelled to conduct what is called 'legal review' to make sure that national laws are consistent with the international commitments the deal seeks to support. The legislative convergence of Vietnamese law with international standards promoted through the trade deal is largely the function of material inducement. Convergence is the consequence of national compliance with international legal standards to attract foreign investment and development cooperation.

III. LEGISLATIVE REFORM

A. The Legislature

The Vietnamese legislature plays a key role in legal reform. Since the launch of the Renovation policy, it has enacted hundreds of laws, which include legal codes, statutes, and ordinances. The legislative enactments created, amended, and replaced legal rules to improve Vietnamese law and legal institutions.

The Vietnamese legislature is well institutionalized, making it capable of legislating to support legal reform. The legal framework governing the formation, function, and process of legislative power comprises the 2013 Constitution and constitutional statutes. The Constitution has a chapter on the NA (Chapter V) dealing with the legislature's position, structure, powers, and the assembly deputies. Several new laws have been passed to give effect to these constitutional provisions. The 2014 Law on Organization of the National Assembly details the provisions on the Constitution on this institution's structure and operation. The 2015 Law on Election of Deputies to the National Assembly and People's Councils establishes principles and procedures for national and local elections. The 2015 Law on Enactment of Normative Legal Documents provides for principles, authority, and procedures for lawmaking of various institutions, including the NA. The 2015 Law on Supervisory Activities of the National Assembly and People's Councils provides detailed procedures for the exercise of the supervisory power of the NA and local assemblies. The NA enjoys the power to supervise the conformity of administrative regulation with its statutes.

Like China's National People's Congress (NPC), Vietnam's NA is unicameral, comprising of a standing committee and special committees. The NA has ten special committees: Ethnic Council; Law Committee; Judicial Committee; Economic Committee Financial and Budget ; Committee; Culture, Education, Adolescents, and Children Committee; Foreign Affairs Committee; National Defense and Security Committee; Science, Technology, Environment Committee; and andSocial Committee. The departmentalization of the legislative structure is instrumental to enhancing its legislative capacity. One comparative point should be noted. While in China the NPC's standing committee is the main lawmaking body due to the huge size of the NPC, in Vietnam the NA is the main lawmaking body meeting twice a year and with each meeting lasting around one to one-and-a-half months, although its standing committee is also delegated some legislative power.

Functionally, the Vietnamese legislature is conventionally viewed as a formalistic platform to institutionalize the Party lines,[51] but it is in fact the most open national institution in Vietnam for the representatives to deliberate national affairs and consider citizens' views. The openness of the legislature renders it a suitable place to carry out legal reform projects.

The system of lawmaking in Vietnam is governed by the Law on Enactment of Normative Legal Documents (hereinafter, Law on Legislation), which is comparable to China's 2000 Law on Legislation. Vietnam's Law on Legislation was first enacted in 1996. After nearly a decade of legal reform in Vietnam, legislative enactments were increasingly extensive. This generated the need for the enactment of law to govern legislative enactment. The Law on Legislation was replaced by subsequent versions in 2004, 2008, and 2015. The 2015 version was amended in 2020. The speedy legislative development induces the frequent replacements and amendments of the Legislation Law.

The Law on Legislation differentiates types of legal instruments, distributes the lawmaking power among state agencies from central to local levels, and establishes the procedures for lawmaking. Table 5.1 shows types of legal instruments and the distribution of lawmaking power according to Article 4 of the current version of Law on Legislation.

Table 5.1 Types of Legal Instruments and the Distribution of Lawmaking Power

Legal Document	Issuing Authority
Constitution	National Assembly
Code and Statute	National Assembly
Ordinance, Resolution	Standing Committee of the National Assembly
Joint Resolution	Between Standing Committee of the National Assembly and Management Board of Central Committee of Vietnamese Fatherland Front

[51] Paul Schuler, *United Front Projecting Solidarity through Deliberation in Vietnam's Single-Party Legislature* (Stanford University Press 2021).

Table 5.1 Continued

Legal Document	Issuing Authority
Order, Decision	President of State
Decree Joint Resolution	Government Between the Government and Management Board of Central Committee of Vietnamese Fatherland Front
Decision	Prime Minister
Circular Joint Circular Decision	Judicial Council of the People's Supreme Court; the Chief Procurator of the Supreme People's Procuracy; Ministers, Heads of ministerial agencies Between Judicial Council of the People's Supreme Court and the Chief Procurator of the Supreme People's Procuracy; between Ministers, Heads of ministerial agencies and Judicial Council of the People's Supreme Court, the Chief Procurator of the Supreme People's Procuracy State Auditor General
Resolution	People's Councils of Local Government
Decision	People's Committees of Local Government

Thus, formal legal rules can be enacted not only by the legislature but also various administrative and judicial bodies. The 2015 Law on Legislation seeks to limit administrative and judicial lawmaking powers by providing for a comprehensive list of issues within the scope of the lawmaking power of the legislature. According to Article 15 of the Law on Legislation, the NA shall promulgate laws to prescribe:

- Structure and operation of the National Assembly, the President, the Government, the people's courts, the People's Procuracies, the National Election Council, the State Audit Office of Vietnam, local governments, administrative-economic units, and other agencies established by the National Assembly;
- Human rights, fundamental rights, and obligations of citizens, restrictions on human rights and citizens' rights; crimes and punishments;
- Basic policies on national finance and state budget; imposition, adjustment, or cancellation of taxes;
- Basic policies on culture, education, healthcare, science, technology, and the environment;
- National defence and security;
- Policies on ethnics and religions of the State;
- Ranks in the People's Armed Forces; diplomatic ranks; other state ranks; medals and honourable titles of the State;

- Basic diplomatic policies;
- Referendum;
- Mechanism for protection of the Constitution;
- Other issues within the competence of the National Assembly.

Nearly every aspect of social relations must be covered by legislation, from state institutions, fundamental rights, and domestic social–economic relations, to international relations. Consequently, institutional reform and substantive legal reform are based on legislation.

The legislative process includes the steps outlined below.[52]

Initiative: The following actors have the right to submit a bill to the NA: president, Standing Committee, Ethnic Council and committees of the NA, assembly deputies, government, SPC, Supreme People's Procuracy, State Audit Office, Central Committee of the Vietnam Fatherland Front, and central bodies of the Front's member organizations (Constitution, Article 84). Thus, the right to legislative imitative is vested not only in state actors but also in certain non-state actors aligned with the Party.

Programming: Based on the legislative initiatives, at the first meeting session of the previous year, the NA shall decide on a legislative programme for the next year. The programme is planned annually according to policies of the Communist Party and the state, as well as socio-economic development strategy (Law on Legislation, Article 31). Notably, given the Party's leading role in the state and the society, the Party's policy is an important source for the state's legislative programme.

Drafting: For bills proposed by the NA institutions and deputies, its Standing Committee shall establish a Drafting Board. For bills proposed by the government, the prime minister shall appoint a ministry or ministerial agency as the drafting agency, which will establish a Drafting Board. For bills proposed by other institutions, these institutions shall establish a Drafting Board (Law on Legislation, Article 52).

Review: Bills will be reviewed by the NA's specific committees to check their constitutionality, legality, consistency, and feasibility, among other things. The Standing Committee will offer opinions on bills. The review body will present the review report, and then the Standing Committee will discuss. Depending on the features and contents of the bill, the Standing Committee may offer opinions once or many times (Law on Legislation, Article 71).

[52] The below paragraphs on legislative process are adapted from Bui Ngoc Son, 'The National Assembly of Vietnam' in Po Jen Yap and Rehan Abeyratne (eds), *Routledge Handbook of Asian Parliaments* (Routledge 2023) 401.

Discussion and approval: Bills will be discussed and approved by the NA. The NA will consider approving the bill after one or two meetings; if the bill is long and contains complex clauses, the institution may consider approving it after three meetings (Law on Legislation, Article 73).

Announcement: The president of state shall announce the law within fifteen days from the day on which it is approved (Law on Legislation, Article 80). The president has no veto power against laws passed by the NA due to the NA's supremacy.

The well-established process involving agenda setting, professional drafting, internal multiple review, and open deliberation and approval renders legislation a suitable method of legal reform.

B. Patterns of Legislative Reform

Like China, Vietnam has developed a sophisticated system of formal legal rules, which cover almost every aspect of the society. After thirty years of Renovation, the number of legislative laws is eight times higher than forty years before Renovation. Vietnam enacted only 64 statutes and ordinances between 1945 and 1986, while the country enacted 483 statutes and ordinances between 1987 and 2013.[53] The NA term IX (1992–97) enacted forty-one statutes and forty-three ordinances; the NA term X (1997–2002), thirty-four statutes and forty ordinances; the NA term XI (2002–07), eighty-four statutes and codes; the NA term XII (2007–11), sixty-seven statutes and fourteen ordinances; and the NA term XIII (2011–15), thirty-seven statutes and seven ordinances from 2011 to September 2013.[54]

Vietnamese legal scholar Đình Dũng Sỹ differentiates three periods in the development of the Vietnamese legal system after Renovation: transition between 1986 and 2002; transition and international integration between 2002 and 2013; international integration and developmentalism from 2013 to now.[55] In fact, transition and convergence are the two regular patterns in legislative development in post-Renovation Vietnam.

[53] Trần Ngọc Đường, 'Nhìn Lại Những Thành Tựu Của Quốc Hội Việt Nam Trong 10 Năm (2005–2015)' ['A Review of the Achievements of the National Assembly of Vietnam for 10 Years (2005–2015)'] in Vietnam National Assembly's Standing Committee, *Quốc Hội Việt Nam: 70 Năm Hình Thành Và Phát Triển 1946–2016 [Vietnam National Assembly: 70 Years of Establishment and Development 1946–2016]* (National Politics Publishing House 2015) 118.

[54] Lê Minh Thông, 'Đổi Mới, Nâng Cao Chất Lượng Công Tác Lập Pháp Của Quốc Hội' ['Renovating and Enhancing the Quality of the NA's Law-making'] (Tạp Chí Cộng Sản, 10 February 2014) <http://www.tapchicongsan.org.vn/Home/Xay-dung-nha-nuoc-phap-quyen/2014/25793/Doi-moi-nang-cao-chat-luong-cong-tac-lap-phap-cua-Quoc.aspx>accessed 6 June 2024.

[55] Đinh Dũng Sỹ, 'Hệ thống pháp luật Việt Nam trong tiến trình đổi mới và phát triển đất nước' ['The Vietnamese Legal System in the Country's Renovation and Development'] (2020) 401 Nghiên cứu Lập pháp 4–5.

Legislative transition occurred from the introduction of the Renovation policy in 1986 to the 1990s. This is the consequence of the transitional project for legal reform. Transitional laws are both aversive and transformative. On one hand, retrospectively, they dismantled some elements of the centrally planned economy. On the other hand, prospectively, they constructed a legal framework to facilitate the incremental economic transformation into the socialist market economy.[56]

During the early stage of economic transition between 1986 and 1992, several economic laws were enacted to incrementally dismantle elements of the centrally planned economy and adopted elements of a socialist market economy (such as foreign investment, private contract, and private enterprises).[57] These include the Law on Foreign Investment (1987), the Economic Contracts Ordinance (1989), the Ordinance on the State Bank of Vietnam (1990), the Ordinance in Banking, Credit Cooperatives and Financial Companies (1990), the Company Law (1990), and the Private Enterprise Law (1990).[58]

In the late 1990s, Vietnamese transitional laws were still aversive to the centrally planned economy and more transformative to the socialist market economy. Legislative enactments continued to dismantle the centrally planned economy and consolidated the socialist market economy. In 1992, a new constitution was adopted replacing the 1980 Constitution. The 1992 Constitution created a stable framework for socialist-oriented market economy.[59] It provides for multiple economic sectors, including the state economic, collective economic, private and small-owner economic, and private capitalist economic sectors.[60] The Constitution also establishes multiple types of ownership, including people's ownership (state's ownership), collective ownership, and private ownership.[61] In addition, the Constitution is committed to law-based governance.[62]

On the new base of constitutional economy and the commitment to legality, laws on investment, businesses, budget, taxes, banking, business, trade, and land were revised or newly adopted. The Labor Code was adopted in 1994. The first Civil Code of the Vietnamese socialist state was promulgated in 1995.[63] New laws have been enacted in the areas of culture, science and technology, and education, including the Law on Cultural Heritage, Law on Universalizing Primary Education, Law on Education, Law on University Education, Law on Vocational Training, and Law on Science and Technology.[64] Other new laws are promulgated to deal with

[56] ibid 4.
[57] ibid 4.
[58] Pham Huu Nghi, 'Vietnam's Legislation: Seventy Years of Development' (2016) 172 Vietnam Soc Sci 6.
[59] Constitution of the Socialist Republic of Vietnam (1992), art 15.
[60] ibid art 16.
[61] ibid art 15.
[62] ibid art 12.
[63] Pham Huu Nghi (n 57) 7.
[64] ibid.

emerging social issues—such as laws on social insurance, health insurance, unemployment insurance, social sponsorship, social concessions, and people with disabilities.[65]

Vietnamese legislation internalizes global norms deriving from comparative and international law, in a pattern of *legislative convergence*. The actual development of legislative convergence is the consequence of the project of legal convergence. The convergent patten started at the turn of the twenty-first century. That Vietnam concluded the Bilateral Trade Agreement with the United States in 2000 and joined the WTO in 2006 generated the need to incorporate global legal norms into domestic law to facilitate trade liberalization.[66] The Constitution was amended in 2001 to incorporate the concept of rule of law, although the concept had been accepted by the Party in 1994.[67] Since the Party adopted a comprehensive plan for legal reform in 2005, new legislative enactments, replacements, and amendments rely on global legal standards as a convergent point. However, in the first decade of the twenty-first century, global convergence in Vietnam was cautious and occurred mainly in economic law.[68]

In the second decade of the twenty-first century, legislative convergence has been more extensive, including public law and private law. A decade of international integration provides extensive experience for Vietnam to move further to engage with global legal regimes. In early 2013, the Party adopted a resolution on Vietnam's comprehensive international integration in various areas (economy, national defence, science, education, society, environmental protection, etc.).[69] The political willingness of comprehensive integration enables extensive convergence of laws in these areas. In addition, in late 2013, the NA adopted a new Constitution. The 2013 Constitution itself is an example of convergence with international human rights law and creates a fundamental framework for the convergence of human rights-related laws such as criminal, civil, and family laws.

Vietnamese legislation has comprehensively covered nearly every area of social relations. Many legislative documents were enacted to facilitate *state-building*. Apart from the amendment and replacement of the Constitution, many constitutional statutes have been amended and replaced several times during the last decades, including the Law on Organization of the National Assembly (2014), Law on Organization of the Government (2015), Law on Organization of the People's Courts (2014), Law on Organization of the People's Procuracies (2014), and Law on Organization of the Local Government (2015).

65 ibid.

66 Đinh Dũng Sỹ (n 55) 5.

67 Nguyễn Văn Cương, 'Nhà Nước Pháp Quyền Xã Hội Chủ Nghĩa Việt Nam Trong Dòng Chảy Lịch Sử' ['The Socialist Rule of Law State of Vietnam in the Course of History'] (Ministry of Justice, 2 February 2023) <https://moj.gov.vn/qt/tintuc/Pages/nghien-cuu-trao-doi.aspx?ItemID=2631>accessed 6 June 2024.

68 Đinh Dũng Sỹ (n 55) 5.

69 Nghị quyết số 22-NQ/TW ngày 10/4/2013 của Bộ Chính trị về hội nhập quốc tế [Resolution No 22-NQ/TW dated 10 April 2013 of the Politburo on International Integration].

The implementation of the Renovation policy requires a formal legal framework for the operation of the emerging market, which explains the enactment of many laws for *the market*. Important statutes for the market have been enacted, revised, and replaced several times in the last decades. The current important laws for the market include:

Civil Code (2015)
Enterprise Law (2014)
Investment Law (2014)
Real Estate Business Law (2014)
Securities Law (2006, amended 2011)
Intellectual Property Law (2005, amended 2009)
Law on the State Bank of Vietnam (2010)
Law on Finance (2005)
Commercial Law (2015)
Competition Law (2005)
Bankruptcy Law (2014)
Law on Commercial Arbitration (2010)
Corporative Law (2012)
Labor Code (2012)
Land Law (2016)

To facilitate and to response to market development, Vietnam codified and recodified civil law every decade in the last thirty years. The Vietnamese socialist state adopted the first Civil Code in 1995. This was replaced by the second Civil Code in 2005, which was in turn replaced by the third, current Civil Code in 2015 (effective in 2017).[70] The official justifications are that the enactment of the 2015 Civil Code is to institutionalize the 2013 Constitution's new commitments to human rights, to create a complete legal framework conductive for market development, and to facilitate international integration.[71] The 2015 Civil Code consists of 689 articles, 27 chapters, and 6 parts:

- Part One-General Provisions includes Chapter I-General Provisions; Chapter II-Establishment, Implementation and Protection of Civil Rights; Chapter III-Individuals; Chapter IV-Legal Entities; Chapter V-The State of the Socialist Republic Of Vietnam, and Central and Local State Agencies in Civil Relations; Chapter VI-Family Households, Co-Operative Groups and

[70] See Hong Hai Nguyen, 'A Study on the Civil Code Revision: The 2015 Civil Code of Vietnam' in Yuka Kaneko (ed) *Civil Law Reforms in Post-Colonial Asia* (Springer 2019) 85

[71] Vietnam's Ministry of Justice, Tờ Trình Về dự án Bộ luật dân sự (sửa đổi) [Proposal on The Project of a Civil Code (Revised)] (2014).

Other Organizations without Legal Entity Status in Civil Relations; Chapter VII-Property; Chapter VIII-Civil Transactions; Chapter IX-Representation; Chapter X-Time-Limits and Limitation Periods.

- Part Two-Ownership Rights and Other Rights Related to Property includes Chapter XI-General Provisions; Chapter XII-Possession; Chapter XIII-Ownership Rights; Chapter XIV-Other Rights Related to Property.
- Part Three-Obligations and Contracts includes Chapter XV-General Provisions; Chapter XVI-Common Contracts; Chapter XVII-Promises of Rewards and Prize Competitions; Chapter XIII-Performance of Acts without Authorization; Chapter XIX-Obligations to Return Due to Unlawful Possession or Use of Property or Deriving of Benefits from Property; Chapter XX-Liability for Compensation for Non-Contractual Damages.
- Part Four-Inheritance includes Chapter XXI-General Provisions; Chapter XXII-Inheritance Under Wills; Chapter XIII-Inheritance under Law; Chapter XXIV-Settlement and Distribution of Estates.
- Part Five-Law Applicable to Civil Relations Involving Foreign Elements includes Chapter XXV-General Provisions; Chapter XXVI-Law Applicable to Individuals and Legal Entities; Chapter XXVII-Law Applicable to Property Relations and Personal Relations.
- Part Six-Implementing Provisions.

Economic transformation has generated many social, cultural, and environmental problems, which explains the high number of formal laws enacted to deal with these. Important laws for *society* include the Law on Social Security (2014), the Housing Law (2014), the Law on Residence (2013), the Law on Environmental Protection (2014), the Ordinance on Population (2008), and the Ordinance on Anti-Prostitution (2003).

Criminal law reform is also notable. Like civil law, since the introduction of the Renovation policy, the Vietnamese socialist state codified and recodified criminal law three times. The first Criminal Code was adopted in 1985, replaced by the second Criminal Code in 1999, which was then replaced by the third, current Criminal Code in 2015.[72]

Vietnam also enacted important civil and criminal *procedure laws*. These procedural laws were enacted, amended, and replaced consistent with the development of civil and criminal substantive laws. The Vietnamese socialist state adopted the first Civil Procedure Code in 2004. The Code was amended in 2012 and replaced by a new Civil Procedure Code in 2015. The Vietnamese socialist state adopted the first Criminal Procedure Code in 1988, which was amended several

[72] Lê Cảm (ed), *Pháp Luật Hình Sự Việt Nam Từ Thế Kỷ X Đến Nay—Lịch Sử Và Thực Tại [Criminal Law of Vietnam from the Tenth Century to the Present—History and Presence]* (Vietnam National University/Hanoi Press 2018).

times in 1990, 1992, and 1999. It was replaced by a new Criminal Procedure Code in 2004, which was then replaced by the current Criminal Procedure Code in 2015.

C. Legislative Convergence

Overall, legislative development resulted in the incorporation into Vietnamese law global legal concepts and institutions unconventional to the socialist legal tradition. These global legal concepts and institutions may have their roots in Western modern law but have spread widely around the world. They are largely derived from two sources: comparative and international law. First, Vietnamese law adopts ideas and institutions from civil law and common law mainly from developed countries in the West and Asia (particularly Japan). Second, Vietnamese law integrates norms from international treaties. Sections III.C.1–7 describe global legal convergence in Vietnam in various areas of public and private law.

1. Constitutional Convergence

The convergence of Vietnam's Constitution with international human rights (IHR) law is evident. Vietnam ratified four IHR treaties in 1982: International Covenant on Civil and Political Rights (CCPR); International Covenant on Economic, Social, and Cultural Rights (CESCR); Convention on the Elimination of All Forms of Discrimination against Women (CEDAW); and International Convention on the Elimination of All Forms of Racial Discrimination (CERD). As the reflection of the treaty ratification, the 1992 Constitution provided that 'In the Socialist Republic of Vietnam human rights in the political, civic, economic, cultural and social fields are respected.'[73] After the adoption of the 1992 Constitution, Vietnam ratified more IHR treaties, including the Optional Protocol to the Convention on the Rights of the Child on the involvement of children in armed conflict (2001) and the Optional Protocol to the Convention on the Rights of the Child on the sale of children, child prostitution, and child pornography (2001).[74]

The greater engagement with IHR treaties has encouraged Vietnam to further incorporate the treaties into its Constitution. On 4 August 2011, the NA of Vietnam decided to comprehensively revise the 1992 Constitution. One of the main concerns of constitutional reformers is to reflect in the Constitution the IHR treaties to which Vietnam is a party. The new bill of rights in the final Constitution adopted in 2013 includes many human rights reflective of the IHR treaties Vietnam has signed. The new bill of rights is renamed as Human Rights, Fundamental Rights, and Obligations of Citizens. The word 'human rights' is added in the new title to

[73] Constitution of the Socialist Republic of Vietnam (1992), art 50.

[74] 'Ratification Status for Viet Nam', UN Human Rights, <https://tbinternet.ohchr.org/_layouts/15/TreatyBodyExternal/Treaty.aspx?CountryID=192&Lang=EN> accessed 6 June 2024.

emphasize the state's commitment to human rights as universal rights inherent to human beings. The Constitution also includes new rights: right to not be expelled and delivered to another state (Article 17); right to life (Article 19); right to social security (Article 34); right to enjoy and access cultural values, participate in cultural life, and use cultural facilities (Article 41); right to determine one's ethnicity, use one's mother tongue, and choose one's language of communication (Article 42), and right to live in a clean environment (Article 43).

The national bill of right in Vietnam is convergent with IHR law. The formal (or textual) convergence is clear: Vietnam's Constitution includes many rights found in IHR law. Domestic scholars juxtapose thirty rights in the 2013 Constitution with the rights provided in the Universal Declaration of Human Rights, the International Covenant on Civil and Political Rights, and the International Covenant on Economic, Social, and Cultural Rights. They conclude that constitutional rights in Vietnam are basically consistent with IHR law.[75] Ideational convergence is also evident. The Constitution provides that human rights 'shall be recognized, respected, protected and guaranteed' (Article 14). This provision ideationally embodies rights universalism: human rights not as things granted to individuals by the state's consent but inherent to human beings, which require the state's recognition, respect, and protection.

2. *Criminal Law Convergence*

The criminal law convergence is evident.[76] This trend means the incorporation of international law and comparative criminal law into Vietnamese criminal law. The trend is attributed to the need to internalize international treaties signed by Vietnam (such as the UN Convention against Transnational Organized Crime, UN Convention against Corruption, and UN Convention against Torture), the need to deal with transnational crimes, and the impact of harmonization of criminal law.[77] For example, the 2015 Criminal Code provides for criminal liability for commercial legal entities. This provision is a response to the recommendations of international treaties on combating corruption, money laundering, human trafficking, terrorism, and terrorist financing. The provision is also based on a comparative study of criminal liability for legal entities in 119 countries carried out by the committee drafting the 2015 Criminal Code.[78]

[75] Vu Cong Giao and Nguyen Minh Tam, 'Quyền Con Người Trong Luật Quốc Tế, Hiến Pháp Năm 2013 Và Pháp Luật Việt Nam' ['Human Rights in International Law, the 2013 Constitution and Vietnamese Law'] in Trịnh Quốc Toản and Vũ Công Giao (eds), *Thực Hiện Các Quyền Hiến Định Trong Hiến Pháp Năm 2013 [Implementing Fundamental Rights in the 2013 Constitution]* (Hồng Đức 2017) 32, 48.

[76] Đào Lệ Thu, 'Xu Hướng Quốc Tế Hóa Của Luật Hình Sự Việt Nam Và Vấn Đề Đặt Ra Cho Lập Pháp Hình Sự' ['The Internationalization Trend of Vietnamese Criminal Law and the Problem Posed to the Criminal Legislature'] 2020 (12) Nghiên Cứu Lập Pháp 3.

[77] ibid 3–4.

[78] ibid 5.

The 2015 Criminal Code also abolishes the death penalty for seven crimes (surrendering to the enemy, opposing order, destruction of projects of national security importance, robbery, drug possession, drug appropriation, and the production and trade of fake food). This abolition is based on the Vietnamese legislators' study of IHR law and comparative criminal law on the death penalty in countries such as the United States, Russia, China, Japan, Thailand, Indonesia, and Malaysia.[79]

Procedural criminal law also adopts global ideas and institutions. For example, both the 2015 Civil Procedure Code and the 2015 Criminal Procedure Code include rules supporting adversarial trials. Although criminal trial in Vietnam has been predominantly inquisitorial, the 2015 Criminal Procedure Code adopts adversarial elements, such as the defence's right to collect and present evidence, the principle of litigation and examination of evidence at trial, and the accused's right to silence.[80]

3. *Business Law Convergence*

The laws for the market also adopt global ideas and institutions. For example, the 1991 Company Law enacted in the initial stage of Renovation was meant to liberalize the economy by allowing the establishment of private economic sectors while the 1980 Constitution, which prohibited this, had not been revised. The 1991 Company Law was therefore a kind of economic constitutional law. Later, the 1999 Enterprise Law:

> introduced comprehensive Western corporate governance rules. Principally borrowing Anglo-American company law principles, in one hundred and thirty-four articles the EL [Enterprise Law] regulates directors' duties, disclosure, members' rights (especial those of minority shareholders), boards of management and inspection board rights and duties, dividend payments, conversion among corporate entities, dissolution, dissolution merger and liquidation.[81]

The 1999 Enterprise Law was replaced by the new Enterprise Law in 2005, which was the base for the development of the private economic sectors and the market economy in Vietnam during the last decades. The 2005 version was then replaced by the new Enterprise Law in 2014. The 2014 version was replaced again by the new Enterprise Law in 2020, which aims to further foster the development of enterprises, particularly private enterprises. New features of the 2020 Enterprise Law include, among other things, reducing administrative procedures

[79] ibid 8.

[80] Võ Minh Kỳ, 'Các Yếu Tố Tranh Tụng Trong Mô Hình Tố Tụng Thẩm Vấn Truyền Thống Của Việt Nam' ['Adversarial Elements in the Traditional Model of Inquisitorial Procedure Model in Vietnam'] (2020) 7 Nghiên cứu Lập pháp 13, 16.

[81] John Gillespie, 'Transplanted Company Law: An Ideological and Cultural Analysis of Market-Entry in Vietnam' (2002) 51 ICLQ 649.

and creating more favourable conditions for enterprise registration and market entry; improving the legal framework for corporate governance and increasing the protection of investors and shareholders according to international standards and practices; and improving governance effectiveness and operational efficiency of state-owned enterprises.[82]

Many other laws are enacted to protect private property and contract rights, and to facilitate domestic and foreign investment and international trade, which were influenced by comparative and transnational experience. For example, John Gillespie observes that 'the key provisions of the Vietnamese Competition Law [2004], which prohibit anti-competitive behaviour, abuse of market dominance and other monopolistic activities, were loosely modelled on the European Union Competition Law'.[83]

4. *Civil Law Convergence*

The adoption of global ideas and institutions is also evident in civil law. The influence of comparative law on the development of Vietnamese civil law has been documented. The 1995 Civil Code was strongly influenced by Russian Civil Code, although influence also came from the French and Japanese Civil Codes. The 2005 Civil Code departed from the Russian model of civil law. It was adopted when Vietnam was preparing for the accession to the WTO, and hence to facilitate this process the Code adopted norms of international treaties and experiences of developed countries.[84] The 2015 Civil Code adopts 'new approaches, reflecting a reform in legal thinking' such as the perspective of the Civil Code as the general law creating a coherent legal framework for private law, the protection of human rights in the civil sphere, and as the law for market relations.[85] The 2015 Civil Code continues the trend of incorporating international and comparative legal norms into Vietnamese civil law. For example, the Code allows for the application of judicial precedents (Article 6). This indicates the influence of common law in Vietnamese law and is a significant departure from the traditional socialist positivist conception, which emphasizes the written, legislative sources of law. To detail the constitutional rights and to domesticize IHR treaties that Vietnam has signed, the

[82] Quỳnh Trang, 'Luật Doanh Nghiệp: Những Bước Tiến Quan Trọng' ['Enterprise Law: Important Developments'] (Thời báo Ngân Hàng, 17 July 2020) <https://thoibaonganhang.vn/luat-doanh-nghiep-nhung-buoc-tien-quan-trong-104187.html> accessed 6 June 2024.

[83] John Gillespie, 'Localizing Global Competition Law in Vietnam: A Bottom-Up Perspective' (2015) 64 ICLQ 938.

[84] Phạm Trí Hùng, 'Ứng Dụng Của Luật So Sánh Trong Xây Dựng Bộ Luật Dân Sự Việt Nam' ['The Application of Comparative Law in Drafting Vietnam's Civil Code'] (*VIBonline*, 12 July 2010) <http://vibonline.com.vn/bao_cao/ung-dung-cua-luat-so-sanh-trong-xay-dung-bo-luat-dan-su-viet-nam> accessed 6 June 2024.

[85] Nguyen Hong Hai, 'The 2015 Civil Code: A More Humane and Feasible Legal Foundation for Civil Relations' (Vietnam Law & Legal Forum, 9 November 2016) The 2015 Civil Code: A more humane and feasible legal foundation for civil relations (vietnamlawmagazine.vn) accessed 6 June 2024.

Civil Code provides for a wide range of personal rights, including the new right to gender reassignment (Article 37).

Procedural civil law also adopts new ideas and institutions. The 2015 Civil Procedure Code provides for adversarial trials by emphasizing the role of courts as neutral arbiters and the parties' right to collect and present evidence.[86] The adoption of adversarial elements in Vietnamese procedural law is largely inspired by comparative experience of common law tradition.

5. *Labour Law Convergence*

Convergence is evident in labour law. Vietnam ratified six out of eight International Labor Organization (ILO) fundamental conventions, including:

Forced Labor Convention (in 2007)
Right to Organize and Collective Bargaining Convention (in 2019)
Equal Remuneration Convention (in 1997)
Discrimination (Employment and Occupation) Convention (in 1997)
Minimum Age Convention (in 2003)
Worst Forms of Child Labor Convention (in 2000)[87]

The EVFTA commits Vietnam to ratify the Abolition of Forced Labor Convention and the Freedom of Association and Protection of the Right to Organize Convention, which the Vietnamese government has planned to ratify in 2020 and 2023 respectively.[88]

Domestically, Vietnam modified the bill of rights and labour law to conform to the ratified labour conventions. The country's 2013 Constitution includes new rights to equal and safe working conditions, payment, and rest; prohibition of discrimination, forced labour, and employment of workers under minimum age; and prohibition of abuse and exploitation of child labour (Articles 35 and 37). In addition, the Vietnamese legislature adopted a new Labor Code in 2019, replacing the previous 2012 one.[89] Enforced since January 2021, one of the striking features of the new Code is workers' right to form independent unions at the workplace

[86] Đặng Thanh Hòa and Đặng Huyền Phương, 'Về Thực Hiện Nguyên Tắc Đảm Bảo Tranh Tụng Theo Pháp Luật Tố Tụng Dân Sự Hiện Hành' ['On the Implementation of the Principle of Ensuring Adversarial Trial in Accordance with the Current Civil Procedure Law'] (Tạp Chí Tòa Án Nhân Dân Điện Tử, 18 July 2021) <https://tapchitoaan.vn/ve-thuc-hien-nguyen-tac-dam-bao-tranh-tung-theo-phap-luat-to-tung-dan-su-hien-hanh> accessed 6 June 2024.

[87] International Labour Organization, Ratifications for Viet Nam, <https://www.ilo.org/dyn/normlex/en/f?p=NORMLEXPUB:11200:0::NO::P11200_COUNTRY_ID:103004> accessed 6 June 2024.

[88] 'Hội thảo tham vấn Dự thảo Kế hoạch chiến lược về Thúc đẩy gia nhập và thực hiện các tiêu chuẩn lao động quốc tế tại Việt Nam' ['Consultation Workshop on Draft Strategic Plan for Promoting Accession and Implementation of International Labor Standards in Vietnam'] Bộ Lao Động—Thương Binh Và Xã Hội, 17 June 2019) <http://www.molisa.gov.vn/Pages/tintuc/chitiet.aspx?tintucID=29682> accessed 25 April 2020.

[89] Bộ luật lao động [Labour Code] (2019).

beyond the national trade union (the Vietnam General Confederation of Labor).[90] Vietnamese lawmakers explained that this new right is 'in accordance with ILO Conventions and other international commitments facilitating international integration'.[91] That means the right to trade association is included to facilitate free trade deals like the Comprehensive and Progressive Agreement on Trans-Pacific Partnership and the EVFTA.

6. *Environmental Law Convergence*

Vietnamese environmental law also converges with global standards. Vietnam ratified twenty-eight multilateral agreements on environmental protection generally and climate change and biological diversity particularly, including:

Basel Convention (13 March 1995)
Cartagena Protocol (21 January 2004)
Convention on Biological Diversity (16 November 1994)
Convention on International Trade in Endangered Species of Wild Fauna and Flora (20 April 1994)
Kyoto Protocol (25 September 2002)
Minamata Convention on Mercury (23 June 2017)
Montreal Protocol (26 January 1994)
Nagoya Protocol (23 Apr 2014)
Nagoya—Kuala Lumpur Supplementary Protocol (23 April 2014)
Paris Agreement (3 November 2016)
Ramsar Convention (20 September 1988)
Rotterdam Convention (7 May 2007)
Stockholm Convention (22 July 2002)
UN Watercourses Convention (19 May 2014)
UN Convention to Combat Desertification (25 August 1998)
UN Framework Convention on Climate Change (16 November 1994)
UN Convention on the Law of the Sea (25 July 1994)
Vienna Convention (26 January 1994)[92]

Domestically, the country's 2013 Constitution newly provided for 'the right to the right to live in a clean environment' and 'the duty to protect the environment' (Article 43). To implement this constitutional right and duty, the NA promulgated the new Law on Environmental Protection in 2014, replacing the 2005 version.

[90] ibid art 3.
[91] 'Quốc Hội Thông Qua Bộ Luật Lao Động (Sửa Đổi)' ['The National Assembly Passes the Labour Code (Amended)'] (Bộ Lao Động—Thương Binh Và Xã Hội, 20 November 2019] <http://www.molisa.gov.vn/Pages/tintuc/chitiet.aspx?tintucID=221042> accessed 6 June 2024.
[92] InforMEA, Vietnam <https://www.informea.org/en/countries/VN/parties> accessed 6 June 2024.

In 2019, the legislature decided a plan to amend the law, and one of the rationales is to comply with commitments in the free agreements and international environmental commitments.[93] In addition, the legislature enacted the Biodiversity Law in 2008 and Environmental Protection Tax Law in 2010; and the government and other administrative bodies issued some 177 regulations on national resources and environment.[94] Vietnamese reformers seek to converge domestic environmental law with global environmental legal standards.

7. IP Law Convergence

Vietnam has also actively engaged with international regimes on IP.[95] The country joined the World Intellectual Property Organization (WIPO) in 1976, and became a member of major WIPO treaties, including:

Berne Convention (26 July 2004)
Brussels Convention (12 October 2005)
Hague Agreement (30 September 2019)
Madrid Agreement (Marks) (17 September 1956)
Madrid Protocol (11 April 2006)
Paris Convention (7 April 1981)
Patent Cooperation Treaty (10 December 1992)
Phonograms Convention (6 April 2005)
Rome Convention (1 December 2006)
UPOV (Union for the Protection of New Varieties of Plants) Convention (24 November 2006)
WIPO Convention (7 April 1981)[96]

Domestically, Vietnam has rapidly developed a comprehensive legal framework for IP (including the Intellectual Property Law and related legislation such as the Competition Law, Civil Procedure Law, Customs Law, and administrative regulations on IP), which is generally compatible with international standards provided

[93] Bộ Tài nguyên và Môi trường, Tờ Trình: Dự Án Sửa Đổi, Bổ Sung Một Số Điều Của luật Bảo Vệ Môi Trường [Report: The Project on Amending and Supplementing Some Articles of the Law on Environmental Protection] (*Dự Thảo Online*) <http://duthaoonline.quochoi.vn/DuThao/Lists/DT_DUTHAO_LUAT/View_Detail.aspx?ItemID=1792&TabIndex=2&TaiLieuID=3825> accessed 6 June 2024.

[94] Văn Phòng Bộ Tài Nguyên Và Môi Trường, 'Văn bản Quy phạm Pháp luật Hiện hành về Tài nguyên và Môi trường' ['Current Legal Documents on Natural Resources and Environment'] <http://vanban.monre.gov.vn/DocViewer.aspx?IDLV=4>.

[95] Sy Luong Nguyen and Van Anh Le, 'Diffusion of Geographical Indication law in Vietnam: "Journey to the West"' (2023) 54 IIC—Int'l Rev IP & Comp L 176; Van Anh Le, 'Second Medical Use Patents and Compensation for the Delay in Marketing Authorisations: The Curious Case of Vietnam' (2022) 71 GRUR Int'l 1048.

[96] Vietnam <https://www.wipo.int/directory/en/details.jsp?country_code=VN> accessed 6 June 2024.

in the Agreement on Trade-Related Aspects of Intellectual Property Rights (TRIPS).[97] Particularly, when the EU–Vietnam FTA was about to be finalized, a review report found that Vietnamese IP law is compatible with the majority of the trade deal's commitments on IP, including general principles, standards of protection of rights, and enforcement of rights.[98] That means Vietnamese domestic IP law converges with international commitments on IP.

D. The Limits of Legislative Reform

Formal legislative convergence in Vietnam does not necessarily mean that the convergent laws will be fully implemented in practice. When convergence occurs through material inducement rather than persuasion, this may be particularly prominent in the textual level of domestic laws but does not guarantee the complete realization of the international norms and institutions in domestic practices. To be sure, when international legal norms have become a part of national formal law, they will be subject to the influence of a wide range of international and domestic actors. The complex influence may incrementally transform formal legal convergence into some level of practice. In this regard, in the long term, due to external pressure stemming from continuing international and regional integration, and the increasing demands of local citizens (including through legal mobilization), formal convergence in Vietnamese law may influence functional legal development.

Despite formal convergence, legislation in Vietnam still diverges from the global legal standards, particularly the universal norms of internal morality of law. To illustrate, an empirical survey of the Central Institute for Economic Management in 2012 identified 'Nine Nos' in the Vietnamese legal system: no sufficiency; no clarity; no stability; no consistency; no transparency; no predictability; no reasonableness; no effectiveness; and no validity.[99] The Party and state leadership also explicitly acknowledge shortcomings of the legal system. For example, Vương Đình Huệ, President of the NA, states:

> Although the legal system is basically extensive and comprehensive, specific fields have not promptly met the requirements of development and has not really

[97] Nguyễn Bích Thảo, 'Hoàn Thiện Pháp Luật Sở Hữu Trí Tuệ Trong Bối Cảnh Việt Nam Đẩy Mạnh Hội Nhập Kinh Tế Quốc Tế Và Tham Gia Các Hiệp Định Thương Mại Tự Do Thế Hệ Mới' ['Improving Intellectual Property Law in the Context of Vietnam Promoting International Economic Integration and Joining New-Generation Free Trade Agreements'] (Nghiên Cứu Lập Pháp, 1 February 2017]) <http://www.lapphap.vn/Pages/tintuc/tinchitiet.aspx?tintucid=208003> accessed 6 June 2024.

[98] Nguyễn Thị Thu Trang (ed), *Rà Soát Pháp Luật Việt Nam Với Các Cam Kết Của Hiệp Định Thương Mại Tự Do Việt Nam—EU Về Sở Hữu Trí Tuệ [Review of Vietnamese Law with the Commitments of Vietnam—EU Free Trade Agreement on Intellectual Property*] (Nhà Xuất bản Công Thương 2016) 16.

[99] Nam Nguyễn, 'Tiêu chí xác định chất lượng của hệ thống pháp luật' ['Criteria of the Quality of the Legal System'] (Ministry of Justice, 10 August 2012) <http://moj.gov.vn/qt/tintuc/Pages/nghien-cuu-trao-doi.aspx?ItemID=1538> [<https://perma.cc/AAG2-8N5M>] accessed 29 October 2017.

> adapted quickly to the strong development of the Fourth Industrial Revolution, and the stability is not high. Some major views and orientations are set out in the Party documents and provisions of the Constitution, but the institutionalization is still not timely and complete. The uniformity and feasibility in the provisions of a number of legal documents are not high; and the overlap, contradiction, and inconsistency between some legal documents have not completely been overcome. The adaptability of the legal system to the rapid changes in practice is limited. Some regulations are inadequate, inhibiting, and hindering development but slow to be studied, modified and dismantled.[100]

Let us consider in greater detail major limitations of legislation in Vietnam as acknowledged by domestic political leaders, officials, and domestic scholars.[101]

1. Insufficiency

While the Vietnamese legal system has comprehensively covered various aspects of society, there has been a lack of law in some areas. Some Vietnamese scholars have discussed the issue of the 'legal loophole' (*lỗ hổng pháp luật*) in the Vietnamese legal system.[102] Drawing on Russian legal scholarship, they understand legal loopholes as the lack of law to regulate negative social relations stably lasting for a considerable period of time.[103] Two factors account for legal loopholes in the Vietnamese legal system. One is internal: economic reform led to social change and the emergence of new social relations, which have not been legislated. Another factor is external: the impact of globalization induces the rise of new areas lacking legislation.

For example, some Vietnamese commentators explore the lack of legal regulations on the mechanism to supervise the contractor management agency and the contractor, and the lack of transparent regulations of the allocation of land, lease of land, and determination of land prices, which were the roots of corruption cases.[104] Also, local commentators contend that Vietnam lacks a legal framework

[100] Vương Đình Huệ, 'Tiếp Tục Đổi Mới Hoạt Động Lập Pháp Của Quốc Hội Nhằm Hoàn Thiện Đồng Bộ Thể Chế Phát Triển, Tạo Lập Khung Khổ Pháp Lý Vững Chắc Để Đất Nước Phát Triển Và Hội Nhập' ['Continuation of Renovation of Legislation Activity of the National Assembly for Synchronous Improvements of Institution Development, Solid Legal Framework for Development and Integration of the Country'] (2022) 450–51 Nghiên Cứu Lập Pháp 7.

[101] Hoàng Thị Kim Quế and Lê Thị Phuong Nga, 'Những Hạn Chế Chủ Yếu Và Giải Pháp Khắc Phục Nhằm Nâng Cao Chất Lượng Xây Dựng Pháp Luật Ở Nước Ta Hiện Nay' ['The Main Limitations and Solutions to Improve the Quality of Law Making in Our Country Today'] (Trang Thông Tin Điện Tử Tổng Hợp Ban Nội Chính Trung Ương, 11 February 2022) <https://noichinh.vn/nghien-cuu-trao-doi/202202/nhung-han-che-chu-yeu-va-giai-phap-khac-phuc-nham-nang-cao-chat-luong-xay-dung-phap-luat-o-nuoc-ta-hien-nay-310649> accessed 6 June 2024.

[102] Nguyễn Minh Đức, 'Khắc Phục Những Xung Đột Và Lỗ Hổng Trong Pháp Luật' ['Overcoming Conflicts and Loopholes in The Law'] (2009) 24 Nghiên Cứu Lập Pháp 38; Hoàng Thị Kim Quế, Bàn Về 'Lỗ Hổng Pháp Luật' [Discussion about 'Legal Loopholes'] (2017) 6 Nghiên Cứu Lập Pháp 3.

[103] Nguyễn Minh Đức (n 102) 40.

[104] Nam Kiên and Vũ Lê Minh, 'Từ Các Vụ Án Kinh Tế Tham Nhũng Trọng Điểm: Nhận Diện Những Chiêu Thức, Thủ Đoạn Của Tội Phạm Và Kiến Nghị Bịt Những Lỗ Hổng Pháp Luật Về Đất

for the Fourth Industrial Revolution. An official from the Ministry of Justice lamented that Vietnam lacks a legal framework for cryptographic assets (eg virtual money); but in practice virtual currency trading is quite common, which is the cause of numerous cases of fraud and people's using virtual currencies to cover illegal multilevel business.[105] Thus, legal loopholes have generated negative consequences. Individuals have exploited legal loopholes to make profits, including engaging in corruption.

2. Inconsistency

The political and legal elites have a strong concern that the Vietnamese legal system has included many conflicting legal rules. According to a review in 2020 by the Ministry of Justice, conflicting legal rules have concentrated on areas relating to production and business, including:

conditions for entering the market, management organization, and operation of enterprises;
approval, implementation, organization of implementation, and termination of investment projects;
financial regulation;
taxes;
management and use of state capital invested in production and business at enterprises and equitization of state-owned enterprises;
land, natural resources, environment, construction, and real estate business;
labour, employment, and social security;
contracts, settlement of disputes arising in business, and bankruptcy of enterprises;
specialized examinations;
judicial assistance and access to law by enterprises;
law meeting the requirements of the Fourth Industrial Revolution; and
assignment, decentralization, and authorization in the state management of the economy.[106]

Đai, Đấu Thầu, Đấu Giá . . .' ['From Key Economic Corruption Cases: Identify the Moves and Tricks of Criminals and Propose to Close the Loopholes in the Law on Land, Bidding, Auction . . .'] (Pháp lý, 31 August 2022) <https://phaply.net.vn/tu-15-vu-an-kinh-te-tham-nhung-trong-diem-nam-2020-nhan-dien-nhung-chieu-thuc-thu-doan-cua-toi-pham-va-kien-nghi-bit-nhung-lo-hong-phap-luat-ve-dat-dai-dau-thau-dau-gia-a245263.html> accessed 6 June 2024.

[105] Bảo Hân, Vừa Thừa, Vừa Thiếu [Both Redundant and Lacking], (Báo Đại biểu Nhân dân, 5 August 2020), (Vừa thừa, vừa thiếu - Báo Đại biểu Nhân dân (daibieunhandan.vn) accessed 6 June 2024.

[106] Lê Sơn, 'Xử Lý Kịp Thời Các Quy Định Mâu Thuẫn, Bất Cập, Không Phù Hợp Thực Tiễn' ['Promptly Handle Contradictory, Inadequate and Practically Inconsistent Regulations'], (Ministry of Justice, 17 September 2020), Xử lý kịp thời các quy định mâu thuẫn, bất cập, không phù hợp thực tiễn (moj.gov.vn)accessed 6 June 2024.

The 2019 Report by the Vietnam Chamber of Commerce and Industry (VCCI) points out many conflicts in legislation, including:

conflict on procedures for approval of investment policies for housing construction projects between the Law on Investment and Law on Housing;
conflict over bidding for investor selection in land use projects and land use right auctions between the Law on Investment, Law on Bidding, and Law on Land;
conflict on procedures for introduction of investment locations and construction sites between the Law on Construction, Law on Housing, and Law on Investment;
overlapping procedures for applying for permission to transfer real estate projects between the Law on Investment and Law on Real Estate Business;
discrepancy in the right to transfer real estate projects between the Law on Investment, Law on Real Estate Business, Law on Housing, and Law on Land; and
differences in the order and procedures for investment in projects with a scale of VND 5,000 billion or more between the Law on Investment, Law on Management of Use of State Capital at Enterprises, and Law on Construction.[107]

For example, consider the conflict on procedures for approval of investment policies for housing construction projects between the Law on Investment and Law on Housing. According to the Law on Housing, any housing construction project must carry out relevant procedures to seek the government's approval of investment policy before implementing a project. However, the Law on Investment provides that projects not subject to approval of investment policies and foreign-invested projects in which foreign investors own less than 51% will not have to carry out any procedures related to government's agreement on investment policies before implementing investment projects. The two laws therefore have conflicting rules on procedures for government's approval of investment policies for housing construction projects.[108]

[107] Thạch Huê, VCCI Báo Cáo Nhanh Về 20 Điểm Xung Đột, Chồng Chéo Lớn Của Pháp Luật [VCCI Quickly Reports on 20 Major Conflicts and Overlaps of the Law], (BNEWS/TTXVN, 6 August 2019) <https://bnews.vn/vcci-bao-cao-nhanh-ve-20-diem-xung-dot-chong-cheo-lon-cua-phap-luat/130330.html> accessed 6 June 2024.

[108] Vietnam Chamber of Commerce and Industry, *Báo cáo: Chồng chéo Pháp luật về Đầu tư Kinh Doanh [Report: Overlapping Laws on Business Investment]* (2019) 2 <http://vibonline.com.vn/wp-content/uploads/2020/02/VCCI-B%C3%A1o-c%C3%A1o-ch%E1%BB%93ng-ch%C3%A9o-PL-2019.12.26.pdf> accessed 6 June 2024.

3. *Framework Law*

Vietnamese legislative leaders, legislators, and legal scholars have had major concerns over what is called *luật khung, luật ống* (framework law or pipe law).[109] Framework laws refer to statutes that include vague and generic provisions. The implementation of such statutes depends on the enactment of many administrative instruments.[110]

Vietnamese scholars point out many reasons for the existence of the framework law. Unstable social relations due to the transitional nature of Vietnamese society require generic statutes to accommodate the rapid social change. Pressures of law-making to meet the demands of economic reform and international integration render legislators to make generic law. The fact that the NA is composed of mainly unprofessional members and convenes only twice a year makes statutes generic.[111]

The consequences of framework law are multifaced. A fewer number of statutory laws can only be implemented through a huge number of administrative regulations. To implement hundreds of legislative laws, legal institutions at different levels from central government to communal governors have enacted thousands of by-law documents. The use of regulatory legal instruments in administrative governance indicates both negative and positive aspects. Regulatory governance is an important reform. This indicates the instrumental adherence to legality in governance, which is better than governing through personal fiats. The goals of the legal regulations of administrative agencies are to facilitate economic development, institutional building, and international integration, not merely to control individuals' actions. However, administrative bodies can rely on regulatory instruments to expand their power, which makes it difficult for legislators to control them.

Vietnamese law is therefore popularly described as a 'jungle of law'.[112] Legislative law includes very general rules that allow a wide space for administrative regulation. And the administrative regulation does not simply interpret legislation. Administrative agents seize the legislation space to extend their discretionary power. Although the legislative institutions have the constitutional power to supervise the consistency between administrative regulations and legislations, it is difficult for them to do so, given the gigantic amount of administrative regulation

[109] Nguyễn Thị Hạnh, 'Ban Hành "Luật Khung" Hay "Luật Chi Tiết"' ['Promulgation of "Framework Law" or "Detailed Law"'] (2005) 4 Nghiên Cứu Lập Pháp 30; Đinh Dũng Sỹ, 'Thực Trạng Và Giải Pháp Khắc Phục Vấn Đề "Luật Khung" Ở Việt Nam' ['Current Situation and Solutions to Overcome the Problem of "Framework Law" in Vietnam'] (2006) 4 Nghiên Cứu Lập Pháp 33.

[110] Song Hà, 'Hạn Chế Tối Đa Luật "Khung", Luật "Ống"' [Minimize the Law of "Framework" Law, the "Pipes" Law'] (Đại Biểu Nhân Dân, 30 March 2022) <https://daibieunhandan.vn/Chinh-sach-va-cuoc-song/Han-che-toi-da-luat-khung-luat-ong-i283507> accessed 6 June 2024.

[111] Nguyễn Thị Hạnh (n 109); Đinh Dũng Sỹ (n 109).

[112] Đan Thanh, 'Lạc giữa... "rừng luật"' ["Missing the Way in . . . 'The Jungle of Law] (Báo An Ninh Thủ Đô, 27 May 2008) <http://anninhthudo.vn/chinh-tri-xa-hoi/lac-giua-rung-luat/325550.antd> accessed 6 June 2024.

and the part-time working hours of the majority of the legislature's members. Consequently, they have never practiced this power. Within the administrative system, the Ministry of Justice is in charge of checking the consistency of administrative regulation. This body is rather active in this work; but its work is only advisory. Instead, the issuing institutions retain the power to revise the challenged laws. In practice, challenges by the Ministry of Justice have resulted in the issuing institutions revising or withdrawing the questioned regulation.[113]

The consequence of the extension of the administrative discretionary power through administrative regulation is significant. Legislative laws may grant more freedom to citizens, but administrative regulation narrows it down. For example, the 2005 Enterprise Law guaranteed the freedom of business, but administrative regulation restricted this freedom by numerous rules regarding requirements, conditions, and licences of conducting business, which gave more discretion to administrative agencies.[114] As a matter of socialist arrangement, judicial review is absent, and citizens are not allowed to challenge an administrative regulation with general effect in the courts because it violates their rights protected in the Constitution and/or by legislation. The administrative courts are only allowed to hear appeals to administrative decisions affecting individual cases.

Another consequence of generic law's dependence on administrative interpretation is policy corruption or the inclusion of group interests in administrative regulation.[115] Group interests can be the institutional interests of the issuing institution in the administrative system. But group interests can also be based on relationships 'formed by the collusion between those who have power in the political system with an individual, business or group of outsiders, in order to make decisions or seek to influence policy to achieve their own interests'.[116] For example, signs of including group interests have appeared in a number of administrative provisions regulating procedures for importing and exporting goods, and projects to exchange land for infrastructure.[117]

[113] For more details, see Bui Ngoc Son, 'Constitutional Developments in Vietnam in the First Decade of the Twenty First Century' in Albert Chen (ed), *Constitutionalism in Asia in the Twenty First Century* (CUP 2014) 207.

[114] Nguyên Tấn, 'Tinh thần Luật Doanh nghiệp còn không?' ['The Spirit of the Enterprise Law Disappears'], (*Thời Báo Kinh Tế Sài Gòn Online*, 25 August 2011) <http://www.thesaigontimes.vn/59939/Tinh-than-Luat-Doanh-nghiep-con-khong.html> [<https://perma.cc/94LV-PV52>] (archived 29 October 2017) accessed 6 June 2024.

[115] Nguyễn Mạnh Cường, 'Hoàn Thiện Cơ Chế Kiểm Soát Quyền Lực Để Phòng, Chống "Lợi Ích Nhóm" Trong Hoạt Động Xây Dựng Chính Sách, Pháp Luật' ['Improve the Power Control Mechanism to Prevent and Combat "Group Interests" in Policy and Law Formulation Activities'], (Cổng Thông Tin Điện Tử Chính Phủ, 14 July 2022) <https://xaydungchinhsach.chinhphu.vn/hoan-thien-co-che-kiem-soat-quyen-luc-de-phong-chong-loi-ich-nhom-trong-hoat-dong-xay-dung-chinh-sach-phap-luat-11922071310492704.htm>.

[116] Trí Dũng, 'Không Để "Lợi Ích Nhóm" Trong Xây Dựng Văn Bản Pháp Luật' ['Do Not Include "Group Interests" in the Development of Legal Documents'] (Hànộimới, 27 December 2022) <https://hanoimoi.com.vn/ban-in/chong-tu-dien-bien/1021045/khong-de-loi-ich-nhomtrong-xay-dung-van-ban-phap-luat> accessed 6 June 2024.

[117] ibid.

4. *Poor Enforcement*

As admitted by the Party itself, the weakest point in the Vietnamese formal legal system concerns legal enforcement. Vice-President and later President of the NA Nguyễn Thị Kim Ngân lamented:

> In Vietnam, there is a very fine and strange law that the world does not have, namely the Law on Legal Propaganda and Education. That means when there are laws, people do not follow them. Therefore, the Law on Legal Propaganda and Education must be enacted, but the people still do not follow.[118]

This situation is significantly divorced from the formalist rule of law ideal's requirement that law must be obeyed. An empirical survey by the authors of the 2015 Justice Index confirms the popular culture of turning against legal institutions because of the problems associated with these institutions:

> Local authorities play an important role in receiving and dealing with citizens' legal matters. Unclear procedures for dispute settlement, lengthy processing time and inefficiency in dispute resolution are the main reasons why disputants choose to solve problems by themselves or opt to use informal measures, instead of turning to local judicial institutions.
>
> The assistance offered by local state agencies in settling disputes and complaints has not been as effective as the assistance of lawyers and legal aid providers.
>
> Access to the court is still limited due to disputants' concerns about costs, procedures and confidence in the integrity of judges and court staff.[119]

So, one of the reasons for the people turning against formal law is the poor quality of the authoritarian legal institutions in delivering justice. Yet, this is not the whole story. Another reason concerns legal history and legal culture. Formal law has a complex relationship with legal legacy. Formal law is just located at the top of a Vietnamese legal pyramid that includes multiple legal layers. Pre-existing legal layers and informal social norms may render formal law ill-enforced. Vietnamese people are more familiar with living with their traditional legal culture, customs, and habits than with newly enacted formal legal rules. Vietnam is an agricultural country, and the majority of the population (around 70%) lives in rural areas. For them, village law, customary law, and traditional social-moral norms are more relevant than the Constitution and legislations. Regarding formal law, they may

[118] 'Việt Nam Có Một Luật Rất Lạ Mà Thế Giới Chưa Có' ['Vietnam Has a Strange Law That the World Does not Have'] (Báo Lao Động, 21 September 2013) <Việt Nam có một luật rất lạ mà thế giới chưa có... (thuvienphapluat.vn) > (Retrieved) accessed 6 June 2024.

[119] VLA and UNDP, *2015 Justice Index: Towards a Justice System for the People* (2016) 12–13 <https://www.undp.org/sites/g/files/zskgke326/files/migration/vn/EN---Chi-so-cong-ly.pdf> accessed 6 June 2024.

be concerned with administrative regulations enacted by communal governments directly relevant to their daily life. Urbanization has brought thousands of peasants to more modern cities together with their village mindset, which makes the legal culture of the emerging middle class in urban areas resonant with their hometown's culture. Consequently, even in modern cities, informal rules prevail over formal rules in many cases. For example, in economic transactions, personal relationships and social networks are in many cases more relevant than formal legal rules. In the administrative system, there is a popular saying about the hierarchy of influential factors in appointment and promotion: 'Nhất hậu duệ, nhì tiền tệ, ba quan hệ, bốn trí tuệ' ['Descendants first; money second; relationship third; intelligence fourth'].

5. *Law, Non-Development, and Anti-Development*

Law and development scholars underline the importance of law and legal institutions in social-economic development. Legal reform in Vietnam was driven by economic reform, but then new legal institutions might contribute to economic development. Although it is difficult to measure empirically, it is safe to say that without legal protections of private property, freedom of contract, and freedom of business, Vietnam could not have achieved economic development in the last decades. However, the law and development story in Vietnam also has negative aspects.

The first is law and non-development. The party-state and legal scholars have often lamented that legislative laws are ineffective, which means the laws fail to create meaningful social-economic development. The source of ineffectiveness of Vietnamese laws is 'law out of context',[120] to borrow Alan Watson's words. Political leaders and many commentators state that Vietnamese statutes do not meet the demands of the society. As law does not meet the need of the society, it fails to create meaningful development. This echoes Watson's account of dysfunction of law or the gap of law and society.

The source of law and non-development in Vietnam is largely legal transplants. While legal transplants contribute to the creation of a formal legal system in Vietnam comparable with legal systems of developed countries, importing external legal sources has generated laws divorced from Vietnamese society. Some commentators describe such laws as 'laws in heaven', which are distant from the actual needs on Earth. Rampant legislation to meet the requirements of international integration leads to the enactment of laws departing from the local context. Borrowing laws from developed countries or transnational institutions (such as the European Union) also contributes to the gap between borrowed laws and the Vietnamese society.

[120] Alan Watson, *Law Out of Context* (University of Georgia Press 2012).

The second aspect is law and anti-development. The Vietnamese government and commentators acknowledge that some elements of Vietnamese laws impede development.[121] The Vietnamese government believes that 'the legal system also has been conflicting, overlapping, inconsistent, unfeasible, inconsistent with practice, causing obstacles and difficulties for investment, production, business and people's lives'.[122] The law and anti-development are therefore connected to other limitations of legislation mentioned above. Particularly, legal transplants also account for law and anti-development. The massive borrowing of laws from various countries and international institutions leads to the adoption of conflicting legal rules, which hinder development.

IV. ADMINISTRATIVE REFORM

A. Public Administration Reform

Like China, Vietnam has constructed a modern bureaucracy in response to the demands of macro-management of the new socialist market economy. The party-state has launched several important programmes to reform the administrative system. To illustrate, in 2001, the government introduced the Administrative Reform Master Programme for the Period 2001–2010. The government believed that economic development is one of the main reasons for a comprehensive programme for administrative reform: 'The demands of building and perfecting the socialist market economy push a forceful pressure on administrative reform which is associated with economic reform.'[123] The Programme comprehensively covers four components: procedural institutions, structural institutions, human resources, and public finance.

The implementation of this Programme has resulted in significant changes to the Vietnamese bureaucracy. Changes to procedural institutions include the simplification or removal of burdensome administrative procedures.[124] Structural changes involve redefinition of administrative functions, rearrangement of

[121] 'Cần Khẩn Trương Sửa Đổi Các Quy Định Gây Cản Trở Sự Phát Triển Kinh Tế' ['It is Urgently Necessary to Amend Regulations That Hinder Economic Development'], (TTXVN/Vietnam+, 3 December 2021) <https://www.vietnamplus.vn/can-khan-truong-sua-doi-cac-quy-dinh-gay-can-tro-su-phat-trien-kinh-te/757824.vnp> accessed 6 June 2024.

[122] Khánh Vy, 'Rà Soát, Sửa Đổi Quy Định Cản Trở Đầu Tư, Kinh Doanh' ['Review and Amend Regulations Hindering Investment and Business'], (VnEconomy, 22 April 2021) <https://vneconomy.vn/ra-soat-sua-doi-quy-dinh-can-tro-dau-tu-kinh-doanh.htm> accessed 6 June 2024.

[123] Quyết Định Của Thủ Tướng Chính Phủ Số 136/2001/Qđ-Ttg Ngày 17 Tháng 9 Năm 2001 Phê Duyệt Chương Trình Tổng Thể Cải Cách Hành Chính Nhà Nước Giai Đoạn 2001–2010 [Prime Minister's Decree No 136/2001/Qđ-Ttg, dated 17 September 2001 Approving the Administrative Reform Master Programme for the Period 2001–2010].

[124] Ngo Thanh Can, 'Public Administration Reform in Vietnam: Current Situations and Solutions' (2013) 3 Sch J Bus Adm 110, 111.

ministerial bodies, and decentralization in central–local relations.[125] On human resource developments, one commentator demonstrates that:

> Results of implementation plans of training civil servants for 2001to 2010 shows that 4,884,506 civil servants have been trained in the past ten years; of which 883,718 has been trained in political theory; 1,230,536 in knowledge of state management; 2,122,702 in specialized knowledge; 97,858 in foreign languages and 224,254 in informatics.[126]

Public finance reforms have resulted in 're-arrange [sic] apparatus, staff downsizing, improving working effectiveness, well fulfilling assigned tasks, saving budget, strengthening material facilities, and gradually modernizing management technology, increasing income for cadres and civil servants'.[127]

In 2011, the government introduced the Administrative Reform Master Programme for the Period 2011–2020,[128] with both economic and political objectives. It underlines first the objectives of further administrative reform 'to build and perfect the socialist-oriented market economy' and to 'create the equal, ventilating, favourable, and transparent business environment'.[129] The Programme also attempts to reform the administrative system to promote the rule of law in public administration and to protect human rights.[130] On the scope of reforms, again, this is comprehensive, ranging from procedural and structural institutions to human resources and public finance. One important new component is the attempt at 'modernizing the administrative system' by applying new digital technology and the Internet in public governance.[131]

In 2021, the government issued a report on the achievements of administrative reforms for the period 2011–20 and the directions for administrative reforms for the period 2021–13 (hereinafter, the Report).[132] The Report surveys five aspects of the achievements of administrative reforms: regulatory, procedural, institutional, personnel, and public finance.

First, the Report underlines that administrative agencies at both central and local government levels have issued numerous regulatory instruments on various

[125] ibid 112.
[126] ibid 113.
[127] ibid.
[128] Nghị Quyết Của Chính Phủ Ban Hành Chương Trình Tổng Thể Cải Cách Hành Chính Nhà Nước Giai Đoạn 2011–2020 [Government's Resolution Issuing the Administrative Reform Master Programme for the Period 2011–2020.
[129] ibid.
[130] ibid.
[131] ibid.
[132] Vietnam Government, Báo Cáo Tổng Kết Chương Trình Tổng Thể Cải Cách Hành Chính Nhà Nước Giai Đoạn 2011–2020 Và Định Hướng Giai Đoạn 2021–2030 [Report Summarizing the Overall Programme of State Administrative Reform in the Period 2011–2020 and Orientation for the Period 2021–2030], No 128/BC-CP, issued on 19 April 2021.

areas to provide a legal framework for the development of the socialist market economy, the building of state apparatus, and international integration. To illustrate, between 2011 and 2021, ministerial bodies issued over 8,600 legal documents. Local governments enacted thousands of legal documents to implement central government's legal documents in localities. For example, from 2011 to May 2022, provincial governments issued 385,826 legal documents.[133]

The second aspect of administrative reform is procedural. The Report emphasizes the simplification or deletion of many administrative procedures. For example, 4,527 out of 4,723 administrative procedures have been simplified. The goals of procedural simplification or deletion are to create a better legal environment for market development and increase national competitiveness.[134]

Third, the Report summarizes institutional administrative reform, including the reduction of administrative departments of central government, the clarification of administrative functions, and the rearrangement of local governments (such as reducing administrative local units) and increasing the autonomy of public service agencies (such as public universities).[135]

Fourth, efforts to improve the quality of administrative public servants include reforms of staff recruitment, education, and training. To illustrate, competitive examinations for appointment to leadership and management positions have been implemented. In addition, in the period between 2016 and 2020, nationwide, there was training and retraining for more than 5.4 million turns of officials, civil servants, and public employees.[136]

Finally, reforms of public finance include increasing the base salary of public servants from VND 730,000 per month in 2011 to VND 1,490,000 per month in 2021; supervising state expenditures by internal spending regulations to increase the efficiency of public spending and to limit corruption and waste in the use of the state budget; and facilitating financial autonomy of public service agencies.[137]

Despite achievements, the Report acknowledges many shortcomings of the administrative system, including conflict in administrative regulations, cumbersome administrative procedures, the cumbersome bureaucracy, the weakness of public servants, and the wasteful and inefficient use of budgets and public investment capital. The Report therefore anticipates directions for further administrative reform, including reviewing and handling conflicting regulatory instruments; reducing and simplifying regulations related to enterprises to remove barriers and promote production and business development; decentralization in central and

[133] ibid.
[134] ibid.
[135] ibid.
[136] ibid.
[137] ibid.

local government relations; pilot implementation of administrative contracts of public servants; and building a digital/e-government.[138]

Administrative corruption remains a serious problem in Vietnam. In 2009, the Vietnamese government initiated and implemented the National Strategy on Anti-Corruption until 2020.[139] Particularly, since the Party launched the largest anti-corruption campaign known as 'burning furnace' in 2016, thousands of public officials, including numerous high-ranking officials, were arrested for corruption. According to a Party report on corruption crimes, over ten years (2002–22), procedural agencies nationwide have investigated 19,546 cases with 33,868 defendants, prosecuted 16,699 cases with 33,037 defendants, and heard first-instance trials of 15,857 cases with 30,355 defendants.[140] The Party is concerned that 'corruption remains one of the threats to the survival of the Party and the regime'.[141] The anti-corruption campaign therefore seeks to retain and enhance the legitimacy of Party leadership and the socialist regime in Vietnam.

Administrative reform in Vietnam has been instigated by economic development and social change. In particular, the imperative of a more effective administrative system to manage the transforming market-oriented economy has resulted in governmental efforts at administrative reform. The government can implement administrative reform and macroeconomic policies and ensure public security and peaceful environment. Yet, administrative reform in Vietnam is ongoing. Administrative corruption in particular remains a grave issue that Vietnam has to deal with.

B. Administrative Law Reform

Major laws have been enacted to support administrative reform. Administrative law in Vietnam is no longer merely an instrument for the state to control citizens' behaviour. Like the case of China, major administrative laws in Vietnam empower citizens to claim their rights and constrain administrative power. These include, among others, the Law on Administrative Procedures, the Law on Complaints, the Law on Denunciations, the Law on State Compensation Liability, the

[138] ibid.

[139] Nghị Quyết Của Chính Phủ Ban Hành Chiến Lược Quốc Gia Về Phòng Chống Tham Nhũng Đến Năm 2020 [Government's Resolution Issuing National Strategy on Anti-Corruption Till 2020].

[140] Nguyễn Xuân Trường, 'Một Số Vấn Đề Về Kiểm Soát Quyền Lực Để Phòng, Chống Tham Nhũng, Tiêu Cực Ở Việt Nam Hiện Nay' ['Some Issues on Controlling Power to Prevent and Combat Corruption and Negativity in Vietnam Today'] (Trang Thông Tin Điện Tử Tổng Hợp Ban Nội Chính Trung Ương, 27 January 2023), https://noichinh.vn/nghien-cuu-trao-doi/202301/mot-so-van-de-ve-kiem-soat-quyen-luc-de-phong-chong-tham-nhung-tieu-cuc-o-viet-nam-hien-nay-312112> accessed 6 June 2024.

[141] Lê Xuân Lịch, 'Tình hình tham nhũng ở Việt Nam' ['The Situation of Corruption in Vietnam'], (Tạp chí Xây dựng Đảng, 18 July 2022) <https://xaydungdang.org.vn/ly-luan-thuc-tien/tham-nhung-va-nhung-giai-phap-phong-chong-tham-nhung-bai-2-17222> accessed 6 June 2024.

Anti-Corruption Law, and the Law on Access to Information. Let us consider these statutes in greater detail.

1. Law on Administrative Procedures

Before 1996, the socialist state in Vietnam refused to allow courts to review administrative actions due to the influence of socialist legal theory. Socialist legal theory rejected judicial review of administrative actions as the product of the bourgeois doctrine of separation of powers, which is inconsistent with the socialist principle of democratic centralism. In addition, judicial review of administrative actions was considered unnecessary under a socialist society, in which presumably there are conflicting interests between the governors and the governed.[142]

Things have changed since Vietnam introduced the Renovation policy. In 1996, administrative tribunals were created within the provincial people's courts and the SPC, and district courts were allowed to hear administrative cases (although there were no administrative tribunals at the district level). The Ordinance on Procedure for Resolving Administrative Law Cases was enacted in 1996, which allowed for citizens to bring legal cases against certain administrative actions.[143] An enumerative clause in the Ordinance provided for a parsimonious list of administrative actions subject to judicial review, including:

- decisions to impose fines against administrative violations or to apply measures for the compulsory dismantlement of the illegally-built dwelling houses, projects or firmly-structured objects;
- decisions to apply administrative measures in the form of re- education at communes, wards or townships, putting into re-education schools, educational establishments, medical establishments or administrative custody;
- decisions on dismissal, except those concerning the People's Army and decisions on dismissal in accordance with the provisions of the Labour Code;
- administrative decisions or administrative actions concerning the grant and withdrawal of permits and licences in the fields of capital construction, production, business and land management;
- decisions on forcible requisition, forcible purchase and confiscation of assets;
- decisions on tax collection and tax arrears collection;
- decisions on the collection of charges and fees.[144]

Vietnamese lawmakers believed that the enumerative clause was suitable for the Vietnamese socialist context in which there was no experience of judicial review

[142] Van Quang Nguyen, 'Judicially Reviewable Administrative Actions: The Development of Vietnamese Administrative Justice' (2013) 46 Verfassung Und Recht in Übersee 368.

[143] Nguyễn Thị Thủy, 'Pháp Luật Tố tụng Hành chính-Quá trình hình thành và Phát triển' ['Administrative Litigation Law: Creation and Development'] (2007) 5 Tạp chí Luật học 49.

[144] The Ordinance on Procedure for Resolving Administrative Law Cases, art 11.

of administrative law, administrative law was nascent, and there were insufficient judges with expertise to hear administrative law cases.[145] The limited scope of judicial review of administrative actions indicates the Vietnamese socialist state's cautious reform towards empowering courts to review administrative law. The cautious reform is not merely due to legal and personal reasons as provided by the lawmakers but also stems from ideological and political reasons. As judicial administrative review contradicts the socialist principle of democratic centralism, which is hostile to the aggressive confrontation between judicial and administrative agencies, it is understandable that Vietnamese lawmakers were modest in granting courts some limited powers to review administrative actions. Politically, judicial administrative review would provide a mechanism for citizens to challenge administrative agencies. This could encourage citizens' aggressive behaviours vis-à-vis the government, generate social instability, and make it difficult for the government to control citizens' behaviours. These potential consequences explain why Vietnamese legislators were cautious in authorizing courts to review administrative actions.

More than ten years since the Ordinance on Procedure for Resolving Administrative Law Cases was enacted in 1996, the need to reform the system of administrative adjudication arose due to internal and external reasons. Internally, as Van Quang Nguyen observes, 'there were many cases in which the courts dismissed applications for judicial review because the impugned administrative decision or act did not belong to the list of categories for judicial review'.[146] In other words, the limited scope provided by the Ordinance on Procedure for Resolving Administrative Law Cases failed to meet the growing demand from society for expanding the scope of judicial review of administrative actions. Externally, judicial review of administrative actions is the requirement of international agreements (such as the US–Vietnam FTA and the WTO agreement) that Vietnam has signed.[147]

In response to the internal demands and external requirements, the Law on Administrative Procedures was enacted in 2010. The Law significantly expanded the scope of judicial review of administrative actions. It replaced the enumerative clause by a general clause, which provides for judicial reviewability of nearly all specific administrative decisions. The Law also includes comprehensive rules of administrative procedures. The implementation of the 2010 Law on Administrative Procedures resulted in the increasing number of administrative law cases. The number of first-instance administrative cases heard by district and provincial courts in seven years from 2011 to 2017 is indicated in Figure 5.1.[148]

[145] Van Quang Nguyen (n 142) 377.
[146] ibid 379.
[147] ibid 373.
[148] This chart is created by the author based on the sources in Thân Quốc Hùng, Chất Lượng Xét Xử Các Vụ Án Hành Chính Của Tòa Án Nhân Dân Cấp Tỉnh Ở Việt Nam Hiện Nay [The Quality of Hearing Administrative Case of Provincial People's Courts in Vietnam Today] (PhD Dissertation, Ho Chi Minh National Academy of Politics 2018) 84.

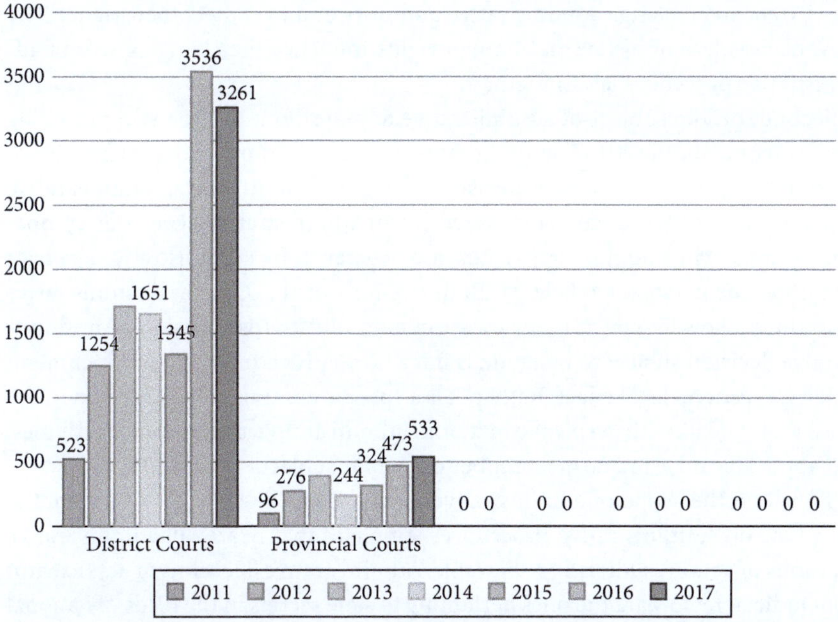

Figure 5.1 Number of First-Instance Administrative Cases 2011–17

The 2010 Law on Administrative Procedures was replaced by a new version in 2015. The replacement was mainly due to the need to reflect the 2013 Constitution's commitment to human rights protection in administrative procedure law. The 2015 version continued substantive features of the 2010 version. Below are important legal issues of Vietnamese administrative adjudication according to the 2015 Law on Administrative Procedures.

First, on the role of administrative procedure law, the 2015 Law on Administrative Procedures provides that the Law 'contributes to safeguarding justice, human rights, citizens' rights, the socialist regime, interests of the State, and lawful rights and interests of agencies, organizations and individuals; educates people in strictly abiding by law; and ensures the stability, continuity and effectiveness of the national administration' (Article 1). On one hand, this provision illustrates socialist legal instrumentalism. The administrative procedures law is an instrument for the state to protect the existing socialist regime and the state's interests and to educate the people. On the other hand, as a reflection of the constitutional commitment to human rights, the 2015 Law on Administrative Procedures seeks to protect 'justice' and 'human rights', which is underlined as the foremost function of the Law. The two preceding legal instruments did not define the role of administrative procedure law in protecting justice and human rights. The 2015 Law on Administrative Procedures tends to recognize that administrative procedure law is not merely an instrument of the state but also a legal framework for the citizens to challenge administrative authority and to protect their rights. The universalist ideas of justice and human rights influence the changing role of administrative procedure law in Vietnam.

Second, on the subject of administrative adjudication, like the two preceding legal instruments, the 2015 Law on Administrative Procedures provides for the distinction between administrative decisions and administrative acts. Administrative decisions are written documents issued by an administrative agency or competent persons, while administrative acts are acts taken by administrative agencies or competent persons (Article 3). Both versions of the Law on Administrative Procedures allow for courts to review specific administrative decisions. An administrative decision subject to litigation is not a normative administrative document, which has general legal effect. Rather, it is a specific administrative decision in the sense that it deals with 'a specific matter in administrative management activities, and applicable once to one or a number of specific subjects' (Article 3).

Third, on the scope of administrative adjudication, like the 2010 version, the 2015 Law on Administrative Procedures stipulates that nearly all administrative decisions or acts are judicially reviewable. Administrative decisions or acts exempt from judicial review are the ones pertaining to state secrets in the fields of national defence, security, and foreign affairs in accordance with law; and internal administrative decisions or acts of agencies and organizations (Article 30). In addition, courts can also review disciplinary decisions on dismissal of civil servants holding the position of general director of a general department or equivalent or lower position; decisions on settlement of complaints about decisions on handling of competition cases; and voter lists (Article 30).

After the enactment of the 2015 Law on Administrative Procedures, the number of administrative law cases continue to rise. During the 2016–20 term, the courts accepted 36,354 cases and handled 32,466. In 2020, the people's courts accepted 12,470 cases and handled 8,582.[149] The administrative cases are mainly related to administrative decisions and acts on land management.[150] The places of administrative litigation have been mainly concentrated in large provinces and cities with rapid economic development such as Hanoi, Ho Chi Minh City, Ba Ria—Vung Tau, Bac Giang, Kien Giang, Long An, Quang Ninh, and Thanh Hoa.[151] The problem is an increasing number of unenforced administrative judgments. The

[149] Vietnam's Supreme People's Court, Báo Cáo Tổng Kết Công Tác Năm 2020 Và Nhiệm Kỳ 2016–2020; Phương Hướng, Nhiệm Vụ Trọng Tâm Công Tác Năm 2021 Của Các Tòa Án [Summary Report of Work in 2020 and Term 2016–2020; Orientation, Key Tasks of the Courts in 2021].

[150] ibid.

[151] Bảo Yến and Nghĩa Đức, 'Ủy Ban Tư Pháp Giám Sát Việc Chấp Hành Pháp Luật Trong Giải Quyết Án Hành Chính—Rõ Thực Trạng, Rõ Địa Chỉ' ['The Judicial Committee Supervises the Observance of the Law in the Settlement of Administrative Judgments—Clear Status, Clear Address'] (Cổng Thông Tin Điện Tử Quốc Hội, 29 July 2022) <https://quochoi.vn/uybantuphap/giamsat/Pages/giam-sat.aspx?ItemID=239>.

number was 224 in 2018, increasing to 339 in 2019, 463 in 2020, and 489 in 2021.[152] Most of the unenforced administrative judgments are in the field of state management of land. Land disputes and complaints have often spanned many years and involved different levels of administrative bodies, which makes it difficult to implement administrative judgments.[153]

2. Laws on Complaints and Denunciations

In 1981, the Vietnamese socialist state already adopted the Ordinance Providing the Consideration and Settlement of Citizen's Complaints and Denunciations, which specified the rules for citizens to lodge complaints against and denounce administrative agencies. In the post-Renovation period, Vietnamese law on complaints and denunciations has been frequently reformed. The 1981 Ordinance was replaced by the new Ordinance on Citizen's Complaints and Denunciations in 1991. This Ordinance was then replaced by the Law on Complaints and Denunciations 1998, which expanded the right to complain and denunciate to individual citizens, public servants, and organs The Law was amended in 2004 and 2005.[154]

In 2011, the Vietnamese legislature adopted two separate laws: the Law on Complaints and the Law on Denunciations. The 2011 Law on Complaints includes seventy articles divided into eight chapters. It establishes a legal framework for the settlement of complaints against administrative decisions and acts (Article 1). The 2011 Law on Denunciations was replaced by the current version in 2018, which was then amended in 2020. The 2018 Law is comprised of sixty-seven articles divided into nine chapters. It codifies legal rules for the settlement of denunciations of legal violations in the performance of administrative duties and state management (Article 1).

The Law on Complaints and the Law on Denunciations both create a legal framework for constraining the abuse of administrative power. However, they are different in nature, which explains their separate enactments. The Law on Complaints allows a citizen, agency, organization, or civil servant to request a competent agency, organization, or person to review an administrative decision or act that they believe is unlawful and infringes upon their rights and lawful interests (Article 2). The Law on Denunciations empowers individuals to notify a

[152] Trần Thị Ngọc Trang, 'Xét Xử Và Thi Hành Án Hành Chính: Quy Định Và Thực Tiễn' ['Adjudication and Execution of Administrative Judgments: Regulations and Practice'] (Vietnam Lawyer Journal, 6 July 2022) <https://lsvn.vn/xet-xu-va-thi-hanh-an-hanh-chinh-quy-dinh-va-thuc-tien1657119359.html> accessed 6 June 2024.

[153] ibid.

[154] Nguyễn Huy Hoàng, 'Quá Trình Hình Thành, Phát Triển Của Hệ Thống Pháp Luật Về Khiếu Nại, Tố Cáo Ở Việt Nam (Phần 2)' ['The Process of Formation and Development of the Legal System on Complaints and Denunciations in Vietnam (Part 2)'] (Trường Cán bộ Thanh Tra, 20 April 2018) <https://truongcanbothanhtra.gov.vn/qua-trinh-hinh-thanh-phat-trien-cua-he-thong-phap-luat-ve-khieu-nai-to-cao-o-viet-nam-phan-2> accessed 6 June 2024.

competent organ or individual of a legal violation committed by any organization or individual in the performance of administrative duties and the management of state affairs (Article 2). The nature of complaints is to request an administrative review of an administrative decision or act that allegedly violates the rights of the complainant. The nature of denunciation is to notify authority of a legal violation (which can be criminal or administrative) in the performance of administrative duties or state management, which does not necessarily infringe on the rights of the denunciator. The complainant can be an individual or an institution, while the denunciator can only be an individual.

The frequent amendments and replacements of the Law on Complaints and Denouncements in Vietnam stem from the growing complaints and denouncements against the abuse of administrative power. To illustrate, in ten years from 1999 to 2008, competent administrative agencies received 129,321 denunciation cases.[155] The number of cases increased and decreased over the years as follows: 1999 (16,216 cases); 2000 (25,132 cases); 2001 (13,385 cases); 2002 (12,128 cases); 2003 (11,496 cases); 2004 (11,153 cases); 2005 (8,841 cases); in 2006 (11,798 cases); 2007 (9,860 cases); 2008 (9,312 cases).[156] The denunciations were against various forms of abuse of administrative power such as corruption, contravening policies and laws in land management, aiding in smuggling and illegal business, hindering up violations of inferior officials, and the unfair implementation of state policies.[157]

The implementation of the two laws on complaints and denunciations resulted in positive protection of citizens' rights. According to a government report in 2016, 'state administrative agencies handled more than 386,500 complaints lodged in 268,225 cases . . . resuming rights for 13,617 citizens who was given back 512 billion VND and 418.6 hectares of land'.[158] However, as documented in a report by the NA on the implementation of the laws on complaints and denunciations from 1 July 2016 to 1 July 2022, complaints and denunciations have been complicated in many areas: particularly land acquisition in localities promoting large public investment projects; real estate business for tourism and commercial real estate projects; production and business establishments that use raw materials; and emissions and wastes causing environmental pollution near residential areas.[159]

[155] Hồ Thị Thu An, 'Áp Dụng Pháp Luật Tố Cáo Và Giải Quyết Tố Cáo – Thực Trạng Và Hướng Hoàn Thiện' ['Applying the Law on Denunciations and Settlement of Denunciations—The Current Situation and Directions for Improvement'] (Nghiên cứu Lập pháp, 1 September 2009) <http://www.lapphap.vn/Pages/TinTuc/211145/Ap-dung-phap-luat-to-cao-va-giai-quyet-to-cao---thuc-trang-va-huong-hoan-thien.html> accessed 6 June 2024.

[156] ibid.

[157] ibid.

[158] 'Laws on Complaints, Denunciation Prove Effectiveness' (Vietnam Pictorial, 16 December 2016) <https://vietnam.vnanet.vn/english/tin-van/laws-on-complaints-denunciation-prove-effectiveness-135823.html>.

[159] 'Quốc Hội Giám Sát Chuyên Đề "Việc Thực Hiện Pháp Luật Về Tiếp Công Dân Và Giải Quyết Khiếu Nại, Tố Cáo Từ Ngày 01/7/2016 Đến Ngày 01/7/2021"' ['The National Assembly Supervises

3. *Law on State Compensation Liability*

Like China, Vietnam has developed a legal framework for citizens to claim state compensation when their rights and interests are infringed upon by state authority. Vietnam adopted the Law on State Compensation Liability in 2009, although before that several legal instruments (such as the 1992 Constitution and the 1995 Civil Code) had provided for state compensation liability. The 2009 version was replaced by another version in 2017.[160]

According to the 2017 Law on State Compensation Liability, individuals and organizations can claim state compensation when they suffer damage caused by legal violations in the exercise of the administrative and judicial powers (Article 1). Article 17 of the Law establishes an extensive scope of compensation liability in administrative management. Accordingly, individuals and organizations can claim state compensation on the ground of the administrative authority's unlawful issuance of decisions on penalties for administrative violations, and unlawful application of measures to prevent and handle administrative violations (Article 17).

In addition, according to the 2017 Law on State Compensation Liability, state compensation can be claimed when administrative agencies and individuals illegally apply remedial measures for administrative violations, including forced dismantling of facilities or parts of facilities that are constructed without licences or inconsistently with the licence; forced elimination of infringement on products, packages, business facilities, or articles; and enforced recall of unqualified products and goods (Article 17).

According to the Law, the state shall also be liable for compensation in the case of unlawful enforcement of decisions on penalties for administrative violations and unlawful application of the measures for administrative violations, including education at communes, wards, district-level towns; and sending individuals to reformatory schools, correctional facilities, and compulsory detoxification centres (Article 17).

The 2017 Law on State Compensation Liability provides that compensation can be claimed when administrative authority fails to apply or illegally applies the measures to protect denouncers according to the Law on Denunciation. These measures include, among others, suspending administrative decisions infringing legitimate rights and interests of denouncers; and resuming positions, income, and other legitimate interests for denouncers at their workplace; and prevention

the Topic "The Implementation of the Law on Receiving Citizens and Settling Complaints and Denunciations from 01/7/2016 to 01/7/2021"'] <https://www.sav.gov.vn/Pages/chi-tiet-tin.aspx?ItemID=39481&l=TinTucSuKien> accessed 6 June 2024.

[160] On the overall development of the law on state compensation liability, see Lê Thái Phương, Trách Nhiệm Bồi Thường Của Nhà Nước Theo Pháp Luật Việt Nam [State Compensation Liability in Vietnamese Law] (PhD Dissertation, Hanoi University of Law 2019) 78–123.

against infringement or threats of infringement on life, health, assets, honour, prestige, and reputation of denouncers (Article 17).

The Law's grounds for the claim of state compensation also include, among others, the administrative authority's committing prohibited acts prescribed in the Law on Information Access—such as providing falsifying information; unlawful issuing, revoking, and non-issuing of certificates of enterprise registration, certificates of household business registration, certificates of registration for investment, licences, and licence-equivalent documents; unlawful imposing of taxes, fees, and charges; unlawful collecting of taxes, fees, and charges; unlawful collecting of tax arrears, paying tax refunds; unlawful collecting of land levies; unlawful applying of customs procedures; unlawful allocating of land, leasing land, or recovering land, permitting land use purpose change, compensating for and supporting ground clearance and resettlement; granting or revoking certificates of rights to use land and own houses and other assets attached to land; and unlawful issuing of decisions on handling of competitions cases (Article 17).

In practice, from 1 January 2010 to 31 December 2015, agencies have received 258 cases claiming damages, of which 204 cases were solved with the state payment of over VND 111 billion (around USD 4.6 million) for compensation.[161] According to the government's annual reports, the number of compensation cases over the years is shown in Table 5.2.

Table 5.2 Number of Compensation Cases[162]

Years	Cases received	Cases handled
01/10/2012–30/09/2013	82	21
01/10/2013–30/09/2014	94	53
01/10/2014–30/09/2015	94	41
01/10/2015–30/09/2016	105	44

In a legislative debate in 2016 on the revised Law on State Compensation Liability, some members of the NA questioned whether the number of compensation cases presented in the government's reports accurately reflect the reality and why some compensation claims were not accepted.[163] In reality, there may be a higher number of compensation cases than the one officially reported. The law and

[161] Lê Thái Phương (n 160) 217.

[162] Author's creation drawn on the data in Lê Thái Phương (n 160) 218–21.

[163] 'Ủy Ban Pháp Luật Thẩm Tra Dự Án Luật Trách Nhiệm Bồi Thường Của Nhà Nước (Sửa Đổi') ['The Law Committee Examines the Project of the Law on State Compensation Liability (Amended)'], (Cổng Thông Tin Điện Tử Quốc Hội, 6 September 2016) <https://quochoi.vn/uybanphapluat/lapphap/pages/home.aspx?ItemID=122>.

practice indicate that Law on State Compensation Liability is an important reform of administrative law in Vietnam.

4. Transparency Laws

The Anti-Corruption Law and the Law on Access to Information were enacted to support transparent governance in Vietnam.

The Anti-Corruption Law was enacted in 2005, amended in 2007 and 2012, and replaced by a new version in 2018. The Law provides rules for good conduct of officials and mechanisms to combat corruption. It does not lay down specific sanctions for non-compliance. For non-compliant acts, the Anti-Corruption Law refers to the Penal Code, the Law on Cadres and State Officials, and the Law on Public Servants for criminal and administrative sanctions.[164]

The 2018 Anti-Corruption Law deals with measures to prevent and discover corruption committed by office holders in both state and non-state organizations (eg state-owned enterprises). I will focus on some main legal issues in the Law regarding corruption committed by office holders in state organizations. According to Article 1 of the Law, acts of corruption committed by office holders in state organizations include:

- Embezzlement;
- Taking bribes;
- Abuse of one's position or power for illegal appropriation of assets;
- Abuse of official capacity during performance of tasks or official duties for personal gain;
- Acting beyond authority in performance of one's duties for personal gain;
- Abuse of official capacity to influence another person for personal gain
- Impersonation for personal gain;
- Bribing or brokering bribery for taking advantage of one's influence over a state organization or for personal gain;
- Illegal use of public assets for personal gain by abuse of official capacity;
- Harassment for personal gain;
- Failure to perform or correctly perform one's duties for personal gain;
- Abuse of official capacity to screen violations of law for person gain; illegally intervening or obstructing supervision, inspection, audit, investigation, prosecution, adjudication or judgment enforcement for personal gain.

The 2018 Anti-Corruption Law establishes numerous mechanisms to prevent corruption committed by office holders in state organizations. These include

[164] Frederick Burke, Chi Anh Tran, and Thuy Duong Van, 'Anti-Corruption in Vietnam' (Baker Mckenzie blog) <https://www.globalcompliancenews.com/anti-corruption/anti-corruption-in-vietnam> accessed 6 June 2024.

information disclosure, implementation of the code of conduct for public holders (which includes social norms, permissible and prohibited actions that are meant to maintain integrity, and responsibility and ethics of office holders) (Article 12); reassignment of managerial officials (Article 24); application of financial and technological measures to reduce use of cash in transactions (Article 29), surveillance of assets and income of public holders (Article 30), public holders' obligation to declare assets and income (Article 33), and inspection of assets and income (Article 41).

The 2018 Anti-Corruption Law also provides for mechanisms to discover corruption committed by office holders in state organizations. These include inspection by regulatory authorities (Article 55); self-inspection by state agencies (Article 56); inspection of anti-corruption activities in inspection agencies, state audit agencies, investigation agencies, the people's procuracies, and people's courts (Article 57); supervision by elected institutions and delegates (Article 59); audit activities (Article 60); and individuals reporting corruption (Article 65).

A related law for transparent governance is the Law on Access to Information enacted in 2016, effective in 2018. The Law allows Vietnamese citizens to enjoy the right to access to government information. It provides that 'All citizens are equal and are not discriminated during the exercise of the right to access to information' (Article 3). More specifically, the Law provides that citizens shall have the rights to be fully, precisely, and timely provided with information, and to file complaints, lawsuits, and denunciations against violations of provisions of the Law on Access to Information (Article 8). Citizens shall have free access to information published by state agencies and can request state agencies to provide information (Article 10).

However, the Law excludes certain information from being accessible to citizens. The inaccessible information comprises information classified as state secrecy, including important information in politics, national defence, national security, foreign affairs, economy, sciences, technology, and other fields as regulated by law (Article 6). Moreover, the inaccessible information includes:

> information which, if published, can cause harm to state interests, cause bad effect to national defense, national security, international relationship, social order and safety, social ethics, social health; likely to cause serious damage to lives, life and property of individuals; information classified as work secrecy, information about internal meetings of state agencies, documents created by state agencies for internal works (Article 6)

The Law on Access to Information presents a cautious move. On one hand, it signals the move to global legal norms promoting information rights and transparent government. On the other hand, the Law adheres to statist ideology. Particularly, it uses broad and vague language to exclude information accessible to individuals for the purpose of state and public interests. The clauses on inaccessible information provide ample room for administrative agencies to regulate access to government information.

C. Convergence and Continuity

The Vietnamese laws on administrative litigation, complaints, denunciations, and state compensation, anti-corruption, and access to information are interrelated. They together provide legal tools for Vietnamese citizens to limit the arbitrary use of administrative power and to hold administrative authority accountable for their misuse of power. Not only can Vietnamese citizens challenge the administrative authority through litigation, complaints, and denunciations: they also enjoy the right to claim state compensation for the damages caused by legal violations in the exercise of administrative power. The citizens are also entitled to report government corruption and they are allowed to access to government information.

Reforms lead to the adoption of global norms of public governance in Vietnamese administrative law. The global norms of transparency, protection of fundamental rights, rule of law, and accountability have been accepted as the standards of administrative law in Vietnam.[165] Particularly, Vietnamese administrative law reform has been strongly informed by the language and concepts of rights and good governance. Consequently, administrative law is now a framework for Vietnamese citizens to subject the use of administrative power to the rule of law, to claim their rights, to challenge the arbitrary use of administrative power, and to hold administrative agencies accountable to the public.

That said, Vietnamese administrative law retains its socialist, instrumentalist, and statist nature. Administrative law in Vietnam does not just empower citizens to curb government action; it also strongly empowers the government to issue regulatory measures to control citizens' behaviours. As indicated, the Law on Access to Information both enables and disables citizens' access to government information. Similarly, various administrative laws allow citizens to litigate, complain, denunciate, and claim state compensation, but they are at the same time the legal tools for the government to control citizens' litigation, complaints, denunciations, and compensation claims. Administrative agencies enjoy the discretion to issue regulatory legal instruments not only to implement the relevant laws but also to control the practice of the relevant rights.

[165] Vũ Thư, 'Tổng Quan Tình Hình Nghiên Cứu Về Lĩnh Vực Luật Hành Chính Trong Hơn 30 Năm Qua' ['An Overview of the Studies of Administrative Law in the Last Over 30 Years'] in Nguyễn Như Phát (eds), *Tổng Quan Tình Hình Nghiên Cứu Về Pháp Luật Ở Việt Nam Trong Hơn 30 Năm Qua [An Overview of Legal Studies in Vietnam in the Last Over 30 Years]* (Social Science Publishing House 2021) 177.

V. JUDICIAL REFORM

A. Judicial Reform Project

Between the 1990s and the early 2000s, Vietnam introduced some sporadic reforms to the court system. After the adoption of the 1992 Constitution, which replaced the 1980 Constitution, the Vietnamese legislature adopted a new Law on Organization of People's Court (LOPC) in 1993, which replaced the 1981 version. Despite constitutional and legal replacements, in the 1990s, the structure of Vietnamese courts was basically the same as the one established by the 1980 Constitution and the 1981 LOPC. Accordingly, the three-tiered court system included the SPC and the local people's courts at provincial and district levels. The local courts were organized according to administrative units. However, some important reforms to the court system occurred in response to the emergence of the socialist market economy. Notably, reforms functionally expanded the jurisdictions of the courts to hearing economic and administrative disputes, and structurally created special economic, labour, and administrative courts.[166] In the early 2000s, the Party proposed measures to deal with emerging judicial issues such as judicial corruption (or the so-called 'negativity' in the courts) and the shortage and low quality of judges.[167] Concomitantly, the new LOPC was enacted in 2002, replacing the 1993 version. The 2002 LOPC introduced major reforms, including chief justices' appointments of local judges, and the requirement of a Bachelor of Laws degree for appointment of judges.[168] The above reforms indicate that the political elite adopted the classical incremental strategy to introduce some sporadic adjustments to the court system.

In 2005, the Party issued the long-term judicial reform campaign called The Strategy for Judicial Reform until 2020.[169] The Strategy is a neo-incremental strategy of judicial reform, which projects an overall plan for judicial reform to be implemented gradually over fifteen years. The Party recognized that after the Renovation the judicial reform had been achieved to a certain extent, which contributed, among other things, to 'creation of state environment for economic development, and international integration'.[170] Yet, there remained serious problems that the Party attempted to tackle, for which it issued the Strategy. One of the fundamental positions of the Strategy is that: 'judicial reform must stem from

[166] Nguyễn Thu Hiền (ed), *Giáo trình Lịch sử Tòa án Việt Nam [Textbook on The History of Vietnamese Courts]* (Vietnam National University-Hanoi Publishing House 2019) 32–40.

[167] Bộ Chính Trị, 'Nghị Quyết Về "Một Số Nhiệm Vụ Trọng Tâm Công Tác Tư Pháp Trong Thời Gian Tới"' ['Resolution on "Some Urgent Tasks of Judicial Work in the Next Time"' Số 08-Nq/Tư (2002).

[168] Nicholson, 'Renovating Courts' (n 5), 531–32.

[169] Nghị Quyết 49-Nq/Tw Của Bộ Chính Trị Về Chiến Lược Cải Cách Tư Pháp Đến Năm 2020 [Politburo's Resolution No 49-Nq/Tw on the Strategy for Judicial Reform Until 2020].

[170] ibid.

the imperatives of socioeconomic development and building up equality, democracy, and civilization, and must contribute to the promotion of socio-economic development'.[171] So, the Party explicitly attempted to reform the judicial institution to promote socio-economic development. On that basis, the Strategy focused on reorganizing the court system to make it more independent from the local government, increasing the quality of judicial staff and ensuring financial conditions for judicial activities, among others.[172]

To assist the implementation of this programme, in 2011 the Party created the Steering Central Commission for Judicial Reform headed by the president of state. In 2014, the Commission reviewed eight years of implementation of the judicial reform campaign and recommended moving forward. The Politburo then issued a Conclusion on the continuing implementation of the programme and clarified further directions.[173] In the Party's review, the judicial reform has been achieved to a certain extent, including consolidation of the court system, clarification of judicial functions and duties, empowerment of the district courts, extension to hearing administrative litigations, increase in the quality and quantity of judicial staffs, renovation of judicial infrastructure, and others.[174] But several policies proposed in the Strategy have not yet been implemented, and new policies arise. The Conclusion therefore attempts to accelerate judicial reform by separating local courts from local administrative units to promote judicial independence from local government's interference, 'mutual controlling' among different bodies (such as the courts, procuracies, and investigation agents), and enhancing the material conditions for the judicial system.[175]

B. New Legislation for Court Reform

Following the adoption of the 2013 Constitution, a new LOPC was enacted in 2014, replacing the 2002 version. The 2013 Constitution and the 2014 LOPC introduce significant conceptual, structural, and functional changes to the Vietnamese court system. The reform of the constitutional and legal framework for the Vietnamese courts is conceptually underpinned by global norms on the rule of law, human rights, justice, judicial power, judicial independence, adversarial trials, and legal equality.

[171] ibid.
[172] ibid.
[173] Kết Luận Về Việc Tiếp Tục Thực Hiện Nghị Quyết Số 49-Nq/Tw, Ngày 2/6/2005 Của Bộ Chính Trị Khóa Ix Về Chiến Lược Cải Cách Tư Pháp Đến Năm 2020 [Conclusion on the Continuing Implementation of Politburo's Resolution No 49-Nq/Tw on the Strategy for Judicial Reform Until 2020].
[174] ibid.
[175] ibid.

The first change concerns the reconceptualization of the nature and role of Vietnamese courts. The 2014 LOPC redefines courts as 'judicial bodies' that 'exercise judicial power' (Article 2) echoing Article 102 of the new 2013 Constitution. In the context of Vietnam's rejection of the separation of power in favour of concentrated power,[176] the new definition of judicial power has a substantive meaning: institutions other than courts cannot exercise judicial power, which enables the operational independence of the judicial power. Vietnamese leadership also recognizes this operational dimension of judicial independence.[177] The recognition of functional independence of courts is a response to the reality that non-judicial bodies (including the governmental institutions and the party institutions) have often interfered into the practice of the judicial power by courts.[178]

The second jurisprudential change concerns the role of the courts in upholding justice and protecting human rights. The 2014 LOPC states that the foremost role of the courts is 'to safeguard justice, [and] human rights' (Article 2), which echoes Article 102 of the 2013 Constitution. In the context of Vietnamese authoritarianism where courts were normally conceived as the instrument to protect the regime and state interests, the constitutional and legal mandate of courts as the bodies to protect justice and human rights presents a significant jurisprudential development.

In addition to new concepts about the nature and role of the courts, the 2013 Constitution and the 2014 LOPC also introduce new principles and concepts about judicial procedure, namely judicial independence, adversarial trials, and legal equality.

First, the 2013 Constitution further consolidates the operational independence of the judiciary, providing that 'During a trial, the Judges and Assessors are independent and shall obey only the law. Agencies, organizations or individuals are prohibited from interfering in a trial by Judges and People's Assessors' (Article 103). The 2014 LOPC goes further to provide for the protection for this principle: 'Individuals, agencies and organizations that commit acts of interfering in trials conducted by judges and assessors shall, depending on the nature and severity of their acts, be disciplined, administratively sanctioned or examined for penal liability in accordance with law' (Article 9).

[176] Bùi Văn Học, 'Tam Quyền Phân Lập Không Phù Hợp Với Thể Chế Chính Trị Ở Nước Ta' ['Separation of Three Powers is Not Suited to Our Political System'] (An Ninh Thủ đô, 9 September 2013) <http://anninhthudo.vn/chinh-tri-xa-hoi/tam-quyen-phan-lap-khong-phu-hop-voi-the-che-chinh-tri-o-nuoc-ta/515038.antd> [<https://perma.cc/7BP8-UGK2>] accessed 6 June 2024.

[177] Trương Hòa Bình, 'Độc Lập Tư Pháp Trong Nhà Nước Pháp Quyền XHCN, Bảo Đảm Cho Tòa Án Thực Hiện Đúng Đắn Quyền Tư Pháp' ['Judicial Independence in the Socialist Rule of Law, Ensuring the Proper Exercise of Judicial Power by the Court'] (Nhân Dân, 9 September 2014) <https://nhandan.vn/doc-lap-tu-phap-trong-nha-nuoc-phap-quyen-xhcn-bao-dam-cho-toa-an-thuc-hien-dung-dan-quyen-tu-phap-post212835.html>accessed 6 June 2024.

[178] See Mark Sidel, 'Property, State Corruption, and the Judiciary: The Do Son Land Case and Its Implications' in Hue-Tam Ho Tai and Mark Sidel (eds), *State, Society and The Market in Contemporary Vietnam: Property, Power and Values* (Routledge 2013) 124.

Second, the 2013 Constitution introduces the principle of adversarial trials: 'The adversarial principle shall be guaranteed in trials' (Article 103). This is also confirmed in Article 13 of the 2014 LOPC. The introduction of the principle of adversarial trials, a feature of common law, into the Vietnamese socialist legal system characterized by highly inquisitorial trials,[179] is notable.

Third, the 2013 Constitution guarantees the principle that 'all people are equal before law' (Article 16) and the 2014 LOPC further provides for the application of the principle of equality in legal proceedings: 'Courts shall conduct trials on the principle that everyone is equal before law, regardless of his/her ethnicity, sex, belief, religion, social class and position; individuals, agencies and organizations are all equal before court' (Article 12).

According to the 2014 LOPC, the overall structure of the Vietnamese court system has been significantly reformed. While the 2002 LOPC provided for a three-tiered system of ordinary courts (Article 2), the 2014 LOPC establishes a four-tiered system comprised of: (1) the SPC; (2) the high people's courts (the courts of appeal); (3) the provincial people's courts (the courts of appeal and first instance); and (4) the district people's courts (the courts of first instance) (Article 2). Notably, there are important changes to the SPC. The general trend is to make the apex court not a court of ordinary trials but the institutional locus to ensure the uniform application of law, develop precedents, and supervise and manage lower courts. This is achieved by the following reforms.

First, according to the 2014 LOPC, one of the foremost functions of the SPC is to develop judicial precedents, that is '[t]o select its cassation trial decisions and judgments and decisions of courts which have taken legal effect and are of standard nature, summarize and develop them into court precedents and publicize court precedents for courts to study and apply in trial' (Article 22). Second, the court no longer hears appellate trials, and therefore the internal structure of the highest court no longer has special courts.

Third, as the consequence of the two former changes, the number of judges in the court has been significantly reduced from 120, according to the previous law, to a maximum of 17 pursuant to the current law.[180] Fourth, the appointment process has changed: the chief justice is appointed by the NA as done previously,[181] but the rest of the judges of the court must be approved by the NA before being appointed by the president sf State.[182] In reality, the presidential appointment is formalistic.

[179] Tim Lindsey and Pip Nicholson, *Drugs Law and Legal Practice in Southeast Asia: Indonesia, Singapore and Vietnam* (Hart Publishing 2016) 252.

[180] Nam Phương, 'Tòa Án Nhân Dân Trong Tiến Trình Cải Cách Tư Pháp' [People's Courts in the Judicial Reform Process] (Công Lý, 14 September 2016) <http://congly.vn/hoat-dong-toa-an/cai-cach-tu-phap/toa-an-nhan-dan-trong-tien-trinh-cai-cach-tu-phap-172960.html> [<https://perma.cc/7WUQ-966U>] accessed 6 June 2024.

[181] Compare Law on Organization of People's Courts (2002), arts 40(1) and 40(3) with Law on Organization of People's Courts (2014), arts 26 and 72

[182] Law on Organization of People's Courts (2014), arts 26 and 72.

Backed by the approval of the NA, the highest body of the state, which is popularly elected by the people according to the 2013 Constitution (Article 69), the seventeen judges of the SPC, constituting the Council of Justices, have a more legitimate base to exercise their judicial power.

C. Trends in Court Reform

After decades of reform, Vietnam has established a stable court system capable of handling various types of social disputes. Major trends in court reform in Vietnam include structural institutionalization, structural specialization, personal professionalization, and functional legalization.

1. *Structural Institutionalization*

A notable trend is structural institutionalization: the creation and consolidation of a stable court system in Vietnam. After decades of reform, the Vietnamese four-tiered people's court system now includes the SPC, three high people's courts, sixty-three provincial people's courts, and 702 district people's courts.[183] The high people's courts are created in 2015, based in Hanoi, Danang, and Ho Chi Minh City, which are respectively responsible for twenty-eight provinces in the North, twenty-one provinces in Central and Central Highlands, twenty-three provinces in the South.[184] The high courts are regional courts with each court hearing appeals from different provinces. The provincial people's and district people's courts are not regionally created: rather, they are created corresponding to administrative units. Each provisional or district court will hear cases within the respective administrative unit. Apart from the people's courts, military courts are created at various levels within the Vietnam People's Army.

The internal structure of the Vietnamese courts is also well institutionalized. It generally includes three types of institutions: managerial institutions (eg the justice council or judge committee), adjudicating institutions (eg civil and criminal courts), and supporting institutions assisting adjudication and court management.

2. *Structural Specialization*

Like China, the creation and consolidation of *special courts* is a notable trend in Vietnamese judicial reform. Before the Renovation, there were only civil and

[183] Vietnam's Supreme People's Court, Báo Cáo Tổng Kết Thực Tiễn Thi Hành Luật Tổ Chức Tòa Án Nhân Dân Năm 2014 [Draft Report on Summary of Implementation Practices Law on Organization of People's Courts 2014] (2023) 3.

[184] Nghị quyế t số 957/NQ-UBTVQH13 Thành Lập Tòa Án Nhân Dân Cấp Cao, ngày 28/5/2015 của Ủy ban Thường vụ Quốc hộI [Resolution No 957/NQ-UBTVQH13 on the Establishment of High People's Court, issued by the National Assembly's Standing Committee, dated 28 May 2015].

criminal courts created according to the 1981 LOPC. In the Renovation era, four other special courts were created, including the Economic Court, the Labor Court, the Administrative Court, and the Family and Juvenile Court. Before the 2014 LOPC, the special courts were created within the SPC and the provincial people's courts. The 2014 Law adopts significant changes to special courts. Accordingly, the special courts are not created at the SPC since this court is no longer a trial and appellate court. In addition, the special courts are created at the three lower levels of the people's courts, with the exception that the Economic Court and the Labor Court are not established at the district people's courts.

The creation and consolidation of the special courts in Vietnam is animated by the emergence of various disputes between citizens and between citizens and government agencies as the consequence of domestic social and economic transformation and international integration in the Renovation era. To illustrate, the Economic Court was created in 1994 in response to the growing economic disputes generated by the post-Renovation development of various public and private economic sectors and various forms of ownership. Market development also generated growing labour disputes on various issues (eg employment, salary, and work conditions), which led to the creation of the Labor Court in 1993. The Administrative Court was created in 1996 in response to the growing disputes between the citizens and administrative agencies around the late 1980s and the early 1990s. More recently, the 2014 LOPC provided for the creation of the Family and Juvenile Court in response to domestic dynamics, particularly the growing minor offences, child sexual abuse, family violations, and divorces. The Family and Juvenile Court was also created to implement Vietnam's international commitments to the protection of children's rights according to the Convention on the Rights of the Child, which Vietnam ratified in 1990.[185]

3. *Personal Professionalization*

In the Renovation era, Vietnam implemented measures of judicial reform to deal with the dearth of judges after wars. Consequently, the numbers of court judges and staff have increased, especially after the launch of the Party's judicial reform strategy in 2005. In a decade, the number of judges increased from 4,141 in 2006 to 4,957 in 2015.[186] By April 2022, the Vietnamese people's courts were staffed by 13,360 people, including: 6,179 judges; 6,819 examiners, clerks, and the

[185] Nguyễn Thu Hiền (n 166) 34–37; Pip Nicholson and Minh Duong, 'Legitimacy and the Vietnamese Economic Courts' in Andrew Harding and Pip Nicholson (eds), *New Courts in Asia* (Routledge 2010) 31; Vũ Thư, 'Sự Hình Thành Và Phát Triển Của Tư Pháp Hành Chính Ở Nước Ta' ['The Creation and Development of Administrative Adjudication in Our Country'] (2003) 33 Nghiên Cứu Lập Pháp 23–28; Lữ Thị Hằng, 'Mô Hình Toà Gia Đình Và Người Chưa Thành Niên Ở Việt Nam Và Hàn Quốc—Nhìn Từ Góc Độ Luật So Sánh' ['The Model of the Family and Juvenile Court in Vietnam and Korea: A Comparative Perspective'] (2019) 377 Nghiên Cứu Lập Pháp 59.

[186] Nicholson, 'Renovating Courts' (n 5) 536; Nguyễn Thu Hiền (n 166) 190.

equivalent; and 504 other titles. The SPC has 405 people, including: 16 justices; 389 examiners, clerks, and the equivalent. The 3 high people's courts have 312 people, including: 101 high judges; 210 examiners, clerks, and the equivalent; and 1 other title. The 63 provincial people's courts have 3,284 people, including: 1,186 Judges; 1,996 examiners, clerk, and the equivalent; and 102 other titles. The 702 district people's courts have 9,306 people, including: 5,156 judges; 3,983 examiners, clerks, and equivalents; and 167 other titles.[187] The SPC still reported a shortage of judges and court staff due to the courts' huge workload.[188]

As the consequence of judicial reform, Vietnamese courts are staffed with more professional personnel. Due to the shortage of judges after wars, the organic laws on courts in 1981 and 1993 did not require judges to have a law degree. However, law graduates increasingly replaced soldiers to become judges. Since 2002, the reformed law requires judges to have a Bachelor of Laws, legal experience, and competent adjudicating training.[189] Nowadays, 100% of first-time appointed judges have degrees in law and adjudicating trainings.[190]

Many reform measures were carried out to increase judicial training and qualifications. The judicial examinations were introduced in 2014 for the selection and promotion of judges.[191] For example, in 2020, 243 candidates passed an exam for selecting primary judges.[192] Also, the Court College created in 1994 was upgraded to the Court Academy in 2015, which conducts legal training (undergraduate and postgraduate), adjudicating training, and vocational training for court leaders, judges, and court staff.[193] The Academy is composed of thirteen faculties and departments and eighty-eight staff and lecturers. It has 5 undergraduate courses in law with 1,428 students.[194]

Other efforts to foster professionalism among judges and court staff include overseas, foreign languages and informatics, and monthly online professional skills training.[195] Finally, to enhance judicial professionalism, in 2018, the Chief Justice of the SPC promulgated the Code of Ethical Standards and Conduct of Judges as the basis for judges to train themselves and for managerial agencies to evaluate, reward, and discipline judges.[196] The ethical standards covered in the

[187] Vietnam's Supreme People's Court (n 183) 7.
[188] ibid.
[189] Nicholson, 'Renovating Courts' (n 5) 4.
[190] Vietnam's Supreme People's Court (n 183) 8.
[191] P Nicholson and NH Quang, 'Independence, Impartiality and Integrity of the Judiciary in Vietnam' in HP Lee and Marilyn Pittard (eds), *Asia-Pacific Judiciaries: Independence, Impartiality and Integrity* (CUP 2017) 379–80.
[192] 'Công Nhận 243 Thí Sinh Trúng Tuyển Kỳ Thi Tuyển Chọn Thẩm Phán Sơ Cấp' ['Recognition of 243 Candidates Who Passed the Primary Judge Selection Exam'], [Tạp Chí Tòa Án Nhân Dân Điện Tử, 28 April 2020] <https://tapchitoaan.vn/cong-nhan-243-thi-sinh-trung-tuyen-ky-thi-tuyen-chon-tham-phan-so-cap> accessed 6 June 2024.
[193] Vietnam's Supreme People's Court (n 183) 13–14.
[194] ibid 14–15.
[195] ibid 14; Nguyễn Thu Hiền (n 166) 59.
[196] Vietnam's Supreme People's Court (n 183) 13.

Code include independence, integrity, impartiality, objectivity, fairness, equality, decency, dedication without delay, competence, and diligence.[197]

4. Functional Legalization

Vietnamese courts are now not merely a tool for political control but a legal institution for resolving legal disputes. Judicial reform efforts lead to the legalization of the functions of Vietnamese courts. The functional legalization of the Vietnamese courts is demonstrated in the courts' capacity to resolve a huge number of legal cases (including civil and commercial cases), legal protections of judicial independence, the adoption of adversarial trials and fair trial rights, the publication of courts' judgements and decisions, and the creation of the judicial precedents system.

Vietnamese courts have the capacity to resolve a vast number of legal disputes. In ten years (2005–15), the people's courts accepted 2,999,747 cases and decided 2,844,515 cases.[198] From 1 June 2015 to 30 April 2022, the courts handled 3,187,285 cases of all kinds.[199] The courts are capable of resolving different types of legal cases, including: criminal; civil, marriage, family, business, commercial, and labour (collectively categorized as civil); and administrative. To illustrate, during the term 2016–20, the courts solved 384,209 criminal cases, 1,842,684 civil cases, and 32,466 administrative cases. [200] The courts are capable of deciding increasing numbers of different types of cases they have accepted. To illustrate, consider the numbers of cases the courts accepted (labelled as A) and decided (labelled as D) over five years from 2018 to 2022, as shown in Table 5.3.

Table 5.3 Case Numbers of Different Types: 2018–22[201]

Years	2022	2021	2020	2019	2018
Criminal	93,452 A 91,312 D	88,607 A 79,409 D	89,726 A 87,770 D	83,239 A 80,280 D	83,118 A 80,566 D
Civil	444,402 A 386,944 D	411,299 A 324,813 D	471,581A 419.793 D	432,666 A 379,441 D	439,546 A 386,923 D
Administrative	11,746 A 8,524 D	10,728 A 5,693 D	11,470 A 8,582 D	10,785 A 7,142 D	10,506 A 6,575 D

[197] Bộ Quy tắc về chuẩ n mực đạo đức và ứng xử của Thẩm phán [Code of Ethical Standards and Conduct of Judges] (2018), arts 3, 4, 5, 6, 7, 8, and 9.

[198] Nguyễn Thu Hiền (n 166) 64.

[199] Vietnam's Supreme People's Court (n 183) 9.

[200] Vietnam's Supreme People's Court, Báo Cáo Tổng Kết Công Tác Năm 2020 Và Nhiệm Kỳ 2016–2020; Phương Hướng, Nhiệm Vụ Trọng Tâm Công Tác Năm 2021 Của Các Tòa Án [Report on Summary of Work in 2020 and Term 2016–2020; Direction, Central Tasks of the Courts' Work in 2021] (2020).

[201] Sources: author's compilation from Vietnam's Supreme People's Court's Annual Reports from 2018 to 2022 (in Vietnamese).

The numbers of civil cases are highest. The fact that the courts can handle hundreds of thousands of civil, marriage, family, business, commercial, and labour cases indicates that they function as legal institutions resolving private legal disputes, rather than merely as political institutions for the regime's stability. The rate of court decisions is high in criminal and civil cases, while it is lower in administrative cases. For example, in 2022, the rate of the decision courts of criminal, civil, and administrative cases is 97.71%, 87.07 %, and 72.6% respectively. The rate in 2021 is 98.62% (criminal), 79% (civil), and 53.1% (administrative).[202] The high rate of decided cases denotes that the courts are capable of handling the numerous legal disputes brought to them. The rate is lower in administrative cases due to their complications as mentioned above. However, thousands of decided administrative cases suggest that the courts can function as the legal arbiters of disputes between the citizens and government agencies.

Some important measures of judicial reform were implemented to provide for legal protections of the courts' independence from political and administrative influence, making courts legal institutions. Judicial independence is not merely confirmed as a constitutional principle. Some limited reforms provide concrete legal protections of courts from administrative and political influence. These reforms include, for example, the extension of judges' second terms from five to ten years since 2014[203] and the change from political (by the president of state) to judicial (by the chief justice of the SPC) appointments to and dismissals from district and provincial courts' judges since 2002.[204]

Another aspect of the legalization of the courts' function is that, while Vietnamese inquisitorial trial model remains dominant, judicial reform led to the incorporation of elements of the common law style of adversarial procedure. For example, the 2015 Criminal Procedure Code adopts the defence's right to collect and present evidence, the principle of presenting arguments and examination of evidence at trial, and the accused's right to remain silent.[205] Adversarial trials make courts function as legal institutions. They subject courts to the control of legal procedures and reduce the administrative and political influences on courts' decisions behind the scenes.

The legal aspect of Vietnamese courts is also demonstrated by the limited publication of court adjudgments and decisions. The SPC has published its legally effective judgments and decisions on its website. By June 2024, 1,432,070 judgments and decisions had been published, including: 295, 222 criminal judgments; 265,328 civil judgments; 721,227 marriage and family judgments; 25,267 business

[202] Vietnam's Supreme People's Court's Annual Reports in 2022 and 2021 (in Vietnamese).

[203] Law on Organization of People's Courts (2014), art 74.

[204] Nicholson, 'Renovating Courts' (n 5) 532.

[205] Võ Minh Kỳ, 'Các Yếu Tố Tranh Tụng Trong Mô Hình Tố Tụng Thẩm Vấn Truyền Thống Của Việt Nam' ['Adversarial Elements in the Traditional Model of Inquisitorial Trial in Vietnam'] (2020) 407 Nghiên Cứu Lập Pháp 16.

and commercial judgments; 17.168 administrative judgments; 5.690 labour judgments; 140 decisions declaring bankruptcy; and 102.028 decisions on applying administrative measures.[206] The publication of the judicial judgments and decisions seeks to enhance publicity and transparency in judicial functioning, to prevent judicial corruption, and to implement the constitutional right to access to information.[207] Efforts to enhance courts' publicity and transparency make them function according to pronounced legal rules.

The judicial precedents also demonstrate the legal functions of the Vietnamese courts. Since 2015 the SPC of Vietnam (SPCV) has created a formal system of precedent, issuing sixty-three precedents by March 2023, which have been widely applied by other courts throughout the country. Precedents in Vietnam are defined as

> arguments and rulings written on effective judgments or decisions of the courts that are selected by the Council of Justices of the Supreme People's Court and published by the Chief Justice of the Supreme People's Court in order for other courts to study and adopt them when deciding later cases.[208]

The Vietnamese precedent system indicates the role of the judiciary in protecting justice or fairness. Precedents are selected on the basis of whether they can protect justice. Most precedents are based on the highest court's repeal of appeal decisions or judgments, mainly for the reasons that they fail to protect the legitimate rights and interests of the parties and other concerned persons.[209] Upon examination, the precedents try to protect the interests of parties and concerned persons.

5. *Judicial Convergence*

Judicial reform in Vietnam has been undertaken corresponding to the economic reform. Economic growth has engendered social complexity, which in turn creates more economic and civil disputes. The conventional informal dispute resolution mechanisms like meditations and social negotiations may still be employed but are insufficient to resolve new disputes. The court system has therefore been reformed to meet with new demands generated by socio-economic development, although it does not replace the conventional informal mechanisms. The introduction of the

[206] Trang Thông tin Điện tử Công bố Bản án, Quyết định của Toà án [Website for Publication of Court Judgments and Decisions] <https://congbobanan.toaan.gov.vn> accessed 6 June 2024.

[207] Vietnam's Supreme People's Court (n 183) 10.

[208] Nghị quyết về quy Trình Lựa Chọn, Công Bố Và Áp Dụng Án Lệ [Resolution Regarding the Selection, Announcement and Application of the Order] (issued by the Council of Justices of the Supreme People's Court, effective 18 June, 2019) art 1.

[209] Nguyen Hong Hai, 'Court Precedents in Vietnam: A View from the Building of the 2015 Civil Code' (Vietnam Law & Legal Forum, 31 July 2017) <http://vietnamlawmagazine.vn/court-precedents-in-vietnam-a-view-from-the-building-of-the-2015-civil-code-5959.html> [<https://perma.cc/EEZ2-GKLH>] accessed 6 June 2024.

economic courts in Vietnam to deal with economic disputes is a specific example. Political leaders in Vietnam expressly realize the need of judicial reform to promote socio-economic development.

Judicial reform in Vietnam is informed by global judicial norms. Consequently, the Vietnamese court system now converges with common judicial norms unconventional to socialist courts. These norms include the nature of courts as the body exercising judicial power, the function of courts as legal institutions to protect justice and human rights, judicial independence, adversarial trials, fair trial rights, and judicial precedents.

Convergence in Vietnamese judicial reform is a part of the broader picture of legal convergence in Vietnamese legal reform. Judicial convergence is shaped by political elites' internal intention to move the Vietnamese courts closer to universal norms. For example, writing in a Party journal, Chief Justice Trương Hòa Bình proposes that 'It is necessary to refer to the universal international conception of judicial power in countries around the world to perfect the [Vietnamese] legal institutions.'[210] This convergent attitude explains why Vietnamese judicial reform is receptive to universal judicial norms.

Judicial convergence in Vietnam is also due to external influences of foreign governments and international agencies. A wide range of international donors provided 'technical assistance' for Vietnam's SPC. These donors included Japan International Cooperation Agency (JICA), Korea International Cooperation Agency (KOICA), UNDP, UNICEF, US Agency for International Development (USAID), Australian Agency for International Development (AusAID), Danish International Development Agency (DANIDA), Canadian International Development Agency (CIDA), World Bank, and World Financial Corporation.[211] South Korea is particularly active in supporting judicial reform in Vietnam. Since 2008, KOICA implemented many projects to support judicial and legal trainings educations in Vietnam, including supporting the facilities of the Court Academy and sending Vietnamese judges and court staff to South Korea for judicial and legal trainings and educations.[212] International involvement in Vietnamese judicial reform results in the incorporation of common judicial norms into the Vietnamese court system.

[210] Nguyễn Hòa Bình, 'Đổi Mới Tổ Chức Và Hoạt Động Của Tòa Án Nhân Dân Các Cấp Trong Xây Dựng, Hoàn Thiện Nhà Nước Pháp Quyền Xã Hội Chủ Nghĩa Việt Nam' ['Renovating the Organization and Operation of People's Courts at All Levels in Building and Perfecting the Socialist Rule-of-Law State of Vietnam'] (Tạp chí Cộng Sản, 7 February 2023) <https://www.tapchicongsan.org.vn/web/guest/media-story/-/asset_publisher/V8hhp4dK31Gf/content/doi-moi-to-chuc-va-hoat-dong-cua-toa-an-nhan-dan-cac-cap-trong-xay-dung-hoan-thien-nha-nuoc-phap-quyen-xa-hoi-chu-nghia-viet-nam#> accessed 6 June 2024.

[211] Nguyễn Thu Hiền (n 166) 71; Vietnam's Supreme People's Court (n 183).

[212] Interview with a lecturer of the Court Academy, 15 May 2023, Vietnam.

D. Vietnamese Socialist Courts

Despite convergence, the Vietnamese courts remain socialist courts. They are the institutional embodiment of socialist legal concepts and principles, particularly legal instrumentalism, party vanguardism, and democratic centralism. This section explores the general embodiment of socialist principles in the Vietnamese courts and specific embodiment in the personal judicial power and judicial precedent system.

1. The Socialist Courts

The Vietnamese courts are the institutional embodiment of legal instrumentalism. Pip Nicholson rightly observes that 'The contemporary Vietnamese court is concurrently a legal and political institution. Legal in that ideally it is bound by law, political in that ultimately it works for the Party-state and must resolve matters in accordance with a complex hierarchy of influences, only one of which is law.'[213] The 2014 LOPC provides that 'People's courts have the duty to safeguard justice, human rights, citizens' rights, the socialist regime, the interests of the State, and the lawful rights and interests of organizations and individuals' (Article 1). Thus, Vietnamese courts are not merely legal institutions for delivering justice; they are also political institutions to protect the socialist regime and state interests. The socialist courts serve political-instrumental purposes through their adjudicative function. Particularly, the adjudications of politically sensitive cases are instrumental to the regime's security and the state's interests.

However, due to its instrumental nature, the socialist courts in Vietnam do not merely have adjudicative function. They also have educational function. The 2014 LOPC provides that: 'Through their activities, courts shall contribute to educating citizens in the loyalty to the Fatherland, strict observance of law, respect for rules of social conduct and the sense of struggle to prevent and combat crimes and other violations' (Article 1). This provision presents the legacy of socialist, Soviet law in contemporary Vietnam.[214] The socialist courts in Vietnam are an instrument to foster the civic loyalty to the country. The socialist courts educate the citizens to facilitate the state's rule of the citizens by law through the demands of strict observance of law and punishments of violations of law. The educational function of the courts in Vietnam has been performed by the courts' organizing mobile trials in the areas where the offences occurred (not in the court buildings), the courts' conducting meetings to propagandize new laws, and even the TV show *Sentencing Court*.[215]

[213] Nicholson, 'Renovating Courts' (n 5) 562.
[214] Harold J Berman, 'The Educational Role of the Soviet Court' (1972) 21 Int'l & Comp LQ 81, 83.
[215] Vũ Hùng, 'Tòa Án Đã Làm Tốt Phổ Biến, Giáo Dục Pháp Luật' ['Courts Have Done Well in Legal Education and Popularization'] (Tạp Chí Tòa Án Nhân Dân Điện Tử, 9 August 2019) <https://www.tapchitoaan.vn/toa-an-da-lam-tot-pho-bien-giao-duc-phap-luat>accessed 6 June 2024.

The instrumental nature of the Vietnamese socialist courts creates the political limits for court reform. On one hand, the party-state has carried out measures of court reform to make the courts a better legal venue to deliver justice. On the other hand, the party-state would make sure that court reform should not go so far as to make the courts an independent venue for the citizens to challenge the party-state. Consequently, court power is limited: the courts are not allowed to adjudicate the constitutionality and legality of legislation and the government's normative legal instruments. This means the socialist courts in Vietnam are not the platform for the citizens to challenge the legislative and executive actions. In addition, the courts are placed under political-institutional control. The highest court is subject to political supervision of the legislature. Local courts are subject to the political supervision of corresponding local people's councils. Consequently, court reform can improve some functional independence of the courts, while the structural dependence of the courts to political institutions is reserved.

The Vietnamese courts are also the embodiment of Party vanguardism. The Party decides policy for court reform. The courts operate under Party leadership. The Party nominates senior party members to hold key leadership positions in the court system. The current chief justice is a member of the Political Bureau, the Party's top decision-making body. This enables the Party to control the chief justice particularly and the whole court system generally. Every judge must be a Party member, although this is not explicitly stated in law. The political requirement of Party membership is to ensure that judges are committed to the protection of the socialist regime.[216] Party groups are set up within the courts to direct the courts to implement Party lines. Courts normally report to and request guiding opinions from party groups with respect to 'big, politically sensitive cases'.[217] These cases include not only criminal cases but also civil cases, which may have a broader effect in the society.[218]

The Vietnamese court structure is underpinned by the principle of democratic centralism. Democratic centralism generates two important consequences to the courts. First, Vietnamese courts are subordinate institutions. Second, to control the court system, the party and the government must control its highest body. The SPC becomes a weak institution externally and a strong institution internally. Externally, the Court is subordinate to the Party and the executive, operating as an instrument for the latter to control the society and behaviours of citizens to make sure that party policy is implemented consistently throughout society and citizens

[216] Interview with a local judge, 19 April 2023, Vietnam.

[217] Vietnam's People' Supreme Court, 'Báo cáo Kết Quả Cải cách tư pháp Tại Tòa án Nhân dân trong Gian Đoạn 2005–2021' ['Report on Judicial Reform Outcomes at People's Courts in Interval 2005–2021'] in Nguyễn Hòa Bình(ed), *Cải cách Tư pháp tại Tòa án Nhân Dân Việt Nam trong giai đoạn mới [Judicial Reform in the Vietnamese People's Courts in the New Period]* (National Politics Publishing House, 2022) 71.

[218] Interview with a judge of the Vietnam's People's Supreme Court, on 15 March 2023, Vietnam.

cannot use the courts to change Party and government actions. Internally, the SPC is the powerful institution that controls the whole court system.

To be more specific, let us consider the embodiment of democratic centralism in the Vietnamese system of judicial precedents. Democratic centralism determines the instrumental rationale for the socialist precedent system. The precedent system operates as the centralized tool for the SPCV to control the work of local courts to improve the quality in their decisions given the grave concerns about a number of unjust cases decided by local courts. Democratic centralism also determines the centralized creation of precedent. The formal mechanism for selection, review, and approval of the guiding cases and precedent clearly illustrates this feature. The mechanisms allow a wide range of actors to propose precedent and open discussions, which exemplifies the 'democratic' aspect of this principle. But after that 'democratic' discussion, the decision is centralized: only the highest court has the power to determine and release the precedent. Another feature of the socialist precedent system defined by the principle of democratic centralism is paternalistic application of precedent. As the superior institution vis-à-vis local courts as the inferior institutions, the SPCV instructs the local courts nationwide on how to apply the precedents it has issued.[219] Local courts are also encouraged to seek guidance from the SPCV on how to apply precedents. A related feature is the mandated effect of precedent. The principle of democratic centralism requires centralized action: the inferiors have to obey the decisions by the superiors. In the socialist judiciary, this means lower courts have to follow the decisions by the highest court. In addition, the requirement of application of precedent is authoritative: lower courts 'must study and adopt' precedent.[220] Yet, as a 'democratic' matter, the formal system allows lower courts to choose not to apply a precedent if they provide an explanation.[221]

Finally, democratic centralism defines the forced departure of the socialist precedent: precedent can be terminated by statute, regulation, or decree. Democratic centralism shapes the external institutional relationship of the courts. Accordingly, courts are subordinate to the legislature in the socialist constitutional order. As a 'democratic' matter, subordinate institutions like courts are allowed to develop their own decisions to handle their departmental enterprises. However, as the 'centralized' matter, courts are subordinate to the legislature, and consequently precedent is only supplementary and subordinate to legislative law. In addition, under the centralized 'democratic' constitutional arrangement, courts are inferior to the executive or the government. Consequently, precedents can be forcibly terminated by governmental regulations and decrees.

[219] Law on Organization of People's Courts (2014), art 22.
[220] Resolution No 03/2015/NQ-HDTP (n 208), art 8.2.
[221] ibid.

VI. LEGAL PROFESSION REFORM

Let us now turn to the reform of legal profession, particularly the lawyer system in Vietnam. A body of domestic scholarship has well documented the historical development of lawyers in Vietnam from French colonialism, to Vietnam War, to post-Renovation.[222] International writings have canvassed the education, functions, and reforms of lawyers in Vietnam.[223] This part explores the legislative development, major reforms, and socialist boundary of the Vietnamese lawyer system.

A. The Legislative Development of the Vietnamese Lawyer System

The legal profession was established in Vietnam in 1876 by French colonial authority.[224] A colonial decree created the Bar Associations in Saigon and Hanoi, consisting of lawyers that graduated from law schools in France with French nationality. In 1911, colonial authority expanded the legal profession to Vietnamese with Vietnamese nationality. In 1930, a colonial decree considerably extended the legal profession. The decree provided for the creation of bar associations in Hanoi, Saigon, and Da Nang. It also allowed lawyers to defend both French and non-French clients in both the French and the Vietnamese courts. Consequently, the period between 1930 and 1945 witnessed the proliferation of the legal profession in Vietnam with lawyers returning from France along with numerous lawyers being trained domestically at Indochina University, Hanoi.[225]

After national independence in 1945, the Democratic Republic of Vietnam temporarily retained the colonial lawyer system with some modifications of the standards required to become a lawyer. In 1949, to deal with the lawyer shortage, the new

[222] Trương Thị Hòa and Phan Đăng Thanh, *Lịch Sử Nghề Luật Sư Ở Việt Nam [The History of legal profession in Vietnam]* (Ho Chi Minh City General Publishing House 2015); Ngô Thị Ngọc Vân and Nguyễn Thị Thu Minh, 'Lịch sử Phát triển Nghề Luật sư ở Việt Nam' ['Historical Development of Legal Profession in Vietnam'] (2021) 3 Nghệ Luật 72; Xuân Anh, 'Luật sư trong Cải cách tư pháp' ['Lawyer Work in Judicial Reform'], (2005) 50 Nghiên cứu Lập pháp 12; Liêu Chí Trung, 'Luật Sư Trong Các Chính Phủ Và Chính Quyền Cách Mạng Trước Năm 1975' ['Lawyers in Governments and Revolutionary Administrations before 1975'] (Vietnam Lawyer Journal, 9 November 2022) <https://lsvn.vn/luat-su-trong-cac-chinh-phu-va-chinh-quyen-cach-mang-truoc-nam-19751667920194.html>.

[223] Ho Nhan Ai, 'The Training of Would-be Lawyers in Vietnam: The Current System, Recent Developments and Potential Transformation' (2023) 57 Law Teacher 171; Pip Nicholson and Hai Ha Do, 'Vietnam: From Cadres to a 'Managed' Profession' in Richard Abel and others (eds), *Lawyers in 21st-Century Societies* (Hart Publishing 2020) 855; Nguyen Hung Quang and Kerstin Steiner, 'Ideology and Professionalism: The Resurgence of the Vietnamese Bar' in John Gillespie and Pip Nicholson (eds), *Asian Socialism and Legal Change: The Dynamics of Vietnamese and Chinese Reform* (ANU Press 2005) 191.

[224] Nicholson and Do (n 223) 856.

[225] Trương Anh Tú, 'Thăng Trầm Nghề Luật Sư Ở Việt Nam' ['Ups and Downs of the Legal Profession in Vietnam'], (Dân trí, 10 October 2013) <https://dantri.com.vn/ban-doc/thang-tram-nghe-luat-su-o-viet-nam-1381868408.htm> accessed 6 June 2024.

government allowed the accused to ask a citizen who was not a lawyer to defend for him or her before ordinary courts and special courts for misdemeanours and felonies.[226] This provided the base for the creation of a unique institution called the 'people's advocate', which was regulated in detail by the Ministry of Justice's decree in 1950. Several years after national unification, the institution of 'people's advocate' continued to exist, and private law practices were not allowed.[227] Scholars observed that 'the people's advocates were civil servants and received their salaries out of the state budget. It can, therefore, be said that in the period between 1960 and 1980, the legal profession virtually did not exist as it had been replaced by that of the people's advocates.'[228]

Things changed after the introduction of the 1986 Renovation policy. In 1987, the Ordinance on Lawyer Organizations was adopted, providing for the establishment of bar associations at the provincial level (Article 1). The Ordinance (Article 2) states:

> lawyer organizations shall actively contribute to the protection of socialist legality, strengthening economic management and social management according to the law; protect the legitimate rights and interests of citizens and organizations; contribute to the settlement of cases in an objective and lawful manner; contribute to the realization of the equal rights of all citizens before the law, and the realization of socialist democracy; educate citizens to obey the Constitution, the law, and to respect the rules of socialist life

Thus, the function of the bar associations was predominantly political and partially legal. The bar associations were political institutions for protecting the socialist political regime and promoting socialist values. At the same time, the bar associations performed a legal function by contributing to the settlement of legal cases among citizens. The Ordinance requires lawyers to have a law degree or an equivalent legal qualification (Article 11). The Ordinance allows lawyers to participate in legal proceedings as a defence counsel for the accused or defendants; to represent victims and other litigants in criminal cases; to represent parties in civil, marriage, family, and labour cases; and to provide legal consultancy for state,

[226] Sắc Lệnh Của Chủ Tịch Nước Việt Nam Dân Chủ Cộng Hoà Số 69/Sl Ngày 18 Tháng 6 Năm 1949: Những Bị Can Có Thể Nhờ Một Công Dân Không Phải Là Luật Sư Bào Chữa Cho, Trước Các Toà Án Thường Và Toà Án Đặc Biệt Xử Việc Tiểu Hình Và Đại Hình [Decree of the President of the Democratic Republic of Vietnam No 69/SL of 18 June 1949: The Accused May Ask a Citizen Who is Not a Lawyer to Defend for, before Ordinary Courts and Special Courts for Misdemeanours and Felonies].

[227] On the history of the people's advocate institution in Vietnam, see Phan Trung Hoài, 'Chế Định Bào Chữa Viên Nhân Dân- Nhìn Từ Lịch Sử Và Hiện Tại' ['The People's Advocate Institution: History and Present'] <http://www.hcmcbar.org/NewsDetail.aspx?CatPK=2&NewsPK=181>.

[228] Nguyen and Steiner (n 223) 194–95 (internal citation omitted).

collective, and private economic organizations, including foreign economic organizations (Article 13).

The 1987 Ordinance is a transitional step in the creation of the lawyer system in Vietnam. Although it has not yet created a framework for a professional system of lawyers, it allows for the private legal practices (representing parties in private legal disputes and providing legal consultancy for private economic entities) as the consequence of the introduction of economic reform policy, which enables the development of the private economic sectors. To implement the 1987 Ordinance, 'by 1989, 16 bar associations had been established, replacing the former people's advocate organisations'.[229] In 1989, the government issued a decree on the establishment of local bar associations. This creates a legal framework for the development of bar associations in the subsequent years. Consequently, by 30 September 2001, sixty-one bar associations with eighty-two branches had been created.[230]

A major step in the development of a professional system of lawyers in Vietnam is the enactment of a new Lawyers Ordinance in 2001, replacing the 1987 Ordinance. The 2001 Ordinance was enacted as a part of the broader legal reform project to create a socialist rule of law state in the context of Vietnam's increasing integration into the international economic order. Scholars comment that 'the most significant change in the 2001 Ordinance was the recognition of the career as a lawyer as a professional career'.[231] The Ordinance emphasizes the legal nature of lawyers (to participate in the legal proceedings and to provide legal consultancy and other legal services, Article 1) and their legal function (contributing to the defence of justice, social equitability and socialist legality, Article 1). The 2001 Ordinance deleted the references to lawyers' political functions that appeared in the 1987 Ordinance. The 2001 Ordinance sought to bring Vietnamese lawyers closer to international standards. To enhance professionalism, the Ordinance requires that lawyers must not be concurrently civil servants, must have a law degree, and must graduate from a lawyer vocational training course. It also provides for the establishment of the Bar Association as the professional organization of lawyers.

The implementation of the Ordinance led to the increase of law firms and lawyers. More than 1,000 law firms were established. In nine years (2001–10), the number of lawyers has increased by 250% compared to those prior to the enforcement of the 2001 Ordinance. The number of lawyers increased from 1,883 in 2005 to nearly 4,200 in 2008 to almost 8,600 in 2011. In terms of functions, apart from litigation, legal consulting activities of lawyers—especially advising clients in the fields of investment, business, and trade—have developed.[232]

[229] ibid 195.

[230] ibid.

[231] ibid 196.

[232] Đặng Văn Cường, 'Sự Hình Thành Và Phát Triển Nghề Luật Sư Ở Việt Nam' ['The Formation and Development of Legal Profession in Vietnam'], (Dan Luat, 21 September 2022) <https://thuvienphapluat.vn/cong-dong-dan-luat/su-hinh-thanh-va-phat-trien-nghe-luat-su-o-viet-nam-77706.aspx> accessed 6 June 2024.

In 2006, the Lawyers Law was enacted, replacing the 2001 Ordinance. Apart from domestic reasons (eg lawyer shortage vis-à-vis population), the enactment of the 2006 Lawyers Law was to facilitate Vietnam's integration into to the global market, especially to prepare for Vietnam joining the WTO (which it did in 2007). One justification for the enactment of the law is that the quality of Vietnamese lawyers does not meet the requirements of international economic integration. Vietnamese lawyers lacked knowledge of international law, foreign language proficiency, and intensive practice in the fields of investment, business, and international trade. The enactment of the Lawyers Law is to enhance the international professionalism of Vietnamese lawyers to facilitate international economic integration. In addition, the accession to the WTO necessitates a comprehensive legal framework for the practice of both Vietnamese lawyers and foreign lawyers in Vietnam.[233]

Major new features of the Lawyers Law include the provisions for the practice of foreign lawyers, foreign law firms in Vietnam, and in-house lawyers. The Lawyers Law was amended in 2012 to enhance the autonomy of bar associations, lawyers' professional responsibilities and legal liabilities, lawyers' obligation to strictly abide by relevant rules in their relationship with the agencies conducting the proceedings, lawyers' obligation to participate in mandatory training, among others.[234]

B. Trends in Lawyer Reform

I underline structural-personnel and functional trends in the reform of Vietnamese lawyer system in post-Renovation.

Like the case of China, a structural-personnel trend in legal profession reform in Vietnam is the rapid growth of the number of lawyers and law firms. Table 5.4 indicates the increasing rise in the number of lawyers since the introduction of the Renovation policy, although the rate of lawyers per capita in Vietnam is still low compared with other Asian countries such as Thailand, Singapore, and Japan.[235]

[233] Ministry of Justice, 'Đề Cương Giới Thiệu Luật Luật Sư Năm 2006' ['Outline Introduction to the 2006 Lawyers Law'], (Luat Minh Khue, 11 November 2010) <https://luatminhkhue.vn/de-cuong-gioi-thieu-luat-luat-su-nam-2006.aspx> accessed 6 June 2024.

[234] Nhuận Phát, 'Giới Thiệu Một Số Điểm Mới Của Luật Sửa Đổi, Bổ Sung Một Số Điều Của Luật Luật Sư', (*Bạc Liêu Online*, 8 May 2013) <https://www.baobaclieu.vn/toa-soan-ban-doc/gioi-thieu-mot-so-diem-moi-cua-luat-sua-doi-bo-sung-mot-so-dieu-cua-luat-luat-su-15027.html> accessed 6 June 2024.

[235] Nguyen Hung Quang, 'Lawyers and Democratic Centralism in Vietnam' in Helena Whalen-Bridge (ed), *The Role of Lawyers in Access to Justice: Asian and Comparative Perspectives* (CUP 2022) 231.

Table 5.4 Lawyer Development in Vietnam[236]

Year	Lawyers	Population	Lawyers per capita
1989	186	64,774,000	1:348,247
2001	2,100	78,620,500	1:37,438
2009	5,700	86,025,000	1:15,092
2011	6,250	87,860,300	1:14,058
2015	10,000	91,713,300	1:9,171
2019	13,563	96,462,106	1:7,094

By 2021, Vietnam had over 16,000 lawyers and 4,000 law firms. On average, the country gains 1,000 new lawyers annually. Vietnamese lawyers are mainly concentrated in two big cities—Hanoi (4,752 lawyers) and Ho Chi Minh City (6,489 lawyers)—accounting for more than two thirds of the country's total lawyers; the remaining 61 bar associations have 4,893 lawyers.[237]

Functionally, Vietnamese lawyers are professional persons providing legal services for clients.[238] From 2015 to 2020, Vietnamese lawyers participated in 81,072 criminal cases; 67,339 civil cases; 52,885 economic, commercial, and business cases; 4,097 administrative cases; 1,854 labour cases; 490,570 cases of legal advice; 22,887 cases of non-judicial representation; 22,880 cases of other legal services; and 161,996 cases of free legal aids.[239] Pip Nicholson and Do Hai Ha explain that 'the increasing involvement of lawyers in civil and commercial transactions has gradually reinforced the importance of law in the eyes of their clients, further increasing demand'.[240] The involvement of lawyers in civil and commercial cases indicates that they are not merely political agents of the state[241] but professional persons providing legal services.

In addition, Vietnamese lawyers have functioned as 'reform agents'.[242] Individual lawyers assisted 'the poor and vulnerable in criminal cases and large-scale environmental and land conflicts with the state or corporate actors'.[243] Pro

236 Source: ibid 231 (internal citations omitted).

237 Trần Tuấn, 'Cả Nước Có Hơn 16,000 Luật Sư, 4,000 Tổ Chức Hành Nghề Luật Sư' ['The Country Has More Than 16,000 Lawyers, 4,000 Law Firms'], (Lao động 22 February 2021) <https://laodong.vn/phap-luat/ca-nuoc-co-hon-16000-luat-su-4000-to-chuc-hanh-nghe-luat-su-987234.ldo>accessed 6 June 2024.

238 Focus group interviews with twelve Vietnamese lawyers, 22 August 2022, Vietnam.

239 Trần Tuấn (n 237).

240 Nicholson and Do (n 223), 872.

241 On the Soviet lawyer as an agent of the state, see GM Razi, 'Legal Education and the Role of the Lawyer in the Soviet Union and the Countries of Eastern Europe' (1960) 48 Calif L Rev 793.

242 Nicholson and Do (n 223), 872.

243 ibid.

bono lawyers created groups like For-Justice Project and Defence Panel. In some cases, pro bono lawyers 'have successfully helped wrongly convicted or powerless plaintiffs in criminal proceedings'.[244] Moreover, Vietnamese lawyers have engaged in legislative reform. They have contributed comments to important laws such as the Civil Code, the Penal Code, the Criminal Procedure Code, the Law on Administrative Procedure, the Code of Civil Procedure, the Law on Property Auction, the Law on Legal Aid, the Law on State Compensation Liability, and the Law on Anti-Corruption.[245] Particularly, lawyer advocacy contributed to the reforms of the 2015 Criminal Procedure Code, including the compulsory use of video recording in interrogation.[246] Vietnamese lawyers are therefore important actors of legal reform. They have engaged in the consultation process of legislation and even in legal mobilization to advocate for legal reform.

The development of the lawyer system in Vietnam is shaped by normative, internal, and external gaps. First, the party-state's normative commitment building to the rule of law animates legal professional reform. Legislative reform of the lawyer system and the increase in the numbers of lawyers and law firms occurred after the party-state had committed to rule of law construction. The gap between the commitment to the rule of law and the lack of lawyers induces reformation of the lawyer system. Second, the gap between domestic social and economic development and the underdevelopment of the lawyer system engenders legal professional reform. The growing number of lawyers and law firms stems from the expandingdemands of legal services.[247] The expansion of the legal service market in turn is due to domestic social and economic change. The transition to the rule-based market economic system has generated the need for legal services as economic actors rely more on law. The supply-side expansion of lawyers is a response to the demand from the market.[248] Social changes generate more social disputes (particularly land, environmental, and family disputes), which require the involvement of professional lawyers. Finally, the gap between the Vietnamese lawyers and international standards of lawyers results in efforts to bring the former closer to the latter. Consequently, the Vietnamese lawyer system converges with international professional standards of lawyers to some extent. By nature, lawyer is now a profession in Vietnam. Structurally, bar associations are created. Personally, law degrees and additional professional training are required to become a lawyer. Functionally, Vietnamese lawyers discharge common legal services like litigation and consultation.

[244] ibid.

[245] Trần Tuấn (n 237).

[246] Hai Ha Do and Pip Nicholson, 'Vietnamese Deliberative Authoritarianism and Legality' in Weitseng Chen and Hualing Fu (eds), *Authoritarian Legality in Asia: Formation, Development and Transition* (CUP 2020) 252.

[247] Nicholson and Do (n 223), 871.

[248] ibid.

C. The Socialist Lawyers

Despite professional convergence and reform, the Vietnamese lawyer system remains essentially socialist. Like the court system, the lawyer system in Vietnam is underpinned by principles and concepts of socialist law, particularly, legal instrumentalism, party vanguardism, and rights statism.

First, the Vietnamese lawyers are basically socialist lawyers as they are still instrumental agents of the socialist state. Vietnamese lawyers do not merely serve their clients' interests; they also serve the state's interests. The Lawyers Law provides that 'professional activities of lawyers contribute to protecting justice, freedoms and democracy of citizens, legitimate rights and interests of individuals, agencies and organizations, socio-economic development, building the socialist rule of law State of Vietnam, and democratic, fair, civilized society' (Article 3). Thus, Vietnamese lawyers must serve the socialist state's social, economic, and legal objectives.

The Lawyer Law prohibits lawyers from 'abusing law practice or the lawyer's title to cause harms to national security, social order or safety, infringing upon the State's interests, public interests or legitimate rights and interests of agencies, organizations or individuals' (Article 9). This ambiguous prohibition provides ample space for the state to discipline lawyers if they are perceived as a threat to the regime's security and the state's interests.

To ensure that lawyers work for the state's interests, they are placed under the state's regulatory, administrative, and political control. The government uses regulatory power to control lawyers. Apart from the Lawyers Law, administrative agencies (particularly the government and the minister of justice) have issued many legal instruments to regulate lawyers' structure and actions. These include, among others, the government's Decree on the implementation of the Lawyers Law (2013); the minister of justice's Circular guiding the implementation of the Lawyers Law and the Decree on the implementation of the Lawyers Law (2011); the minister of justice's Circular on law-practice probation (2013); the minister of justice's Circular on professional training for lawyers (2014); the ministers of finance and justice's joint Circular on remuneration and payment of expenses for lawyers in case lawyers participate in proceedings at the request of the procedural agency (2014); the minister of justice's Circular on sample documents on lawyers and law practice (2015).[249] These legal instruments seek to subject the lawyers to the government's stringent regulatory control.

[249] Nguyễn Thị Trà, 'Hệ Thống Các Quy Phạm Pháp Luật Đang Còn Hiệu Lực Về Luật Sư Và Tổ Chức Hành Nghề Của Luật Sư' ['The System of Valid Legal Regulations on Lawyers and Their Organizations'] (Cổng Thông Tin Điện Tử Pháp Điển) <https://phapdien.moj.gov.vn/qt/tintuc/Pages/nghien-cuu-trao-doi.aspx?ItemID=19> accessed 6 June 2024.

Vietnamese lawyers are placed under the strict hierarchical management of administrative organs. The Lawyers Law includes a chapter on administrative management of lawyers. At the central level, the Ministry of Justice is the regulator of lawyers. The institution enjoys the powers to:

provide the framework programme for lawyer training;
grant and withdraw law-practice certificates;
grant, withdraw, and extend permits for foreign lawyers' professional practice in Vietnam;
grant and withdraw permits for establishment of foreign law-practicing organizations in Vietnam;
approve the charter of the national lawyers' organization;
inspect, examine, and handle violations;
settle complaints and denunciations about lawyers' organizations and law practice.[250]

At the local level, lawyers are subject to the administrative management of provincial governments. Provincial governments are authorized to:

permit the setting up of bar associations and decide on their dissolution;
approve charters of bar associations;
inspect, examine, and handle violations;
settle complaints and denunciations about the organization and operations of bar associations and law-practicing organizations.[251]

The government strictly manages lawyers to ensure they work for state interests, not the forces challenging the state.

Vietnamese lawyers are also subject to political control. The state uses different tactics to ensure the compliance of lawyers with the state's objectives. These tactics include repression, indoctrination, coercive distribution, and infiltration.[252] First, the repressive tactic involves, for instance, criminal punishment of activist lawyers who oppose the socialist regime and the state's objectives.[253] Indoctrinative tactics include, for example, the state's approval of legal professional training programmes and its control of the lawyers' public discourse to limit their criticism of the state.[254] The state also uses distributive tactics to create material inducement for lawyers'

[250] Lawyers Law, art 83.
[251] ibid.
[252] These general tactics of political control are theorized in Mai Hassan, Daniel Mattingly, and Elizabeth R Nugent, 'Political Control' (2022) 25 Ann Rev Pol Sci 158.
[253] John Gillespie, 'The Juridification of Cause Advocacy in Socialist Asia: Vietnam as a Case Study' (2013) 31 Wisconsin Int'l LJ 680–85.
[254] Vietnam Lawyer Association is largest association of Vietnamese jurists. Vietnam Bar Federation created in 2009 is the social-professional body of legal practitioners. Do and Nicholson, (n 246) 253.

compliance with the state's objectives—such as the state sponsorship of legal education and legal professional training, the state-funded legal aid centres, and the state's funding of certain criminal defendants.[255] Finally, the state uses infiltrative tactics to foster the compliance of lawyers with the state's goals. For example, the state tightly controls the Vietnam Lawyer Association (VLA) and the Vietnam Bar Federation (VBF) to ensure that they operate as institutional platforms to implement the state's policy on lawyers and legal propaganda.[256]

Another socialist legal identity shaping the Vietnamese lawyer system is Party vanguardism. Lawyers in Vietnam are under Party leadership.[257] The VLA's Charter explicitly states that the organization 'is placed under the leadership of the Communist Party of Vietnam'.[258] The Party decides policy for legal professional reform. The Party nominates senior party members to head key bodies of lawyers: the VLA and VBF. The heads of the VLA and VBF are normally concurrently the heads of the Party groups created with these institutions. The Party cells are set up within bar associations.[259] The meetings of the Party cells are the platform to indoctrinate lawyers with the party lines and ideology.[260] Functionally, Vietnamese lawyers 'are strictly forbidden to take advantage of the practice of lawyers and legal consultancy in order to undermine the guidelines and policies of the Party and the laws of the State'.[261] In other words, Vietnamese lawyers are agents for implementing Party lines.

The Vietnamese lawyer system is also shaped by rights statism. The statist rights regime generates important institutional and functional consequences to the lawyer system. The fundamental right to counsel is itself statist: its practice is strictly regulated by the state and must be balanced with the state's interests. For example, to defend a case, lawyer must obtain a certificate of defender with complicated conditions such as presenting the lawyer card, a letter from the law firm, and a request for a lawyer by the accused.[262] These regulatory conditions sought to ensure that the right to counsel would not be used to oppose the state interest or to impede the activities of the state institutions in criminal proceedings. Lawyers in Vietnam must protect the rights of their clients and the state's interests at the same time, and when there is a conflict between these two roles the latter should trump. Activist lawyers have 'faced strong pressure, threats of disciplinary action,

[255] Nicholson and Do, (n 223) 870.

[256] ibid 857.

[257] Lê Đức Bính, 'Vai Trò Lãnh Đạo Của Đảng Đối Với Tổ Chức Và Hoạt Động Của Luật Sư Việt Nam' ['The Leadership of the Party in the Organizations and Activities of Vietnamese Lawyers'] (Vietnam Lawyer Journal, 22 April 2021) <https://lsvn.vn/vai-tro-lanh-dao-cua-dang-doi-voi-to-chuc-va-hoat-dong-cua-luat-su-viet-nam1619107545.html>accessed 6 June 2024.

[258] Charter of the Vietnam Bar Federation, Preamble.

[259] Interviews with a lawyer in Hanoi, 13 March 2023.

[260] Lê Đức Bính (n 257).

[261] ibid.

[262] These conditions are recently removed in a reform to the Criminal Procedure Law in 2015, effective in 2028.

and prosecution'.[263] This is to ensure that lawyers cannot invoke individual rights to oppose the state.

Vietnamese lawyer Nguyen Hung Quang argues that the lawyer system (and the court system) in Vietnam is influenced by the socialist principle of democratic centralism, stating that:

> As a result of the continued relevance of the principle of democratic centralism, judges adjudicating criminal cases often obtain opinions from court leaders, senior courts, or other agencies before hearings are held. This practice means that many judgments are already decided before adjudication, and therefore even though litigants are represented by a lawyer, there is little opportunity for litigants to effectively exercise their right to counsel. The practice of consultation with others prior to hearings is maintained to the present day, and some lawyers even characterize their presence at a hearing as just a 'dien vien' (actor or actress) for a 'vo kich' (drama).[264]

Democratic centralism is the principle for the party and state institutions, not lawyers. The lawyer system is not the institutional embodiment of democratic centralism. However, this principle may have an indirect functional effect on lawyers as the lawyers are under the state's instrumental control and the party's vanguard leadership. The formalistic role of lawyers in criminal proceedings is in part due to the indirect functional effect of the centralized court system.

VII. CONCLUDING ANALYSIS

A. Universal Intention

After nearly four decades of legal reform, Vietnam has constructed a sophisticated and functional legal system. Legal reform in Vietnam is therefore shaped by the Party's *intention*: their interests, purposes, and aspirations. Legal reform in Vietnam is a top-down project initiated and led by the Party. To be sure, Vietnamese legal reform is influenced by different domestic actors (legal scholars, lawyers, activists, members of civil society) and international actors (foreign governments, international agencies, foreign legal advisors). However, the Party remains the dominant actor shaping legal reform. The Party launched legal reform projects, articulated measures for legal reform, created Party agencies to monitor legal reform, and authoritatively decided on how far legal reform can go. Consequently, legal reform in Vietnam is controlled by the political elite, not the legal elite. The Party's

[263] Do and Nicholson, (n 246) 250.
[264] Nguyen Hung Quang (n 235) 233.

prevailing attitude to legal reform is legal universalism, an attitude on reforming domestic law according to common norms rooted in international and comparative law. Legal reform embodies the Party's competing purposes and aspirations: to reform the legal system according to universal legal standards and to retain the socialist identity of the legal system.

B. Incremental Strategies

The Party adopts both *classical and neo-incremental strategies* of legal reform. Between 1986 and 2004, the Party adopted the classical incremental strategy to introduce some sporadic adjustments to the existing socialist legal system in response to immediate needs of economic reform. Since 2004, after two decades of legal reform with considerable achievements, the Party turned to neo-incrementalism to formulate an overall plan for comprehensive legal reform to be undertaken within several decades. Among other things, the single leadership of the Party over the state and society is the institutional and political condition for the Party to adopt an overall plan for legal reform.

C. Legislative Method

The main method of legal reform in Vietnam is through *legislative enactment*. Rules in substantive laws in nearly all aspects of society are newly introduced, amended, or deleted through the lawmaking process of the NA. Institutional reforms (the reform of the legislature and the administrative, court, and legal professional systems) are also based on the legislative enactments of the relevant organic laws. The NA is not merely formalistic but increasingly a platform for deliberating reform issues. This in part explains why legal reform is based on legislative enactment.

D. Positive Change

The implementation of measures of legal reform induces *positive change* to the Vietnamese legal system. Generally, legal reform leads to the creation of a sophisticated and functional legal system. Thanks to legal reform, the Vietnamese legal system now acquires some formal qualities of the rule of law. In addition, some substantive legal norms have been integrated into Vietnamese law and legal institutions such as private property, transparent governance, and functional judicial independence. To some extent, legal reforms contribute to realizing the party-state's commitments to the legality of governance and socio-economic development.

E. Factors

Legal reform in Vietnam is animated by normative, internal, and external *gaps*. The gap between the party-state's commitments to socialism, socialist legality, and socialist rule of law and the reality of the under-development of the legal system generates the need for its reform. Legal reform is therefore carried out to bring the legal system closer to the party-state's commitments. In addition, social-economic change as the consequence of the Renovation policy creates new social relations, disputes, and institutional tasks; and improvement of the legal system is required to deal with these issues. Finally, legal reform in Vietnam is generated by the gap between Vietnamese law and comparative and international law. Legal reform efforts seek to bring Vietnamese law closer to the external legal norms, consolidate the international and domestic legitimacy of Vietnamese law, and facilitate the country's international integration.

F. Continuity of Socialist Law

Legal reform in Vietnam is therefore legally and politically *bounded*. Despite significant reform, the Vietnamese legal system remains essentially socialist. Vietnamese law and legal institutions are generally an instrument for the party-state to achieve socialist goals: the stability and security of the socialist political regime and social-economic development towards the direction of socialism. The construction, operation, and development of the whole legal system is under the vanguard leadership of the Party. Law is the institutionalization of the Party line. The Party nominates party members to hold key positions in the legislature, the government, courts, and legal professional organs. Party groups are set up within the legal institutions to ensure the implementation of the Party lines in the legal system. The Vietnamese legal system is shaped by the principle of democratic centralism. Legislative laws and the government's regulatory instruments are judicially unquestionable. The Supreme Court is a powerful institution to control lower courts. Law and legal institutions protect individual rights to the extent that the protection does not contradict the state interests. Law and legal institutions can facilitate the market development to the extent that the state remains the dominant controller of the economy (through the state economic sectors and state regulatory power).

Legal reform in Vietnam is a dilemma. The Party seeks to converge the domestic legal system with the global legal standards to adapt the socialist legal system in line with the changing domestic and international environment. The adaption of the socialist legal system is crucial to its survival and resilience. At the same time, global legal identity may undermine socialist legal identity. To deal with this dilemma, the Party sets down legal-political limits of legal reform. Legal reform is legally limited by the grand constitutional norms: instrumentalism, vanguardism, democratic centralism, rights statism, and economic statism. In addition, legal reform is politically limited. The party-state employs various tactics to control actors involving legal reform to ensure the conformity of legal reform with the Party's socialist goals: the security and stability of the socialist regime and social-economic development towards the direction of socialism.

G. Prospects

As discussed, there remains numerous problems of formal laws, the administrative, judicial, and lawyers systems. The party-state is committed to continuing legal reforms as indicated in the 2022 Rule of Law Resolution. The aspiration to international integration and legal convergence continue to shape legal reforms. Yet, the reforms will be limited by the socialist ideology and institutions and therefore largely formalist and technical.

6

Laos: Legal Reform and External Assistance

I. INTRODUCTION

Since the introduction of the reform policy in 1986, Laos—officially the Lao People's Democratic Republic (PDR) has embarked on legal reform, leading to the creation of a stable, functional legal system. Lao legal reform is a cooperative project: the project of comprehensive legal reform with the strong support of various sectors of the international community. Laos seeks external assistance internationally for its legal reform and sectors of the international community are willing to support its legal reform. This chapter explores legal reform in Laos from 1986 to today. It examines the rule of law reform plan and achievements of legislative, administrative, judicial, and legal professional reforms.

This chapter is empirically supported by my two field trips to Laos. During those trips, I conducted extensive interviews with a former justice of the Lao People's Supreme Court, an incumbent justice of the Lao People's Supreme Court, an assistant of the Lao People's Supreme Court, several Lao lawyers, a local government officer, and a lecturer at the Faculty of Law and Political Science of the National University of Laos.[1] The chapter also uses academic writings on Lao law and legal institutions in Vietnamese. There are many Lao graduates of Vietnamese law schools and other departments who wrote their theses and journal articles in Vietnamese. This study also relies on Vietnamese and English translations of Lao legislation. Finally, it uses scant English literature on Lao law, society, and politics. Some legal scholars explore Lao law and legal reform,[2] while social scientists discuss some legal aspects of Lao transformation.[3]

[1] The languages used during the interviews include English and Vietnamese. Some interviewees studied in Vietnam and therefore I could communicate with them in Vietnamese.

[2] Michael Bogdan, 'Legal Aspects of the Re-Introduction of a Market. Economy in Laos' (1991) 17 Rev Social Law 108; Kazuo Fukuda, 'Human Rights Council's Universal Periodic Review as a Forum of Fighting for Borderline Recommendations? Lessons Learned from the Ground' (2022) 20 Nw J Hum Rts 63; Katsunori Irie, 'The Reform for Secured Transactions Regime with the Doing Business Indicator: A Case of Laos' (2023) 16 Law Dev Rev 225; Perrine Simon, 'The Role of Law in the Rule of Law, the Contribution of Academics in Lao PDR' (2019) 103 Critical Quarterly for Legislation and Law 206.

[3] Simon Creak and Keith Barney, 'The Role of "Resources" in Regime Durability in Laos' (2022) 55 CPCS 35; Martin Stuart-Fox, 'Politics and Reform in the Lao People's Democratic Republic' (2005) Working Paper No 126, Asia Research Center.

Legal Reform in the Contemporary Socialist World. Ngoc Son Bui, Oxford University Press. © Ngoc Son Bui 2024.
DOI: 10.1093/9780191948053.003.0006

II. THE COOPERATIVE PROJECT OF LEGAL REFORM

Legal reform in Laos is a top-down project initiated and led by the Party. The Party plays a leading role in legal reform. It initiates directions for legal reform to be carried out by state actors.

A. 'New Thinking' and Legal Transition

Although Laos introduced some market reform policies from 1979, it was not until 1986 that the breakthrough comprehensive policy of market economic reform known as New Economic Mechanisms (NEM) was adopted by the Fourth Congress of the Lao People's Revolutionary Party (the Party).[4] Inspired by reform policies in China, Vietnam, and the Soviet Union, the NEM policy sought to transform the planned economy into a socialist market economy under the slogan *Chin Thanakaan Mai* ('New Thinking'). The reform policy promoted the development of private economic sectors, foreign investment, autonomy of state-owned enterprises, and prices determined by the market, among other things.[5]

Market development requires legal underpinnings. Understandably, the Fourth Congress adopted policy for the reform of state institutions, making a constitution, lawmaking, and governing the economy according to the law.[6] One of the objectives of the Second Five-Year Plan adopted in the Fourth Congress is to improve the legal system.[7] Thus, the Party acknowledges the significance of law in state building and economic development.

Since 1986, the Party continued to emphasize the significant role of law in governance and social-economic development. Consequently, legal reform has been the main concern of the Party's Congresses. According to a Lao communist leader, the Party's Congresses proposed measures for constitutional and legislative reform (including constitution making, constitutional amendment, enactment, and revision of statutes), administrative reform (including change of the Council of Minister into the government and reforms of local government), and judicial reform.[8] However, before 2009, Laos did not have a separate, overall plan for legal

[4] Norihiko Yamada, 'Legitimation of the Lao People's Revolutionary Party: Socialism, Chintanakan Mai (New Thinking) and Reform' (2018) 48 J Contemp Asia 717.

[5] Bogdan (n 2) 104.

[6] Vangseng Keobounphanh, Xây dựng Nhà nươc Pháp quyền Công hòa Dân chủ nhân dân Lào của Dân, Do Dân và Vì Dân [Building the Rule of Law State in Lao People's Democratic Republic of the People, by the People and For the People] (PhD Dissertation, Ho Chi Minh Academy of National Politics 2016) 110.

[7] Bogdan (n 2) 110.

[8] Ki-kẹo Khảy-khăm-phị-thun, Xây dựng Đảng và hệ thống chính trị của chế độ dân chủ nhân dân tại Lào trong tình hình mới [Party-Building and the Political System of People's Democracy in Laos in New Situation] (*Tạp chí Tổ chức Nhà nước*, 13 August 2019) <https://tcnn.vn/news/detail/43990/Xay-dung-Dang-va-he-thong-chinh-tri-cua-che-do-dan-chu-nhan-dan-tai-Lao-trong-tinh-hinh-moi-1-.html> accessed 6 June 2024.

reform. Rather, legal reform was incorporated into the Party's plans for political, social, and economic development. The measures of legal reforms aim to introduce sporadic adjustments to the legal system.

B. The 'Master Plan' for Rule of Law Reform

For the first time, in 2006, the Eighth Party Congress adopted the policy to create a 'rule of law state' (*lat haeng kotmai*) in Laos, although this concept had been discussed by Party leader Kaysone Phomvihane before that.[9] The Eighth Party Congress proposed 'incremental creation of the Rule of Law State in the Lao People's Democratic Republic under the leadership of the Lao Revolutionary Party'.[10] For this purpose, the Party Congress urged improving state institutions, governing society and the economy according to the law, clearly distributing state power, and preventing the abuse of state power, among others.[11] The adoption of the rule of law reflects the Party's previous acknowledgement of the role of law in governance and social-economic development.

To implement the Party's policy, in 2009, the Lao government adopted a systematic plan for rule of law reform entitled the Master Plan on Development of the Rule of Law in the Lao PDR toward the Year 2020 (hereinafter, Master Plan).[12] The Master Plan was prepared by state institutions (Ministry of Justice, Office of the Supreme People's Prosecutor, People's Supreme Court, and Ministry of Security) to implement the Party policy for rule of law reform. The Party therefore plays a leading role in the introduction of the rule of law reform project.

The Master Plan sought to tackle the weaknesses of the Lao legal system. In a 2005 paper, Martin Stuart-Fox discussed many shortcomings of the Lao legal system from the perspective of the rule of law. One is the lack of institutional and public awareness of law. The proliferation of new laws since 1986 made it difficult for officials, lawyers, and citizens to know about them.[13] In addition, 'some of the laws drafted by foreign experts, in English or French, remain untranslated into Lao for years',[14] which rendered laws unknowable. The consequence of poor legal awareness is poor legal enforcement. 'Indeed even high-ranking officials in the Justice Ministry concede that few, if any, of the laws so far passed have been fully implemented.'[15] Another problem is judicial corruption. 'It has been estimated by

[9] Vangseng (n 6) 104.
[10] ibid 112.
[11] ibid 112.
[12] Laos' Ministry of Justice, Office of the Supreme People's Prosecutor, People's Supreme Court, and Ministry of Security, Master Plan on Development of the Rule of Law in the Lao PDR toward the Year 2020 (2009).
[13] Stuart-Fox (n 3) 24.
[14] ibid 25.
[15] ibid 24–25.

one legal practitioner that one in ten decisions taken by the courts in Vientiane is on the basis of corrupt payment or personal influence.'[16] Finally, courts lacked independence due to political control of the Party and private interference. According to Stuart-Fox:

> Law in Laos is determined on three levels: by reference to Party policy (in Lao *nayobay*, a term which has taken on the additional meaning of bending the law in cases where a 'policy ruling' is made in favour of an individual); by reference to the written text as passed by the National Assembly; and in response to those who are in a position to influence a legal outcome. The third is the most efficacious and widespread means, but as a result legal authorities may find themselves evaluating a case not on the basis of the law as it stands, but on which of two conflicting sets of phone calls and other private interventions represents the more powerful political interests. Failure to get this right has cost some justice officials their jobs.[17]

The Master Plan acknowledges the weaknesses of the Lao legal system, including inconsistency of laws, poor legal enforcement, widespread violations of law, and customs prevailing law. To deal with these shortcomings, the Master Plan attempts to create a 'rule of law state' in Laos by 2020.[18] It defines that 'Rule of Law State is the State that regards Laws as supreme governing rules above all and legal consciousness of citizens should become customary practices in daily life.'[19] This definition reflects the formal conception of the rule law: the adherence to legality by all. The particular emphasis on social internalization of law as the nature of the rule of law is due to the prevailing evasion of law in Laos. Some substantive aspects of the rule of law are addressed as follows:

> the main objective of the development of the Rule of Law State is to secure the extension of ownership of Lao and Ethnic People, rights of citizens, rights and interests of children, equality between men—women, ethnic groups, as well as for ensuring the implementation of obligations under international treaties to which Lao is a party.[20]

This substantive conception of the rule of law largely reflects the local concerns (eg promoting ethnic diversity). Some of these local concerns (such as the protection of children's rights and general equality) echo universal concerns; but the Lao government does not frame them in universal terms, like human rights. The

[16] ibid 25.
[17] ibid 28.
[18] Simon (n 2) 210.
[19] Master Plan (n 12).
[20] ibid.

official discourse on the substantive aspect of the rule of law state employs the distinctive local discourse—such as 'ownership of Lao and Ethnic People'—rather than liberal-democratic discourse—such as popular sovereignty or democracy.

The Master Plan anticipates specific objectives and measures of legislative, administrative, judicial, and legal professional reforms. On legislative reform,[21] it aims to achieve formal features of the rule of law such as uniformity, coherency, clarity, credibility, predictability, and accessibility. The Master Plan seeks to improve both the procedural and substantive quality of legislation. It anticipates the creation and improvement of the procedures and standards of lawmaking, including the enactment of a law on legislation. Substantively, the Master Plan proposes legislative enactments to ensure the operation of state institutions under the Constitution and the laws, protect human rights, and support market development. The Master Plan proposes the enactments of many laws, including the laws on stock market, natural resources and environment, education, science-technology, health, culture-information, sport, tourism, ethnics, religion, citizenship, family, national defence, national security, social order and social safety, and detention camp, among others.[22] The Master Plan therefore seeks to create a legal framework that can comprehensively cover various aspects of social life.

The Master Plan particularly underlines that:

> the attention must be paid to creation and improvement of local Laws to harmonize with international treaties that Lao PDR is a party to and international customary practices; developing a legal framework that harmonizes with ASEAN [Association of Southeast Asian Nations] framework agreements and for accession to the WTO [World Trade Organization] by incorporating these international treaties into a domestic legal framework.[23]

Thus, the Lao rule of law reform plan seeks to promote international and regional convergence of laws.

On administrative reform, the Master Plan aims to improve the quality and efficiency of administrative agencies and their respect for the laws. Particularly, it proposes the creation of 'legal units' in every administrative organ. The main functions of the legal units include promoting civic legal awareness, monitoring the observation of law in the administrative organ, providing legal advice to administrative leaders, responding to citizens' complaints, and collecting legal data, among others.[24]

[21] The Master Plan does not articulate measures for reform of the structure of the legislature because this institution has its own plan for its structural reform.

[22] Master Plan (n 12).

[23] ibid.

[24] ibid.

The Master Plan seeks to improve the quality and efficiency of the court system and courts' functional independence in deciding cases. It anticipates measures for court reform such as:

> consolidating the role of the People's Supreme Court in reviewing cassation, developing case law (or judicial precedents), and instructing the local courts; increasing the terms and qualifications of judges to ensure judicial independence;
> strengthening the ethical code for the judges;
> establishing special courts; strengthening the management of local courts;
> widely publicizing all the court's decisions and judgments; and
> promoting adversarial trials.[25]

On legal professional reform, the Master Plan proposes some measures to improve the Lao Bar Association (LBA)—such as enacting a law on this body, developing a Code of Ethics of the Lawyer, promoting the public interest to use the service of the LBA, expanding LBA membership, and mobilizing international funds. The Master Plan also anticipates the establishment of governmental legal advice offices. In addition, it proposes the extension of the private legal advice offices in big cities.[26]

The measures for rule of law reform are consistent with the formal and procedural conception of the rule of law the Lao government adopts. Legislative reforms seek to achieve formal features of good law. Measures for institutional reforms largely focus on technical, formal, and procedural dimensions of the legal institutions. Measures of rule of law reforms do not target substantive aspects of the rule of law such as protection of individual rights, democracy, and the separation of powers (despite the inclusion of judicial independence).

Although rule of law reform is an ambitious project, the party-state has no intention to radically change the socialist legal-political principles. The general goal of rule of law reform is to create legal underpinnings for social-economic development towards socialism under the Party leadership. Rule of law reform must secure 'political stability' for the socialist political regime.[27] Within that grand goal, the Master Plan establishes six 'general principles' of rule of law reform, three of which explicitly seek to protect the socialist legal-political principles of the Lao legal system.

The first principle is 'ensuring the transforming of directives, strategic plan, policy of the Party and provisions of the Constitution into Laws and regulations promptly, fully, correctly'.[28] This means law must be an instrument to

[25] ibid.
[26] ibid.
[27] ibid.
[28] ibid.

institutionalize Party lines. This embodies socialist legal instrumentalism and vanguardism. The second principle is 'ensuring the creation of a favourable environment for the basis for expansion of the market economy with a socialist orientation'.[29] On one hand, legal reform must support market development. On the other hand, legal reform must protect the socialist direction of the economic development. This principle seeks to entrench economic statism. Law may support private economic sectors, but the state must retain the power to regulate the economy to ensure the socialist direction of economic development. The third principle suggests legal reform must guarantee the use of local potential resources 'on the basis of securing the independence, sovereign integrity, national security and socialist orientation'.[30] The improvement of the laws supporting the use of local resources for developmental projects mush ensure the socialist orientation of the political regime.

The Master Plan is supposed to end in 2020. The Ninth Five-Year National Socio-Economic Development Plan (2021–25) proposed directions for further legal reforms, including developing a new Master Plan on the Development of the Rule of Law. In addition, the Ninth Plan prioritizes activities of legal reform such as:

improving laws in a systematic and comprehensive manner;
enhancing the role of the National Assembly (NA) and Provincial People's Assemblies in improving and adopting legislation;
improving the awareness of respect for the law by the people;
disseminating laws, including the penal and civil codes; strengthening the capacity of law enforcement agencies; providing capacity building for justice experts, judges, prosecutors, and lawyers; and
strengthening the LBA.[31]

Thus, the Lao government is committed to continued rule of law reform.

What explains Laos' adoption of the rule of law reform project? The party-state has institutional interests to promote the rule of law. Martin Stuart-Fox observed in 2005 that:

> the Party and government have made it clear on innumerable occasions that they are committed to establishing the rule of law in Laos. Increasingly educated and informed Lao in the urban centres do refer to the law to defend themselves or others against arbitrary decisions or actions by Party and government officials.

[29] ibid.
[30] ibid.
[31] Ninth Five-Year National Socio-Economic Development Plan (2021–25) 97–98.

> But these educated few constitute a small minority. In rural areas the Party determines the law.[32]

So, the adoption of the rule of law is not generated by the bottom-up pressure from society but is a top-down initiative of the party-state due to institutional interests.

The party-state needs to rely on promulgated legal rules to govern the emerging market economy. The party-state could govern the planned economy by policy or even personal fiats but could not do so with complex social relations emerging from the transition to market economy. Market relations are rules-based relations. Therefore, law presents a useful tool for the party-state to manage the emerging market. Law is also a useful tool for the party-state to attract foreign investments that require legal protection of private property of the investors. In addition, the party-state needs to control state officials. The prevailing evasion of law by state officials has made it difficult for the party-state to implement its reformist policy. Undertaking rule of law reform to subject state officials to law becomes necessary. Moreover, the party-state needs to control society to achieve its developmental policy embedded in law. The popular neglect of law is an obstacle for the party-state to implement its developmental law. Therefore, rule of law reform becomes necessary to facilitate the social internalization of law.

Like the legal reform projects in China and Vietnam, the Master Plan in Laos seeks to coordinate legal reform activities, express the party-state's commitments to legal reform, and establish the limits for legal reform to preserve the socialist legal identity. However, different from China and Vietnam, Laos pursues a general version of the 'rule of law state' not a specific model of 'socialist rule of law state', although the rule of law reform project insists on the socialist orientation of legal development. The Lao political elite may not have a clear vision of a socialist model of the rule of law state. In addition, the political elite may adhere to the general idea of the rule of law to attract the broader support from the international community.

C. Cooperative Legal Reform

Legal reform in Laos can be understood by a cooperative project: domestic political elites seek to work with international donors to formulate and implement measures of legal reforms. The combination of both the external influence of the law and development movement and domestic needs induces cooperative legal reform in Laos.

[32] Stuart-Fox (n 3) 24.

Cooperative legal reform is shaped by the extensive spread of the law and development movement in Laos. Since Laos introduced the reform policy in 1986, various international agencies and foreign governments have supported legal reform to facilitate socio-economic transformation in the country. Before the introduction of the 2009 rule of law reform plan, international actors had already been involved in legal reform in Laos. After the introduction of the plan, many donors then actively supported its implementation.[33] The United Nations Development Programme (UNDP) has supported the rule of law reform in Laos for many years, particularly public access to justice and legal consciousness. The German Society for International Cooperation supported good governance and people's access to justice in the country. The Luxembourg Agency for Development Cooperation supported legal education at the National University of Laos and the National Institute of Justice (NIJ). The Asia Foundation supported public access to justice in Laos. The Ministry of Justice of Vietnam supported the skills and abilities of the NIJ instructors and staff and improving the curriculum. The International Finance Corporation supported the drafting of the Securities Part of Laos' Civil Code. Since 1998, Japan has provided ongoing support to legal reform in Laos. The Japan International Cooperation Agency has supported various projects, including legal personnel and the making of the Civil Code.[34]

In response to the spread of the law and development movement, Lao political elites are willing to cooperate with external actors to formulate and implement measures of legal reform. The political willingness to cooperate with external actors is shaped by cognitive, personal, and financial constraints. The political elites may lack knowledge about possible legal resolutions for new emerging social relations (particularly market relations), and hence they need the support of the international community to gain comparative and international legal knowledge. In addition, as the country has lacked human resources (eg legal experts and government staff) to formulate and implement measures of legal reforms, it needs to cooperate with sectors of the international community. The financial constraints also require international legal cooperation. Despite economic reform, Laos remains one of the least developed countries in the world. The country needs financial assistance from donors to undertake many legal reform activities such as drafting laws, training legal personnel (legal experts, government officials, judges,

[33] 'Support to the Implementation of the Legal Sector Master Plan' <https://www.undp.org/laopdr/projects/support-implementation-legal-sector-master-plan>accessed 6 June 2024; 'U.S. Launches New Program to Strengthen the Rule of Law in Laos' <U.S. Launches New Program to Strengthen the Rule of Law in Laos | Press Release | Laos | Archive - U.S. Agency for International Development (usaid.gov) /> accessed 6 June 2024; Ministry of Justice, 'Laos' <https://www.moj.go.jp/EN/housouken/houso_houkoku_laos.html>; Support Programme for Legal Teaching and Training and to the Promotion of the Rule of Law Concept in Laos, LuxDev—LAO/031 <https://luxdev.lu/en/activities/project/LAO/031> accessed 6 June 2024.

[34] 'The Current Situation and the Challenges of Japan's Legal Technical Assistance to Laos' (*JICA*, 2 November 2020) <https://www.jica.go.jp/laos/english/office/topics/201102.html>.

and lawyers), improving facilities (eg buildings and computers) of legal institutions, and distributing legal materials to the public.

III. LEGISLATIVE REFORM

A. Legislative Process

Since the enactment of the first socialist constitution in Laos in 1991, the NA has been the country's legislature. According to the 2015 Constitution, the NA is 'the legislative branch to perform the role to adopt the Constitution and laws' (Article 52). The NA is a unicameral legislature created by election for a five-year term. In the election for its ninth term in 2021, 224 candidates contested the 164 seats in the NA.[35] Its internal structure includes a Standing Committee and eight specialist committees, namely:

Law Committee;
Economy, Technology, and Environment Committee;
Planning, Finance, and Audit Committee;
Cultural and Social Committee;
Ethnic Affairs Committee;
National Defence and Security Committee; the Judicial Committee; Foreign Affairs Committee.[36]

Despite considerable constraints (eg the limited choice of candidates in one-party elections, the limited duration of sessions, and the lack of capacity, experience, and resources),[37] recent changes rendered the NA a more active institution for legislation. The NA

> is beginning to assume a much more assertive role in the consideration of laws and the scrutiny of government and budgets. There has been a gradual change in the functioning of the Assembly over the years with more critical debates on issues of national concern such as logging, corruption, lack of budget transparency, land concessions etc.[38]

[35] Lao People's Democratic Republic Election for Sapha Heng Xat (Laotian National Assembly) (*ElectionGuide*, 21 February 2021) <https://www.electionguide.org/elections/id/3623> accessed 6 June 2024.
[36] Lao Law on National Assembly (revised 2015), art 44.
[37] Richard Slater and Khamlouang Keoka, 'Trends in the Governance Sector of the Lao PDR' (Swiss Agency for Development and Cooperation SDC February 2012) 17.
[38] ibid.

In other words, the NA is not merely a formalist institution to approve the Party policy. It has incrementally transformed into a deliberate platform, making it a legitimate institution for legislative enactments supporting legal reform.

In the period 1975–91, Laos lacked legal rules governing the legislative process. The legislative process from setting the agenda for lawmaking, to preparing the draft law, to submitting the draft law for adoption, to publishing the law was basically the task of the Standing Committee of the Supreme People's Council.[39] After the enactment of the 1991 Constitution, the legal framework for the legislative process incrementally developed. The government issued two legal instruments in 1994 and 1996 respectively to govern the procedures of law drafting. On the basis of these two legal instruments, in 2003, the president of state issued a Decree on legislative procedure.[40] The fact that the executive issued legal instruments to govern the lawmaking process seems unusual but is understandable in the Lao context. As the Lao socialist state did not adopt the principle of separation of power, laws were initiated by the government and its lawmaking process can be regulated by the government.

In 2012, the NA adopted the Law on Legislation to provide a comprehensive legal framework for governing the legislative process. According to the law, the types of legal instruments include:

- Constitution
- National Assembly Law
- National Assembly Resolution
- Standing Committee Resolution
- Presidential Ordinance
- Government Decree
- Government Resolution
- Prime Minister Order and Decision
- Ministerial Order, Decision and Instruction
- Provincial Decision and Instruction
- District Order, Decision and Instruction
- Village Regulation.[41]

The process of making legislative law (or NA law) is provided in Part III of the Law on Legislation. Institutions and individuals eligible to propose drafting a law include: the president; the Standing Committee of the NA; the government; the

[39] Sự hình thành và phát triển chế định lập pháp nước CHDCND Lào <http://www.lapphap.vn/Pages/tintuc/tinchitiet.aspx?tintucid = 209005>.
[40] Master Plan (n 12).
[41] Lao Law on Legislation, art 4.

People's Supreme Court; the People's Supreme Prosecutor; and the Lao Front for National Construction and National Mass Organizations (Article 18).

The procedures of legislation making include these steps:

planning for lawmaking and amendment;
drafting a law;
reviewing the consistency of the draft law by the Ministry of Justice;
reviewing the draft law by the government;
reviewing the draft law and adoption of the law by the NA; and
promulgation of a law by the president (Article 19).

A notable feature is the planned legislation making. This includes a five-year plan of lawmaking adopted by the first session of each NA, and an annual plan determined by its Standing Committee on the basis of the five-year plan (Article 21).

The Law on Legislation introduces notable reforms, including the establishment of these requirements of legislation making: transparency (eg the publication of the laws in the Official Gazette), public participation (eg public consultation workshops and posting all contents of the draft law, Article 36), impact assessment, and systemization (eg the hierarchy of normative legal documents, and formats for the content of laws).[42]

B. Achievements of Legislative Reform

The trajectory of legislative reform in Laos since 1986 can be divided into three periods: incipient transition (1986–91), consolidated transition (1991--2009), and rule of law reform (2009–today).

The first period is from the introduction of the reform policy in 1986 to before the enactment of the 1991 Constitution. During this period, Laos lacked a constitution, but the introduction of the reform policy in 1986 induces the legislative enactment to support incipient transition from a centralized to a socialist market economy. These include the following laws:

Law on Foreign Investment (1988);
Law on Property (1990);
Inheritance Law (1990);
Contract Law (1990);
Law on Establishing of the Bank of the Lao PDR (1990);
Law on Labour (1990);

[42] UNDP, 'The Law-Making Process in Lao PDR: A Baseline Study' (Ministry of Justice and UNDP Lao PDR 2015) 10.

Law on Insurance (1990);
Law on Accounting System for Enterprises (1990); and
Law on Promotion, Protection, and Management of Foreign Investment (1990).[43]

Particularly, the Law on Foreign Investment is considered 'one of the first legislative measures leading to the re-introduction of market economy'.[44] The law creates a legal framework for foreign organizations and individuals to invest in Laos. It recognizes the property right of the foreign investors and promises that their property shall not be requisitioned under administrative procedures.[45] Apart from law for the market, Lao legislature also enacted several other laws to facilitate the reform of criminal justice system and judicial reform. In 1989, the Supreme People's Assembly adopted the Penal Law, the Penal Procedure Law, the Law on People's Courts, and the Law on People's Prosecutors.[46]

The second period is from the enactment of the 1991 Constitution to before the adoption of the 2009 rule of law reform plan. During this period, Laos enacted the first socialist constitution in 1991, replaced by the second socialist constitution in 2003, and enacted eighty laws. The constitutions and the laws consolidated state and market institutions, and deal with social issues generated by economic transition. In 1991, Laos adopted the first socialist constitution and twenty-two laws.[47] The 1991 Constitution provides the base for the creation of state institutions, including the NA (the legislature), the government (the executive), the court system, the public prosecution institutions, and local government. This provides the foundations for subsequent institutional reform. The constitution also codifies policy of market reform, including the multi-sectoral economy, and the commitment to the state's protection of private ownership of domestic capitalists and foreigners (Articles 13 and 14). These provisions seek to foster market development and attach foreign investments.

After the enactment of the 1991 Constitution, Lao legislature enacted many news laws to support the continuing transition into the socialist market economy. These include the following major laws:

Law on Labour (1994);
Law on Business (Company) (1994);
Law on Customs (1994);

[43] Bogdan (n 2) 117.
[44] ibid 115.
[45] ibid; Lao Health Master Planning Study, 'Final Report Volume 4: Sector Review, Appendix 3 Social-Economic Reform, A3-2' <https://openjicareport.jica.go.jp/pdf/11707338_07.pdf> accessed 6 June 2024.
[46] Bogdan (n 2) 117.
[47] Sự hình thành và phát triển chế định lập pháp nước CHDCND Lào (lapphap.vn).

Law on Budget (1994);
Law on Bankruptcy (1994);
Law on Secure Transaction (1994);
Law on Foreign Investment (1994);
Law on Taxation (1995);
Law on the Bank of the Lao PDR (1995);
Law on Enterprise (1995);
Law on Domestic Investment (1995);
Law on Forestry (1996);
Law on Water and Water Resources (1996);
Law on Land (1997);
Law on Electricity (1997);
Law on Land Transportation (1997);
Law on Commerce (1997);
Law on Mining (1997);
Law on Agriculture (1998);
Law on Industrial Manufacturing (1999);
Law on Environmental Protection (1999);
Law on Urbanism (1999);
Law on Highways (1999);
Law on Drugs and Pharmaceutical Products (2000);
Law on Education (2000); and
Law on Road Traffic (2000).[48]

The third period is from the adoption of the 2009 rule of law reform plan to today. This period is marked by efforts of legal reform to create a rule of law state. The implementation of the Master Plan led to the rapid legislative enactments. The Sixth NA approved fifteen new laws, giving Laos a total of eighty-three laws by 2011.[49] The seventh NA adopted thirty new laws, including the Law on Civilians, the Law on Prevention of Terrorism, the Law on State Property, the Law on Sports and Physical Activity, the Law on State Audit, the Law on Cross-Border Trade, and the Law on Agriculture.[50] The eighth NA amended forty-seven laws and adopted thirty-four new laws.[51] According to the *Lao Official Gazette*, there are 153 effective laws as of May 2023.

Lao law now comprehensively covers various aspects of social life. A body of public law was developed to support institution building. Following constitutional reforms, several organic laws were newly enacted or amended. Existing laws

[48] Lao Health Master Planning Study (n 45).
[49] Seventh Five-Year National Socio-Economic Development Plan (2011–15) 59–60.
[50] Eighth Five-Year National Socio-Economic Development Plan (2016–20) 64.
[51] Ninth Five-Year National Socio-Economic Development Plan (2021–25) 24.

supporting institutional building include the Law on the National Assembly (revised 2015), the Law on Government (revised 2017), the Law on Judges (2017), the Law on The People's Court (revised 2017), the Law on The People's Prosecutors (revised 2017), and the Law on Local Government (revised 2015), among others. These laws at least suggest that the party-state seeks to govern the use of the state power within a legal framework. Some of these laws will be explored later in the sections IV and Von institutional legal reforms. Sections III.B.1–4 provide an overview of legislative development in Laos in criminal, civil and commercial, social, and agrarian law.

1. Criminal Law

Since 1986, criminal law in Laos has experienced several rounds of reform. During the early stage of transition, the Supreme People's Assembly adopted the Penal Law in 1989. Later, as the transition had been consolidated, the NA adopted the revised versions of the Penal Law in 1990 and 2005. The implementation of the rule of law plan led to the enactment of the first Penal Code in 2017, effective from 2018, which replaced the Penal Law of 2015.

The Penal Code is 'the compilation of provisions related to criminal offences and punishments into a single law' (Article 2). It incorporated and invalidated criminal provisions in twenty other laws, including:

Anti-Corruption Law;
Law on Preventing and Combating Violence against Women and Children;
Law on Protection of the Rights of Children;
Law on Anti-Money Laundering and Financing of Terrorism;
Law on the Prevention of Cyber Crimes; and
Law on Anti-Human Trafficking.[52]

The 2017 codification of criminal law thus seeks to systematize the discursive legal rules of criminal offences and penalties.

The Penal Code, however, did not simply copy relevant provisions in these laws but 'amended most of these laws by imposing increased penalties or stipulating additional acts that constitute offences'.[53] For example, operating an unregistered business can be sanctioned by fine under the Enterprise Law but by both fine and imprisonment under the Penal Code.[54] Some argue that the new sanctions regime 'signals the strong determination of the Lao Government to deter criminal activities and advance the rule of law in the country'.[55]

[52] Lao Penal Code (2017), art 425.
[53] New Penal Code Implemented in Laos (*ZICO Law*, 30 November 2018) <https://www.zicolaw.com/resources/alerts/new-penal-code-implemented-in-laos>.
[54] ibid.
[55] ibid.

2. Civil and Commercial Law

Laos enacted a set of civil and commercial legislation, including:

Civil Code (2018);
Law on Competition (2015);
Enterprise Law (revised 2013);
Consumer Protection Law (2010);
Enterprise Rehabilitation and Bankruptcy Law (2019);
Law on Securities (revised 2019);
Law on Settlement of Economic Disputes (revised 2018);
Law on Intellectual Property (2017); and
Law on Investment Promotion (2017).

This body of law is particularly necessary for market development in Laos.

A notable development is the adoption of the first Civil Code in Laos in 2018, effective from 2020. Before the enactment of the Code, Lao civil law included separate laws such as those on contract, property, and family. The enactment of the Civil Code seeks to deal with the shortcomings of Lao civil law such as 'insufficient stipulations, discrepancies between multiple laws and some laws too old to apply to modern life'.[56]

The Ministry of Justice created the Civil Code Drafting Committee in 2012. The first draft of the Civil Code was completed and sent for public consultation in 2016. The second draft of the Civil Code, after the government's endorsement, was submitted to the NA for first reading in 2017. The Drafting Committee then continued to work on the second draft, taking into account the concerns raised by Assembly delegates and citizens in public consultation . Then, the third draft of the Civil Code was submitted to the NA for deliberation and adoption. The Civil Code was adopted by the NA in August 2018 and pronounced by the president in January 2019.[57]

The making of Lao Civil Code involves comparative study of civil codes and international engagement, especially the assistance from Japan. Mr Xaysy Santivong, Minister of Justice, remarks that:

> The Lao Civil Code is also the remarkable outcomes of the research and studies of civil codes of different countries . . . The Lao Civil Code is also a result of the evolution, legal development from the lessons of regional and international Civil Code, which is an invaluable contribution from professors and foreign experts

[56] 'Rule of Law for Sustainable Development and Access to Justice for All: Laos (January 2017) JICA's World 4.

[57] Remarks by Mr Xaysy Santivong, Minister of Justice, in Lao Civil Code: Unofficial Translation, printed by Lao Ministry of Justice 2021 <https://www.jica.go.jp/activities/issues/governance/portal/laos/ku57pq00002khhw3-att/civil_code_03.pdf>accessed 6 June 2024.

from neighboring countries especially from Japan International Cooperation Agency (JICA).[58]

Nalonglith Norasing, Director of Planning and Cooperation Department of the Ministry of Justice of Laos, appreciates Japan's support, saying that 'experts both from Japan and Laos join the projects, and Laotian experts are learning and absorbing the way of thinking from the Japanese experts'.[59] During the process of drafting the Lao Civil Code, under JICA's support, some Lao officials were sent to Japan for some training on civil law issues.[60]

The Civil Code is 'a systematic code combining with several provisions of laws related to establishment, variations, cessation of rights and obligations of individuals, juristic persons, organisations in the civil relationships that relate to things, ownerships, family, contracts and non-contractual obligations, inheritance and other civil relationships' (Article 2). Like China's Civil Code, Laos' Civil Code incorporates and replaces preceding laws dealing with similar civil and commercial issues, including the Law on Contract and Tort, the Law on Family, the Law on Property, the Law on Succession, and the Law on Secured Transactions. The Civil Code is comprised of 630 articles divided into nine parts, namely:

(i) General Provisions
(ii) Personal and Juristic Person
(iii) Family
(iv) Property, Proprietorship, and other Property Rights
(v) Contractual Obligations
(vi) Non-Contractual Obligations (Tort, Undue Enrichment, and Management without Mandate)
(vii) Secured Transaction
(viii) Succession
(ix) Final Provision[61]

The codification of civil law in Laos responds to the need for a coherent and comprehensive framework to facilitate civil and commercial transactions and to attract foreign investment. As a commentary puts it:

> previously, it had been relatively difficult for those unfamiliar with Lao legal system to identify provisions of law that are relevant and applicable to their activities, given that laws and regulations governing civil and commercial transactions

[58] ibid.
[59] 'Rule of Law for Sustainable Development' (n 56).
[60] Interview with a Lao local official, 18 August 2022, Vientiane, Laos.
[61] 'Snapshot of the Lao Civil Code 2020' 6 June 2024 <https://www.zicolaw.com/resources/alerts/snapshot-of-the-lao-civil-code-2020>.

> and relationship are set out in numerous instruments . . . This codification of domestic private law would thus have an indirect affect in simplifying such process, thereby attracting more foreign investment.[62]

In addition, the Civil Code is substantively a systematic framework for the protection of civilian rights, including the right to marriage, children's rights, the rights to freedom of contract, private property rights, and the right to inheritance.

While the Civil Code is an important legislative achievement in the formal sense, it is not yet well implemented.[63] This may be due to the lack of public awareness of the Civil Code and citizens' conventional reliance on customs rather than law in dealing with civilian issues. The Lao government has worked on disseminating knowledge about the Civil Code, including through music video, to improve public awareness. However, it will take time for the Lao citizens to establish the culture of relying on civil law to deal with civilian matters.

3. Social Law

Social-economic transition generated issues such as working conditions, family violence, drugs, and diseases. Therefore, Laos enacted many social laws to deal with these issues, including the following laws:

Labour Law (revised 2013);
Law on Prevention of Violence against Women and Children (2014);
National Drug Law (2007);
Law on Prevention and Control of Infectious Diseases (2017);
HIV/AIDS Control and Prevention Law (2010);
Food Law (revised 2013); and
Law on Gender Equality (2019).

To illustrate, consider the reform of labour law. Lao adopted the Labour Law in 1994, 'providing labour protection, labour contracts, dismissal of labour contracts, working hours, rest hours, protection of woman and child labour, wage, social security, safe working conditions and enforcement measures'.[64] A revised version of the Labour Law in 2006 sought to improve 'worker compensation for work related injury, the monitoring and supervising of labour and complimenting workers with good performance'.[65] The current revised Labour Law adopted in 2013 attempted

[62] ibid.
[63] Interview with a Lao Lecture on Civil Law, 22 March 2023, Vientiane, Laos.
[64] Apirat Petchsiri and others, 'The Research of Legal system of Lao People's Democratic Republic and Legal Information Related to Social, Culture, Political and Security of Lao People's Democratic Republic' (Khon Kaen University 2016) 155.
[65] ibid.

to increase the effectiveness of labour skills by building the labour development system.[66] The system includes skills courses, evaluation and certification of labour skills, and competitive skills through the participation of labour skills development locations and labour units.[67]

4. Agrarian Law

Despite market development and urbanization, Laos 'remains an agrarian economy with most of the population dependent on agriculture'.[68] Reportedly, 'most people in Lao PDR live in rural areas and work in an agriculture sector dominated by subsistence farming. Lao PDR's economy relies heavily on its natural resources, with over half the country's wealth produced by agricultural land, forests, water and hydropower and mineral resources'.[69] To support the development of the agrarian economy, a body of Agrarian Law is enacted, which regulates and organizes the allocation, use, and protection of natural resources mainly in rural sectors, including the Land Law (revised 2021), the Forestry Law (2019), and the Law on Water and Water Resources (2017), among others.

The Land Law seeks to regulate and manage the protection, development, and use of land to improve people's livelihood; to ensure peace, social order, and social security; to facilitate national socio-economic development; and to protect the environment, the national borders, and territorial integrity (Article 1). Land includes land surface, underground land, mountains, islands, and submerged land (Article 2). The state is the owner of land, and Lao citizens and legal persons enjoy the land use rights (Article 3). The scope of the land use rights includes the rights to protect, use, and gain benefits from the land; the right to transfer land use; and the right related to inheritance of land use (Article 133).

The Forestry Law provides rules and principles for the management, protection, development, utilization, and inspection of forests and forestland to increase the richness of forest resources as a source for tourism and for sustainable use in people's livelihoods; to protect soil quality, air quality, water sources, biodiversity, and environmental protection in a green and sustainable manner; and to facilitate socio-economic development (Article 1). The Forestry Law defines that 'Forests are invaluable national resources with a unique ecology, comprising biodiversity, water sources and land with various tree species growing naturally or planted in an area of at least zero point five (0.5) hectares and a crown cover of at least 20 percent (20%)' (Article 2). The state is the owner of the natural forest and forestland and shall manage the forest and forestlands in a uniform

[66] ibid.

[67] Lao Labour Law (2013), art 8.

[68] Asian Development Bank, 'Lao People's Democratic Republic: Agriculture, Natural Resources, and Rural Development Sector Assessment, Strategy, and Road Map' (Country Sector and Thematic Assessments 2018) 2.

[69] Laos, Landlinks <https://www.land-links.org/country-profile/laos>accessed 6 June 2024.

and centralized manner (Article 4). However, individuals, households, and legal entities are vested with the right to use forests, forestland, and forest ecosystem services (Article 125).

The Law on Water and Water Resources creates a legal framework for the management, use, protection, development, rehabilitation, monitoring, inspection of water resources for the purposes of sustainability in terms of quantity and quality of water resources, national socio-economic development, national defence, security, and protection of the environment (Article 1). Water resources include natural and manmade resources such as rivers, streams, ponds, lakes, reservoirs, ground water, as well as water in the atmosphere, mud, stones, minerals, sand, sand islands, islands, banks, wetlands, lands under water, and others (Article 2). The state is the owner of water resources and shall manage water resources in a centralized and uniform manner, while individuals, entities, and organizations are entitled to use water resources for activities of production, businesses, and livelihoods (Article 6). The use of water resources includes these activities: the diversion, abstraction, separation, or impoundment of water resources; the extraction and use of stones, minerals, and sand from water sources; the construction of permanent structures on riverbanks; the alteration of riverbanks, beds, or the course of a water source; and aquaculture structures in a water source (Article 18).

The common functions of Lao agrarian laws are to protect and facilitate the use of natural resources for sustainable development. Given that the Lao agrarian economy heavily relies on natural resources, it is understandable that the agrarian laws seek to facilitate the use of natural resources for social-economic development. However, the use of natural resources may generate issues such as environmental pollution and ecosystem imbalance. The agrarian laws therefore attempt to balance the facilitation of economic development with the preservation of natural resources.

The ownership regime established by Lao agrarian laws shares some common features. The state is the owner of land, forests, and water resources, but individuals and legal entities are vested with the rights to use these natural resources. The consequence is that although Lao agrarian laws are highly regulatory, the language of rights informs these laws to some extent. The state manages and directs the use of natural resources in a centralized manner to pursue developmental purposes. At the same time, individuals and legal entities enjoy the right to use and gain benefits from the natural resources.

C. Limitations of Legislative Reform

Although Laos enacted numerous laws, legal enforcement remains a serious limitation. Richard Slater and Khamlouang Keoka point out that:

> Whilst the legal system in Laos has a substantial and growing body of law, there are many weaknesses and loopholes in the operation of the present system which undermine the degree of legal certainty and the establishment of a fully functioning rule of law. Part of the problem lies in poorly defined and applied procedure and part in low levels of capacity and resources.[70]

In the same vein, Simon Creak and Keith Barney explain that 'The legal sector lacks human resources, legal coordination and harmonization is poor, public awareness of the law remains low, and state officials have demonstrated an uneven commitment to upholding the law.'[71]

The Lao government acknowledges that 'the lack of strict implementation of laws and regulations' resulted in 'violations and misuse of authority'.[72] The government then is committed to further legislative reforms. To illustrate, the Ninth Plan (2021–25) anticipates the directions to:

> strengthen the role of the National Assembly and Provincial People's Assemblies in improving and adopting legislation . . . [;] develop strong and effective rule of law, focusing on developing and improving laws and subordinate legislations in a systematic and comprehensive manner and in line with the actual situation; improve law dissemination via different means in line with the actual conditions of the target audience; and create awareness of respect for the law by the people, and engage the public in the dissemination of laws'[73]

The continued commitment to legislative reforms is shaped by the government's continued commitment to rule of law reform, the political need to improve legislative law as a tool for the government to foster economic development, and the continued influences of international donors in legislative development in Laos.

D. Lao Socialist Law

Despite significant reform, Lao law remains essentially socialist. Lao law is an instrument for the party-state to pursue socialist development. Simon Creak and Keith Barney contend that 'the quest for a rule-of-law state appears to reflect the value the LPRP [Lao People's Revolutionary Party] attaches to making its rule—and guardianship over natural resources—more systematic, even while acknowledging that governance challenges are too complex to be solved through

[70] Slater and Keoka (n 37) 31.
[71] Creak and Barney (n 3) 47–48.
[72] Ninth Plan (n 31) 37.
[73] ibid 97–98.

laws alone'.[74] In other words, legislative reforms towards the direction of the rule of law are instrumentalist, not normative. The Lao state needs to use coherent and accessible legislation as an instrument to govern the emerging market relations and natural resources to foster social-economic development. The state appreciates norms of formal rule of law (such as coherence and accessibility) not because of their internal values but because of their necessity for external outcomes, such as state building, regime security, social order, and state-led economic development.

Public law is an instrument to consolidate the state power and to protect the state interests. For example, the 2017 Criminal Code provides that:

> the Penal Code intends to safeguard the political, economic and social regimes of the Lao PDR, to protect interests of the State, the legitimate rights and interests of citizens, the life, health, dignity, rights and freedom of Lao people, national security and social order; to prevent and counter offences; and to teach all citizens to be aware of the laws (Article 1)

Thus, criminal law is a means to protect the socialist regime and state interests, in addition to individual interests. The Penal Code includes specific offences to protect the socialist regime. For example, Article 117 of the Code punishes with imprisonment up to five years and fines up to twenty million kip:

> any person conducting propaganda activities against and slandering the Lao PDR, or distorting the guidelines of the Party and policies of the government, or circulating false rumors causing disorder by words, in writing, through print, newspapers, motion pictures, videos, photographs, documents, electronic media, or by other means, which are detrimental to the Lao PDR or are for the purpose of undermining or weakening State authority[75]

This vague provision vests the government with broad discretion to impose criminal sanctions on dissidents and other individuals criticizing the ruling Party and the government. For example, in 2019, a woman was jailed according to Article 117 of the Penal Code for five years for her online criticism of the government.[76]

Private law is an instrument for the state to direct social-economic development to socialism. For example, the Civil Code seeks to protect the 'rights and the legitimated interests of individuals, juristic persons, organisations, State and

[74] Creak and Barney (n 3) 49.

[75] Lao Penal Code (2017), art 117

[76] 'Woman Jailed for Five Years for Criticizing the Government Online (Press Release, International Federation for Human Rights, 22 November 2019) <https://www.fidh.org/en/region/asia/laos/woman-jailed-for-five-years-for-criticizing-the-government-online>accessed 6 June 2024.

collectives', maintain the 'unity of all Lao ethnics and fine national customary practices', and strengthen 'social-economic development' (Article 1). Thus, the Civil Code is enacted to protect not only individual interests but also state interests. It is also a means for general ends (ethnic unity, fine customs, and social-economic development) defined by the state.

The instrumental aspect of Lao legislation is also embodied in the legislative plan. Legislative planning indicates that the socialist culture of planning extended from the economic to the legal field. Like economic planning, legislative planning suggests that socialist legal development is not evolutionary but a designed change directed by the party-state in a systematic and rational way. Legislative planning is an instrument for the party-state to subject legal development to the party-state's intention. Planning allows the party-state to ensure that legislative development will process to the direction of socialism. Planning is therefore a means for controlling legislative development to achieve socialist ends. Legislative planning has both inclusive and exclusive instrumental functions. As Laos needs to make many laws under limited resources, legislative planning enables the party-state to prioritize the making of certain laws perceived as more necessary for the developmental goals. Legislative planning also allows the party-state to exclude proposed laws perceived as unnecessary or even inimical to the developmental goals.

Lao legislation is under the Party's vanguard leadership. The Party adopts policy for general development of law. It even directs the adoption of specific laws.[77] The Legislation Law establishes the principle that legislative development must be 'consistent with political orientation' (Article 7). 'Political orientation' means the Party's orientation normally embodied in the Party's political documents. Consequently, law is the embodiment of Party lines in legal forms.

Despite market reform, the features of the statist economy remain in the Lao legal system. The Civil Code protects state's ownership of 'lands, minerals, water resources, airs, forest products, wildlife, aquatic animals, mineral resources, and other natural resources' (Article 263). As mentioned above, the agrarian laws establish the state's centralized management of natural resources (land, water, and forests). The state ownership and centralized management of natural resources (crucial means of production) enables the state to control the economy.

The statist economy is also embedded in the role of the state economic sector. The state economic sector in Laos has been less dominant than those in China and Vietnam as Laos has privatized most state-owned enterprises.[78] However, the state retains its domination in the sectors of strategic importance, including electricity

[77] Vangseng (n 6) 113.
[78] Creak and Barney (n 3) 44.

and water.[79] Even private enterprises are under the state's regulatory control. The 2013 Enterprise Law provides that:

> the State encourages persons and organizations, whether foreign or domestic, to establish enterprises or engage in operating businesses in all business sectors that are not prohibited, by facilitating measures for them through tax incentives, regulations, information support and other services. This policy aims at promotion of all enterprises to make their contributions to develop the socio-economy (Article 7)

This provision suggests that private enterprises should not only pursue private gains but also contribute to the implementation of the state's social and economic developmental objectives. Section 2 of the Enterprise Law includes many rules for enterprise registration. This allows bureaucratic agents to control the creation of private enterprises to ensure enterprise creation conforms with the state's developmental objectives.

Statist rights are embodied in Lao legislation. The practice of rights depends on the state's paternalistic policy. For example, Article 4 of the Civil Code provides that 'Government creates favourable conditions to facilitate the conduct of civil relationship by issuing rules, conducting campaigns to raise the law awareness among citizen to raise the common acknowledge and understanding of Civil Code.' The practice of civilian rights thus depends on the government's benevolent regulatory policy. The popular awareness of legal rights is shaped by the state's propaganda. The consequence is that the practice and the public understanding of civilian rights would conform to the state's objectives. Some laws provide a framework for the state to control the rights practice. To illustrate, Article 124 of the Penal Code punishes with imprisonment up to five years and a fine up to fifty million kip 'any person organizing or participating in the gathering of groups of persons to conduct protests, marches, demonstrations or similar activities with the intention of causing social disorder'. Article 124 further adds that 'any preparation or attempt to commit such an offence shall also be punished'. Article 124 creates a legislative base for the state to control the practice of the fundamental rights to association and demonstration promised in Article 44 of the 2015 Constitution.[80] The state controls the practice of these rights to subordinate individual rights to state interest (eg regime security, social order, and social-economic development).

[79] Bertelsmann Stiftung, 'BTI 2022 Country Report—Laos' (Bertelsmann Stiftung 2022) 24.

[80] Lao 2015 Constitution, art 44 ('Lao citizens have the right and freedom of speech, press and assembly; and have the right to set up associations and to stage demonstrations which are not contrary to the laws.').

IV. ADMINISTRATIVE REFORM

A. Public Administration Reform

Since 1986, an important trend in Lao administrative reform has been the legalization of the administrative system. The party-state seeks to create a legal base for a stable administrative system. The enactment of the 1991 Constitution lays down the foundation for the reform of the Lao administrative system. The laws on central and local governments were enacted and revised following the constitutional replacements. According to the existing constitutional-legal framework, the administrative structure in Laos includes the central government and local governments at provincial, district, and village levels. 'At the central level, the Council of Ministers was replaced by the Members of Government and at the provincial and district levels, the provincial and district administrative committee was replaced by governor and district mayor and cancellation of Commune (Taseng) and replaced the village committee by the village chief.'[81] These reforms sought to modify the Soviet-collective style of administrative governance by improving the power and accountability of individual administrative leaders.

Another trend is organizational reconstructing, which involves ministerial merging and new establishment. For example, the Ministry of Industry and Crafts and the Ministry of Commerce were merged into the Ministry of Industry and Trade; the Ministry of Energy and Minerals was newly created; and the Committee on Planning and Investment was transformed into the Ministry of Planning and Investment.[82] Consequently, the number of ministries increased to eighteen 'to provide greater policy direction and management over a more comprehensive range of sectors and services than in the past'.[83] The eighteen ministries are:

Ministry of Justice
Ministry of Internal Affairs
Ministry of Defense
Ministry of Finance
Ministry of Health
Ministry of Agriculture and Forestry
Ministry of Education and Sports
Ministry of Foreign Affairs

[81] Master Plan (n 12).

[82] Vanlaty Khamvanvongsa, 'Cải cách hành chính nhà nước ở Cộng hòa Dân chủ nhân dân Lào' [Administrative Reform in Lao PDR] (*Tạp chí điện tử Tổ chức nhà nước*, 9 October 2014) accessed 6 June 2024 <https://tcnn.vn/news/detail/6919/Cai_cach_hanh_chinh_nha_nuoc_o_Cong_hoa_Dan_chu_nhan_dan_Laoall.html>.

[83] Slater and Keoka (n 37) 86.

Ministry of Public Security
Ministry of Energy and Mines
Ministry of Natural Resources and Environment
Ministry of Post, Telecom and Communication
Ministry of Industry and Commerce
Ministry of Public Work and Transportation
Ministry of Labour and Social Welfare
Ministry of Information, Culture, and Tourism
Ministry of Planning and Investment
Ministry of Science and Technology[84]

Another achievement in administrative reform is the development of civil servants. By 2021, the number of civil servants grew to 176,151, of whom 83,102 were women and 42% were public school teachers.[85] The government had made some efforts to improve the cost of living for civil servants such as salary reform.

Since the 1990s, the Lao government introduced reform measures to improve the functional performance of the public administration. In 1997, the government adopted the Governance and Public Administration Reform (GPAR) programme. Supported by the UNDP, the GPAR programme aimed to improve the delivery of public administration and accessibility of public services. In 2011, the Lao government and its international donors launched a new GPAR programme to continue efforts of service delivery.[86] Reportedly:

> as a result of the GPAR programme, ongoing since 1997, the governance sector in Lao PDR has already been transformed. The programme has strengthened the public administration's capacity to plan, finance, manage, and monitor governance reform. It has also enabled civil servants to deliver services to Lao citizens in effective, accountable, and transparent ways, allowing the public administration to increasingly fulfil its role in alleviating poverty and achieving national development goals.[87]

An important trend in central–local relations in Laos is decentralization. In 2012, the Lao government adopted the decentralization policy known as the Sam Sang ('Three Builds'). Sam Sang sought to improve local delivery of public services by fostering autonomy and accountability of socio-economic (particularly natural

[84] Apirat Petchsiri and others (n 64) 249

[85] Manyphone Vongphachanh, 'Laos Ranks 4th in the List of ASEAN Countries with Most Civil Servants' The Laotian Times (14 September 2022) accessed 6 June 2024 <https://laotiantimes.com/2022/09/14/laos-ranks-4th-in-the-list-of-asean-countries-with-most-civil-servants>.

[86] Governance and Public Administration Reform (GPAR), Federal Department of Foreign Affairs FDFA accessed 6 June 2024 <https://www.eda.admin.ch/eda/en/fdfa/suche/suchresultat.html/content/dezaprojects/SDC/en/2003/7F03181/phase3>.

[87] ibid.

resource) management at provincial, district, and village levels.[88] Several legal instruments were enacted to support and guide the implementation of this decentralization policy, including a Standing Committee Resolution in 2012, a Prime Minister Ordinance in 2012, and instructions issued by central and line ministries.[89] Simon Creak and Keith Barney point out that 'despite its putative focus on administrative devolution, the Three Builds aims at strengthening central coordination to permit "correct" and "appropriate" decentralization, in order to strengthen centralization'.[90] In other words, Sam Sang is a project of administrative, not political, decentralization.

Laos needs to reform the administrative system to facilitate the formation and implementation of development policy. There was 'a growing interest on the part of the Party and senior government functionaries of the need to develop an efficient and effective public administration capable of formulating strategic policies and plans in line with national priorities'.[91] In addition, public governance reform in Laos was instigated by the external normative influence and support of international agents. International donors did not just provide fanatical assistance they also diffused norms of good governance (eg participation, accountability, and transparency) in Laos, which informed the country's public administration reforms.

The Lao administrative system, however, has been confronted with significant shortcomings. The government acknowledges that:

> Public administration and governance by the rule of law, despite the attention and effort, have not been as effective as expected. There have been violations of the law and violations of individual rights on a regular basis, as well as interference by organisations or individuals in the public administration process . . . Management mechanisms and the division of responsibilities between the vertical and horizontal lines of organisational structure are not clear-cut . . . The division of management responsibilities according to the Sam Sang Directive has not yet been transformed.[92]

The government then is committed to continuing administrative reforms. For example, the Ninth Plan (2021–25) proposes measures to 'reform the public administration system and civil service management regulations to simplify and improve consistency', 'redefine the mandates and duties of some ministries and

[88] Creak and Barney (n 3) 47.
[89] Vongsakda Vongxay and Yangsoo Yi, 'Sam Sang Rural Community Development Model of Lao PDR in Approach to Successful Implementation-Lessons from Korea's Saemual Undong' (2017) 24 J Agri Exten Comm Dev 145–46.
[90] Creak and Barney (n 3) 47.
[91] Slater and Keoka (n 37) 88.
[92] Ninth Plan (n 51) 35–36.

agencies more clearly to avoid duplication and overlap', and 'establish the Sam Sang Directive work as a regular work of sectors and local administrations nationwide by assigning authority and responsibility to localities at each level in the decision-making process under a clear regulatory and legal framework'.[93]

B. Administrative Law Reform

Administrative law reform has also witnessed some achievements. Several laws were enacted to check the use of the administrative power and to empower citizens.

Laos enacted the Law on Handling of Petitions in 2005, which enabled citizens and organizations to present a petition to a relevant authority for it to review action or decision arguably infringing the law, which affects their interests and state interests (Article 2). A new version of the Law on Handling of Petitions was adopted in 2014, which includes eighteen new articles, revises forty articles and retains eight articles of the 2005 version.[94] Like the 2005 version, the 2014 Law on Handling of Petitions distinguishes three types of petitions: a request presented to a state administrative authority; a claim presented to an investigation organization, the Office of the Public Prosecutor or the People's Courts; and a petition for justice presented to the NA (Article 2).[95] The Law provides that the petitioner has the rights to present the petition in person or by a legal representative, receive a written response to the petition from the concerned authority, be protected from threats and suppression and disclosure of personal information (eg name and address), and have the infringed rights restored and receive compensation from the person who has violated the law (Article 8).[96] In administrative petitions, if the petitioner is not satisfied with the decision, he or she can propose it to a higher public administrative authority to consider. If the petitioner is not satisfied after all administrative procedures are exhausted, he or she may make a claim in court or present a petition for justice to the NA (Article 19).[97]

Corruption remains a major problem in the Lao administrative system. Therefore, the state has developed a legal framework for combating corruption. Important legal instruments to deal with corruption in Laos include the Anti-Corruption Law (2012), the Penal Code (2017), the Law on Anti-Money Laundering and Counter-Financing of Terrorism, the Decree on Asset Declaration

[93] ibid 94–95.

[94] Chaovang Toudouachi, Hoàn Thiện Pháp Luật Về Khiếu Nại Và Giải Quyết Khiếu Nại Của Cộng Hòa Dân Chủ Nhân Dân Lào—Bài Học Kinh Nghiệm Từ Việt Nam [Improving the Law on Petition and Petition Settlement of the Lao People's Democratic Republic—Lessons learned from Vietnam] (PhD Dissertation, Hanoi Law University 2019) 57.

[95] Cited in ibid 58.

[96] Cited in ibid 60.

[97] Cited in ibid 63–64.

(2013), and the Decision on Prohibitions and Disciplining State Employees in the Finance Sector (2017).[98]

Lao legislature adopted the Anti-Corruption Law in 2005 and replaced it with another version in 2012. The 2012 Anti-Corruption Law covers the following acts:

embezzlement of state property or collective property;
swindling of state property or collective property;
bribes;
taking bribes;
abuse of position, power, and duty to take state property, collective property, or individual property;
abuse of state property or collective property;
excessive use of position, power, and duty to take state property, collective property, or individual property;
cheating or falsification relating to technical construction, standards, designs, calculations, and others;
deception in bidding or offering concessions;
forging documents or using forged documents; and
disclosure of state secrets for personal benefit.[99]

Corruption is defined by an official committing any of the above acts to 'benefit himself, or his family, relatives, friends, clan or group, and causes damage to the interests of the State and society, or to the rights and interests of citizens'.[100] Depending on the severity of the offence, individuals who have committed corruption can be sanctioned under the Anti-Corruption Law with educational measures, a warning, and disciplinary measures (such as criticism, suspension from any promotion, and removal from position).[101]

The government attempted to implement the Anti-Corruption Law. According to a Party report in 2017:

> corrupt practices over the past five years have involved payments totalling more than 4,807 billion kip, and 734 officials were found to have been involved. Additionally, between 2011 and 2015, more than 130 police officers were dismissed from their tenure in the province of Oudomsay for taking bribes and benefits related to their position, in a clear abuse of power.[102]

[98] Dino Santaniello, 'Laos: Anti-Corruption Laws Key to Economic Development', Global Investigations Review (21 September 2018) accessed 6 June 2024 <https://globalinvestigationsreview.com/review/the-asia-pacific-investigations-review/2019/article/laos-anti-corruption-laws-key-economic-development>.
[99] ibid.
[100] ibid.
[101] ibid.
[102] ibid.

In 2018, Prime Minister Thongloun Sisoulith dismissed two provincial governors accused of profiteering from the timber trade. 'These are high-ranking dismissals, which have rarely happened in the past.'[103]

Apart from the Anti-Corruption Law, Laos enacted several other laws and regulations to deal with corruption. The Penal Code includes a chapter on corruption (Chapter 10). The Code prosecutes different types of individuals (eg leader, administrative, technical, or enterprise staff member, civil servant, military officer, police officer, and foreign or international organization staff member) who commit an act of corruption. In addition, in 2014, Lao legislature enacted the Law on Anti-Money Laundering and Counter-Financing of Terrorism. The Law requires banks to report suspicious transactions to the Anti-Money Laundering Intelligence Office (Article 31). Moreover, in 2013, the government issued the Decree on Asset Declaration in 2013. The Decree defines legal rules and principles for asset and income declaration of officials, soldiers, and police officers working under the party-state organizations, the Lao Front for National Construction, mass organizations, state enterprises, state-mixed enterprises, and state-partnerships 'to prevent and combat corruption in the party-state institutional organizations and the aforementioned organizations' (Article 1). Reportedly, by mid-January 2017, 'more than 1,900 officials and civil servants at the central level, 98,000 people under the supervision of ministries, and 142,000 officials and civil servants under provincial administrations, have declared their assets.'[104] In 2017, the Ministry of Finance issued the Decision on Prohibitions and Disciplining State Employees in the Finance Sector. The Decision includes ten prohibitions applicable to its own officials and civil servants, which aim to sanction false and incorrect reporting.[105]

The legal framework for anti-corruption is substantive, but legal enforcement remains a major problem. One reason is institutional: 'Laos' judiciary is weak and inefficient, and officials are rarely prosecuted' for corruption.[106] Another reason is cognitive: Lao citizens, who have mainly resided in rural areas, have lacked awareness of anti-corruption laws, which has prevented them from referring to the laws to combat administrative wrongdoings.[107]

Several other pieces of legislation were enacted to check the use of administrative power. The Law on State Inspection adopted in 2007 aims to strengthen

[103] Lào Quyết Tâm Phòng Chống Tham Nhũng [Laos is Determined to Combat Corruption] (*Tạp chí Lào—Việt*, 21 August 2022) accessed 6 June 2024<https://tapchilaoviet.org/cam-nang-lao-viet/lao-quyet-tam-phong-chong-tham-nhung-49853.html>.

[104] Santaniello (n 98).

[105] Dino Santaniello, 'Lex Mundi Global Anti-Corruption Compliance Guide: Laos' (Tilleke & Gibbins, the Lex Mundi member firm for Thailand, 27 November 2018) accessed 6 June 2024<https://www.tilleke.com/wp-content/uploads/2018/12/Anti-Corruption-Global-Guide-Laos.pdf>.

[106] 'Impoverished Laos Has Lost More Than $760 Million To Corruption Since 2016: Report' (*Radio Free Asia*, 18 April 2022) accessed 6 June 2024 <https://www.rfa.org/english/news/laos/corruption-losses-04182022171408.html>.

[107] Martin Stuart-Fox, 'The Political Culture of Corruption in the Lao PDR' (2006) 31 Asian Stud Rev 69.

the investigation of legal infringement, corruption, and weak administration and management. The Law on Audit adopted in 2007 creates rules for the inspection and management of the state budget, business organizations, and non-profit organizations.[108]

Thus, Laos has legislated to reform administrative law. The country now has a substantive framework of formal administrative legal rules and principles. The body of the formal administrative law at least suggests political elite's reformist efforts to subject the use of the administrative power to legality. Particularly, several pieces of legislation seek to curb arbitrary administrative power and empower citizens to challenge the legality of administrative agents. The party-state has institutional interests to control the legality of administrative power. First, administrative law reform can consolidate the legal legitimacy of the party-state. Second, the party-state has the incentive to control the legality of the administrative power to implement its development policy pronounced in legislation. Third, the party-state needs to ensure that the use of administrative power adheres to law to attract foreign investors and international aids.

C. Socialist Administrative Law

Despite significant reforms, public administration and administrative law in Laos remain essentially socialist. The law and legal institutions of public administration are instruments to facilitate the interventional role of the government in social-economic development to achieve socialist objectives. Lao administrative law therefore is more about empowering than constraining the regulatory power of administrative agents. Administrative agents from central to various local levels enjoy the power to issue different kinds of regulatory instruments.

The public administrative agents in Laos are under the vanguard leadership of the Party. The Party nominates Party members to hold key positions in the administrative system. Party cells operate with every ministry and provincial administrative body.[109] The Party decides policy that will be implemented by the administrative agents. 'The Party and Government are essentially one and the same and there is no distinction between the political and executive arms of government. The main function of the Party is to provide direction, formulate policy and provide guidance on all aspects and across all branches of government.'[110] The Party adopts policy for administrative reform. Consequently, administrative reforms are limited within the Party's vanguard role in the administrative system.

[108] Apirat Petchsiri and others (n 64) 265–67.
[109] Stuart-Fox (n 3) 12
[110] Slater and Keoka (n 37) 12.

The principle of democratic centralism is embodied in Lao public administration and administrative law. The Law on the Government provides that 'The Government carries out its affairs based on the principle of democratic centralism by integrating collective responsibility with personal accountability. The meeting of the Government is the main form by which the government conducts its activities.'[111] The meeting of the government provides the forum for 'democratic' discussions. Collective decisions made by the central government at its meeting must be centrally implemented by its individual members and local governments. In the same vein, the Law on Local Administration provides that:

> The organisation, functions and operational procedures of the local administrations are implemented in accordance with the principle of democratic centralism [with devolution of responsibility to the local administration level], which divides responsibility among management levels. The village level reports to the district level, the district level reports to the provincial level and the provincial level reports to the government under the guidance and responsibility of the party committee based on the Constitution and the laws.[112]

Despite the greater decentralization to local governments according to the Sam Sang polity, the principle of democratic centralism subordinates the inferior institutions of local governments to the hierarchical control of the superior institutions of local and central governments.

Statist rights are embodied in the Law on Handling of Petitions. The Law indicates that the state tends to subordinate the individual rights to petition to the state interests. The state allows citizens and organizations to exercise the right to petition to protect their own interests and the state interests to ensure transparency and effectiveness of the state administration.[113] However, the Law provides that the state shall promote mediation according to customs and the law to prevent petition and mitigate social conflicts.[114] On one hand, the state needs to accommodate the increasing petitions (particularly petitions against land confiscations for developmental projects[115]) and to check the misuse of administrative power. On the other hand, the state needs to avoid the aggressive use of petitions to pursue personal interests and challenge the administrative power. To deal with this dilemma, the Law on Handling of Petitions seeks to subordinate the use of petition to the state interests and encourages communal mediation or conciliation to prevent petition.

[111] Amended Law on the Government of the Lao People's Democratic Republic (2003), art 30.

[112] Law on Local Administration (2003), art 5.

[113] Chaovang Toudouachi (n 94) 57.

[114] ibid.

[115] Chaovang Toudouachi, Sự Cần Thiết Khách Quan Của Việc Hoàn Thiện Pháp Luật Về Khiếu Nại Và Giải Quyết Khiếu Nại Ở Nước Cộng Hòa Dân Chủ Nhân Dân Lào [The Objective Necessity of Perfecting the Law on Petition and Petition Settlement in the Lao People's Democratic Republic] (2018) 6 Tạp chí Công Thương 43.

Administrative law provides the legal basis for the state's domination of the national economy. Despite market reform, Lao economy is under the government's control with legal underpinnings. The Law on the Government empowers the government to determine strategic plans and socio-economic development plans and to issue legal regulatory instruments (decrees and resolutions) on socio-economic management (Article 7). The government can use its planning and regulatory power to direct the economy to socialist objectives. Consider, for example, the Negative List issued by the Prime Minister Decree in 2008. This is 'the list of the businesses which are highly sensitive notably to the national security, public order, fine tradition and culture and environment, and which shall be scrutinized and authorized by the relevant authorities prior to enterprise registration.'[116] This regulation allows the state to stringently supervise and control (not prohibit) the operation of business in a wide range of areas (agriculture, forestry, fishing, electricity, gas, water supply, transportation, information and communication, banking, finance, health, social works, art, entertainment, etc.) to protect state interests. Generally, the development of private economic sectors is possible but planned and regulated by the state to achieve the state's goals. Consequently, the Lao economy is partially capitalist but principally statist.

V. JUDICIAL REFORM

A. Achievements of Court Reform

Since 1986, Laos introduced measures for judicial reforms. After several decades of reforms, Laos now has a functional court system structurally separate from the government. The courts are staffed by more professional judges. They also perform legal functions and are not merely a tool for political control. Constitutional and legislative enactments supporting indicial reforms include the Constitution (last updated 2015), the Law on People's Courts (last updated 2017), the Law on Judges, and the Law on Court Fees (last updated 2019).

Lao courts have changed from being a component of the executive established by administrative regulation to a separate system under the Constitution and statutory law. As mentioned previously, in the early years after the creation of the Lao PDR, courts were part of the executive. Since the introduction of the NEM policy in 1986, Laos has carried out judicial reforms leading to structural separation of the courts from the government. In 1989, the NA adopted the Law on the People's Court and elected the president of the Supreme People's Court. The Law provided for the creation of the Supreme People's Court and local courts at provincial

[116] Decree on Adoption of the Negative List, No 68/PM, 2008.

and district levels. The Supreme People's Court was accountable to the Supreme People's Assembly, which means it was structurally separate from the Ministry of Justice. However, the organizational structure and administration of the local courts were still under the Ministry of Justice.[117]

The enactment of the 1991 Constitution provides the legal basis for the continued structural reform of the court system separate from the government. According to the Constitution, the court system included the Supreme People's Court, provincial and prefecture courts, district courts, and Military Court. Local courts were still administered by the Ministry of Justice. In early 2001, 18 prefecture and provincial courts and 136 district courts were established.[118]

Constitutional replacement in 2003 created important changes to the court system, which consolidated its structural separation from the government. The court system established by the 2003 Constitution includes the People's Supreme Court; the appellate courts; the people's provincial courts and city courts; the people's district courts; and the military courts (Article 79). Notably, the Constitution transferred the management of local courts from the Ministry of Justice to the People's Supreme Court (Article 80). This transfer is a further move to separate the courts from the executive. In practice, the transfer took place on 5 September 2003. Three appeal courts were established in the northern, middle, and southern parts of Laos. Eight new district courts were created. To implement the amended Law on People's Court (2003), specialist chambers (including the Civil Chamber, Criminal Chamber, Commercial Chamber, Family Chamber, and Juvenile Chamber) were created at the People's Supreme Court, the appellate, provincial, and capital city courts. By 2009, the Lao court system included a Supreme Court, 3 appeal courts, 17 provincial and capital city courts, 103 district courts, 1 High Military Court, and 3 regional military courts. By the same year, the court system was staffed by 393 judges in total.[119]

The 2015 Constitution further strengthens courts' independence, providing that 'the People's Courts are judicial organs; only courts have the power to adjudicate [and] judge cases in the Lao People's Democratic Republic' (Article 90). This provision seeks to assert the independence of the judicial branch and prevent the interference of other branches in the courts' adjudication.

After several decades of reforms, Lao courts are now rather well organized under a solid legal framework established by the Constitution (2015) and the Law on People's Courts (last updated 2017). The Constitution provides that 'The People's Courts of the Lao People's Democratic Republic consist of the People's Supreme Court, Local People's Courts and Military Courts as provided by the laws. In the event that it is deemed necessary, the National Assembly Standing Committee may

117 Master Plan (n 12).
118 ibid.
119 ibid.

decide to establish a special court' (Article 91). The revised Law on People's Court (2017) specifies that the local people's courts include district people's courts; provincial or capital people's courts and children's courts; and people's regional courts.[120] District courts have been merged into area courts with at least two courts per province.[121] Laos currently has a People's Supreme Court, 3 regional courts, 18 provincial courts, and 149 area courts.[122] The creation of the regional courts and the area courts, which do not correspond to administrative units, may facilitate more convenient access to justice and some independence of local courts from local governments.

The Law on People's Courts (2017) specifies three levels of court authority, namely court of first instance, court of appeal, and Supreme Court. Accordingly, the district people's court is the court of first instance. The provincial or capital people's court is the court of first instance and the court of appeal for the appeal against the judgment of the district people's court. The regional people's court is the court of appeal for the appeal against the judgment of the provincial people's and capital people's courts. The People's Supreme Court functions as the supreme court for appeal against judgment on appeal of the regional people's court or other high court.[123]

There has been progress in the quantity and quality of the judges. Several years after the launch of the 2009 rule of law reform plan, the number of judges grew to 576 (including 163 females) by 2023.[124] Lao courts are now staffed by more professional judges. The Judicial Training Institute was established in 1997 to build the capacity of officials working in the legal and judicial sector, including judges.[125] The enactment of the Law on Judges in 2017 is an important step to foster judicial professionalism. Apart from moral and political requirements, the Law establishes general professional requirements (legal education and judicial training) and specific professional requirements for four ranks of judges.[126]

Formal law provides a framework for Lao courts to perform legal, not merely political function. The Law on Courts protects fair trial rights and legal principles for the court proceedings, including the equality of citizens before law and court, the rights of citizens to defend their cases, independence during the court proceeding, compliance with the law in the conduct of legal proceeding, holding court proceedings at an open venue, and compliance with the final court decision.[127]

[120] Aristotle T David, Novah Rose S De Leon-David, and Tuchakorn Kitcharoen, 'Legal System of the Lao People's Democratic Republic' Hauser Global Law School Program accessed 6 June 2024 <https://www.nyulawglobal.org/globalex/Laos1.html#_edn122>.

[121] Slater and Keoka (n 37) 24.

[122] Personal communication with Khamphaeng Phochanthilath, 5 June 2023.

[123] David, De Leon-David, and Kitcharoen (n 120).

[124] Personal communication with Khamphaeng Phochanthilath, 5 June 2023.

[125] Master Plan (n 12).

[126] Lao Law on Judges, arts 11, 12, and 13.

[127] David, De Leon-David, and Kitcharoen (n 120).

These formal legal commitments at least render the operation of the courts to look like a legal process. Procedural laws such as the Law on Criminal Procedure Law (last updated 2018), the Law on Civil Procedure (last updated 2024), and the Children Procedure Law (2014) provide the framework for the operation of the courts as legal institutions.

To some extent, Lao courts have operated as arbiters to resolve legal disputes, rather than as mere political tools to suppress anti-revolutionary forces. The courts are capable of dealing with a large number of legal disputes. To illustrate, between 2006 and 2010, some 13,898 cases were resolved at the courts in the provinces and the capital Vientiane; 3,420 cases were resolved in the appellate courts; and 3,451 cases were resolved in the People's Supreme Court. So, in total, the courts throughout the country resolved some 20,764 cases during the above period. In the same period, there were 11,448 criminal and civil cases of which 2,332 cases were resolved, 8,641 cases were under process, and 475 cases were pending.[128]

According to the Eighth Plan adopted in 2016, during the past two and a half years, the courts received 36,492 cases and settled approximately 36,076 cases (95.32%). The most frequent cases were criminal cases (19,151 cases, 50.6 %), especially concerning possession and selling of illicit drugs. There were 19,151 civil cases (30.6 %), especially about land disputes (11,583 cases) or trade (1,907 cases). There are also 4,296 family cases; 881 children cases related to theft of civilians' assets and use of illicit drugs; and 28 cases related to labour issues, particularly wage and agreement.[129]

Between 2016 and 2020, courts at all levels received 41,699 cases of which 38,497 were resolved (92.32%). Of the 9,043 court judgments that were enforced 4,079 were civil cases and 4,964 were criminal cases. There were 279 cases involving economic disputes of which 237 cases were resolved.[130]

The number of cases increased significantly in the five-year periods. The number of cases during the 2016–20 period was nearly double that of the 2006–10 period. The implementation of the 2009 rule of law plan may result in the increased number of cases as this plan may put pressure on the courts to accept and decide cases and encourage citizens to approach courts to resolve legal disputes. In addition, market development generated more legal disputes, especially civil and commercial disputes, which led to the increase in number of cases.

Laos now has a functional court system. The courts were able to decide thousands of cases annually. Particularly, the number of decided civil, commercial, and family cases suggests that Lao courts have operated as arbiter of legal disputes among private sectors. Law has been implemented by courts. The courts have

[128] Seventh Plan (n 49) 61.
[129] Eighth Plan (n 50) 66.
[130] Ninth Plan (n 51) 24.

therefore performed the legal function: to adjudicate legal disputes and to enforce the law.

Lao courts, however, are still faced with important shortcomings. Despite the formal commitment to judicial independence, the actual functions of the courts have been subject to various interferences. Richard Slater and Khamlouang Keoka report that:

> in practice, the outcome of a case may be decided less by technical analysis than by individual connections, offers of consideration, family ties and other interventions. Reaching a decision can be even more tricky where it involves competing interventions, each desirous of a different outcome and where a case may thus have to be evaluated on the basis of competing influence rather than the weight of evidence.[131]

Other problems involve judicial corruption and extra-legal adjudication. 'Some judges reportedly accepted bribes; others reportedly decided guilt or innocence in advance of trials, basing their decisions on police or prosecutorial investigation reports.'[132] Another issue is the poor enforcement of court decisions. The Lao government acknowledges that 'the enforcement of court judgments in some cases has not been straightforward or fully executed, with the issue of social justice not having been fully addressed'.[133] The Lao government is committed to further reforms of the court system. For example, the Ninth Plan (2021–25) prioritizes providing capacity building for judges and improving enforcement of court judgments. It targets providing modern equipment for the People's Supreme Court and implementing 80% of pending court judgments and new court judgments.[134]

B. The Socialist Courts

Like courts in China and Vietnam, Lao courts remain essentially socialist despite considerable reforms. To begin with, instrumentalism is embodied in the court system. Although the courts have legal functions thanks to reforms, they remain political institutions to protect the state interests. The courts therefore do not just have adjudicative function. They have various political functions as provided by the Law on People's Courts such as to educate citizens, promote and disseminate law, and 'increase political conscience, respect and compliance with law of citizen'.[135] The courts are political institutions to inculcate in the civic conscience

131 Slater and Keoka (n 37) 31.
132 US Department of State, 'Laos 2021 Human Rights Report' 5.
133 Ninth Plan (n 51) 36.
134 ibid 97–98.
135 David, De Leon-David, and Kitcharoen, (n 120).

with socialist ideology, propagandize law, and foster citizens' compliance with the law. The courts are the instruments for political control of the civic compliance and loyalty to the socialist regime and socialist law.

Lao courts also embody party vanguardism. Like the cases in China and Vietnam, although there is no formal legal requirement, a judge in Laos must be a Party member.[136] The Party decides major policy on the judicial institutions and directs judicial reforms.[137]

> [Functionally,] judgments on all important cases are routinely submitted to senior Party leaders, which in the provinces means to the provincial governor, before being handed down. Just as there is no distinction in Laos between the Party and the government or administration, so there is no distinction between the Party and the judiciary.[138]

This means the operation of the courts is under Party leadership.

The principle of democratic centralism is also embodied in Lao courts, particularly the powers of the People's Supreme Court as provided by the Law on People's Courts. The People's Supreme Court's powers are externally weak and internally strong. Externally, the Court must report to the NA and is not allowed to review the constitutionality and legality of statutes. Internally, the People's Supreme Court is a powerful institution to manage and control local courts in a centralist manner. In this regard, the People's Supreme Court has the power to review the legal aspects of the decisions by local courts, advise and monitor the legal compliance and uniformity in the conduct of legal proceeding of local courts, compile minutes of the general meeting of judges to ensure the understanding and implementation of all courts, direct the education of judges, and monitor court operations, among other things.[139] Judges of the People's Supreme Court regularly go to localities to supervise and advise the work of local courts.[140] Local courts are placed under the centralized control of the People's Supreme Court.

VI. LEGAL PROFESSIONAL REFORM

A. Achievements of Lawyer System Reform

Reform of the lawyer system is an important part of rule of law reform in Laos. After several decades of reform, the country has a functional lawyer system governed

[136] Interview with a Lao lawyer, 21 March, 2023, Vientiane, Laos.
[137] Vangseng (n 6) 114.
[138] Stuart-Fox (n 3) 27.
[139] David, De Leon-David, and Kitcharoen (n 120).
[140] Interview with a judge of Lao People's Supreme Court, 20 March 2023, Vientiane, Laos.

by the Law on Lawyers adopted in 2016 and recently replaced by another version in 2023.

Shortly after the introduction of the reform policy, there were some efforts to create a lawyer system in Laos. The government approved the establishment of the LBA in 1989. However, the Association was suspended due to the limited understanding of the role of lawyers in the legal system and the public distrust of lawyers.[141] In 1996, the LBA was re-established. Reportedly, 'After its establishment, the LBA concentrated on increasing the capacity of its members, and provided legal assistance to its clients by strengthening morality, ethics and more appropriate application of Laws, and its activities were supervised by the Minister of Justice, who appoints and removes lawyers.'[142] By the time of the adoption of the rule of law plan in 2009, the LBA had 105 members.[143]

The implementation of the rule of law plan resulted in the increase in the number of lawyers and law firms in Laos. As of 2019, there were 243 lawyers (including 59 females) and 64 law firms in Laos, including both local and international firms.[144] Nowadays, there are 372 registered lawyers in Laos.[145] Lao lawyers are concentrated in Vientiane as indicated in Table 6.1.

Table 6.1 Distributions of Lao Lawyers as of 2019[146]

Province	No. of Lawyers	Female
Vientiane	206	58
Bokeo	1	0
Oudomxay	3	1
Luang Prabang	7	0
Xayyabouly	1	0
Vientiane Province	4	0
Xiengkhuang	5	0
Khammuane	2	0
Savannakhet	6	0
Champasak	5	0
Salavan	2	0

[141] Master Plan (n 12).
[142] ibid.
[143] ibid.
[144] Sophia Cason, 'Laos Legal Aid Support Activity' Quarterly Report, The Asia Foundation (2019) 12.
[145] 'USAID Legal Aid Support,' USAID, <USAID Legal Aid Support | Laos | Fact Sheet | U.S. Agency for International Development> accessed 6 June 2024.
[146] Source: ibid. Cason (n 144), 12.

To some extent, Lao lawyers are professional persons proving legal services for the citizens, not merely agents of the state. This is demonstrated by the professional requirements to become a lawyer in Laos as established by the Law on Lawyers. A lawyer must not concurrently be a civil servant, soldier, or police officer.[147] Apart from being a Lao citizen and the ethical requirements, to become a lawyer an individual must have a higher degree of legal education, receive professional training as a lawyer or judge, complete legal training, and pass the bar exam.[148] Higher legal education is provided at the Faculty of Law and Political Science of the National University of Laos, the Faculty of Law of Champassak University, and Lao Law College under the Ministry of Justice. A lawyer must also receive professional training at the NIJ according to the curriculum set by the Ministry of Justice,[149] complete six months of legal training with a certificate offered by the LBA, and pass the bar exam. A lawyer must be appointed by the Ministry of Justice and register as a member of the LBA to receive a lawyer card.[150]

As professional persons, Lao lawyers can provide legal services, including giving legal advice and representing clients in litigation.[151] In reality, lawyering in Laos involves more legal advice than litigation.[152] Lao law firms work mainly in the areas of civil, commercial, and foreign investment law.[153]

The Lao lawyer system, however, has been confronted with considerable shortcomings. Quantitatively, by 2023, Laos has less than 400 lawyers 'to respond to the needs of the people which prompts the need for more lawyers and enhanced capacities'.[154] Qualitatively, some lawyers believe that the bar examinations are easy to pass, which weakens lawyers' professionalism. The lawyers' skills are also not strong.[155] In addition, 'most defendants chose not to have attorneys or trained representatives due to the general perception that attorneys could not influence court decisions'.[156] This is in part due to the limited role of attorneys 'in most trials to such actions as asking the court for leniency in sentencing or appealing a technical matter, rather than arguing the merits of the case, challenging evidence, or mounting a true defense'.[157] In response to the limitations, the Lao government

[147] Lao Law on Lawyers (2023), art 9.
[148] ibid art 9.
[149] ibid art 11.
[150] ibid arts 13, 14, 15, and 16.
[151] ibid art 20.
[152] Focus group interviews with Lao Lawyers, 17 August 2022, Vientiane, Laos.
[153] Focus group interviews with Lao Lawyers, 17 August 2022, Vientiane, Laos; Law Firms in Laos, Thai Law Forum <http://www.thailawforum.com/laos-lawyer.html>accessed 6 June 2024.
[154] 'Lawyer Project Launched to Strengthen the Role of Lawyers in Advancing Rule of Law and Access to Justice of Lao PDR' (UNDP Lao PDR, 3 April 2023) <https://www.undp.org/laopdr/press-releases/lawyer-project-launched-strengthen-role-lawyers-advancing-rule-law-and-access-justice-lao-pdr>accessed 6 June 2024.
[155] Focus group interviews with Lao lawyers, 17 August 2022, Vientiane, Laos.
[156] US Department of State, Laos 2021 Human Rights Report, 5.
[157] ibid.

is committed to further legal professional reform. To illustrate, the Ninth Plan attempts to 'support the LBA to provide quality services to clients and train a new generation of legal professionals in collaboration with universities and law firms'.[158]

The reform of the lawyer system in Laos stems from three factors. First, the government's normative commitment to building the rule of law results in the development of lawyers. In other words, legal professional reform is a part of the broader rule of law reform in Laos. Lawyers are important to facilitate better access to justice and the creation of society governed by law. In addition, legal professional reform responds to the need of the society. Particularly, as Laos heavily relies on foreign investments, the country needs to facilitate the development of lawyers and law firms to provide legal services for foreign investors.[159] Domestic market development has also generated more private legal disputes and services, which necessitate the improvement of the lawyer system.

Legal professional reform in Laos is also driven by external influences of international donors. Particularly, the US Agency for International Development has supported the Lao Ministry of Justice and LBA.[160] Recently, in April 2023, the Lawyer Project in the capital Vientiane was launched. This project is funded by the US Government's Bureau of International Narcotics and Law Enforcement Affairs and will be implemented for three years under the management of the UNDP in close partnership with the Ministry of Justice and the LBA.[161] The project aims to strengthen the institutional capacity of the LBA, empower lawyers by fostering a network of leading lawyers committed to professionalism, and deliver practical tools for learning and professional development.[162] Ms Catherine Phuong, Deputy Resident Representative of UNDP, underlines that 'Lawyers help foster stability, enhance accountability, and contribute to a society that is governed by the rule of law in which everybody can enjoy access to justice. Supporting lawyers, therefore, is of critical importance to the inclusive and comprehensive development of Lao PDR.'[163] International donors do not just provide financial support. They also diffuse norms of the legal profession (such as the role of lawyers in the rule of law), which shape legal professional reforms in Laos.

B. The Socialist Lawyers

The Lao lawyer system retains socialist features. Given the limited access to resources, I focus on the manifestation of instrumentalism in the Lao lawyer system

[158] Ninth Plan (n 31) 98.
[159] Focus group interviews with Lao lawyers, 17 August 2022, Vientiane, Laos.
[160] Cason (n 144) 5.
[161] 'Lawyer Project Launched' (n 154).
[162] ibid.
[163] ibid.

as evident in the Law on Lawyers. The lawyers are both professional persons and instrumental agents of the Lao socialist state. Lawyers and their organizations are expected not only to protect their clients but also contribute to state interests such as social-economic development, attracting foreign investments, and regional and international integration.[164]

To ensure that they will serve the state interests, lawyers are placed under the centralized management of the government, particularly the Ministry of Justice. The Law on Lawyers provides that 'the government manages the work of lawyers in a centralized and unified manner throughout the country'.[165] The management agencies include the Ministry of Justice and department of justice at local governments.[166] To manage lawyers, the Ministry of Justice enjoys extensive power to formulate policy for lawyer development, publicize internal rules of the LBA, decide on courses for lawyers' professional training, appoint and withdraw a lawyer, suspend or withdraw (legal) business licence, grant and revoke permission for foreign lawyers to practice law in Laos, adopt an ethical code for lawyers, and manage and monitor the activities of the LBA, among others.[167] The provincial departments of justice are responsible for implementing the central government's policy on lawyers, monitoring the work of the LBA office, and reporting the departments' work to the Ministry of Justice.[168] The department of justice at the district level has the responsibility to implement the policy on lawyers, monitor the work of lawyers, and report its work to the provincial department of justice.[169] Thus, Lao lawyers are subject to the state's hierarchical control.

The LBA is an institutional agent for the government to manage lawyers. The Law on Lawyers defines the Bar Association as a body to promote the legal profession and to contribute to the creation of the rule of law state in Laos.[170] Thus, the LBA must serve the state's broader legal reform project. The Law on Lawyers provides that 'the Lao Bar Association operates professionally and is organizationally and financially independent under the laws and the internal rules of the Bar Association'.[171] However, in reality, the LBA is unlikely to be a body independent from the government as the Ministry of Justice has the power to manage and monitor it.

The state's regulatory management of lawyers is driven by conflicting motivations. On one hand, the state needs to reform the lawyer system so that lawyers become professional persons meeting the demands of legal services from the

[164] Lao Law on Lawyers (2023), art 1.
[165] ibid art 71.
[166] ibid art 71.
[167] ibid art 72.
[168] ibid art 73.
[169] ibid art 74.
[170] ibid art 33.
[171] ibid art 33.

emerging market, particularly from foreign investors. On the other hand, professional lawyers may invocate law and rights discourse to challenge the arbitrary use of the state power, including corruption. To deal with this dilemma, the state would support legal professional reform but at the same time place lawyers under the state's control to ensure that they work for rather than oppose the state.

VII. CONCLUDING ANALYSIS

After several decades of legal reforms, Laos has transformed a legal system based on Party resolutions and administrative decrees into a legal system based on legislation. Legal reform in Laos can be generalized as a cooperative project: domestic actors work together with international actors to formulate and implement measures of legal reform. The international cooperation is prominently embodied in the intention, method, strategy, and content of legal reform.

A. Intentional Nature

Lao legal reform is a top-down project animated by domestic political elites' intention to create a state governed by law while retaining the fundamental socialist principles of the legal system. International cooperation is embodied in the intention of legal reform. Domestic and international actors intend to work together towards a common goal: legal reform. The legal reforms present the mixed aspirations of domestic and international actors. The legal reform presents the aspiration of international actors to introduce norms of international rule of law in Laos, which is sometimes incongruent with the domestic intention of creating a rule of law state under the Party's leadership.

B. Legislative Method

Legislation is the main mechanism of legal reforms. Legislative reform involves making, amending, replacing, and codifying legal rules by the NA. The Party may adopt policy for legislative reforms, but once adopted, the policy is materialized by legislative enactments. In the same vein, institutional reforms of the administrative, court, and lawyer systems rely on legislative enactments. These institutions and the Party may propose measures for institutional reforms, but once approved, the measures are implemented by the NA's enactment of institutional laws such as laws on anti-corruption, courts, judges, and lawyers. Legislation is the legitimate method of legal reform as it derives from the authority of a nationally elected body. Although the NA is under the Party's control, it is elected by the people and hence the legitimate platform for deliberating and approving measures for reforms, including legal reforms.

International cooperation is prominently embodied in the legislative method of legal reform. International cooperations in legislative enactments are explicitly confirmed. This political willingness is even expressed in law. The Law on Legislation adopted in 2012 includes a provision supporting international aids to Lao legal reform. Article 14 states that:

> the State promotes relations and cooperation with foreign countries and with regional and international organizations in relation to the development of legislation by exchanging experiences, sharing data and information, organizing seminars, upgrading knowledge and technical capacity and assisting in the development of legislation and implementation of international conventions and treaties that Lao PDR is a party to

This provision reflects the reality of the active engagement of various sectors of the international community into Lao legal reform. The provision also signals the Lao government's intention to seek to attract further international assistances to Lao legislative reform.

C. Incremental Strategy

Political elites adopt incremental strategies of legal reform. Before 2009, the Lao state adopted the classical incremental strategy to provide sporadic adjustments to the legal system in response to the immediate needs of the emerging market economy and state building. Since 2009, political elites have turned to the neo-incremental strategy. The state adopted an overall plan for rule of law reform to be implemented incrementally over a decade. Some preceding achievements of legal reform create the base for the state's confidence to proceed systematically but slowly in undertaking legal reforms. After several decades of market development, the demands for legal consolidation of the market are more extensive, which requires systematic legal reform. The demands for legal underpinnings of state building are also more extensive. The systematic demands necessitate more systemic strategy for legal reform. The state's understanding of systematic problems of the legal system (conflicts of existing laws, the lack of many laws, the prevalence of legal ignorance, poor enforcement of law) also prompts the change from sporadic to systematic reforms of the legal system. The domination of a single party constitutes the institutional condition for political consensus necessary for the adoption of an overall legal reform project. At the same time, the plan must be implemented step by step due to the lack of financial and human resources and the unanticipated effects of the reforms.

International cooperation is particularly expressed in the neo-incremental strategy of legal reform. The legal reform plan is constructed of and constructive to international cooperation. The rule of law reform plan was launched with international cooperation. More specifically, the Lao government worked with UNDP to design and launch the rule of law plan. The introduction of the rule of law plan then facilitates the further cooperation not only with UNDP but also many donors. The rule of law plan provides the base for attracting and coordinating international cooperation in incremental implementation of the legal reform measures.

D. Positive Content

The implementation of measures for legal reform, particularly, for the rule of law reform since 2009, significantly improves the Lao legal system. Laos now has hundreds of statutes covering nearly every aspect of social life. The administrative system is better organized based on laws. Some laws even empower citizens to claim their rights and challenge administrative authority. The country also has a functional, rather well-structured court system capable of handling thousands of cases annually and staffed by more professional judges. The lawyer system has also been improved. Lao lawyers are not merely state workers but professionals offering legal services.

International cooperation is embodied in the contents of legal reform. The Lao government adopts the rule of law as a normative framework for legal reform, which is in part due to international cooperation. The rule of law is the dominant idea of the 'new' law and development movement in post-Cold war Laos. International organizations and foreign developed countries have employed the rule of law as the framework to promote legal reform in developing countries.[172] The influence of the law and development movement explains why the idea of the rule of law is adopted as the dominant framework for regal reform in Laos. As Laos heavily relies on international aid, the party-state has the incentive to adhere to the rule of law ideals to attract international assistance to its legal reform.

However, the content of legal reform in Laos is cooperative, not convergent with the international ideals of the rule of law. The content of cooperative legal reform is mainly about technical features of formal rule of law such as uniformity, coherency, clarity, credibility, predictability, and accessibility. This explains why international actors tend to focus their cooperations on technical activities supporting formal rule of law such as legal education, legal aids, and dissemination of legal knowledge. The Lao government's understanding of the substantive rule of law is

[172] David M Trubek, 'The "Rule of Law" in Development Assistance: Past, Present, and Future' in David M Trubek and Alvaro Santos (eds), *The New Law and Economic Development: A Critical Appraisal* (CUP 2006) 74.

divergent from international ideals of the rule of law (such as human rights and separation of power). This limits international cooperation in substantive and political contents of legal reform such as human rights law reform and constitutional reform.

E. Factors

Legal reform in Laos iscaused by the gap factors. First, internal legal disharmony drives efforts of legal reforms. The gap between the political elites' normative commitment to the formal ideal of the rule of law and the reality of the existing legal system (the lack, poor enforcement, and low public awareness of law) induces efforts to reform the legal system to implement the rule of law promise. The internal conflicts of existing laws also drive efforts or legal reforms to mitigate and eliminate the conflicts. Additionally, functional dissonances trigger institutional legal reforms. Administrative reforms are undertaken to mitigate the competing functions of the administrative law as the tool to consolidate the administrative power and to empower the citizens. Judicial reforms are carried to reconcile the competing functions of courts as institutions to protect the state interests and justice. The reform of the lawyer system is also animated by the competing functions of lawyers as agents of the state and as professionals delivering legal services.

Lao legal reform is also driven by the gap between law and societal change. The transition from command to market economy induces the enactment of laws (particularly contract, property, business, and commercial law) to sustain economic liberalization. The development of the agrarian economy results in the enactment of agrarian laws. Market development creates social and family issues (eg unemployment, drugs, and divorces), which impels legislating to deal with these issues. Societal change also triggers institutional legal reforms. The emergence of new social and economic relations due to market transition requires more effective public governance, which animates administrative reform. The emergence of more legal disputes due to social-economic transition also requires improvement of the court system. Market development also generates more demands for the legal services, which puts pressure on legal professional reforms.

Another factor of Lao legal reform is the gap between the domestic legal system and transnational law. Laos improves its legal system to adjust it to the external legal environment. This is in part due to the domestic motivation to reform domestic law according to international legal standards to attract foreign investments, particularly given that the Lao economy heavily relies on foreign investments. The adjustment of the Lao legal system to the external legal environment is also animated by the influence of law and development movement in the country. Law and development actors do not simply provide technical and financial assistances.

They also spread transnational legal norms (eg norms of formal rule of law, transparent governance, judicial independence, human rights, and access to justice) in Laos, which informs legal reform in the country to some extent. This demonstrates the prominent presentation of international cooperation in the factors of legal reform. The gap between domestic law and comparative and international law provides the base for international legal cooperations.

F. Continuity of Socialist Law

Despite considerable reforms, the Lao legal system remains socialist. It is underpinned by fundamental principles of socialist law. Institutionalism shapes the functions of law and legal institutions. Law remains an instrument for the state to pursue social-economic development towards the direction of socialism. The administrative bodies, courts, and lawyers are instruments for implementing the state interests—such as social-economic development, attracting foreign investment, regime security, social order, and regional and international integration. The Party leadership shapes the contents of legislation and penetrates all state institutions. Law is the legal embodiment of the Party lines. The Party nominates Party members to hold key state positions. The operation of state institutions is placed under the Party leadership, particularly through Party cells operating within the institutions. The Party formulates policy for legal institutional reforms. The structure of legal institutions is shaped by the principle of democratic centralism. The executive and judicial bodies are subordinate to the legislature. Local governments are under the control of the central government, despite administrative decentralization. Courts are not allowed to review legislation. Local courts are under the centralized control of the People's Supreme Court. Private laws are shaped by the public ownership and the state's dominant role in the economy. The practice of rights depends on the state's paternalistic policy and is under the state's regulatory control.

G. Prospects of Legal Reform

There is considerable space for continuing legal reforms in Laos due to the existing shortcomings, continued commitments to reform, and ongoing international cooperation. Legal reform in Laos continues to face many pressures. The proliferation of laws makes it difficult for government officials to know and enforce the laws. The public awareness of laws remains low in part due to the existence of many laws and regulations. Many courts judgments are not enforced. The number of lawyers is low to respond to social demands. Lawyers' professional skills are also weak. In response to these shortcomings, the Lao government is committed to continuing legal reforms, including the possible formation of a new rule of law reform plan. Law and development actors continue to engage in Lao legal reform and the Lao government continues to work with sectors of the international community to improve its socialist legal system.

7

North Korea: Legal Reform and Self-Reliance

I. INTRODUCTION

North Korea or the Democratic People's Republic of Korea (DPRK) has carried out legal reform since the 1980s. However, unlike China, Vietnam, and Laos, North Korea has not implemented a comprehensive programme of legal reform. The lack of comprehensive legal reform in North Korea is largely because the *Juche* ideology (self-reliance) constrains the regime from opening up the country domestically and internationally. The country has not yet opened the doors for domestic citizens to set up business, which prevents the need for comprehensive legal reform to support the market. Due to the isolation policy and international sanctions, the emerging market economy has been limited mainly to socialist neighbours (particularly China). This means North Korea does not have an incentive to carry out comprehensive legal reform to incorporate international legal norms to facilitate foreign investments.

Rather, relying on domestic sources, North Korea introduces some sporadic changes to improve some aspects of the existing legal system. This chapter argues that North Korean legal reform can be described as a self-reliant project. North Korea's self-reliant project of legal reform refers to intentional sporadic adjustments through legislative enactments to improve the existing socialist legal system to facilitate better economic development, more effective public management, amelioration of its regime's harsh treatment of its citizens, and institutional building.

The study of North Korean legal reform has significant challenges. The regime's isolation makes it difficult to access legal resources in the country. However, since the 1980s, North Korea has introduced important legislative reform and officially released legislation particularly in the areas of foreign investments, which has generated interest from Western and Korean academics. Consequently, a large body of scholarship in English on North Korean law focuses on foreign investment law.[1]

[1] Chin Kim, 'North Korean Joint Venture Laws' (1989) 19 Cal W Int'l LJ 175; Chin Kim, 'North Korean and Chinese Joint Equity Venture Laws: A Comparison' (1989) 2 Transnat'l Law 531; Arno Wohlgemuth, 'The Law on Foreign Investment in North Korea' (1993) 1993 Int'l Bus LJ 47; Haksoo Ko, 'Foreign Investment in North Korea: An Assessment of Recent Laws and Regulations' (1998) 38 Va J Int'l L 221; Doo Hwan Kim, 'Legal Aspects of Foreign Investment in Korea' (1992) 15 Hastings Int'l & Comp L Rev 227; Sang-Jick Yoon, 'Critical Issues on the Foreign Investment Laws of North

Legal Reform in the Contemporary Socialist World. Ngoc Son Bui, Oxford University Press. © Ngoc Son Bui 2024.
DOI: 10.1093/9780191948053.003.0007

This international literature explores laws and regulations of foreign investment, assesses their limitations, and anticipates the possible future reforms, particularly whether North Korea could adopt a comprehensive model of legal and economic reforms like China and Vietnam.

Since the mid-2000s, the North Korean regime has attempted to build a 'socialist rule of law state' and hence released more comprehensive compilations of their laws in all fields, which provides the resources for more systemic studies of North Korean law in English. Some studies attempt to classify the sources of laws in North Korea.[2] Others explore the North Korean legal system from the perspective of rule of law.[3] Some look at the relationship between legal change and economic development in North Korea.[4] Further studies deploy quantitative methods to explore 4,000 legal changes enacted from 1945 to 2017 in the country.[5] Apart from systematic studies, other studies deal with specific aspects of North Korean law such as criminal, civil and family, and intellectual property (IP) law.[6]

North Korean law has been well studied in South Korea. 'South Korean scholars have been studying and tracking the DPRK legal developments for years and have produced hundreds of books and articles on this subject.'[7] This chapter, however, relies on the English literature. It is also informed by my exchanges with some South Korean experts on North Korean law.

Korea for Foreign Investors' (1996) 15 Wis Int'l LJ 325; Greyson Bryan, Scott Horton, and Robin Radin, 'Foreign Investment Laws and Regulations of the Democratic People's Republic of Korea' (1998) 21 Fordham Int'l LJ 1677; Patricia Goedde, 'Law of Our Own Style: The Evolution and Challenges of the North Korean Legal System' (2004) 27 Fordham Int'l LJ 1265; Joongi Kim, 'The Challenges of Attracting Foreign Investment into North Korea: The Legal Regimes of Sinuiju and Gaeseong' (2004) 27 Fordham Int'l LJ 1306; Dae-Kyu Yoon, 'Overview of the Legal Structure of Foreign Investment in the DPRK' (2005) 5 J Korean L 1; Hyun Yoon Shin, 'Development and Problems of North Korea's Foreign Investment Legislation and Tasks Ahead' (2011) 2 Yonsei LJ 160; Jeehye You, 'Legislative Reform of the Kaesong Industrial Complex in North Korea' (2011) 29 UCLA Pac Basin LJ 36; Darren C Zook, 'Reforming North Korea: Law, Politics, and the Market Economy' (2012) 48 Stan J Int'l L 131; Robert W Emerson and Jason R Parnell, 'Sanctions, Nukes and Juche: Franchising in North Korea' (2023) 44 U Pa J Int'l L 235.

[2] Hyowon Lee, 'Review on the Form and System of North Korean Law' (2018) 27 Int'l J Korean Unification Stud 71.

[3] Marion P Spina Jr, 'Brushes with the Law: North Korea and the Rule of Law' (2007) 2 Academic Paper Series 1.

[4] Christopher Hale, 'North Korea in Evolution: The Correlation between the Legal Framework and the Changing Dynamic of Politics and the Economy' (2002) 33 Korea Observer 363.

[5] Martin Weiser, 'Unseen Laws—A Quantitative Approach to Developments in North Korea's Legal System' (2018) 17 Eur J Korean Stud 22.

[6] In Sup Han, 'The 2004 Revision of Criminal Law in North Korea: A Take-off' (2007) 5 Santa Clara J Int'l L 122; Eun-Jung Lee, 'Family Law and Inheritance Law in North Korea' (2005) 5 J Korean L 172; Deming Liu, 'Copyright in North Korea: Reality or Hoax' (2018) 18 Chi-Kent J Int'l Comp L 1; Joseph Cho, 'Introductory Note to the English Translation of the Civil Code of North Korea' (2022) 14 J Civ Law Stud 237.

[7] Spina Jr (n 3) 2.

II. THE SELF-RELIANT PROJECT OF LEGAL REFORM

A. The Intention of Legal Reform

Although North Korea does not have a plan for legal reform, the regime has the intention of legal reform: aspirational commitments and realistic considerations to improve the socialist legal system. This intention is expressed in the 1992 amendment to the Constitution. Article 18 of the amended Constitution provides that: 'The State shall perfect the system of socialist law and promote the socialist law-abiding life.' This constitutional provision suggests that the regime intends to improve the legal system and promote legality in social life. Understandably, the constitutional commitment to legal reform was adopted when the regime actively promoted economic development through attracting foreign investment in the wake of the collapse of the socialist regimes in 1991.

Since the mid-2000s, the North Korea regime 'has consistently emphasized the socialist rule-of-law'.[8] Kim Jong Un further underlined the need for improvement of the legal system and the creation of a socialist rule of law state. In a speech at the Supreme National Assembly in 2019, Kim emphasized the necessity to perfect the legal system and to modify and supplement laws in a timely manner.[9] In the report on the work of the Party's Central Committee in 2021, Kim continued to underline the need to 'establish a revolutionary spirit of law observance throughout society as required by the building of a socialist rule-of-law state'.[10] At the Plenary Meeting of the Central Committee in 2022, he stated that 'The work for perfecting the socialist legal system was further prioritized and the legal order was strengthened to bring substantial progress in guaranteeing the economic development and the stabilization of people's living conditions.'[11] The political discourse on the rule of law does not necessarily means the regime is truly committed to the rule of law. However, the discourse suggests that North Korean leaders have the intention to improve the legal system, including by enacting and revising laws, particularly to facilitate economic development and ameliorate living standards.

Consistent with the commitment to improving the legal system, since the 1980s North Korean leaders have implemented sporadic legal reform. The personal

[8] Dae Un Hong, 'North Korean Laws Since 2016: What They Imply for the Country's Future' (*38 North*, 25 February 2021) <https://www.38north.org/2021/02/north-korean-laws-since-2016-what-they-imply-for-the-countrys-future> accessed 6 June 2024.

[9] Suehyun Jung, 'Economic Construction by Means of Legal Institutionalization under Kim Jong Un Regime of North Korea' (2012–21), (2023) J Asian Afr Stud 3 (OnlineFirst).

[10] 'Great Programme for Struggle Leading Korean-style Socialist Construction to Fresh Victory on Report Made by Supreme Leader Kim Jong Un at Eighth Congress of WPK' <https://kcnawatch.org/newstream/1610261416-871234007/great-programme-for-struggle-leading-korean-style-socialist-construction-to-fresh-victory-on-report-made-by-supreme-leader-kim-jong-un-at-eighth-congress-of-wpk> accessed 6 June 2024.

[11] Jung (n 9) 3.

intention of sporadic legal reform is shaped by the *Juche* ideology. Although *Juche* does not underline the legal aspects, its core principles of political, economic, and military self-reliance necessarily result in the intention of legal self-reliance. Legal self-reliance refers to sporadic and autonomous adjustment of the domestic legal system to support economic development and public management. Sections II.B and C consider core principles of *Juche* and their consequence for self-reliant legal reform.

B. *Juche* (Self-Reliance) Ideology

Juche was substantively articulated in Kim Il Sung's speech entitled 'Let Us Defend the Revolutionary Spirit of Independence, Self-Reliance, and Self-defense More Thoroughly in All Fields of State Activities', at the Supreme People's Assembly on 16 December 1967.[12] In that speech, he said:

> The Government of the Republic will implement with all consistency the line of independence, self-sustenance, and self-defense to consolidate the political independence of the country (*chaju*), build up more solidly the foundations of an independent national economy capable of insuring the complete unification, independence, and prosperity of our nation (*charip*) and increasing the country's defense capabilities, so as to safeguard the security of the fatherland reliably by our own force (*chawi*), by splendidly embodying our Party's idea of *Juche* in all fields.[13]

There are three principles of *Juche*:

(i) political self-reliance (a nation's self-determination and non-intervention, and equal and mutual respect of nations);
(ii) economic self-reliance (independent and self-sufficient national economy);
(iii) military self-reliance (independence in national defence).

These principles are interrelated. Political independence is important for economic and military independence. The reliance on foreign powers would threaten national defence. Economic independence is the material base for political and military independence.[14]

Juche, however, is not about complete isolation. On political independence, *Juche* itself is a political ideology developed as the creative application of

[12] Grace Lee, 'The Political Philosophy of Juche' (2003), 3 Stanford J E Asian Aff 105.
[13] Cited in ibid 105–06.
[14] For detailed explanation, see ibid 106–07.

Marxism-Leninism in the special conditions of North Korea. In political practices, *Juche* does not reject North Korea's relations with and learning from other socialist countries such as the Soviet Union and China. To be sure, *Juche* rejects dogmatic application of Marxism-Leninism and mechanical imitation of the experiences of other socialist countries.[15] On the economic aspect, *Juche* does not completely reject international economic relations, which provides space for foreign investment. To illustrate, Kim Il Sung stressed the importance of foreign trade at the First Session of the Fourth Supreme People's Assembly in 1967, stating that:

> The development of an independent, comprehensive economy in our country though our own efforts does not imply that we reject international economic ties or that we produce everything we need for ourselves . . . each country should produce on its own the essentials and those products which are in great demand, and obtain through trade with foreign countries those things which are in slight demand or in short supply, or which cannot be produced at home, on the principle of meeting each other's needs.[16]

Juche derives but also diverges from Marxism-Leninism. While Marxism-Leninism underlines the determination of material conditions of human progress, *Juche* considers humans to be the driving force of historical development.[17] Consequently, the *Juche* ideology underlines the spiritual rather than material forces of historical progress. The *Juche* spirit means 'holding fast to an independent position, rejecting dependence on others, using one's own brains, believing in one's own strength, displaying the revolutionary spirit of self-reliance, and thus solving one's own problems for oneself on one's own responsibility under all circumstances'.[18]

The second, related divergence is that *Juche* denotes a kind of personal vanguardism. Leninist party vanguardism places the working class under the collective and institutional leadership of a Communist Party, while *Juche* stresses that the working class should be under the personal leadership of a single communist Great Leader. The Great Leader is considered the embodiment of the most excellent consciousness, and therefore the working class must be under the absolute guidance of the Greater Leader.[19] Within the *Juche* ideology, the role of the Communist Party is less important than the single Great Leader. 'The Great Leader is the brain that makes decisions and issues orders, the Party is the nervous system that channels information, and the people are the bone and muscle that physically execute the order.'[20]

15 ibid.
16 Cited in Hale (n 4) 376.
17 Lee (n 12) 111.
18 Cited in ibid 105.
19 ibid 111.
20 ibid.

The 1972 Constitution confirms *Juche* as the state's official ideology. It provides that 'The Democratic People's Republic of Korea is guided in its activities by the Juche idea of the Workers' Party of Korea, a creative application of Marxism-Leninism to the realities of our country' (Article 4). The current Constitution does not explicitly specify *Juche* as the state's official ideology but provides that 'The Democratic People's Republic of Korea is guided in its building and activities only by great Kimilsungism-Kimjongilism' (Article 3). Kimilsungism 'is interchangeable with the *juche* idea'.[21] This means *Juche* is still constitutionally entrenched as the guiding ideology of the regime. *Juche* ideology has been embodied in the hermit kingdom's economic, political, and military policies. *Juche* is also embedded in the personal leadership in North Korea: it provides the ideological justifications for the North Korean model of personal authoritarianism in which 'the leader controls key political appointments, pronounces may policy directives, and limits the ruling class to family members and loyal allies'.[22]

C. Self-Reliant Legal Reform

Although the *Juche* ideology does not explicitly address legal aspects, its general principles have shaped legal reform in North Korea. North Korean leaders do not have a systematic plan for legal reform; but the regime in fact implemented some changes to improve the domestic legal system, which can be understood as a self-reliant project of legal reform. The North Korean self-reliant project of legal reform demonstrates the political elites' intention to rely on domestic sources to introduce sporadic adjustments to improve the domestic legal system to facilitate better economic development, public management, and social control.

The self-reliant model of legal reform has three features. First, the sources of self-reliant legal reform are autonomous. Self-reliant legal reform consists mainly of domestic legal innovations without significant reliance on external transnational legal norms. Unlike the cases of China, Vietnam, and Laos, legal reform in North Korea is not considerably influenced by the law and development movement although there are efforts to promote transnational norms (such as human rights norms[23]) in the country. The autonomous aspect of legal self-reliance is shaped by the *Juche* principle of political self-reliance. The emphasis on national

[21] Jae-Cheon Lim, 'North Korea's Hereditary Succession: Comparing Two Key Transitions in the DPRK' (2012) 52 Asian Sur 561.

[22] Andrew Yeo, *State, Society, and Markets in North Korea* (CUP 2021) 17.

[23] Patricia Goedde, 'Human Rights Diffusion in North Korea: The Impact of Transnational Legal Mobilization' (2018) 5 Asian J Law Soc 175

sovereignty, self-determination, and non-intervention logically rejects the intervention of foreign governments and international agencies in domestic legal reform. To be sure, like economic reform, self-reliant legal reform does not completely reject partial learning from the experiences of other socialist countries, particularly China.

Second, the scope of self-reliant legal reform is sporadic. Self-reliant legal reform introduces some occasional, scattered, partial changes to improve the existing socialist legal system. It does not involve systematic legal changes. This feature is mainly shaped by economic self-reliance. The focus on an independent and self-sufficient national economy limits the engagement of the domestic economy with foreign and global economic systems. As the economic system is not open to outsiders, the legal system is closed too. However, as economic self-reliance partially allows for foreign trade, this instigates accidental legal reform to attract foreign investors. Sporadic legal reform to support foreign investment is mainly drawn on domestic self-legal creations, although sporadic legal transplants (particularly from the socialist countries) are possible and contextualized. The independent development of the national economy also requires some sporadic changes to the legal system to facilitate better public management of the economy and national resources.

Third, the content of self-reliant legal reform is mainly domestically embedded legal issues. These issues involve four main kinds of law:

- promoting economic development in specially designated areas of the country;
- facilitating public management of the economy and domestic resources (eg forests, rivers, and ginseng);
- supporting local institutional reform (eg administrative decentralization, the enforcement of court decisions, and the creation of a lawyer system); and
- softening the regime's harsh treatment of its citizens (eg life imprisonment as an alternative to capital punishment, and observation of law in criminal procedure).

III. LEGISLATIVE REFORM

Despite personal authoritarianism, North Korea has many laws. Like authoritarian regimes elsewhere, North Korea relies on laws as a tool to control the compliance of the population. However, beyond social control, the regime has also enacted many laws to support economic development and improve public administration of the economy and natural resources. The regime also attempts to institutionalize the legislative process and publicize laws.

A. Legislative Process

The regime attempts to institutionalize the legislative process, which renders legislative enactments the main method of legal reform. The Constitution institutionalizes the legislative power. The Constitution provides for the creation of a legislature in North Korea following the Soviet style of legislature. It includes the Supreme People's Assembly and its Presidium. The Supreme People's Assembly is the highest organ of state power created by direct elections for a five-year term.[24] Legislative power is exercised by the Supreme People's Assembly, and its Presidium also may exercise legislative power when the Supreme People's Assembly is not in session.[25] Major laws adopted by the Presidium must be subsequently approved by the Supreme People's Assembly.[26] Thus, at least, the Constitution attempts to regularize and distribute the legislative power.

Another important aspect of institutionalizing the legislative process is the enactment of the Law on Legislation in 2012. This enactment suggests that North Korea seems serious about making formal general legal rules rather than merely ruling by personal fiats. The Law on Legislation is an important step to regularize the legislative process. It provides more details about the types of legal instruments and distributes the rule-making power. According to the Law, domestic written laws in North Korea include the Constitution, sector laws, and governmental regulations. Article 2 of the Law on Legislation provides that 'the sector law means the basic legal form by which the supreme sovereign authorities control social relations according to constitutional law'.[27] Thus, sector laws are statuary laws enacted by the Supreme People's Assembly and its Presidium. Since 1998, most legislative laws in North Korea have been adopted by the Presidium.[28] This may be because elections of the Supreme People's Assembly were not regularly held as required by the Constitution.[29]

Laws in North Korea have been publicized to some extent. It is observed that 'in contrast to the current regime's secrecy and disinterest in releasing core information, for almost two decades after its inception North Korea was relatively open about its legal system'.[30] In 1961, North Korea published a selection of around 600 legal texts (including enacted laws and regulations) in 5 volumes. The release of legal information further increased after North Korea promoted foreign investment in the 1980s. The Committee for Promotion of External Economic Cooperation published a multivolume collection of laws and regulations in 1993.

24 Socialist Constitution Law of the Democratic People's Republic of Korea (2019), arts 87 and 90.
25 ibid art 88.
26 ibid art 116.
27 Cited in Lee (n 27) 89.
28 ibid 96.
29 Weiser (n 5) 25
30 ibid 27.

This institution also published the *Compilation of Laws and Regulations for Foreign Investment* in English translation in 2003. In 2004, the Legal Publishing House published a collection of legislation in all fields.[31] It then published updated versions with new and revised legislations in 2006, 2008, and 2016. Legal information has also been published in other venues such newspapers, journals (eg Kim Il Sung University *Journal for History and Law*), monographs, and government documents.[32]

The publicization of laws at least suggests that the North Korean legal system is relatively open. Laws are made knowable to both domestic citizens and international audiences. The North Korean regime needs to publicize their laws to attract foreign investments. This publicization may also serve to demonstrate the country's legislative progress, which might attempt to counter the international criticisms of its personal rule.

B. Legislative Development

Although North Korea has not implemented a comprehensive plan of legal reform, it has enacted many laws since the 1980s. Particularly, the attempt to construct a rule of law state since the mid-2000s led to the enactments and revisions of numerous laws in North Korea. Quantitatively, when Kim Jong Un assumed power in December 2011, the regime had already enacted 205 laws. The number of laws then increased to 236 by December 2015.[33] Depending on their function, North Korean laws can be grouped into four areas: laws for economic development, laws for public management, laws for social control, and laws for institutional building. This functional categorization is relative and for analytical purpose only, as in reality North Korean laws are intertwined and unsystematic. This section discusses three areas of law with a focus on elements of reforms, saving law for institutional buildings for the later parts on institutional reform.

1. *Law For Economic Development*

North Korea also adopted many laws to support economic development. Unlike China, Vietnam, and Laos, North Korea has not adopted the comprehensive reformist model of a socialist market economy and remains a planned economy that rejects private economic sectors. However, in response to economic hardship, the country has introduced some sporadic market reforms to the planned economy, and consequently carried partial legislative reforms to support partial marketization.

[31] ibid 28–29.
[32] ibid 29.
[33] Hong (n 8).

The first to note is the adoption of the Civil Law. North Korea adopted the Civil Law in 1990, which was amended in 1993, 1999, 2007, and 2012. The Law is divided into four parts. Part 1 (General Part) deals with the basics of civil law (Chapter 1), the parties to civil legal relations (Chapter 2), and civil juridical acts (Chapter 3). Part 2 consists of general principles of ownership (Chapter 1), state ownership (Chapter 2), social cooperative ownership (Chapter 3), and private ownership (Chapter 4). Part 3 includes the general principles of obligation (Chapter 1), contracts based on planning (Chapter 2), contracts not based on planning (Chapter 3), and enrichment without cause (Chapter 4). Part 4 deals with civil liability (Chapter 1) and civil prescription (Chapter 2).[34]

Reforms have caused civil law in North Korea to deal with more private matters. 'As a citizen could partake in more transactions and own more property, the civil law dealing with private matters would need to play a more significant role than previously.'[35] For example, the Civil Law provides that 'private ownership is individual ownership by the workers for the purposes of consumption'.[36] Individuals are allowed to own 'basic materials required for a home and family life such as different kinds of household goods, cultural goods, other daily necessities and cars'.[37] North Korean civil law does not allow private ownership of means of productions, including the amendment in 2012.[38]

Apart from the Civil Law, North Korea has also adopted other laws related to civil issues such as the Damage Compensation Law (2001), the Succession Law (2002), the Protection of Handicapped People Law (2003), the Notary Public Law (2004), and the Nationality Law (2017). In the area of IP law, the country adopted the following laws:

Copyright Law (2001);
Industrial Designs Law (1998);
Invention Law (1998);
Name of Origin Law (2003);
Protection of Computer Software Law (2003); and
Trademark Law (1998).

Notably, a body of foreign investment law has been developed to allow foreign enterprises (including the private ones) to invest in specially designated areas of North Korea under the legal framework of joint ventures. North Korea has

[34] Joseph Cho, 'Introductory Note to the English Translation of the Civil Code of North Korea' (2022) 14 J Civ Law Stud 240.
[35] Dae Kyu Yoon, North Korea's Transformation: A Legal Perspective (2009) <http://www.nkeconwatch.com/nk-uploads/microsoft-word-ifes-paper-dae-kyu-yoon.pdf>accessed 6 June 2024.
[36] 민법 2007 [Civil Law of the Democratic People's Republic of Korea (2007)] [tr Daye Gang], art 58.
[37] ibid art 59.
[38] Ung-Yeon Kim, 'From Marketization to a Market Economy in North Korea' (2022) 2 Asia Global Econ 3–4.

developed a sophisticated body of foreign investment law since the 1980s.[39] The reform of foreign trade law expressed the regime's intention to expand trading with not only socialist but also capitalist countries to meet the need of economic development.[40] The country's economic difficulty and default on loans in the 1980s and beyond put pressures on legislative reform to attract foreign investment.[41] In addition, the influence of Chinese reforms on North Korea is considerable. Reportedly, 'When Kim Il-sung visited China in 1982 and 1983, he showed visible interest and listened attentively to Beijing's advice to make similar reforms. When fifty senior DPRK leaders toured China's special economic zone in April and July 1983, they were similarly impressed and showed their backing for opening up special economic zones in North Korea.'[42]

Consequently, North Korea enacted the Joint Venture Law in 1984, modelled after the Chinese model.[43] Running against the prevailing *Juche* ideology, the Law encourages joint ventures between North Korea's companies and enterprises with foreign companies, enterprises, and individuals within its boundary on the principle of equality and reciprocity.[44] The law is considered 'the most important legal development in trade sphere', 'an historic and important step toward an "open-door" policy for North Korea'.[45] The law, however, failed to attract considerable foreign investments due in part to the lack of clear terms to protect investors.[46]

In the early 1990s, in the wake of the collapse of socialist regimes, North Korea took further steps of legislative reform to attract foreign investments while remaining the commitment to socialist regime. In 1991, a free trade economic zone was created in the Raseon-Sonbong region. In 1993, North Korea adopted the Free Economic Trade Zone Law to foster foreign investment in the region.[47] The regime amended the Constitution in 1992 to support the creation of joint venture enterprises, and subsequently enacted several foreign investment-related laws, including:

Foreign Investment Law (1992);
Contractual Joint Venture Law (1992);
Wholly Foreign-owned Enterprise Law (1992);
Foreign Currency Law (1993);
Foreign-invested Enterprise and Foreign Individual Tax Law (1993);

[39] Hale (n 4) 395.
[40] ibid 384.
[41] ibid 385.
[42] ibid 385.
[43] Chin Kim, 'North Korea Joint Venture Laws' (1988–89) 2 Cali Western Int'l Law 175.
[44] Eric Yong-Joong Lee, 'Development of North Korea's Legal Regime Governing Foreign Business Cooperation: A Revisit under the New Socialist Constitution of 1998' (2000–01) 21 Northwest J Internat'l Law Bus 202.
[45] Hale (n 4) 384–85.
[46] ibid 386.
[47] Shin (n 1) 164.

Land Leasing Law (1993);
Foreign Investment Bank Law (1993);
External Economic Contracts Law (1995); and
External Civil Relations Law (1995).[48]

In 1998, North Korea further amended the Constitution to promote business enterprises in a special economic zone. Consequently, several foreign investment-related laws were amended. The Free Economic Trade Zone Law was renamed as the Rajin-Sonbong Economic Trade Zone Law 1999.[49]

In the turn of the twenty-first century, North Korea continued to be confronted with economic difficulty. To facilitate economic development, in 2002, North Korea adopted the Reform Measures for the Economic Management whose contents have been implemented through the special economic zones.[50] Therefore, the country continued to adopt regional legal regimes for special areas. In 2002, it enacted the Basic Law of the Sinuiju Special Administrative Region, modelled on the Hong Kong Basic Law.[51] In the same year, to seek investment and tourism from South Korea, North Korea enacted the Gaeseong Industrial Complex Law and the Geumgang Mountain Tourism Zone Law. In 2005, the country enacted the Law for Economic Cooperation between North and South Korea. The regime also enacted the Foreign-Invested Enterprise Bankruptcy Law in 2000 and the Law on Registration of Foreign-invested Enterprises in 2006 and revised other foreign investment-related laws in the 2000s.[52]

Since Kim Jong Un came to power, the regime has prioritized economic development on the same level as nuclear power, and hence the special economic zones have been significantly expanded. The Economic Development Zone Law was adopted in May 2013. Thanks to this law, the number of special economic zones increased from five in the Kim Jong Il era to twenty-seven in the Kim Jong Un era.[53]

Foreign trade law in North Korea selectively adopts some capital institutions. Christopher Hale demonstrates that three capital institutions, namely private property ownership, taxation, and the payment of monetary compensation to the labour force, have in theory been abolished in North Korea, but in fact they have been applied to venture companies operating in the country.[54] To illustrate,

[48] ibid 165–66.
[49] ibid 164.
[50] Eric Yong-Joong Lee, 'The Special Economic Zones and North Korean Economic Reformation with a Viewpoint of International Law' (2004) 27 Fordham Int'l LJ 1343–44.
[51] For discussion, see Patricia Goedde, 'The Basic Law of the Sinuiju Special Administrative Region: A Happy Medium between the DPRK Constitution and Hong Kong Basic Law' (2003) 3 J Korean L 77; Joongi Kim, 'The Challenges of Attracting Foreign Investment into North Korea: The Legal Regimes of Sinuiju and Gaeseong' (2004) 27 Fordham Int'lLJ 1306.
[52] Shin (n 1) 165–66.
[53] Dongho Jo, 'Kim Jong Un's Economic Opening and Reform: Opportunities, Constraints and Prospects' (2021) 16 Glob Asia 78.
[54] Hale (n 4) 393.

the 1993 Land Leasing Law allows for the land-lease contract, which resembles a real-property sale. The 1985 Joint Venture Income Tax Law requires joint venture companies to pay 25% income tax. The Rajin-Sonbong Free Economic and Trade Zone Employment Authority functions as an employment agency suppling the demands for labour.[55]

Darren C Zook conceptualizes the new body of investment law in North Korea as 'exceptional law' in the sense that 'this new legislation does not replace or reform any existing pieces of state legislation or constitutional law, and because the new areas of economic expansion and regulation occur largely outside the strict context of state-society relations in North Korea'.[56] He further classifies this body of exceptional law into two groups. The first is '*common exceptional law*, which consists of laws that generally address the expansion of marketization and international trade in North Korea and are applicable uniformly throughout North Korea'.[57] This group includes, for example, the Foreign Investment Law and the Wholly Foreign-Owned Enterprise Law. The second is '*specific exceptional law*, which consists of the laws and regulations that apply only to specific areas and projects and delineate the boundaries of permissible action and constrained jurisdiction that pertain only to those areas and projects'.[58] This category includes the basic laws for Raseon, Sinuiju, Kaeseong, and Geumgangsan. Zook points out shortcomings of both common and specific exceptional law in North Korea, 'arguing that the inconsistencies, ambiguities, and contradictions, accompanied by unclear terrains of jurisdiction, collectively represent a fundamental flaw in the process of economic restructuring that will continue to preclude effective economic reform without a concomitant and comprehensive program of legal restructuring and reform'.[59]

The new legislation on investment is better conceptualized as reformative than exceptional law as it continues and improves the socialist principle of the leading role of the state in the economy, including in foreign trade, which shapes North Korean economic law. In a broader sense, this reformative legislation, to some extent, introduces positive changes to improve the existing socialist legal system. Also, the distinction between common and specific investment laws is blurred. On the one hand, some common laws are specially applied to special areas. For example, the Foreign Investment Law is nationally applied but particularly enacted for special economic zones. On the other hand, specific laws are the institutional expression of the national policy for promoting foreign investments.

The co-existence of national laws and regional laws governing foreign investment in North Korea can be understood as a kind of legal pluralism. North Korean legal pluralism is characterized by the co-existence within the territory of North

[55] ibid 393–94.
[56] Zook (n 1) 150.
[57] ibid 156.
[58] ibid.
[59] ibid 157.

Korea of the national legal system dominated (not exclusively) by socialist institutions and the regional legal systems dominated (not exclusively) by capital institutions. In different economic zones, the regional legal systems established by the basic laws vary in terms of their personnel, administration, and substantive rules for foreign investment. Legal pluralism in North Korea is animated by the tension between norms and needs. That is the tension between the normative commitment to internal reliance (*Juche* ideology) and the actual necessity of attracting external capital to facilitate economic development. The state avoids legal monism because to establish a single comprehensive and coherent legal regime for foreign investment for the whole country may lead to the state lacking control over the flow of capital, which would undermine the *Juche* ideology and the entire socialist regime. Instead, legal pluralism can deal with the tension between norms and needs. Allowing for the partial operation of capital legal institutions in specifically designated areas of the territory would meet the need of economic development while retaining the socialist commitments at the national level.

2. *Law for Public Management*

North Korea has also adopted many laws to support public administration of the economy and national resources. They are also relevant to economic development but have different administrative functions and therefore should be discussed separately. The regime has enacted and revised several laws to support the public management of the economy. These laws and their amendments have some developmental intention. For example, the Law on Recycling Resources adopted in 2020 seeks to contribute to the sustained development and protection of the ecological environment.[60] Other laws in this area will be considered later in section IV on administrative reform.

North Korea also adopted several laws on the management of natural resources (eg forest, rivers, water, and ginseng) with developmental intention. The Forest Law (1992) 'is intended to contribute to . . . conserving forests and utilizing forest resources'.[61] The Rivers Law (1992) 'is intended to contribute to utilizing rivers in a comprehensive way and laying out the land in a beautiful way by establishing a strict system and order in improving, conserving and utilizing rivers'.[62] The Law on Water Resources (1997) 'is intended to contribute to supplying sufficient amounts of water needed for national economic development and people's living'.[63] The Law of Insam (2018) seeks to provide the legal guarantee for increasing *insam* (ginseng) production.[64] The enactment of the laws on natural resources to support

[60] Hong (n 8).
[61] The Forest Law of the Democratic People's Republic of Korea (amended through 2001), art 1.
[62] The Law on Rivers of the Democratic People's Republic of Korea (amended through 2004), art 1.
[63] The Law on Water Resources of the Democratic People's Republic of Korea (amended through 1999).
[64] Hong (n 8).

substantiable development is in part due to international sanctions and the deficiency of resources, and therefore 'the regime has focused on primary industries—particularly agriculture, fisheries and forestry—that extract natural resources and generally require less capital, energy or sophisticated technology than other industries, such as manufacturing'.[65] The exploration of natural resources would generate environmental problems. North Korea therefore adopted several laws to protect the environment, including the Environmental Protection Law (1986), the Seawater Pollution Prevention Law (1997), and the Environmental Impact Assessment Law (2005). The laws on natural resources and the laws on environmental protection collectively form a body of substantiable development law in North Korea.

3. *Law for Social Control*

North Korea enacted and revised several laws for controlling its citizens such as the Criminal Law, the Criminal Procedure Law, the Administrative Penalty Law, and the Reactionary Ideology and Culture Rejection Act. These laws are mainly legal tools for the state's political repression of citizens. Particularly, the North Korean criminal system is often criticized for the prevailing violations of human rights—such as the nonjudicial punishment of political offences through *kwanriso* camps.[66] However, there are some sporadic changes to the criminal system, which partially soften the regime's harsh treatment of its citizens.

In the 1990s, North Korea adopted a new Criminal Law and a new Criminal Procedure Law, which have been amended several times. The new Criminal Law was adopted in 1990 and then amended in 1994, 2004, 2010, 2011, 2012, 2013, 2014, and 2015.[67] The New Criminal Procedure Law was adopted in 1992 and amended in 2004, 2011, and 2012.[68] The amendments to these two laws contain some positive changes.

To illustrate, In Sup Han demonstrates that the primary change in the 2004 amendment to the Criminal Law 'lies in the articulation of the principle of legality. Analogy and retroactivity are no longer allowed. Articles are more specified. Legal terms dilute the ideological tone. The Criminal Law is more focused on the control of economic and social offenses rather than on political repression.'[69] The amendment also introduced life imprisonment as an alternative penalty for five capital offences (four 'anti-state' offences and one 'murder offence'), and for thirteen other felony offences.[70] In addition, in response to new policy to expand foreign

[65] ibid.

[66] Tae-Ung Baik, 'Nonjudicial Punishments of Political Offenses in North Korea—With a Focus on Kwanriso' (2016) 64 Am J Comp Law 891.

[67] 형법 2015 [Criminal Law of the Democratic People's Republic of Korea (2015)] [tr Daye Gang].

[68] 형사소송법 2012 [Criminal Procedure Law of the Democratic People's Republic of Korea (2012)] [tr Daye Gang].

[69] In Sup Han, 'The 2004 Revision of Criminal Law in North Korea: A Take-off' (2007) 5 Santa Clara J Int'l L 132–33.

[70] ibid 125.

investments and better economic management introduced by a measure in 2002, the 2004 amendment to the Criminal Law increased the number of economic offences from eight to seventy-four and sought to regulate rather than suppress economic activities such as foreign trade, product quality control, and trademark protection.[71] In Sup Han comments that 'A violation of economic regulations is normally punishable by less than two years' labor training, which indicates that the authorities will be more interested in controlling the abuse of commercial discretion, rather than in wielding omnipotent powers on all the economic matters.'[72]

The Criminal Procedure Law also has some positive changes.[73] The formal changes seek to render the law to have a more legal rather than merely political function. For example, Article 1 of the 1999 version of the Law provides that the Law 'shall safeguard national sovereignty and the socialist system and guarantee self-reliant and creative life of the people through its struggle against crime'.[74] Article 1 of the 2004 version of the Law removed that political statement and provides for the legal function of the Law to 'contribute to the establishment of firm order and a system of procedures at all stages of investigation, preliminary examination, indictment and trial, so that criminal cases may be handled accurately'.[75] The 2004 amendment to the Criminal Procedure Law also has positive changes in the areas of human rights.[76] For example, the amendments shorten the detention period of a suspected or accused criminal, prohibit overnight interrogation, prohibit forced interrogation or leading questions, require that suspect are informed of their rights, and prohibit detaining an accused in court.[77]

In short, at the formal legislative level, there are sporadic changes to improve the criminal system. How formal legislative reforms actually generate functional change to the criminal system is a separate story.

C. North Korean Socialist Law

The embodiment of Marxist-Leninist socialist principles in North Korean law is generally stronger than in the law of China, Vietnam, and Laos. This is mainly because North Korea has only introduced sporadic reforms to the socialist legal system, while the three other countries have implemented a programme of comprehensive legal reform. North Korea's aspiration to develop its own way of socialism under the *Juche* ideology shapes the variation of socialist law in North Korea.

[71] ibid 126.
[72] ibid.
[73] Soo-Am Kim, *The North Korean Penal Code, Criminal Procedures, and the Actual Applications*, Studies Series 06-01 (Korea Institute for National Unification 2006) 10.
[74] Cited in ibid.
[75] Cited in ibid.
[76] ibid 15.
[77] Korean Bar Association, *Report on Human Rights in North Korea 2014* (2015) 56–57.

To begin with, the legislation generally and the reformative legislation particularly are the embodiment of *legal instrumentalism*. North Korean law remains an instrument for the state's socialist interests, particularly to protect the socialist political and economic systems, to achieve the state's socialist goals, and to control the society.

The current Constitution continues to entrench an instrumentalist perception of North Korean law, providing that:

> The law of the Democratic People's Republic of Korea reflects the wishes and interests of the working people and is a basic instrument for State administration. Respect for the law and strict adherence to and execution of it is the duty of all institutions, enterprises, organizations and citizens. The State shall perfect the system of socialist law and promote the socialist law-abiding life.[78]

Thus, the national law is conceived of as the institutional expression of the will and interest of the working class, a tool for the state dominated by the working class to control social compliance and create a socialist society. Law is an instrument to unify people's behaviour.[79] North Korea's numerous legislative enactments are consistent with the intention to promote 'the socialist law-abiding life'.

The body of law for economic development serves the state's instrumental interests. To illustrate, the Civil Law aims to 'ensure a strong socialist economic system'.[80] The Law explicitly puts the state's interests above individuals' interests, providing that 'The State shall prioritize State and social interests while thoroughly guaranteeing the interests of individual institutions, enterprises, organizations or citizens, in establishing and realizing property relationships.'[81] Instrumentalism is also embodied in the emerging body of foreign investment law. Zook demonstrates that:

> the general theme that investment and investment-related activities in North Korea are to serve the political and economic needs of the DPRK first and foremost; the economic needs of the outside investor are not at any point to override these. It is possible, for instance, to establish a wholly foreign-owned enterprise in North Korea, but in nearly every phase of planning and development, including selecting a location, the DPRK would have considerable power of control and supervision.[82]

[78] Socialist Constitution (n 24) art 18.
[79] Lee (n 2) 83.
[80] 민법 [Civil Law] (n 36) art 1.
[81] ibid art 9.
[82] Zook (n 1) 161.

In other words, the foremost function of the legislation on foreign investment is to serve the state's not the investors' interests.

Instrumentalism is particularly prominent in the laws for social control. For example, the Criminal Code 'defends the sovereignty of the State and the socialist system'.[83] Therefore, it includes offences to protect the socialist political regime (eg propaganda against the nation),[84] the socialist economy (eg individuals' profiting from enterprises and business operations),[85] and the socialist culture (eg listening to hostile broadcasts).[86] In addition, the Reactionary Ideology and Culture Rejection Act was adopted in 2020 'as a powerful battle to obstruct the inflow and distribution of reactionary ideology and culture and anti-socialist ideology and culture'.[87] The law imposes criminal sanctions on acts spreading into North Korea 'ideology and culture of hostile forces including South Korean publications'.[88] To illustrate, viewing, listening to, or possessing South Korean movies, video recordings, compilations, books, songs, drawings, or photographs can result in a sentence of five to ten years of reform through labour.[89] Distributing a large amount of movies, video recordings, compilations, and books of 'hostile countries' can carry a sentence of reform through labour for life or the death penalty.[90] Thus, the Reactionary Ideology and Culture Rejection Act is the tool for ideological and informational control.

North Korean law is also the embodiment of *Party vanguardism*. The Constitution establishes the principle of Party vanguardism, stating that 'The Democratic People's Republic of Korea shall conduct all activities under the leadership of the Workers' Party of Korea.'[91] The Presidium of the Supreme People's Assembly 'is by and large composed of' members of the Workers' Party of Korea (WPK), effectively subordinating the North Korean legislature to the Party's control.[92] Consequently, North Korean law is the embodiment of Party policy. Suehyun Jung notes that 'reorganization of the legal system by enacting and amending a series of laws in support of the WPK's policy changes has been remarkable since

[83] 형법 [Criminal Law] (n 67) art 1.
[84] ibid arts 60 and 62.
[85] ibid art 114.
[86] ibid art 185.
[87] Reactionary Ideology and Culture Rejection Act of the Democratic People's Republic of Korea, art 1.
[88] Reactionary Ideology and Culture Rejection Act of the Democratic People's Republic of Korea, art 2.
[89] ibid art 27.
[90] ibid art 27.
[91] Socialist Constitution (n 24) art 11. Apart from the ruling Workers' Party of Korea (WPK), there are two other (non-communist) parties in North Korea (namely the Social Democratic Party and the Chondoist Chongu Party) but, like the case of China, they are allies of the ruling Communist Party. On these two parties, see Fyodor Tertitskiy, 'Being a Minor Party in the North: In a Totalitarian Regime, What Do N. Korea's Other Political Blocs Do?' (NK News, 26 November 2014) <https://www.nknews.org/2014/11/being-a-minor-party-in-the-north>accessed 6 June 2024.
[92] Jung (n 9) 3.

just after Kim Jong Un took power'.[93] In other words, North Korean law, legal institutions, and legal reform are the embodiment of the Party's policies.

North Korean legal institutions are shaped by the principle of *democratic centralism*. The Constitution confirms that 'All State organs in the Democratic People's Republic of Korea are formed and function on the principle of democratic centralism.'[94] The Supreme People's Assembly, the nation's legislature, and the highest organ of state power elect or recall top military, executive, and judicial leaders who are accountable to the former.[95] As will be discussed later, democratic centralism shapes the administrative and court systems.

North Korean law is the strong embodiment of the statist economy. The law confirms the state's dominant ownership of the means of production, the planned economy under the state's centralized control, and the state's strict regulation of the economy. The Marxist-Leninist commitment to planned economy (which limits domestic marketization) and the *Juche* commitment to self-economic reliance (which limits engagement with foreign and international economies) underpin the strong legal embodiment of the statist economy. Apart from the Constitution, the statist economy is embedded in many laws related to the economy.

The National Economic Planning Law establishes principles and rules for the planned economy. The law confirms that the country's economy is a planned economy founded in the socialist ownership of means of production.[96] Administering and operating the national economy must be under the centralist standardized guidance and command of the state.[97]

The Civil Law provides for three types of ownership: state ownership; ownership by social, cooperative organizations; and private ownership.[98] The state is the only owner of underground, forest, and marine resources; railway, aviation transport, communications institutions and important factories, enterprises, ports, and banks; and important cultural and public health facilities.[99] Thus, as the exclusive owner of the major means of production, the state dominates the economy. The Civil Law allows institutions, enterprises, and organizations to conclude 'contracts based on plans' on the basis of the national economic plan.[100] Thus, the state controls planned contractual relations of the state (not private) economic sectors to implement the state's economic plan. North Korea's Civil Law is not merely a private law but a public law regulating statist property and contractual relations.

[93] ibid.
[94] Socialist Constitution (n 24) art 5.
[95] ibid arts 87 and 91.
[96] 인민경제계획법 2015 [National Economic Planning Law of the Democratic People's Republic of Korea (2015)] [tr Daye Gang], art 2.
[97] ibid art 3.
[98] 민법 [Civil Law] (n 36) art 37.
[99] ibid art 45.
[100] ibid art 10.

The Enterprises Law establishes a legal framework for the creation and function of the state-owned enterprises under the state's control. The Law provides that 'The State shall resolutely guarantee standardized guidance from the State to enterprises in conformity with the principle of socialist economic administration.'[101] The organization of enterprises shall be caried out by the state's institutions, including the Cabinet, the central labour administration guidance institution, local governments, and the relevant authorities.[102] Private enterprises are not legally allowed: only the state can create an enterprise. Therefore, the state, through its enterprises, dominates the national economy.

North Korean law also ensures the state's control of international economic activities. The law cautiously allows for foreign investment and provides ample space for the state to control foreign investors to remain committed to self-economic reliance. The Trade Law provides that trade must be conducted according to the state's national economic plan, contractual regulations, and guidance.[103] Trade deals must be approved by the state's central trade guidance institution.[104] The Foreign Economic Contract Law subjects foreign economic contracts to the supervision and control of the state's central trade guidance institution.[105] The Contractual Joint Venture Law provides that contractual joint venture enterprises must be approved by the state's investment management institution and have to register the location of the enterprise with local government or the special economic zones management institution.[106]

The Foreign Enterprise Law provides that foreign investors must observe the state's laws and regulations 'and must not do acts that cause inconvenience to national economic development'.[107] The creation of a foreign enterprise has to be approved by the state's investment management institution.[108] Foreign investors must register with the relevant local government or the special economic zones management institution.[109] Foreign enterprises are required to submit annual and quarterly production and exports and imports plans to the investment management institution.[110] These legal establishments provide the

[101] 기업소법 2015 [Enterprises Law of the Democratic People's Republic of Korea (2015)] [tr Daye Gang], art 8.
[102] ibid art 11.
[103] 무역법 2015 [Trade Law of the Democratic People's Republic of Korea (2015)] [tr Daye Gang], arts 5 and 6.
[104] ibid art 13.
[105] 대외경제계약법 2008 [Foreign Economic Contract Law of the Democratic People's Republic of Korea (2008)] [tr Daye Gang], art 7.
[106] 합작법 2014 [Contractual Joint Venture Law of the Democratic People's Republic of Korea (2014)] [tr Daye Gang], arts 6 and 7.
[107] 외국인기업법 2011 [Foreign Enterprise Law of the Democratic People's Republic of Korea (2011)] [tr Daye Gang], art 5.
[108] ibid art 7.
[109] ibid art 9.
[110] ibid art 15.

base for the state to control the creation and operation of foreign enterprises in North Korea.

Statist rights also strongly feature in North Korean law. In a negative aspect, the law allows the state to control and if necessary curtail individual rights. The Constitution promises many citizen's rights (from freedom of speech to freedom of travel) but provides that these rights 'shall be amplified with the consolidation and development of the socialist system'.[111] This means the implementation of the state's socialist goals is the justification of individual rights. The state can withdraw individual rights if their exercise contravenes the socialist system. This explains the state's prevailing denial of human rights, which the state considers a threat to the socialist system.

In a positive aspect, legal provisions of statist rights establish the socialist state's benevolent duties to protect rights. Particularly, several laws protecting the rights of vulnerable people (eg the elderly, people with disabilities, women, and children) in North Korea strongly emphasize the positive role of the socialist state. The statist rights of vulnerable people are largely aspirational and expressive of the state's socialist ideology. The statist rights embody the socialist conception of the activist state as the key actor of social change. In addition, they are expressive of the socialist state's aspirational commitment to social equality.

The Protection of the Elderly Law aims 'to guarantee the rights and interests of the elderly'.[112] The Law provides that 'the state taking responsibility for and looking after the standard of life and health of the elderly is a superior measure of the socialist system. The State shall systematically increase investment in the protection of the elderly sector to assure a more civilised and good standard of life to the elderly.'[113] It further establishes that 'The State shall strengthen socialist morals education and good customs education so that the ethos of paying attention to, assisting, and respecting the elderly is elevated high all across society.'[114] These provisions are expressive of the state's intention to protect the elderly to demonstrate the superiority of the socialist state and the socialist morality.

The Persons with Disability Protection Law requires the state to assure the social and political rights, freedoms, and interests of people with disability in the same way as healthy people.[115] The law then stipulates that the state shall 'systematically increase investment in the persons with disability protection sector', prevent the occurrence and deterioration of disability, 'regularly investigate the true state of persons with disability', 'strengthen education work among people so that they

111 Socialist Constitution (n 24) art 64.

112 년로자법 2012 [Protection of the Elderly Law of the Democratic People's Republic of Korea (2012)] [tr Daye Gang], art 1.

113 ibid art 2.

114 ibid art 6.

115 장애자보호법 2013 [Persons with Disability Protection Law of the Democratic People's Republic of Korea (2013)] [tr Daye Gang], art 2.

have refined love for other humans, treat people with disability kindly and without discrimination', and give preference to persons with disability.[116] Thus, the law establish the state's positive duties to protect people with disabilities.

The Women's Rights Protection Law provides that 'the State shall raise attention to women across all of society and shall thoroughly assure their rights'.[117] The law even provides for the state's plan to protect women's rights: 'The State shall adopt and execute a foundational plan for women's rights protection. Regional People's Committees shall adopt detailed plans for each year according to the State's foundational plan for women's rights protection, and must correctly execute it'.[118] The socialist planning culture is hence extended to women's rights protection.

The Children's Rights Protection Law considers children as 'the future of the nation that will take on the future fate of the people' and 'the rear guard for the building of socialism'.[119] Therefore, the Law provides that 'the state shall always turn deep attention to the growth and development of children, and shall turn every consideration to allow all children to exercise their rights as much as they like, and so that they grow happily and without an envy in the world'.[120] These provisions express the state's aspiration to support the development of children and to protect their rights to achieve the state's socialist goal.

IV. ADMINISTRATIVE REFORM

North Korea does not have a comprehensive programme of administrative reform. However, it has induced sporadic adjustments to the public administrative system in response to the need for effective management of the changing economy. Particularly under Kim Jong Un, a notable change is decentralization in the administrative management of the economy. The regime also enacted many administrative laws, which contain some sporadic reforms.

A. Public Administration

Since Kim Jong Un came to power, North Korea has reformed its Enterprise Management System by revising key laws on economic management, including:

116 ibid arts 3, 4, 5, 6, and 7.
117 녀성권리보장법 2015 [Women's Rights Protection Law of the Democratic People's Republic of Korea (2015)] [tr Daye Gang], art 3.
118 ibid art 4.
119 아동권리보장법 2014 [Children's Rights Protection Law of the Democratic People's Republic of Korea (2014)] [tr Daye Gang], art 2.
120 ibid art 4.

National Economy Planning Law;
Farm Law;
Enterprises Law;
Trade Law; and
Materials Management Law.[121]

Moon-Soo Yang observes that 'the most notable change was the official overhaul of the allocation system for planning indicators between the central government and individual production and trade units'.[122] As indicated in Table 7.1, the reformed allocation system illustrates administrative decentralization in the sense that it grants more autonomy to individual production and trade units.

Table 7.1 Reallocation of the Roles between the Central Government and Enterprise under the Revised Laws: Decentralization[123]

Related Laws	Revised Provisions (as of 2012~2015)
Economy Planning Law	Indicators were allocated at the central, regional, and corporate levels, meaning the key indicators with strategic significance are managed at the central level while other indicators are allocated to the regional and business levels.
Enterprises Law	Businesses received the right to develop plans independently, which constituted the business indicator.
Farm Law	Farm indicator was divided into the central and farm indicators. Farmers were allowed to plan their own indicator as long as they achieved the central indicator.
Trade Law	The National Planning Commission planned national strategic and limitation indicators in volume terms. Other indicators were set by the key actors in trade in trade-value terms.
Materials Management Law	For the materials supply planning, the National Planning Commission was responsible for developing the central indicator and relevant institutions, businesses, and organizations for other indicators.

The adoption of the 'socialist enterprise responsibility management system' to replace the Party-Centric Taean Work System is illustrative of administrative decentralization. The new system seeks to partially transfer the central government's

[121] Moon-Soo Yang, 'The Economic Reform of North Korea in the Kim Jong-un Era: Status & Evaluation' KDI Working Paper, Korea Development Institute (June 2021) 10.
[122] ibid 10.
[123] Source: ibid 12 (adapted table).

authority to the state-owned enterprises.[124] Accordingly, the enterprises enjoy rights to plan their production, set prices, and sell their products with certain limits, manage their finances, adjust labour, and transfer or rent out unnecessary equipment.[125] The 'socialist system of responsible business operation' was confirmed in the Enterprises Law in 2014 and then in the Constitution through the 2019 amendment.[126]

Decentralization is also evident in efforts to reform the administrative management of the special economic zones under the Kim Jong Un era. Dongho Jo demonstrates that 'the old zones were led by the central government, but in the Kim Jong Un era, they have been divided into central and local levels, with a larger number of local special economic zones'.[127] In addition, the institutions managing special economic zones were restructured to improve efficiency. For example, in June 2014, the Ministry of Foreign Trade, the Joint Venture and Investment Commission, and the State Economic Development Commission were merged into the Ministry of External Economic Affairs within the Cabinet.[128]

Finally, Kim Jong Un's anti-corruption movement, initiated in 2013, is also connected to the implementation of decentralization. Suehyun Jung argues that Kim seeks 'to control corruption to ensure the success of the decentralizing economic reforms and thus bring a decent amount of the economic surplus into state revenue'.[129] In a speech at a Party's meeting in 2013, Kim said that 'those who abuse their power and work in a bureaucratic manner are the major targets of criticism, those whom our Party should punish resolutely'.[130] Under Kim Jong Un, the regime also reinforced legal controls of corruption 'by directly linking them to the decentralizing economic reform'.[131] To illustrate, the 2015 amendment to the Criminal Law increased sentences in cases of particularly large bribes from three (the 2012 version) to five years' hard labour.[132]

B. Administrative Law

Apart from public administration of the economy, North Korea adopted and amended several administrative laws, including:

[124] Suk Jin Kim, 'The Limits of Economic Reform in North Korea under the Kim Jong-un Regime: Lessons from Chinese Experiences' (2021) 30 IJKUS 1.
[125] ibid 4–5.
[126] Jo (n 53) 78.
[127] ibid 79.
[128] ibid 79.
[129] Suehyun Jung, 'Elite-Middle Class Competition for Rent-Seeking in North Korea and Kim Jong Un's Anti-Corruption Movement' (2022) 62 Asian Surv 479.
[130] Cited in ibid 479.
[131] ibid 474–75.
[132] ibid 474.

Civil Service Qualification Law (2005, amended in 2008 and 2011);
Administrative District Law (2008);
Local Organs of State Power Law (1974, amended in 1993, 1999, 2007, 2009, and 2012);
Municipal Administration Law (1992, amended in 1999, 2000, 2006, 2013, 2014, and 2015);
Complaints and Petitions Law (1998, amended 1999, 2000, and 2010); and
Administrative Punishment Law (2004, amended, 2005, 2006, 2007, 2008, and 2011).[133]

The existence of these laws at least suggests that there may be some degree of legality in the exercise of administrative power.

To be sure, commitment to legality does not necessarily mean commitment to the rule of law. Administrative law in North Korea is the instrument to organize and consolidate administrative power. However, as an exceptional case, the Complaints and Petitions Law attempts to empower citizens and curb administrative power to some extent. It is therefore useful to explore this law in greater detail. The law was enacted to deal with 'backward and irrational order which lags behind the developing realities', and low practical qualifications and administrative officials' misinterpretations of the law, which may lead to the encroachment of citizens' interests.[134] Also, the law seems to reflect political concerns. Kim Jong Il said that 'Complaints represent the voice of the people, and every citizen has the right to make a complaint. When their interests are violated by any state organs or individual officials, the people are entitled to lodge a complaint to law-enforcement organs about it.'[135]

The Complaints and Petitions Law therefore aims to both 'protect the rights and interests of citizens' and 'improve the State's administration work'.[136] Complaints are defined as 'acts of preventing the violation of one's rights and interests in advance, or requiring the recovery of violated rights and interests', while petitions are defined as 'acts of raising an opinion to improve the work of institutions, enterprises, organizations, and individual workers'.[137] The Law authorizes citizens to make complaints and petitions to institutions, enterprises, organizations, and individual workers until they reach the highest organ of state power.[138] So,

[133] The English translations of these laws are available at *Law and North Korea* <https://www.lawandnorthkorea.com/about> accessed 6 June 2024.
[134] Kim Kyong Hyon, 'The Complaint and Petition System of the Democratic People's Republic of Korea—The Most Popular Complaint and Petition System' (Kim Il Sung University, 23 September 2021) <http://www.ryongnamsan.edu.kp/univ/en/research/articles/bf764716fe1a58cb07f8a377ec25c16d>.
[135] Cited in ibid.
[136] 신소청원법 2010 [Complaints and Petitions Law of the Democratic People's Republic of Korea (2010)] [tr Daye Gang], art 1.
[137] ibid art 2.
[138] ibid art 8.

there are no restrictions on the content and level of complaints and petitions.[139] The Law requires that institutions, enterprises, and organizations 'receive raised complaints and petitions without exception, and must correctly register them'.[140] Once complaints and petitions are received, there will be investigation and resolutions.[141]

The Complaints and Petitions Law formally empowers citizens to voice their concerns regarding the administrative encroachments of their rights and interests. However, the legal system of complaints and petitions in North Korea is vague and not sophisticated like those in China, Vietnam, and Laos. For example, North Korea's Complaints and Petitions Law does not concretize the administrative actions subject to complaints and petitions. It also does not specify resolutions for administrative violations of citizens' interests and rights.

In practice, the rights to petitions or complaints are not always respected. For example, 'when individuals submitted anonymous petitions or complaints regarding state administration, the Ministry of Social Security and the Ministry of State Security sought to identify the authors and subject them to investigation and punishment'.[142]

However, the legal right to petitions has been used in practice to some extent. To illustrate, consider the Pyongyang Medical University incident in 2020. Four sons of Central Committee cadres at the Pyongyang Medical University sexually abused female students repeatedly. One of the victims committed suicide. Her mother first appealed to the university's party committee to punish the four male students, but the university ignored her appeal. The mother then petitioned to the Ministry of Social Security branch in Chung-guyok, the district where the university is located, but the branch did not respond. The woman then submitted a petition to the Central Committee of the Party. Considering that 'a serious anti-socialist crime' had occurred, the desk clerk and staff received the petition letter and informed Jo Yong Won, first vice director of the Party's Organization and Guidance Department. The Organization and Guidance Department conducted an intensive week-long investigation of the party committee of Pyongyang Medical University. Consequently, some sixty people involved in the incident were exiled from Pyongyang to the provinces. All seven members of the party committee of Pyongyang Medical University who overlooked 'the students' anti-socialist acts' were sent with their families to Chagang Province to work at a calcium carbonate mine. Five officials from the Ministry of Public Security in Chung-guyok who suppressed the petition were exiled with their families to a farm in North

[139] Hyon (n 134).
[140] Complaints and Petitions (n 136) art 15.
[141] ibid ch IV.
[142] 2021 Country Reports on Human Rights Practices: North Korea <https://www.state.gov/reports/2021-country-reports-on-human-rights-practices/north-korea>accessed 6 June 2024.

Hwanghae Province. The four male students at Pyongyang Medical University were executed.[143]

The Pyongyang Medical University incident has generated broader political concern of the petition system. At the Eighth Party Congress in 2021, petition handling was discussed as a major issue.[144] 'Kim Jong-un urged his officials to strengthen the petition system, not just in formality but in practicality.'[145] It is questionable whether the petition system can function as an effective mechanism to check corruption and ease public discontent because citizens may be afraid of the aftermath of petitions, and petitioners may be forced to close the case within the organization.[146] However, the existence of a legal system for petitions or complaints and some practices at least suggests some positive changes to administrative law to empower citizens and contain the abuse of administrative power.

C. Socialist Administrative Law

Administrative law in North Korea is an instrument for the state to control the population and to protect the state's interests. For example, the Administrative Penalty Law, a semi-criminal code following the Russian model, was enacted in 2004 and subsequently amended many times.[147] The Law seeks to establish 'a law-abiding ethos in society'[148] by providing administrative punishments (such as warnings, unpaid labour, labour education, demotion, dismissal, termination, compensation confiscation, and suspension of qualifications)[149] to various unlawful acts committed by institutions, enterprises, organizations, and citizens. For example, Article 153 of the Law imposes a punishment of less than three months of labour education on 'a person who has listened to enemy broadcasts or collected, stored, or disseminated hostile goods without a purpose against the State.'[150] The Administrative Penalty Law is an instrument for the state to punish its citizens to protect the state's socialist ideology and the socialist political regime.

The administrative system is also the institutional embodiment of Party vanguardism. To illustrate, the Party representative is set up in every administrative

143 Ha Yuna, 'N. Korean Authorities Bust Students at Pyongyang Medical University for 'Anti-Socialist Activity' Daily NK (23 November 2020) <https://www.dailynk.com/english/north-korean-authorities-bust-students-pyongyang-medical-university-anti-socialist-activity>accessed 6 June 2024; 'Complaints and Petitions in N. Korea' (KBS WORLD 11 November 2021), <https://world.kbs.co.kr/service/contents_view.htm?lang=e&menu_cate=northkorea&id=&board_seq=414209&page=0&board_code=oth_tnt>accessed 6 June 2024.

144 Hyon (n 134).

145 ibid.

146 ibid.

147 Hong (n 8).

148 행정처벌법 2011 [Administrative Punishment Law of the Democratic People's Republic of Korea (2011)] [tr Daye Gang], art 1.

149 ibid art 14.

150 ibid art 153.

unit, and it will 'transmit policy directives from the Party, evaluate the performance of bureaucrats, and report to the central Party'.[151] This institutional arrangement allows the Party's polices to penetrate the administrative system and places the administrative system under the Party's leadership.

Administrative law is also the embodiment of the principle of democratic centralism. For example, the Local Organs of State Power Law provides that 'Local organs of State power shall embody the principle of democratic centralism in all activities.'[152] The Regional People's Committees (the local administrative organs) are accountable to the respective People's Assemblies (the people's representative organs.) In addition, the Regional People's Committees shall submit to People's Committees at higher levels, the Cabinet, and the Presidium of the Supreme People's Assembly.[153] Thus, local governments are placed under the centralized control of the central government.

Statist rights are also embodied in administrative law. Administrative law empowers administrative agents to regulate the exercise of citizen's rights. To illustrate, consider the administrative regulation of the constitutional right to residence and travel. The Constitution provides that 'citizens have freedom of residence and travel'.[154] However, the Immigration Law requires that 'citizens seeking to exit or enter the country must receive an immigration certificate issued through the Ministry of Foreign Affairs, the immigration work institution, or the authorities concerned'.[155] The requirement of obtaining an immigration certificate allows administrative agents to control and even deny the constitutional right to travel to prevent the spread of ideas challenging the state's ideology.

It is also difficult for North Korean citizens to travel domestically due to the administrative regulation of the right to residence. The Citizen Registration Law provides that 'citizens must do residence registration in the people's safety institutions in the areas they live in'.[156] If citizens seek to move their domicile to a different area, they must submit 'a vacation registration application' to the people's safety institution in that residential area.[157] These provisions allow the 'people's safety institution' to control and even reject the right to residence and movement to avoid the civic formation of domestic collective actions opposing the state.[158]

[151] Sara R Jordan and Eric CY Ip, 'Demystifying the Hermit Kingdom: The Constitution and Public Administration in North Korea' (2013) 79 Int'l Rev Adm Sci 555.
[152] 지방주권기관법 2012 [Local Organs of State Power Law of the Democratic People's Republic of Korea (2012)] [tr Daye Gang], art 5.
[153] ibid art 35.
[154] Socialist Constitution (n 24) art 75.
[155] 출입국법 2012 [Immigration Law of the Democratic People's Republic of Korea (2012)] [tr Daye Gang], art 12.
[156] 공민등록법 2015 [Citizen Registration Law of the Democratic People's Republic of Korea (2015)] [tr Daye Gang], art 4.
[157] ibid art 14.
[158] Yeo (n 22) 23.

V. JUDICIAL REFORM

A. Sporadic Judicial Reforms

North Korea does not have a plan of comprehensive judicial reform but has introduced some sporadic adjustments to improve the judicial system. The Court Composition Law enacted in 1976 was amended several times in 1998, 2009, and 2011.[159] The 1998 amendments soften the political elements of courts in the original 1976 version, although the class nature of the courts remains. To illustrate, the amendment deleted Article 4 of the original Law, which stated that 'the courts shall actively strive to oppose all class enemies and all law violations, and contribute to achieving the historic task of uniformly covering the entire society with the great Juche Ideology'.[160] The current version of the Court Composition Law suggests that the Law attempts to institutionalize the courts as legal institutions. The Law does not heavily feature the political statements but includes legal provisions on structural, personal, and functional aspects of the court system.

On the structural dimension, the Court Composition Law provides that the court system includes the Central Court (the highest court), provincial courts, county people's courts, and special courts (such as military tribunals, railway courts, and military supplies courts).[161] The *North Korea Handbook* (2003) reports that North Korea has a Central Court, twelve provincial courts and around a hundred people's courts.[162]

On the personal aspect, the Court Composition Law deals with the selection, qualification, terms, and dismissal of judges and people's assessors. Judges and people's assessors are selected by political institutions. The judges and people's assessors of the Central Court shall be selected by the Presidium of the Supreme People's Assembly.[163] The judges and people's assessors of the province courts and county people's courts shall be selected by the local People's Assembly at the respective levels.[164] The judges of special courts shall be appointed by the Central Court, and people's assessors of these courts shall be selected at the given soldiers' or employees' meetings.[165]

The Court Composition Law provides that 'Judges and People's Assessors may be citizens of the Republic who have the right to vote. However, people without the

[159] 재판소구성법 2011 [Court Composition Law of the Democratic People's Republic of Korea (2011)] [tr Daye Gang].
[160] Kim (n 73) 17.
[161] Court Composition (n 159) art 3.
[162] Citied in Goedde (n 1) 1276–77.
[163] Court Composition (n 159) art 4.
[164] ibid art 4.
[165] ibid art 5.

given qualifications may not be Judges.'[166] But the law does not specify the qualifications. 'In reality, it is customary for judges to be elected after completing five years of legal education in the law department of Kim Il Sung University and subsequently working in a court as trainees, staff or assistant judges.'[167]

The Court Composition Law also does not specify the term of election of judges and people's assessors but generally provides that it shall be the same as the term of election of the respective People's Assembly.[168] It can be understood that judges and people's assessors of the Central Court will have a five-year term, the same as the term of the Supreme People's Assembly,[169] and local judges and people's assessors have a four-year term, the same as the term of the local People's Assembly.[170] Judges and people's assessors may only be dismissed by the electing and appointing institution.[171]

Functionally, the county people's courts hear the first-instance cases, while the provincial courts hear appellate cases. The Central Court or a provincial court may hear the first-instance cases involving critical matters.[172] First-instance cases shall be heard by a judge and two people's assessors,[173] while appellate cases shall be heard by three judges.[174]

At a textual level, the Constitution protects some fair trial rights such as the right to public trial and the right to defence.[175] The document even protects judicial independence, providing that 'in administering justice, the Court is independent, and judicial proceedings are carried out in strict accordance with the law.'[176] Relatedly, interference with a law enforcement official's performance of duties, threatening a witness or exacting revenge, and non-execution of judgment can be punished.[177]

However, court reform in North Korea is very modest due to the limited function of courts in reality. Courts mainly deal with divorce cases because the law does not allow divorces to be settled by simple agreement of the two parties.[178] 'Criminal cases were also unusual. Political crime is handled through a non-judicial process, while many deviances are resolved through unofficial processes within more local

[166] ibid 6.
[167] Korean Bar Association (n 77) 57.
[168] Court Composition (n 159) art 7.
[169] Socialist Constitution (n 24) art 90.
[170] ibid art 139.
[171] Court Composition (n 159) art 8.
[172] Judiciary and Legal Profession of North Korea (2018) 65 Barun Newsletter, <http://www.naver.com> accessed 6 June 2024.
[173] Court Composition (n 159) art 9.
[174] ibid art 14.
[175] Socialist Constitution (n 24) art 64.
[176] ibid art 66.
[177] Yoon (n 35) 9.
[178] ibid.

organizations.'[179] Due to this limited role of the courts, there is no strong need for comprehensive reform of the court system.

B. The Socialist Courts

Due to the limits of judicial reform, North Korean courts strongly remain socialist features. The courts are the instrument to protect the state's power, the socialist regime, and the state's property, in addition to the lives and property of citizens.[180] The courts also function as an instrument for political control. The Constitution provides that the courts 'ensure that all institutions, enterprises, organizations and citizens abide strictly by State laws and staunchly combat class enemies and all lawbreakers'.[181] The courts are therefore the tool for the state to control the compliance of citizens and punish those opposing the government.

The North Korean court system is also the embodiment of Party vanguardism. The courts are under the Party's control, particularly through the Party's safety committees.[182] 'Trials are reported in advance to the Party's Safety Committee of the city or country, with possible sentence alternatives, before actual trial.'[183] It is testified that 'the Party Chief secretary has the right to pressure the court from behind. If the party instructs, the judicial branch is bound to listen'.[184] In other words, the Party both leads and directly interferes with the exercise of the judicial power.

The North Korean court system strongly embodies the principle of democratic centralism. The whole court system is under the internal supervision and control of the Central Court in a standardized way.[185] The county people's courts and the special courts are subject to the supervision and control of the provincial courts.[186] The courts are subject to the external control of the people's assemblies. At the central level, the Central Court must be accountable to the Supreme People's Assembly.[187] At the local levels, the provincial courts and county people's courts must be accountable to the respective People's Assembly.[188] Thus, the law establishes the internal hierarchical centralization and external hierarchical political control of the judicial power.

179 ibid.
180 Socialist Constitution (n 24) art 162.
181 ibid.
182 Kim (n 73) 22.
183 ibid 48.
184 ibid 48–49.
185 Court Composition (n 159) art 18.
186 ibid art 20.
187 ibid art 19.
188 ibid.

VI. LEGAL PROFESSIONAL REFORM

A. Sporadic Legal Professional Reform

North Korea adopted the Lawyers' Law in 1993.[189] This Law replaced regulations that had been in place since 1948, which 'loosely described the roles of lawyers and their qualifications'.[190] The enactment of the Lawyers' Law can be considered an effort to promote the reform of legal profession in North Korea. To some extent, the Law attempts to establish lawyering as a legal profession. This is demonstrated by the legal rules on the role of lawyers to protect human rights, the normal legal services offered by lawyers, the legal principles of lawyering, the legal qualifications of lawyers, the creation of a lawyers' association, and even the acceptance of foreign lawyers on the basis of reciprocity.

The Law attempts to 'raise the role of lawyers to protect the legal rights and interests of institutions, enterprises and organizations and citizens, and shall serve to assure the correct implementation of the law'.[191] The Law requires lawyers to 'assure human rights through legal activities and legal aid'.[192] Lawyers are, among other things, legal advisors, representatives for lawsuits, and representatives of acts of civil legal affairs, and their activities involve drafting and deliberating on legal advice and documents.[193] The law establishes legal principles of lawyering such as free choice of lawyer, independence, fairness, and the adherence to legality.[194]

The Law provides for the legal rights of lawyers in legal proceedings, including the rights to view the criminal case, confer with witnesses or expert witnesses, collect and confirm evidence required for defending a case, and appeal to a higher court for the first-instance judgment, among others.[195]

Lawyers must have professional legal qualifications and have been working in the legal sector for over five years.[196] Holders of law degrees or legal academic positions at a university or scientific research institution can also work as lawyers as an additional job.[197] The Lawyer Law even allows for foreign lawyers to work in North Korea. It provides that 'Lawyers of other countries may be given lawyer qualifications of the Republic from the principle of reciprocity. Lawyers of other countries who have lawyer qualifications of the Republic may only handle issues related to

189 변호사법 1993 [Lawyers' Law of the Democratic People's Republic of Korea (1993)] [tr Daye Gang].
190 Spina Jr (n 3) 3.
191 Lawyers' Law (n 189) art 1.
192 ibid art 2.
193 ibid art 3.
194 ibid arts 4, 5, and 6.
195 ibid art 9.
196 ibid art 20.
197 ibid art 21.

corporations and individuals of other countries, and laws of other countries.'[198] Michael Hay, a British-French lawyer, was the first and only person to open a foreign law firm in North Korea.[199]

> The firm, Hay, Kalb & Associates (HK&A), specialized in providing legal and investment counsel to foreign investors, entrepreneurs and NGOs wanting to work in North Korea from 2004 to 2016. Along with a handful of North Korean government lawyers who assisted him, Hay represented foreign firms in the country's arbitration courts, which he says operated in fair and equitable ways.[200]

The Lawyers' Law provides for the creation of the Choson lawyers' Association as the lawyers' organization. This body has a committee in the centre, provinces, or relevant sectors.[201] Lawyers' committees at each level will perform duties such as (among others) informing lawyers of the laws and regulations, and educating them; receiving applications of institutions, enterprises, organizations and citizens requiring legal aid; and organizing the division of work.[202] Thus, lawyers do not contract with their clients for a legal service, rather their work is allocated by the lawyers' committees.

Consequently, North Korean lawyers do not receive remuneration from their clients. Instead, they are remunerated by the lawyers' committees. The remuneration depends on the importance, complexity, and results of the work performed by the lawyer.[203] It is not the lawyers but the Central Committee of the Choson Lawyers' Association who determines remunerations for lawyers. 'Local lawyer committees collect all legal representation requests and later pay individual member lawyers in the form of a monthly salary.'[204]

Reportedly, there are 500 lawyers in North Korea, among whom 200 practice law in Pyongyang.[205] Two law firms operate in Pyongyang, and there is one law firm in the Rason free trade zone.[206] Particularly, the Korea Law Firm, associated with the Central Committee of the Chosen Lawyers' Association, established in Pyeongyang in June 2007, is the first law firm in North Korea. It provides local and foreign clients with legal services such as drafting, review, and translation of legal documents, litigation, and legal services.[207]

198 ibid art 23.
199 Shim Kyu-Seok, 'Practicing Law in Pyongyang—And Adoring It' Korea JoongAng Daily (22 June 2019) <Practicing law in Pyongyang—and adoring it (joins.com)> accessed 6 June 2024.
200 ibid.
201 Lawyers' Law (n 189) art 29.
202 ibid art 30.
203 ibid art 25.
204 'Lawyers in N. Korea' KBS WORLD (17 September 2020) <Lawyers in N. Korea l KBS WORLD>.
205 ibid.
206 ibid.
207 Judiciary and Legal Profession (n 172).

Legal education is provided at the law departments of Kim Il Sung University and the National Economic Institute.[208] The creation of the Faculty of Law at the Kim Il Sung University in 1999 was an important step towards improving the legal profession. It enrols fifty students annually.[209] According to its website, the law school has enrolled a thousand students and has eighty lecturers and researchers. The internal structure of the law school includes ten departments:

Department of Political Science
Department of Jurisprudence
Department of Public Administration Law
Department of Criminal Law
Department of Criminal Procedure Law
Department of Civil Law
Department of Legal History
Department of Legal Cybernetics
Department of International Law
Department of International Economic Law

The law school offers the following courses:

Socialist Constitution
Legislation
Labour Law
Civil Law
Stock Law
International Law
International Treaty Law
Law on International Civil Procedure
Law on Foreign Trade
Foreign Civil Law
Law on International Trade
International Arbitration Law
International Private Law
International Political Science
History of International Laws
Criminal Investigation[210]

[208] 'Lawyers in N. Korea' (n 204).
[209] ibid.
[210] Faculty of Law <http://www.ryongnamsan.edu.kp/univ/en/about/organization/faculties/law-faculty> accessed 20 June 2024.

Thus, the faculty's courses have a strong focus on foreign trade and business law, which is in part due to the legislative development in these areas in North Korea.

The enactment of the Lawyers' Law, the existence of 500 lawyers and 3 law firms, and the creation of some law schools illustrate some sporadic changes to improve the legal profession in North Korea. This modest reform stems from instrumental concerns. First, when the regime had carried out limited economic reform to attract foreign investment, it needed lawyers to provide legal services for foreign investors who may not be familiar with the many unusual features of North Korean laws. This explains why the Lawyers' Law was adopted in the wake of North Korea's enactments of many other laws to support foreign investments in the early 1990s. In addition, as the regime pays more attention to legislation, it needs lawyers to assist the state in the law-making process—such as drafting and deliberating legal instruments. Finally, as the regime increasingly relies on law as a tool for social control, it needs lawyers to assist the state in disseminating the law and educating the people about the law to foster their compliance.

However, the lawyer system in North Korea has many shortcomings, including the deficiency of lawyers, law graduates, and institutions for legal education and professional training, and the limited role of lawyers in the judicial system.[211] Particularly, it is said that:

> In North Korea, lawyers can hardly find their job rewarding. Individual rights are not considered important in the socialist country, where lawyers, who are supposed to protect the rights and interests of individuals, exist in name only. In the legal court, a lawyer is nothing but a public official who explains the crime of an individual . . . There is no training system for those who passed the exam, either. Anyone can become a lawyer after graduating from a law school.[212]

The limitations of legal professional reform in North Korea are due to institutional, social, and economic reasons. The lack of broader comprehensive institutional reforms to foster the rule of law and the protection of individual rights limit the scope of legal professional reform. In addition, the limited reform stems from the limited demands of society. As legal disputes are unusual, mainly due to the lack of private economic development, there are no strong demands for legal professional development.

B. The Socialist Lawyers

Due to limited reform, the North Korean lawyer system firmly retains its socialist features, particularly legal instrumentalism. North Korean lawyers are

[211] 'Lawyers in N. Korea' (n 204).
[212] ibid.

partially professionals but principally the workers of the state. The Lawyers' Law provides that lawyers 'shall support the legal system of the State'.[213] This means lawyers cannot challenge the existing legal system; rather they should justify it. The Lawyers' Law requires that lawyers 'explain the laws and regulations of the State to the people'.[214] Thus, lawyers serve as agents to justify and disseminate state law.

That legal provision reflects the actual instrumental role of the lawyers in trials:

> North Korean lawyers are allowed to represent defendants only within the range of justifying the policies and decisions of the party. In other words, they simply explain the defendants' motives behind their suspected crimes and do not speak for the accused. Therefore, lawyers no not represent the accused, even if the defendants are not guilty.[215]

Lawyers are agents for the state to control the citizens by explaining the state law and justifying the state's punishment of the citizens during the judicial process.

VII. CONCLUDING ANALYSIS

A. Self-Reliant Intention

North Korea does not carry comprehensive legal reform due to socialist commitment, the *Juche* ideology, and concomitantly political, economic, and military isolation. However, the regime introduces intentional sporadic changes to improve the existing socialist legal system.

North Korean legal reform is shaped by the political elites' self-reliant intention: the aspirational commitments, hope, willing and pragmatic calculation to rely on domestic sources to introduce sporadic adjustments to improve the domestic legal system to facilitate economic development, more effective public management, the regime's better treatment of the citizens, and institutional building. The self-reliant intention is both principled and pragmatic. On one hand, the regime is committed to independent socialist legal development. On the other hand, the regime is willing to partially modify the socialist legal system by adopting non-socialist elements, which involves learning from external experiences. Principled commitments to independent socialist development remain

[213] Lawyers' Law (n 189) art 2.
[214] ibid art 11.
[215] 'Lawyers in N. Korea' (n 204).

dominant, while pragmatic reforms are peripheral and instrumental to the broader socialist goals.

B. Legislative Method

Self-reliant legal reform in North Korea is carried out mainly through legislative enactments. Despite personal authoritarianism, the regime enacts many statutory laws. The country's legislature (the Supreme People's Assembly and its Presidium) provides the institutional platform for self-reliant legal reform. The legislature enacts new laws and revises or replaces existing laws to support autonomous legal innovations. Legal reforms in substantive areas are undertaken by legislative enactments. Some sporadic reforms to the administrative system, the courts, and lawyers are also implemented by the enactments of relevant statutes. Measures of legal reforms may derive from personal leaders but are institutionalized and legitimatized in the form of the laws enacted by the people's representative. To be sure, due to personal authoritarianism, legislative enactments reflect the personal power of the supreme leaders more than the institutional power of the legislature and the popular power of the people.

C. Incremental Strategy

North Korea adopts the classical incremental strategy of legal reform. The country does not have a coherent plan for legal reform but occasionally and slowly adjusts some aspects of the existing legal system. North Korea's legal incrementalism is largely the consequence of socialist and self-reliance ideology and practice. Legal reforms may generate unexpected and uncontrollable consequences (eg privatization, the flow of foreign capital, civic opposition, the emergence of new legitimacy ideas hostile to the regime's ideology), which may undermine the socialist and self-reliant commitments and practice. Therefore, the regime demonstrates its wariness of legal reform by avoiding systematic reforms and only adapting the legal system gradually and occasionally.

Sporadic legal adjustments partially improve the North Korean legal system. General legal rules are publicly pronounced. Economic law softens the planned economy by innovating legal rules and institutions mixing some capitalist elements with the dominant socialist elements. Administrative law empowers local governments and citizens to a degree. Sustainable development law seeks to better use and protect natural resources. Criminal law partially ameliorates the regime's hash treatment of the citizens. Criminal procedure law better protects some fair trial rights. The courts and lawyers are more institutionalized, which makes them look like legal institutions to some extent.

D. Factors

The self-reliant legal reform is shaped by three factors. First, the normative gap between the regime's commitment to independent development of the socialist economy to improve the living condition of the citizens and the reality of economic difficulty requires the regime to carry out legal reform. To undertake legal reform to somehow narrow that gap is necessary to secure the legitimacy of the socialist and self-reliant ideology and the socialist regime.

Second, legal reform is animated by the gap between the law and economic change. Although the law denies market businesses, informal markets (eg farmers' black markets) have emerged since the 1990s. This is considered 'the single most significant change in North Korea in the past three decades'.[216] To deal with economic hardship, the regime seeks to regulate by law rather than completely supress markets.[217] The development of informal markets therefore triggers legal reform to formalize and facilitate partial marketization and better public management of the economy. The adoption of laws for economic development and better public management is a reformist response to market change. This partial legal adaption to the changing economic environment does not undermine but consolidates the resilience of the socialist legal system.

Third, although self-reliant legal reform is mainly based on domestic innovations, it is in part induced by external influences, particularly the Chinese experiences, as evident by the Joint Venture Law. The legal adaption to the transnational legal environment is induced by the need to attract foreign investment, particularly from China. The transnational gap between domestic and international human rights treaties (eg ICCPR and the ICESCR) that North Korea has signed also results in reform of domestic human rights laws (such as the Criminal Law and the Criminal Procedure Law), although these laws are not largely enforced.[218] The state formally adapts transnational human rights norms to gainsay international criticisms of human rights violations in the country.

E. Continuty of Socialist Law

Due to the lack of comprehensive legal reform, North Korean law remains strongly socialist. The law and legal institutions are instruments for the state to protect the socialist regime and support socialist development. The law is the institutionalization of the Party policy. The administrative and court systems are the embodiment of democratic centralism. Local administrative and judicial agencies are under

[216] Yeo (n 22) 4–5.
[217] ibid 32.
[218] Korean Bar Association (n 77) 31–33.

centralized and hierarchical control. Economic laws strongly embody the socialist model of statist economy: state ownership of the main means of production, command economy, and the state's strong regulatory intervention in the economy. Rights are regulated, controlled, and withdrawn by the state to protect the socialist ideology and political regime. The implementation of social rights depends on the benevolent policy of the socialist state. The contextualized commitment to socialism and the persistence of the socialist political regime explains the continued embodiment of socialist legal principles in the North Korean legal system. Consequently, North Korean law is essentially socialist law, although it has some of the non-socialist elements of other legal traditions.

F. Prospects

Because of the limited reforms, the North Korean legal system continues to have serious shortcomings associated with its formal features (eg vagueness, inconsistency, and uncertainty) and substantive and functional features (eg repressive laws, violations of human rights, deficiency of legal enforcement, corruption, and limited roles of courts and lawyers). Within the existing self-reliant constraints, there is still ample room for North Korea to deal with these limitations. Normative, internal, and external forces of legal reforms remain present. The state's promise to build the 'socialist rule of law state' may lead to further legal reforms. The continued expansion of marketization (in sectors such as consumer foods, service, real estate, finance, and labour) and consequentially social change (eg greater space for social interactions)[219] may put pressure on further legal reforms. The state's efforts to attract foreign investment could necessitate further legal reforms to adapt the domestic legal system to the changing international environment.

[219] Yeo (n 22) 33, 50.

8
Cuba: Legal Reform and Updating Socialism

I. INTRODUCTION

In the late 1980s and early 1990s, Cuba carried out sporadic legal reforms to respond to the challenges of the Special Period. The Communist Party of Cuba's adoption of the reform policy called Updating Socialism in 2011 and the state's enactment of the new Constitution in 2019 have led to extensive and systematic legal reforms. Legal reform is a part of the broader project of Updating Socialism. Cuban legal reform is a top-down project of the party-state. It expresses the political elite's intention to systematically improve the legal system while preserving its socialist legal principles as the consequence of its commitments to the Revolution. Due to the limited scope of substantive legal reforms, Cuba's current legal system strongly embodies the principles of the socialist legal tradition.

This chapter explores legislative, administrative, judicial, and legal professional reform in Cuba since the 1980s. The chapter uses Cuban legislation in Spanish published in the *Gaceta Oficial de la República de Cuba (Official Gazette of the Republic of Cuba)*, with the assistance of English translation. It is also informed by my field visit to Cuba in 2019. The chapter also relies on secondary scholarly and popular literature in English on Cuban law.

II. THE PRESERVATIVE PROJECT OF LEGAL REFORM

A. From the Special Period to the Updating Era

1. *The Special Period*

Between the late 1980s and early 1990s, Cuba undertook sporadic legal reforms to respond to the condition of the Special Period or the time of economic depression due to the demise of the Soviet bloc in 1989 and dissolution of the Soviet Union in 1991. Particularly, as the Soviet Union provided Cuba with material supports (eg subsidies of averaged US$4.3 billion between 1986 and 1990), its fall generated economic difficulty in Cuba: its imports dropped by 75% and its GDP went down

Legal Reform in the Contemporary Socialist World. Ngoc Son Bui, Oxford University Press. © Ngoc Son Bui 2024.
DOI: 10.1093/9780191948053.003.0008

by 33% in the three years before 1993.[1] However, the remedies for the Special Period were not transformative but sought to adapt the socialist model in restricted areas (eg production, trade, and investments) as 'a response to the emergency situation caused by the breakdown of international cooperation'.[2] The response to the situation of the Special Period includes sporadic adjustments to the socialist legal system. Cuba amended its Constitution in 1992 to introduce non-socialist property (joint ventures, corporations, and other economic associations).[3] The Cuban state also expanded legislation to allow for foreign investment, and revised laws concerning private farms and cooperatives.[4]

2. *Initiation*

After the Special Period, at the turn of the twenty-first century, Cuba engaged in extensive economic reform under the framework called 'the update of the Cuban economic model'. The reform was introduced in the global changing context in the new century, which witnessed 'the empowerment of a number of developing countries', including the rise of China, whose reform model inspired Cuba.[5] In addition to the external context, the initiation of Cuba's economic reform was closely connected to the change of domestic politics, particularly the handover of leadership from Fidel Castro to Raúl Castro who became the president of Cuba in 2008.[6]

Under Raúl Castro, charismatic leadership was replaced by a collegial arrangement, and the regime's ideology departed from the centrally planned economy to adopt market socialist features.[7] On ideological change, Raúl Castro introduced the idea of 'the update of the Cuban economic model' in a speech in 2009.[8] A few months later, he explained the idea of 'update' or 'upgrade' (*actualización* in Spanish) in this statement: 'We are convinced that we need to break away from dogma and assume firmly and confidently the ongoing upgrading of our economic model in order to set the foundations of the irreversibility of Cuban socialism and its development.'[9] Thus, updating the economic model involves pragmatic reforms and principled commitments to socialism.[10]

Raúl Castro differentiates Cuba's Updating from China's Reform and Vietnam's Renovation:

[1] Marek Hrubec, 'Strategic Socialism: The Updating of Cuba's Model' (2023) Hum Affairs 4.
[2] ibid.
[3] Bui Ngoc Son, *Constitutional Change in the Contemporary Socialist World* (OUP 2020).
[4] Debra Evenson, *Law and Society in Contemporary Cuba* (2nd edn, Kluwer Law International 2003) 13.
[5] Hrubec (n 1) 5.
[6] ibid.
[7] Ramón I Centeno, 'The Cuban Regime after a Decade of Raúl Castro in Power' (2017) 9 Mex Law Rev 99
[8] ibid 113.
[9] Cited in ibid.
[10] ibid.

> The introduction of demand and supply rules is not at odds with the principle of planning. Both concepts can coexist and complement each other [. . .] as has been successfully demonstrated in the processes of reform in China and renovation in Vietnam, as they call them. We have called it [our process] updating because we are not changing the key goal of the Revolution.[11]

The preservation of the key commitments of the Revolution makes Cuba's Updating different from China's Reform and Vietnam's Renovation. Consequently, Cuba's model of updating does not seek to transform the planned economy (the material condition for realizing the revolutionary commitment to creating socialism in Cuba) into the socialist market economy like the Chinese and Vietnamese models of economic reform.

3. *Adoption*

In 2011, the Sixth Congress of the Communist Party of Cuba adopted the Guidelines of the Economic and Social Policy proposed by Raúl Castro, seeking to materialize the idea of updating Cuba's socialist economic model.[12] The Guidelines introduced measures for economic updating in response to economic challenges such as trade blockade due to US sanctions, decline in exports of goods, losses caused by hurricanes, poor efficiency, deterioration of production infrastructure, and an ageing and growth-stagnant population.[13] The Guidelines states that 'The Party's economic policy will follow the principle that only socialism is capable of overcoming every difficulty and preserve the achievements attained by the Revolution. The updating of the economic model shall be governed by planning, which will take into account the market trends.'[14] On one hand, the planned economy is reserved for realizing the revolutionary commitments to socialism. On the other hand, the planned economy will be updated by integrating some market elements. The Guidelines allow for running small businesses, permit buying and selling cars and homes, and ease foreign travel, among other things.[15]

Economic updating requires legal updating. Therefore, to implement the measures for economic upgrading, the Party agreed 'to recommend to the National People's Power Assembly, the Government and all relevant bodies to draft and approve, as the case may be, the necessary legal rules to create the legal and institutional framework in support of the functional, structural and economic modifications that may be adopted.'[16] Thus, the Party recognized the necessity of legal

[11] Cited in ibid, 123 (italics omitted).

[12] Guidelines of the Economic and Social Policy of the Party and the Revolution, adopted by the Sixth Congress of the Communist Party of Cuba (2011) (hereinafter, Guidelines).

[13] ibid.

[14] ibid.

[15] Lina Forero-Nino, 'The Cuban Government Approves Guidelines to Reform Cuba's Economic Model and Develops an Implementation Strategy' (2011) 17 LBRA 762–65.

[16] Guidelines (n 12).

reform for economic reform. In practice, some sporadic legal reforms were introduced. President Raúl Castro adopted two decrees to allow for the private sales of automobiles and private ownership and sales of homes.[17] A new foreign investment law was adopted in 2014, which is consistent with Raúl Castro's emphasis on the need of foreign capital.[18]

4. *Conceptualization*

The blueprint for updating Cuba's socialist economic model as anticipated in the Guidelines lacks a general conceptual framework for the kind of socialism the Cuban state seeks to build.[19] This deficiency was remedied by the adoption of the Conceptualization of the Cuban Economic and Social Model of Socialist Development at the Party's Seventh Congress in 2016.[20] Legal development is a part of the conceptual framework for updating Cuban socialism. The Conceptualization seeks to develop 'the Socialist State of Law' as a guarantor of equality and freedom, independence, sovereignty, popular participation, sustainable development, territorial integrity, stability and internal security, national identity, the nation's heritage, historical memory, and culture, among other things.[21] The Conceptualization anticipates the exercise and protection of economic, social, cultural, civic-political, individual, and collective rights and duties in accordance with the Constitution and the laws, through responsible, effective, and transparent actions of the institutions and entities in charge.[22] This is the conceptual framework for legal reform. Legal reforms seek to realize the socialist state of law, the protection of rights, the promotion of duties, and institutional accountability, effectiveness, and transparency.

5. *Constitutionalization*

The guidelines and concepts for updating Cuban socialism are institutionalized in the 2019 Constitution.[23] The 2019 Constitution, which replaces the 1976 Constitution, both retrospectively codifies pre-existing sporadic legal reforms and prospectively creates the foundations for more systematic and extensive legal reform in the future. The 2019 Constitution preserves key principles of socialist

[17] Grant JE and others, 'Guide to Cuban Law and Legal Research' (2017) 45 Int'l J Leg Inf 86.
[18] ibid 86–87.
[19] William M LeoGrande, 'Updating Cuban Socialism: The Politics of Economic Renovation' (2017) 84 Soc Res 355.
[20] For an extensive analysis of this document, see Larry Cata Backer, 'Central Planning versus Markets Marxism: Their Differences and Consequences for the International Ordering of State, Law, Politics, and Economy' (2016) 32 Conn J Int'l L 17–35.
[21] Conceptualization of the Cuban Economic and Social Model of Socialist Development, adopted by the Seventh Congress of the Communist Party of Cuba (2016).
[22] ibid.
[23] Hrubec (n 1) 8; Mark Ginsburg, 'Constituting Socialism for the Twenty-First Century: Examining Cuba's 2019 Constitution' (2021) 13 Int'l J Cuban Stud 303.

law but also introduces significant changes, which opens the doors for extensive legal reform, particularly legislative reforms in various areas of private (property, business, foreign investment, and family law) and criminal law, and institutional reforms.

The Constitution's new commitment to creating a 'socialist state of law' (Article 1), a Cuban version of the socialist rule of law state, would require extensive enactments of law generally. The Constitution's recognition of private ownership (Article 22) creates the base for legislative reform of property rights and the development of business law. The Constitution's commitment to the state's promotion of foreign investments and the state's protection of foreign investors' property allows for legislative reform in investment law. The Constitution's recognition of the concept of human rights for the first time and incorporation of many new rights (such as the right to family privacy, the right to information about the government, presumption of innocence, prohibition of discrimination, the right to legal assistance, the right to food safety, and the right to establish family)[24] requires legislative reforms in various areas (particularly family, criminal, and social law), judicial reform, and legal professional reform to realize these constitutional commitments. The Constitution's changes on the state institutions (the creation of personal presidency, the creation of the post of prime minister, the creation of independent institutions, and the vertical distribution of power to local government)[25] create the conditions for institutional legal reforms.

B. Preservative Legal Reform

In the Updating era, Cuba has engaged in extensive, systematic legal reforms. Legal reforms are to realize the aspirations of updating the Cuban socialist model. The systematic reform started with the enactment of the new Constitution in 2019, which lay down the foundations for the subsequent legislative and institutional reforms. The reforms, however, are constrained by the Revolution's commitments to building socialism in Cuba.

After constitutional reform, the government introduced the plan for extensive legal reform. Miguel Díaz-Canel, who succeeded Raúl Castro as President of Cuba in 2018, urged that the birth of the Constitution requires the 'support from laws that facilitate its implementation and strengthen it'.[26] He reported that there are more than seventy laws, 'which we must draft, update, or modify'.[27] Thus,

[24] Bui Ngoc Son (n 3) 271–73.
[25] ibid 269–70.
[26] National News staff, 'May the Constitution Have the Laws Needed for Its Implementation' (Granma, 7 May 2019) <https://en.granma.cu/cuba/2019-05-07/may-the-constitution-have-the-laws-needed-for-its-implementation> accessed 7 June 2024.
[27] ibid.

constitutional reform dictates legislative reform. Consequently, the National Assembly of People's Power in its IX term (2018–23) adopted thirty-five laws.[28] Particularly, the year 2022 is considered a legislative 'marathon without precedents in the previous sixty-two years'.[29] According to the legislative plan for this year, the state intended to adopt twenty-seven laws, which touch on key substantive, procedural and institutional aspects of the legal order.[30] The rapid implementation of this plan of legal reform is shaped by a wide range of factors, including the outdated and exhausted hyper-centralized bureaucracy, the COVID-19 pandemic, US sanctions, and the erosion of the legitimacy of the authorities as indicated in popular protests.[31] As one commentator puts it, 'we [Cubans] are facing the largest, deepest and most ambitious legal reform plan in the last six decades'.[32]

Larry Catá Backer argues that while the Chinese Communist Party '*looks forward* to attainment of a communist society', the Communist Party of Cuba 'assumes that its role is to *preserve* the communist society it achieved at the moment of revolutionary triumph'.[33] The preservation of the revolutionary achievements is a prominent factor shaping legal reform in Cuba. Although legal reforms after the 2019 constitutional reform are more extensive and systematic than the previous reforms since the 1980s, they update rather than transform the socialist legal model. Like economic updating, legal updating in Cuba involves pragmatic adjustments and the principled preservations of the revolutionary commitments of the Cuban socialist legal system. The pragmatic adjustments involve sporadic and then extensive modifications of institutional and substantive aspects of the legal system. At the same time, the ideational aspects of the socialist legal system are strongly preserved as a matter of the commitments to the Revolution.

III. LEGISLATIVE REFORM

A. Legislative Process

The legislative process is institutionalized. Cuba's legislative body includes the National Assembly of People's Power elected for a period of five years and its permanent body called the Council of State created by the former. The National Assembly (NA) is comprised of eleven specialized commissions:

[28] National Assembly of People's Power, IX Legislature (2018–23) <https://www.parlamentocubano.gob.cu/index.php/ix-legislatura-2018-2023> accessed 7 June 2024.

[29] Walter Mondelo, 'The Year of Laws' (*OnCubaNews*, 27 December 2022) <https://oncubanews.com/en/cuba/the-year-of-laws> accessed 7 June 2024.

[30] ibid.

[31] ibid.

[32] ibid.

[33] Larry Catá Backer, 'The Cuban Communist Party at the Cusp of Change' (2016), Working Papers Coalition for Peace & Ethics 13 (SSRN) <https://ssrn.com/abstract=2711907> accessed 7 June 2024.

Food Commission
National Defense and Internal Order Commission
Industry, Construction, and Energy Commission
Commission for Education, Culture, Science, Technology, and the Environment
Committee on Economic Affairs
Health and Sport Commission
Commission for Attention to Youth, Children, and the Equality of Women's Rights
Committee on Constitutional and Legal Affairs
International Relations Commission
Service Attention Commission
Local Bodies Commission

The NA in its tenth term has 470 deputies of which 55.74% are women.[34]

The legislative power is divided between the NA and the Council of State. According to Cuba's 1976 Constitution (amended through 2002), the NA shall enact 'law', while the Council of State can enact decree-law (Articles 75 and 90). The 2019 Constitution also distributes legislative power in the same manner (Articles 108 and 122). However, the new Constitution requires that the decree-laws adopted by the Council of State be ratified by the NA in the upcoming session (Article 120). This provision limits the legislative power of the Council of State. As the Cuban state seeks to advance systematic legal reform, it tends to rely on the NA as the main, legitimate platform for legislation making.

The 2019 Constitution provides that bills can be initiated by central state institutions (legislative, executive, and judicial institutions, and independent institutions); national leadership of social and mass organizations; and citizens with a minimum of ten thousand electors.[35] Once adopted, laws will be published in the *Official Gazette of the Republic of Cuba*. As of August 2023, there are forty-six constitutional and legislative instruments (including the Constitution, laws, and decree-laws) published in the *Gazette*.[36] Cuban laws therefore meet certain requirements of the formal type of the rule of law. The laws include general legal rules promulgated by the people's representatives. The laws are gazetted for public access.

B. Legislative Development

Among laws adopted during the period between 2019 and 2023, several laws deal with *criminal justice*, including:

[34] National Assembly of People's Power <https://www.parlamentocubano.gob.cu> accessed 7 June 2024.

[35] Cuba's 2019 Constitution, art 164; Cuba's 1976 Constitution (amended through 2002), art 88.

[36] *Official Gazette of the Republic of Cuba* (Ministry of Justice) <https://www.gacetaoficial.gob.cu/es/algunas-legislaciones-cubanas> accessed 7 June 2024.

Penal Code (2022); and
Law on Penal Enforcement (2022).

Other laws seek to protect *civil rights*, including:

Family Code (2022);
Law on Protection of Personal Data (2022); and
Law on the Rights of the Author and the Performer (2022).

Many laws respond to the constitutional framework for *state institutions*. Some laws deal with the *legislature*, including:

Election Law (2019);
Law on the Organization and Functioning of the National Assembly of People's Power and the Council of State of the Republic of Cuba (2020); and
Law of Revocation of Those Elected to The Organs of People's Power (2020).

Other laws concern the *administrative system*, including:

Law of the President and Vice President of the Republic of Cuba (2020); and
Law on the Organization and Functioning of the Council of Ministers (2020).
The *judicial system* is provided in the Law on People's Courts (2021). Several laws create principles and rules for *local governments*, including:
Law on Organization and Functioning of the Municipal Administration Council (2021); and
Law on the Organization and Functioning of the Provincial Government of People's Power (2021).

Some laws deal with the *fourth branch*, or independent agencies, including:

Law on the Office of the Attorney General of the Republic (2022); and
Law on the Office of the Comptroller General of the Republic of Cuba, and the System of Superior Control of Public Funds and Administrative Management (2022).

Several *economic laws* have been adopted to create a legal framework for the government to regulate economic activities and resources, including:

Fisheries Law (2020);
Law on the Promotion and Development of Livestock (2022);
Law on Expropriation for Reasons of Public Utility or Social Interest (2022);
Law on Territorial and Urban Planning, and Land Management (2022); and

Law on Food Sovereignty and Food and Nutritional Security (2022).

Other laws deal with *national identity* and *international relations*, including respectively:

Law on National Symbols of the Republic of Cuba (2019); and
Law on the Foreign Service of the Republic of Cuba (2020).

Apart from substantive laws, several laws deal with criminal, civil, administrative, and constitutional *procedures*, including:

Process Code (2021);
Criminal Procedure Law (2021);
Administrative Procedure Law (2021); and
Law on the Process for the Protection of Constitutional Rights (2022).

In 2023, the National Assembly of People's Power in its X term (2023–27) adopted a more ambitious programme of legal reform. Accordingly, the legislature plans to enact fifty-two laws in this term, including twelve in 2023, seventeen in 2024, eight in 2025, seven in 2026, and eight in 2027. The proposed laws will deal with various aspects of social life, including business, commercial companies, consumer rights, tax, state budget, forests, mining, tourism, sports, education, science and innovation, culture, state heritage, work, social security, housing, etc.[37] As the existing laws have extensively covered institutional aspects, the proposed laws tend to focus on market development, sustainable development, and social issues.

This rest of section explores reforms in various areas of both public and private law, particularly criminal substantive and procedural law, family law, and business law. Some sporadic legislative reforms in these areas of law were introduced in response to the situation of the Special Period. The Updating era has witnessed more extensive reforms in these areas of law. After the 2019 constitutional reform, the legislature has adopted plans for systemic legislative reform.

1. *Criminal Substantive and Procedural Law*

Cuba has carried legislative reforms to improve criminal justice. Amendments and replacements of substantive and procedural criminal law include elements protecting individual rights.

Criminal law: In 1987, Cuba adopted a new Criminal Code replacing the 1979 Criminal Code. The 1987 version is considered 'a far more liberal code'.[38] It reflects

[37] Cronograma Legislativo X Legislatura Leyes <https://www.parlamentocubano.gob.cu/sites/default/files/documento/2023-06/cronograma-legislativo-2023.pdf> accessed 7 June 2024.
[38] Evenson (n 4) 166.

the change in jurisprudential thinking, which perceives 'that severe sentences had not only failed to deter crime, but that they carried social costs as well- the human and material price of incarceration'.[39] The enactment of the Criminal Code was also influenced by comparative and transnational engagements. The drafting commission studied criminal codes of both socialist and capitalist countries, including some state codes of the United States. The works of the United Nations on criminal justice also shaped Cuba's new approach to criminal justice. Consequently, the 1987 Criminal Code improves the criminal justice system in various ways such as lowering sentences (eg removing the death penalty for the offence of robbery with the use of force) and decriminalizing many minor offences (eg traffic violations and some misdemeanours).[40] The 1987 Criminal Code was amended in 1997 and 1999 in response to the increase of criminal activity due to economic crise.[41]

In 2022, Cuban legislature adopted a new Criminal Code replacing the 1987 version. The 2022 Criminal Code presents a mixture of reform and regress. It includes positive changes, which indicates the reform of criminal law. In general, the Code seeks to update the legal framework for crimes and penalties in accordance with the 'most recent trends in international penal doctrine' and the principles and rights provided in the 2019 Constitution.[42] More specific reforms include:

exhaustive prohibition of the use of analogy in criminal law;
elimination of the figure of pre-criminal social dangerousness;
limitation of the duration of the deprivation of freedom to a maximum of forty years;
substantial improvement in the definition of criminal offences such as sexual assault; and
new regulations on environmental crimes, cybercrime, gender-based violence, and transnational criminal networks.[43]

At the same time, critics lament that the new 2019 Criminal Code further facilitates government's repression—including criminalizing propaganda against the state, the use of social media, and homeless Cubans—and increases the number of crimes punishable by death penalty from twenty (in the 1987 version) to twenty-four and life imprisonment from twenty-four (in the 1987 version) to thirty-one.[44] These changes indicate legal regress.

[39] ibid 171.
[40] ibid 171–73.
[41] ibid 166.
[42] Mondelo (n 29).
[43] ibid.
[44] Walter Mondelo, 'Society Socialism, Death Penalty And Criminal Punitiveness: Notes On The Penal Code' (*OnCubaNews*, 23 May 2023) <https://oncubanews.com/en/cuba/society-cuba/socialism-death-penalty-and-criminal-punitiveness-notes-on-the-penal-code> accessed 7 June 2024.

Criminal Procedure Law: Shortly after the new 1987 Criminal Code was adopted, Cuban jurists debated the shortcomings of the 1977 Criminal Procedure Law. After over four years of debate, amendments to the Criminal Procedure Law were adopted in 1994.[45] The amendments are not as advanced as the expectations of the Cuban jurists but they include some positive changes to improve the efficiency of the criminal process and protect the accused.[46] One amendment strengthens the supervisory role of the prosecutor during the preparatory phase to protect the accused.[47] Another important amendment introduces abbreviated procedure to deal with 'cases in which the sanction is less than 8 years and the accused is caught in the act of committing the crime or where the accused has confessed and there is other evidence clearly the participation of the accused in a criminal act'.[48] The 1994 amendments also deleted some formalities in the appeal process, which had led to long delays in obtaining a remedy.[49]

In 2021, Cuban legislature adopted a new Criminal Procedure Law, replacing the 1977 version. Supreme Court President Rubén Remigio said that the new law 'draws on the best international experiences and regulations and over 100 doctoral and master's diploma papers in Cuba and abroad'.[50] The 2021 Criminal Procedure Law responds to new constitutional provisions on fair trial rights and better protects the victim's rights. Specifically, the law guarantees the right of the defendant to have legal assistance from the beginning of the process, the presumption of innocence, the right against self-incrimination, the right to be informed of the charges, and the right to be tried by a pre-established court and prior criminal laws, among others.[51]

2. *Family Law*

The 2022 Family Code, which replaced the 1975 version, is considered 'the most advanced piece of legislation in Cuban Law' and 'a modern and comprehensive text, in line with the most recent and advanced legislation in the world on the matter'.[52] The Code presents positive legal changes in both procedural and substantive terms. The Code is adopted through 'a remarkably democratic process'.[53] The reform process includes both public deliberation and referendum. The public

[45] Evenson (n 4) 188–89.
[46] ibid 197.
[47] ibid 196.
[48] ibid 196.
[49] ibid 197.
[50] 'Cuban Parliament Approves New Criminal Procedure Law' (*TeleSUR*, 28 October 2021) <https://www.telesurenglish.net/news/Cuban-Parliament-Approves-New-Criminal-Procedure-Law--20211028-0015.html> accessed 7 June 2024.
[51] ibid.
[52] Mondelo (n 29).
[53] Buchanan Waller, 'Cuba's 2022 Family Code: A Different Model for Social Progress' Minn J Law Inequal <https://lawandinequality.org/2022/11/02/cubas-2022-family-code-a-different-model-for-social-progress> accessed 7 June 2024.

deliberation involves the attendance of over 6 million Cuban people in over 70,000 town hall meetings and over 300,000 public suggestions leading to modifications to 48% of the provisions in the original draft. A wide range of social groups engaged in the public debate on the draft law, including LGBT activists from the Cuban National Sex Education Center, the Committees for the Defense of the Revolution, and the Catholic Church. The Code went through twenty-five versions before it was approved by Cuban voters in the Referendum in September 2022.[54]

Substantively, the 2022 Family Code is considered 'the most inclusive and progressive family code in the world'.[55] The Code is progressive in the sense that it includes many provisions protecting vulnerable people, particularly LGBT people, victims of domestic violence, children, women, the elderly, and the disabled. The Code legalizes same sex marriage and guarantees the right of same sex couples to adopt children, which drew great international attention.[56] The Code defines marriage as 'the voluntarily arranged union of two persons' (Article 201), which effectively allows for same sex marriage. The Code includes many other progressive provisions regarding the recognition of women's household work, child protection, and strong measures against gender violence and discrimination.[57] To illustrate, the Code recognizes 'the value of indirect contributions' and that 'domestic and care work is computable as a contribution to charges' (Article 216). The Code prohibits corporal punishment of children and humiliating treatment or the use of any other forms of violence or abuse of children, including abandonment and neglect (Article 146). The Code prohibits granting guardianship and care to anyone who has been sanctioned by a final sentence in criminal proceedings for crimes related to gender or family violence, against sexual freedom and indemnity, and against children, youth, and the family (Article 155). The Code also provides mediation to resolve family conflicts in most matters and establishes the Family Ombudsman to protect the vulnerable members of families.[58]

Despite progressive features, there were several concerns about the Family Code, such as whether the Referendum was a legitimate instrument, the Code was an instrument of government indoctrination, and the Code might expand the capacity for state intervention in the control of minors, which is linked to the issues of migration.[59] Some commentators believe the Code is connected to broader political contestations. 'The Family Code placed sexual and gender politics at the centre

[54] ibid.

[55] Jos Chathukulam and Manasi Joseph, 'Cuba Family Code towards the Democratisation of Family and Society' (2022) 57 Econ Pol Weekly 20.

[56] 'Cubans Vote in Favour of Family Law Reform that Will Allow Same-Sex Marriage' The Guardian (26 September 2022) <https://www.theguardian.com/world/2022/sep/26/cubans-vote-in-favour-of-family-law-reform-that-will-allow-same-sex-marriage> accessed 7 June 2024.

[57] Chathukulam and Joseph (n 55) 20.

[58] Mondelo (n 29).

[59] Ailynn Torres Santana and Julio César Guanche, 'Cuba's New Family Code is a Window into the Political Ecosystem' (NACLA Report on the Americas, 11 November 2022) <https://nacla.org/cubas-new-family-code-window-political-ecosystem> accessed 7 June 2024.

of the social and political fabric, and this was tied up with other debates and cleavages related to political identities, economic crises, migratory strategies, religious communities, and much more.'[60]

3. Business Law

Business law in Cuba has witnessed important reforms in the last decades. The general pattern of business law reform is the cautious, incremental incorporation of market elements into the centralized economy, particularly foreign investment, private property, and concomitantly private enterprises, and the final autonomy of the state-owned enterprises. These reforms seek to facilitate economic development to respond to social demands and deal with economic hardship caused by the US sanctions and, recently, the COVID-19 pandemic. Reforms of business law are both shaped by and shape the incremental expansion of the private economic sector. However, business law reforms in Cuba are constrained by the reservation of the revolutionary commitment to building socialism and therefore do not indicate the trend to transition from a command economy into a socialist market economy like the cases of China, Vietnam, and Laos.

Foreign investment: Three important legal reforms regarding foreign investment include the enactments of a joint venture law in 1982, the first Law on Foreign Investment in 1995, and the second Law on Foreign Investment in 2014. Cuban legislature plan to enact a new foreign investment law in 2026.

Like socialist China and North Korea, Cuba adopted a joint venture law to attract foreign investment. In 1982, Cuba enacted Decree-Law No 50 on Economic Association between Cuban and Foreign Entities, which allows for the creation of economic cooperations between foreign investors and Cuban state-owned enterprises. The enactment of the law seeks to facilitate rapid industrialization 'to overcome trade deficits and to continue to provide a high level of social services'.[61]

After the 1992 constitutional amendment's commitment to promoting foreign investment, Law No 77 on Foreign Investment was enacted in 1995, which provides for the creation of 100% foreign-owned cooperations, in addition to joint ventures and international association contracts.[62] Law No 77 also extensively permits foreign investments in all sectors of the Cuban economy except health services, public education, and the armed forces. In addition, the Law also allows for the creation of free trade zones and industrial parks. Law No 77, however, did not generate great proliferation of foreign investment deals in part because the

[60] ibid.

[61] Jean G Zorn and Harold A Mayerson, 'Cuba's Joint Venture Law: New Rules for Foreign Investment' (1983) 21 Col J Transnat'l Law 285.

[62] Jorge A Vargas, 'Cuba: Foreign Investment Act Of 1995' (1996) 35 Int'l Legal Materials 331; James D Whisenand, 'Cuba's Legal Structure: How It Affects Foreign Investment and Trade' (1995) 31 Col J World Bus 16; Matias F Travieso-Diaz and Charles P IV Trumbull, 'Foreign Investment in Cuba: Prospects and Perils' (2003) 35(4) George Wash Int'l Law Rev 903.

government considered foreign investment only supplementary to other economic reforms and in part because of the weak infrastructure and the bureaucratic delays in the approval process.[63]

The implementation of the 2011 Guidelines for updating the economic model resulted in the enactment of Law No 118 on Foreign Investment in 2014, which replaced Law No 77.[64] Law No 118 is complemented by a body of regulations by central institutions such as the Central Bank of Cuba, the Ministry of Economy and Planning, the Ministry of Labor and Social Security, the Ministry of Trade and Foreign Investment, and the Ministry of Finance and Prices to create a comprehensive legal framework of foreign investment in Cuba.[65] Law No 118 diversifies markets, offers investors greater protection against expropriation, and introduces tax incentives to investors such as cutting the profit tax in half to 15% and eliminating the labour tax.[66]

Private property: Due to the strong commitment to the preservation of the revolutionary commitment to socialism, the Cuban government is highly cautious in legal reform of private property, which is an element of capitalism. However, in response to economic difficulty, the socialist state has legalized private housing property and recently constitutionalized private property. Some legal reforms regarding housing property were introduced in the 1980s. The 1984 General Housing Law allowed small farmers to sell surplus produce at unregulated prices.[67] More legal reforms regarding private property were undertaken in the context of broader market reforms in the era of Raúl Castro. In response to housing shortage, the Decree-Law No 288 was enacted in 2011 to allow for individuals sell their homes for the first time since the 1959 Revolution. This legalization of private housing ownership creates the basis of a housing market.[68] The pre-existing legal reforms culminated in the constitutionalization of private property in 2019. The 2019 Constitution recognizes private ownership or the ownership of specific means of production by natural or legal persons, Cubans, or foreigners (Article 22). The Constitution also recognizes private property over land (Article 29). The constitutional recognition of private property provides the basis for the reforms of business

[63] Evenson (n 4) 251–59.

[64] Mesa Tejeda and Natacha Teresa, 'Notes on the Categories of Foreign Investment in Cuba' (2017) 29 Florida Journal of International Law 77–78

[65] Marta Moreno Cruz, 'Safeguards in the Cuban Legal System for the Promotion and Protection of Foreign Investment' (2017) 29 Florida J Int'l Law 92.

[66] Karin Paparelli, 'Reforming Foreign Investment Law in Cuba: What Does it Really Mean for Eager Investors?' (2016) Florida Bar Association, International Law Section Journal: International Law Quarterly Special 'CUBA' edition 10–11 (SSRN) <https://ssrn.com/abstract=2678019> or <http://dx.doi.org/10.2139/ssrn.2678019> accessed 7 June 2024; Alyssa K Ortiz, 'Cuba's New Foreign Investment Law Number 118: Can Tax Incentives Buy Foreign Investors' Trust and Be Justified in Increasing FDI' (2015) 21 LBRA 175.

[67] Evenson (n 4) 209.

[68] Renee Monzon, 'Introducing Private-Property Rights to Cuba: How Cuba's New Constitution Paves the Way for Economic Growth' (2020) 52 Case W Res J Int'l L 643–44.

law, including the development of a legal framework for private enterprises, which would foster the development of property market.

Private business: The reservation of revolutionary commitments to socialism constrains the development of private business, an element of the capitalist economic system. However, the Cuban socialist state has cautiously carried out legal reforms that allowed the development of private business in three forms: self-employment; family business; and more recently private enterprises.

Legal reforms facilitate private business under the form of self-employment (or *cuentapropistas*).[69] In 1993, in response to growing unemployment due to economic crisis during the Special Period, the Council of State enacted Decree-Law No 141 to allow for self-employment. Expectedly, about 200,000 Cuban would conduct service activities like repairs of domestic appliances and hair cutting. In 1996, the actual number of the self-employed was 198,000.[70] Since the introduction of economic reform in 2010 and 2011, self-employment has been expanded. In October 2010, the government legalized 178 activities or categories of self-employment, a significant increase from the previous limits. The Decree-Law No 268 adopted in 2010 allowed self-employed workers to simultaneously engage in various types of self-employment activities. The Decree-Law No 289 adopted in 2011 created a new system of microcredits to permit self-employed workers to obtain small amounts of credit financing from state-owned banks.[71] As the consequence of legal measures, the number of licences for self-employment increased to over 550,000 by 2017.[72] Thus, legal reforms supported the expansion of self-employment and the emergence of a private economic sector, albeit within the remit of socialism.

The second form of private business is family businesses known as *paladars*, small private restaurants, which have mainly served tourists. The government granted licences to operate the private restaurants and regulate by law the size and ingredients of foods to be served.[73] *Paladars* started in the Special Period in the 1990s and have been considerably expanded in the Updating era since 2011. *Paladars* take two forms. In the traditional form, individual owners of a house use the living room of the house as the *paladars*. In the more recent form, houses are extended and exclusively used for running the *paladar*.[74] The legalization of

[69] Emma F Phillips, 'Maybe Tomorrow I'll Turn Capitalist: Cuentapropismo in a Workers' State' (2007) 41 Law Soc Rev 305.

[70] Evenson (n 4) 264–65.

[71] Mario A Gonzalez-Corzo and Orlando Justo, 'Private Self-Employment under Reform Socialism in Cuba' (2017) 32 J Priv Enterp 66–67.

[72] Center for Insights in Survey Research, *Cuentapropistas: A Survey of Cuban Entrepreneurs* (2017) 4.

[73] Evenson (n 4) 266.

[74] James Corporal, 'Paladares in Cuba: A Bitesize Story of Some of Cuba's Best Eateries' (Cubania, 10 December 2020) <https://cubaniatravel.com/stories/paladares-in-cuba-a-bitesize-story-of-some-of-cubas-best-eateries> accessed 7 June 2024.

paladars stems from the need to improve the living standard of the domestic population and the expansion of international tourism in Cuba. *Paladars* have fostered family entrepreneurship and expanded the cuisine market.

The third and more extensive form of private business is private enterprise. In a cautious but important reform in 2021, the Cuban government issued a law allowing for the creation of micro-businesses (up to ten employees); small businesses (eleven to thirty-five employees), and medium-sized businesses (thirty-six to a hundred employees).[75] This law is not exclusively applied to private enterprises. However, among 406 enterprises created according to this law, 397 enterprises are private.[76] The legalization of private enterprises is in part a response to economic crises caused by the COVID-19 pandemic.[77] More broadly, this continues and extends the development of the private economic sector since 2011. Compared with two other forms (self-employment and private restaurants), the legalization of private enterprises is a more extensive move to marketize the economy. Cuban legislature planned to enact an Enterprise Law in late 2023. This law may create the legal base for greater extension of private economic sector.

State-owned enterprises: The adherence to the revolutionary commitment to socialism requires the state's control of the economy, including through state-owned enterprises (SOEs). The Cuban state, however, adopted measures of legal reforms to grant more autonomy to SOEs. During the 1970s and 1980s, Cuba's SOEs were heavily subsidized. The situation of the Special Period in the 1990s induced reform of the SOEs: they 'are no longer subsidized, they must operate at a profit or they are dissolved or merged into a successful entity'.[78] In the Updating era, SOEs have witnessed more sporadic reforms. For example, reform measures have been introduced to separate company and state functions, which enables SOEs to have more autonomy—such as the abolition of direct management of SOEs by ministries (with a few exceptions). Cuba now has 2,417 SOEs. The Party has identified many SOE problems, including heavy bureaucratic structures, lack of incentives for workers and credits for the enterprise, and too little innovation. Expectedly, the Enterprise Law scheduled to be enacted in late 2023 will create extensive reforms to SOEs to address these shortcomings.[79]

[75] Michael Davis, 'A Long Awaited Opportunity: Private Businesses are Now Legal in Cuba' (Latina Republic, 1 December 2021) <https://latinarepublic.com/2021/12/01/a-long-awaited-opportunity-private-businesses-are-now-legal-in-cuba> accessed 7 June 2024.

[76] Andrea Rodriguez, 'Cuban Small Business Owners Complain to Biden' (*AP News*, 9 November 2021) <https://apnews.com/article/noticias-2f412556cd220f471cf50b79e631a408> accessed 7 June 2024.

[77] Davis (n 75).

[78] Antonio R Zamora, 'Cuba's Business Enterprises: How Business is Conducted on the Island' (2003) 15 Fla J Int'l L 351.

[79] Marcel Kunzmann, '"We're Not Afraid of the Market": Far-Reaching Reform of State-Owned Enterprises in the Making' Cuba Standard (26 June 2023) <https://www.cubastandard.com/not-afraid-of-the-market-enterprise-reform-cuba> accessed 7 June 2024.

C. Cuban Socialist Law

Due to the preservation of the goal of the Revolution to build socialism, Cuban legislation deeply retains socialist features.

Instrumentalism: Cuban law is an instrument for the state to pursue socialist development. The instrumental concept of socialist legality is still constitutionally embodied. The 2019 Constitution provides that 'All are obligated to strictly adhere to socialist law. Furthermore, the organs of the State, their leaders, functionaries, and employees ensure its respect in the lives of all people and act within the limits of their respective responsibilities' (Article 9). Thus, Cuban law is intentionally defined by socialist law. Law is an instrument for the state to control the compliance of various political and social actors to achieve socialist goals. In general, while revolutionary laws are an instrument to codify the achievements of the Revolution, reformative laws are an instrument to continue to realize the revolutionary commitments and to implement pragmatic reform policies to respond to situations of the Special Period in the 1990s and to update socialism since 2011.

The instrumental nature and function of socialist law is manifested in various areas of law. For example, the 2014 Foreign Investment Law seeks 'to contribute to the country's economic development in the interest of a prosperous and sustainable socialist society' (Article 1). Thus, the law is an instrument to pursue socialist development. The 2022 Criminal Code attempts to protect 'the political, economic and social order established in the Constitution' and contribute to all citizens' 'awareness of respect for the socialist law' (Article 1). In other words, criminal law is the instrument to protect the socialist system and socialist legality. The Code's criminalizing propaganda against the state is a concrete embodiment of this instrumental, repressive nature of socialist criminal law. The instrumental nature of socialist law is also reflected in the 2022 Family Code. As one commentator puts it: 'The Family Code not only protects the most vulnerable in Cuba, it protects the course of Cuban socialism.'[80] The Code's progressive provisions protecting vulnerable people and combating against discrimination are expressive of socialist commitments to social equality. The Code is an instrument for the state to implement the socialist commitments and policy.

Party vanguardism: Cuban law remains deeply socialist in that it is the embodiment of the Party's guidance and policy. The 2019 Constitution continues to confirm the Party's vanguard role:

> The Communist Party of Cuba, unique, Martiano, Fidelista, and Marxist-Leninist, the organized vanguard of the Cuban nation, sustained in its democratic character as well as its permanent linkage to the people, is the superior

[80] Lyn Neeley, 'Cuba's New Family Code, a Law of Love' (*Workers World*, 20 January 2023) <https://www.workers.org/2023/01/68708> accessed 7 June 2024.

> driving force of the society and the State. It organizes and orients the communal forces towards the construction of socialism and its progress toward a communist society. It works to preserve and to fortify the patriotic unity of the Cuban people and to develop ethic, moral, and civic values (Article 5)

The consequence of this constitutional mandate of the Party's vanguard leadership is that ordinary law is enacted to implement the Party's policy for socialist development. In general, reformative laws enacted during the Updating era are the institutional embodiment of the Party's guidelines and conceptual framework for reforming Cuba's socialism. The Party therefore takes the vanguard role in legal reform.

Democratic centralism: Cuban institutional laws are shaped by the socialist principle of democratic centralism. Unlike other Asian socialist constitutions, Cuba's 2019 Constitution does not explicitly mention the principle of democratic centralism. Instead, it establishes the principles of 'socialist democracy' (Article 101), which reflects Cuba's tradition of public participation.[81] However, several particular rules for the exercise of 'socialist democracy', as provided by the Constitution, are the embodiment of democratic centralism, including:

> the orders of the superior State organs are obligatory for the subordinate State organs; the subordinate State organs respond to the superior organs and they submit documentation regarding their management; the liberty of discussion, the exercise of criticism and self-criticism, and the subordination of the minority to the majority govern in all of the collegial State organs (Article 101)

Thus, the inferior institutions are subordinated to the control of the superior institutions. Democratic discussions are followed by centralized actions. Democratic centralism shapes institutional laws on the administrative and judicial systems, as will be discussed later.

Statist rights: Cuban law, particularly the Constitution and rights related laws, continues to reflect socialist tradition of rights given and regulated by the state. For example, the Constitution provides that 'the State creates the conditions necessary to guarantee the equality of its citizens. It educates all people from the earliest age possible in the respect of this principle' (Article 44). Thus, the practice of the right to equality depends on the state's benevolent education. Social and economic rights entail the states' positive duties. The 2022 Law on Protection of Personal Data seeks to 'ensure due respect for personal and family privacy' and to 'regulate the use and effective treatment of personal data and public information' (Article 1). Thus, the Law establishes the state's positive duty in protecting personal data and

[81] Armando Chaguaceda, Djanamé Daubelcour, and Lázaro González, 'Community Participation in Cuba: Experiences from a Popular Council' (2012) 4 Int'l J Cuban Stud 366.

allows the state to use regulatory tools for this purpose. The practice of the right to personal privacy depends on the state's paternalistic duty and regulation. The social-economic rights have generated positive practices such as nationalization of health and education services and free access to high-quality education, including graduate-level university studies, and high-quality health care.[82] Different from social-economic rights, legal establishments of political rights augment the state's power rather than the state's duty. The state regulates political rights for the state interests in socialist development. As one commentator puts it, 'political rights have been limited in a drastic way in Cuba. The government's justification is that they are rights promoted and defended as a strategy to topple the socialist political, economic and social system.'[83] This explains the state's limitation of political rights such as the rights to association, meetings, demonstrations, and freedom of speech and press.[84]

Statist economy: The socialist principle of the statist economy is deeply embodied in Cuban law, particularly the Constitution, business law, and economic law. The Constitution confirms 'a socialist economic system' based on the state's ownership of the fundamental means of production, the planned economy, and the state's direction and regulation of economic activities (Articles 18 and 19). Foreign investment and private businesses (eg self-employment, private restaurants, and private enterprises) are carefully regulated by the state to protect the state's interests in socialist development. The SOEs remain dominant in the economy, although private businesses have been cautiously legalized. The Cuban state adopted several laws to regulate economic activities and resources. The 2019 Fishing Law, for example, seeks to create a regulatory framework for the state to manage and control fishing, based on the conservation and rational use of hydrobiological resources in maritime, fluvial, and lake waters, to contribute to the food sovereignty of the country (Article 1). As the Updating policy does not pursue the transformation into a socialist market economy, the socialist ownership of the means of production and the command economy are preserved and strongly reflected in Cuban law.

IV. ADMINISTRATIVE REFORM

A. Administrative Law Reform

Major legal reforms of the administrative system include the clearer distribution of the executive power, decentralization to local governments, and consolidation

[82] Julio Antonio Fernández Estrada, 'The Ups and Downs of Human Rights in Cuba' Harvard Review of Latin America (22 December 2022) <https://revista.drclas.harvard.edu/the-ups-and-downs-of-human-rights-in-cuba> accessed 7 June 2024.
[83] ibid.
[84] ibid.

of the supervision of the administrative power. These reforms are reflected in the 2019 Constitution and the subsequent related organic laws.

The first important reform is the clearer distribution of executive power. The 2019 Constitution creates the position of prime minister. Subsequently, Law No 134 on the Organization and Operation of the Council of Ministers enacted in 2020 details the power and duty of the prime minister. According to this law, the Council of Ministers, a collegiate body headed by the prime minister (Article 8), is composed of the prime minister, the vice prime ministers, the secretary, the ministers, the minister-president of the Central Bank of Cuba, and the presidents of agencies of the central administration of the state (Article 9). Law No 134 provides that the prime minister is responsible to the NA and to the president of the state (Article 60). Law No 134 empowers the prime minister to, among other things:

> convene and direct the sessions of the Council of Ministers or its Executive Committee;
> control the performance of the activities of the administrative bodies;
> assume, exceptionally and temporarily, the management of any organization of the central state administration;
> give instructions to the provincial governors and control their execution; and
> exceptionally adopt decisions on executive-administrative affairs under the jurisdiction of the Council of Ministers (Article 76).

Thus, the legal reforms tend to individualize the power and accountability of the prime minister. The individualizing of the executive power stems from the need for quicker decision-making and personal accountability in the management of the changing society, including emerging marketization.

Another important reform is decentralization or the transfer of powers from the central government to the local governments. Particularly, the 2019 Constitution creates the framework for the ongoing reforms of territorial decentralization, including reforms strengthening the autonomy of municipal governments.[85] Several laws were then enacted to support decentralization and public participation in governing local affairs.[86] For example, Law No 132 on Organization and Operation of the Assemblies Municipalities of the People's Power and of the Popular Councils guarantees the autonomy of the municipality; includes the election or designation of its authorities; and grants the power to decide on the use of its resources and to issue agreements and necessary regulatory provisions for the exercise of their powers (Article 8). Law No 132 also empowers the Municipal Assembly to approve

[85] Lissette Pérez Hernández, 'The Theoretical and Methodological Framework of Intergovernmental Relations and the Process of Territorial Decentralization in Cuba as an Ongoing Process' (2013) Pub Org Rev 11 (first published online 28 April 2023).
[86] ibid 13.

and control the plan of the economy, the budget, and the comprehensive development plan of the municipality (Article 16). Decentralization reform is induced by the need to strengthen effective management to deal with economic difficulties.

Other reforms of administrative law seek to constrain the arbitrary use of administrative power. These reforms are evident in Law No 134 on Administrative Process (2021), Law No 158 on the Office of the Comptroller General of the Republic of Cuba, and the System of Superior Control of Public Funds and Administrative Management (2022).

Law No 142 empowers citizens to sue administrative agencies and officials for violating their rights and interests. This law allows for judicial review of three types of administrative matters, namely administrative acts, regulatory provisions, and material actions and omissions of administrative functions (Article 1). According to Law No 142 (Article 6), the administrative agencies and individuals subject to administrative litigations are extensive, including:

the Council of Ministers and its Executive Committee;
agencies of the central state administration and their subordinate entities;
national, provincial, or municipal entities and companies that provide public services;
governors of the provincial administration and their subordinate entities;
the councils of the municipal administration and other structures of the municipal Administration.

Law No 142 (Article 35) empowers the courts to decide on the following:

total or partial annulment of regulatory provisions;
annulment of administrative acts;
recognition or restoration of the claimed right;
reparation for damages and compensation for damages;
condemning the public administration;
cessation of material actions contrary to law; and
forced expropriation for reasons of public utility or social interest.

The scope of administrative litigation in Cuba is more extensive than those in China and Vietnam. Particularly, Law No 142 allows judicial review of regulatory provisions having general effects, which is not allowed in China and Vietnam. The implementation of the law remains to be seen.

Law No 158 on the Comptroller General seeks to prevent 'risks, indiscipline, illegalities and manifestations of administrative corruption'.[87] It details constitutional

[87] SAI Internal Editorial Staff, 'The Cuban Parliament Approved the Law of the Comptroller General of the Republic of Cuba and the System of Superior Control of Public Funds and Administrative

rules on the comptroller general. The 2019 Constitution defines the comptroller general as an institution 'to ensure the proper and transparent administration of public funds and the superior monitoring of administrative management' (Article 160). Apart from the constitutional base, Law No 158 allegedly complies with the principles of the UN Convention against Corruption and takes into account the principles of the Lima Declaration on the Basic Guidelines for Auditing and the Mexico Declaration on the Independence of Supreme Audit Institutions.[88] For this purpose, Law No 158 (Article 15) empowers the comptroller general to:

supervise the processes of state budget and check the operation of financial institutions;
supervise and provide methodological advice to the National Audit System, and establish the Cuban audit standards;
supervise the execution of those contractual operations in which the state or a state entity is a debtor or a creditor; and
evaluate foreign trade operations, international cooperation, and business of foreign investment, among others.

In short, Law No 158 aims to ensure legality and transparency in administration of public funds and administrative management.

B. Cuban Socialist Administrative Law

The new administrative laws, despite innovations, reflect features of socialist law, particularly democratic centralism and the instrumental concept of socialist legality.

Cuban bureaucracy is the embodiment of the socialist principle of democratic centralism. As one commentator puts, 'in general, the Cuban system is highly centralized and obscure, which leads to inefficiencies, slows down the decision-making process, and affects the design and implementation of policies'.[89] This centralized administrative system is established by law.

Law No 134 on the Executive is shaped by the principle of democratic centralism. Externally, the Council of Ministers is subordinate to the NA and must

Management' Int'l J Gov Auditing (12 July 2023) <https://intosaijournal.org/the-cuban-parliament-approved-the-law-of-the-comptroller-general-of-the-republic-of-cuba-and-the-system-of-superior-control-of-public-funds-and-administrative-management> accessed 7 June 2024.

[88] ibid.

[89] Tamarys L Bahamonde, 'Cuban Bureaucracy and its Impact on the Economy and Society' (Cuba Capacity Building Project, 11 November 2021) <https://horizontecubano.law.columbia.edu/news/cuban-bureaucracy-and-its-impact> accessed 7 June 2024.

report to the later. Internally, the Council of Ministers is a collegiate body that prioritizes collective decision-making. This institution is called 'Council of Ministers' rather than 'Government', indicating the collective nature of the institution. Law No 134 defines the Council of Ministers as a collegiate body headed by the prime minister (Article 8). Consequently, according to this law, most executive decisions are made collectively by the Council of Ministers (Article 13), although the prime minister enjoys some individual power. In addition, Law No 134 establishes that the Council of Ministers shall function according to rules of 'socialist democracy' (Article 5). Some rules reflect the 'democratic' aspect of democratic centralism such as the people's controlling the activity of their directors and officials, the incorporation of mass and social organizations into government activity, and the freedom of discussion (Article 5). Other rules are the expression of the centralist dimension of democratic centralism such as the binding of the provisions of higher state bodies on the Council of Ministers and the subordination of the minority to the majority rule (Article 5).

Some new administrative laws explicitly confirm the concept of socialist legality. They are an instrument to control the strict compliance of administrative agencies and individuals with the law enacted by top political institutions and leaders. To illustrate, Law No 138 on Organization and Functioning of the Municipal Administration Council provides that the provincial government, its directors, officials, and employees 'have the obligation to strictly comply with socialist legality, ensure their respect in the life of the whole society and act within the limits of their respective competencies the provisions of the law' (Article 7). Law No 138 is an instrument to ensure that municipal government shall strictly observe law promulgated by the central government. In the same vein, Law No 158 on the Comptroller General attempts to 'contribute to compliance with socialist legality' (Article 15). The law is an instrument to control the strict legal compliance in the administration of public funds and administrative management.

V. JUDICIAL REFORM

A. Achievements of Court Reform

In the 1980s, Cuba began to engage in comprehensive reform of the court system following the 1980 retirement of Enrique Hart, who served as the president of the Supreme Court for nineteen years. The Governing Council of the Supreme Court worked closed with the Ministry of Justice to analyse the shortcomings of the court system, including poorly trained judges and inefficient structure and procedures of the courts. In 1990, the new Law No 70 on Courts was enacted, replacing the 1977 law. Law No 77 has revised jurisdictions of the courts, clarified the administration of the courts, and increased access to judicial process. In 1997, Cuba enacted a new Law No 82 on Courts, which replaced Law No 77.[90] In response to the 2019 Constitution, Cuba adopted another new Law No 140 on Courts in 2021, replacing Law No 82. Thus, court reforms require legislative actions. Once measures for judicial reforms were adopted, they were legislated to provide a systematic base for their implementation.

Judicial institutionalization: Reform measures have been introduced to consolidate the institutionalization of the court system. Law No 140 generally retains the court structure established by Law No 82. The court system includes the People's Supreme Court, the popular provincial courts, popular municipal courts, and the military courts (Law No 140, Article 9). The specialization of courts is evident. The People's Supreme Court is comprised of the following specialist chambers:

Chamber for the Protection of Constitutional Rights
Criminal Chamber
Chamber for Crimes against State Security
Civil and Family Chamber
Administrative Chamber
Chamber of Labor and Social Security
Commercial Chamber
Military Chamber (Law No 140, Article 35)

The provincial courts have similar specialist chambers, except the Military Chamber (Law No 140, Article 45). The special Chamber for the Protection of Constitutional Rights is newly introduced in Law No 140 in response to the new provisions on constitutional rights in the 2019 Constitution.

Judicial professionalism: Several reform measures have been implemented to promote professionalism among judges. A reform in 1991 allowed legal professionals to access the judiciary to deal with the shortage of judges. Over 150 lawyers sought judicial positions in 1992. At the same time, the Ministry of Justice introduced competitive examinations for all candidates of judicial positions in the courts.[91] The current law on courts continues to enhance judicial professionalism. Law No 140 establishes 'professionalism' as the guarantee of the judicial functioning, providing that 'judicial personnel are continuously trained and improved; the courts favour the specialization of professional magistrates and judges to raise the quality of their work' (Article 15). Candidates for judges at the Supreme Court and provincial courts must have an academic degree (Law No 140, Article 59). In addition, to be elected as a professional judge of provincial and municipal courts, the candidate must have practiced as a lawyer or have taught in law faculties for

[90] Evenson (n 4) 55.
[91] ibid 58–59.

five years and two years respectively (Law No 140, Article 60). These requirements seek to enhance judicial professionalism.

Judicial independence: Several reform measures have been introduced to support the independence of the courts. Law No 82 in 1997 transferred the administration of the courts from the Ministry of Justice to the Supreme Court, which enhances the Court's autonomy.[92] The law also established the judge's life tenure, which is necessary for judicial independence. In addition, judges are free from Party membership, and in reality, according to a study in 1994, 'a substantial proportion of the professional judges are not members of the Party'.[93] Law No 140 consolidates judicial independence in several ways. It establishes independence as one of the principles of judicial functioning, providing that 'magistrates and judges, in their function of imparting justice, are independent and owe obedience only to the law' (Article 13). Law No 140 prohibits magistrates and judges from receiving instructions or recommendations from other institutions regarding the trial and decision of cases they are hearing (Article 13). Law No 140 also prohibits professional judges, during the exercise of their functions, from performing any other position or employment that entails administrative power or executive function outside the court system, except in the case of teaching, research, or intellectual creation activities that generate copyright, compatible with the judicial function (Article 63). Law No 140 protects the rights of judges to not be transferred from his or her position, suspended, dismissed, or revoked, except in the cases and with the formalities established in this Law; not be detained or prosecuted without the authorization of the Governing Council of the Supreme Court; and to receive the guarantees of due process in disciplinary proceedings (Article 58). The law continues to protect judge's life tenure, providing that professional magistrates and judges are elected with an unlimited term (Article 78). These measures enhance the functional independence of judges.

Judicial review: Cuba is currently the only socialist country to adopt judicial review of constitutionality. In response to the 2019 Constitution's extensive inclusion of new fundamental rights, Law No 153 on the Process for the Protection of Constitutional Rights (2022) empowers citizens to sue state institutions and officials for violating their constitutional rights and to claim damage caused by state institutions and officials due to their improper action or omission of their functions (Article 1). However, the Law excludes the following from judicial constitutional review: claims for disagreement with judicial decisions; the declaration of unconstitutionality of the laws and other normative acts; and claims related to defence and national security, measures taken in exceptional and disaster situations to safeguard independence, the peace, and security of the country (Article 6). Thus, Law

[92] ibid 58.
[93] ibid 59–60.

No 153 does not allow for judicial review of constitutionality of legislation. The law distributes the courts' jurisdictions in handling claims of constitutional violations.

The Supreme Court is competent to hear first-instance cases regarding the claims on violation of constitutional rights (by improper action or omission of functions) by state institutions and officials at the central level, including the NA, the Council of State, the president and vice president of the Republic, the Council of Ministers and the prime minister, their directors, and officials (Article 9). The Supreme Court can also hear appeals on this matter. The provincial courts hear first-instance cases on the claims of violations of constitutional rights by state institutions and officials excluding the ones belonging to the jurisdiction of the People's Supreme Court (Article 10). The implementation of Law No 153 remains to be seen but its enactment suggests the regime's commitment to realizing constitutional rights.

Law No 153 is Cuba's unique contribution to constitutional review. Other socialist countries (namely China, Vietnam, Laos, and North Korea) do not allow judicial review of constitutional claims. Cuba's adoption of judicial constitutional review may be due to the influence of comparative law and constitutional history. Drafters of Law No 153 consulted the experience of this matter in Latin America, Europe, and Cuba's 1940 Constitution, which created the Court of Constitutional and Social Guarantees.[94] Despite a limited scope, Cuba's innovation of judicial constitutional review is an important contribution to comparative constitutional review and may have implications for future development of constitutional review in other socialist countries.

B. Cuban Socialist Courts

The functions and structure of Cuban courts retain socialist features. The courts embody legal instrumentalism, Party vanguardism, and democratic centralism.

Instrumentalism: Like other socialist courts, Cuban courts are an instrument for protecting the state interests and socialist legality. According to Law No 140 (Article 14), the main objectives of the courts include:

(i) enforcing the Constitution and socialist legality;
(ii) safeguarding the economic, social, and political order established in the Constitution, legal certainty, and social discipline;
(iii) protecting the rights and legitimate interests of the people, bodies, agencies and other state entities, political, social, and mass organizations, companies, associations, and other legal entities constituted in accordance with the law;

[94] Mondelo (n 29).

(iv) preventing infringements of the law and antisocial behaviour, and restoring the rule of law provisions when they have been violated;
(v) seeking a harmonious and consensual solution to conflicts;
(vi) promoting the legal culture of people, the conscious and voluntary observance of their duties, and respect for the rules of social coexistence..

Thus, the courts are not merely a judicial institution to resolve legal disputes. Beyond legal functions, the courts are the political tool to maintain the existing socialist regime, to foster the strict compliance with the law (socialist legality), and to promote social duties, social harmony, and the social norms consistent with the socialist objectives.

Party vanguardism: The Party plays a leading role in the judiciary. Although a judge is not required to be a Party member, the judiciary is under the Party's vanguard leadership. At a meeting in 2018, Rubén Remigio Ferro, President of the People's Supreme Court of Cuba, explicitly acknowledged that 'the judges are of the Revolution and of the Party'.[95] The Party can provide guidance for judicial work. To illustrate, Directive 273 (2022) of Cuba's People's Supreme Court states that:

> The top leadership of the Cuban Party and State recently issued several general directives aimed at strengthening the prevention and punishment of crime, corruption, illegalities and social indiscipline significantly affecting the proper functioning of society, calling on the population and the bodies, agencies, entities and organizations in general to increase, each in its field of action, actions to spur and combat this harmful phenomena [sic].[96]

Thus, the Party can issue guidance on the work of the judiciary, which is the judicial embodiment of Party vanguardism.

Democratic centralism: The Cuban courts are also strongly influenced by the principle of democratic centralism. Externally, the courts are subordinate to the legislature. Law No 140 provides that the People's Supreme Court must report to the NA (Article 16). The persistent influence of democratic centralism results in Law No 135's rejection of judicial review of legislation despite the general interests in the protection of constitutional rights. As courts are subordinate to the legislature, they are not allowed to review the constitutionality of legislation. Internally, local courts are under the centralized control of the People's Supreme Court. Through its Governing Council, the People's Supreme Court exercises legislative initiative and regulatory power, makes decisions and rules mandatory for all courts, and

[95] Lucía Alfonso Mirabal, 'Cuban Courts to the Communist Party: "At Your Service"' (*Diario De Cuba*, 7 June 2023) <https://diariodecuba.com/cuba/1686170241_47687.html> accessed 7 June 2024.
[96] Cited in ibid.

issues mandatory instructions to establish uniform judicial interpretation and application of the law (Law No 140, Article 25).

The Governing Council of the People's Supreme Court consists of the president and vice presidents of the Court, and the presidents of the Court's chambers (Law No 140, Article 28). It is a powerful institution to centralize judicial power. The provincial popular courts must report their work to the Governing Council (Law No 140, Article 16). Managers, magistrates and professional judges, lay judges, secretaries, judicial officers, and other court workers must report their work to the Governing Council (Law No 140, Article 17). The Governing Council can issue directives to unify the practice of judicial power, particularly to control the local courts. In practice, jurist Edel González Jiménez, a judge for seventeen years in the province of Villa Clara, states that:

> As long as they are in force, the directives are binding. A supervisory team of the Supreme Court, trained in observing compliance, annually observes, inspects and evaluates compliance. Those who do not comply suffer consequences of various kinds. Individuals may receive demerits or be disciplined. It is not an exaggeration to say that 'badly decided' cases are submitted to the President of the Supreme Court so that he, in accordance with the powers granted to him by the procedural legislation, may immediately order the revision of the sentence and issue a new one in its place, thus protecting the interest of the State that has been undermined.[97]

In short, Cuban courts are essentially socialist courts. The courts do not only have judicial functions but also perform numerous political instrumental functions. The courts are subject to the Party leadership. The court system is under the internal centralized control of the Supreme Court, which in turn is under the external centralized control of the legislature.

VI. LEGAL PROFESSIONAL REFORM

A. The Lawyer System Reform

Background: Cuba has a long history of the legal profession dating back to the colonial age.[98] Following the 1959 Cuban Revolution, the legal profession dramatically declined with many Cuban lawyers leaving the country as the practice of law was considered unnecessary in the 'new sociality' where crime and corruption

[97] ibid.

[98] See generally Gerard J Clark, 'The Legal Profession in Cuba' (2000) 23 Suffolk Transnat'l L Rev 413.

would disappear. In the mid-1960s, the legal profession began to recover to support the institutionalization of the Revolution and the development of the socialist legal system. In 1965, the Ministry of Justice created collective law offices known as *bufetes colectivos*. In 1973, the Law on the Organization of the Judicial System abolished the private practice of law, requiring that all legal services be provided by *bufetes colectivos* and that to practice law a lawyer must join one of the *bufetes colectivos*. In 1974, the National Organization of Bufetes Colectivos (ONBC) was created to organize and supervise the work of collective law offices. Since the 1980s, the lawyer system has been significantly reformed together with other legal system reforms.[99] The legal professional reform is evident in structural, personnel, and functional aspects.

Structural reform: An important structural reform is the strengthening of the independence of the ONBC. Decree-Law No 81 on the Exercise of the Practice of Law and the Organization of the Bufetes Colectivos confirms that 'The ONBC is an autonomous national entity serving social interests and of professional character, with its own judicial personality and property, consisting of jurists who join voluntarily, and governed by the present Decree-Law' (Article 5).[100] Although the ONBC was supervised by the Ministry of Justice, it enjoyed the autonomy to direct its own affairs.[101] Another structural reform is the emergence of new independent law offices. Although independent legal practice was not allowed, since the early 1990s when the government attempted to attract foreign investments, it permitted the formation of new independent legal offices to provide legal services (eg legal work involving registration of foreign firms, contract disputes, intellectual property, and immigration) to foreign investors and tourists.[102]

Personnel reform: A personnel reform is the quantitative development of lawyers. The number of lawyers increased from 634 in 1965 to around 2,000 in 1992.[103] This number remains the same today, according to the ONBC website.[104] Apart from quantitative development, the professional quality of lawyers was also improved. The development of legal education contributes to the professionalization of the lawyer system.[105] In addition, the ONBC has enacted the Code of Ethics, which also contributes to lawyers' professionalism. The Code requires lawyers to remain loyal to their clients and act with independence.[106]

Functional reform: Cuban lawyers are not merely state workers but also perform legal functions: providing legal services to clients. The number of cases handled by

[99] Evenson (n 4) 69–72.
[100] Cited in ibid 73.
[101] ibid 74.
[102] ibid 86.
[103] ibid 81.
[104] Organización Nacional de Bufetes Colectivos <https://portal.onbc.cu>.
[105] Teresa Delgado Vergara, 'Teaching Law in Cuba' (2017) 29 Fla J Int'l L 1.
[106] Clark (n 98) 433.

the ONBC increased from 114,675 in 1980 to 177,015 in 1989.[107] The common cases involved divorces, inheritance, housing matters, and criminal defence.[108] In 2014, lawyers in the *bufetes colectivos* contracted legal services with 300,000 clients.[109] The *bufetes colectivos* provides a wide range of common legal services to individuals on:

(i) civil, administrative, labour, and family matters (eg acknowledgements of marriage, divorces, and liquidation of the matrimonial community of property, and filiation and adoption processes);
(ii) criminal defences; and
(iii) agriculture (eg contractual procedures, economic claims of these entities and their partners, management, appeals, and claims related to inheritance, usufruct, and land tenure).[110]

The *bufetes colectivos* also provide advisory and representation services to state bodies and companies on commercial, economic, financial, banking, and labour matters such as representation in litigation before the Economic Chamber of the People's Courts and the Court of Arbitration of the Chamber of Commerce; advice and representation in economic, commercial, banking, and civil contracts; litigation around copyright violations or claims of rights related to intellectual property, tax matters, and insurance; advice and representation in recognition of rights or litigation in labour matters before administrative instances, justice bodies, and courts.[111] Thus, Cuban lawyers function as legal professionals since they provide common legal services.

B. Cuban Socialist Lawyers

Although Cuban lawyers are now legal professionals, they retain the identity of socialist lawyers. Like other socialist cases, the Cuban lawyer system is still the legal embodiment of legal instrumentalism, vanguardism, and statist rights.

Instrumentalism: Cuban lawyers remain an instrument to protect the state interests. Decree-Law No 81 states that attorneys 'contribute to the realization of justice by means of their observance and strengthening of socialist legality' (Article 2).[112] The *bufetes colectivos* are considered 'Socialism's answer to capitalist law practice

[107] Evenson (n 4) 81.
[108] ibid 81.
[109] Grant and others (n 17) 151.
[110] Organización Nacional de Bufetes Colectivos, 'Asesoría y Representación' <https://portal.onbc.cu/servicio/asesoria-y-representacion>.
[111] ibid.
[112] Cited in Raymond J Michalowski, 'Between Citizens and the Socialist State: The Negotiation of Legal Practice in Socialist Cuba' (1995) 29 Law Soc Rev 79.

and are prized as one of the most distinctive changes in Castro's Cuba.'[113] The abolition of private legal practice and creation of the *bufetes colectivos* 'were to ensure universal public access to legal services and to reshape the practice of law into a system that would place collectivist, socialist goals ahead of the individual goals of attorneys and their clients'.[114] The lawyers working in *bufetes colectivos* therefore cannot merely defend their clients against the state but must also protect the state's interests. A Cuban human rights defender laments that the attorney at the ONBC defends the interest of the state more than those of the clients.[115]

The ONBC itself has the vision to be recognized as an institution that has achieved 'participation in the fundamental activities of the legal, social and economic life of the nation'.[116] The lawyers are more than legal professionals providing legal services to their clients but are expected to contribute to the broader socialist development. The legal instrument creating the ONBC defines the function of this institution as:

> to ease presentation before the courts, to direct the legal profession so that it develops as an assistant in the functioning of the courts and authorities in the realization of the justice of socialist legality . . . to work for the development of legal socialist conscience . . . to raise in its members the spirit of solidarity and internationalism which our revolution practices.[117]

Thus, lawyers are instrumental agents to promote socialist legality and socialist legal ideology.

Vanguardism: The embodiment of Party vanguardism in the lawyer system is evident. The presence of Party members (*militantes*) at law firms allows the Party to supervise the work of lawyers 'to insure [sic] the ideological purity of the work environment'.[118] The possible consequence is that the lawyers do not merely perform professional legal functions; they work as agents to advance Marxist-Leninism, the Party's ideology.

Statist rights: Statist rights are also embodied in the lawyer system. According to one Cuban human rights defender:

> it is very difficult to defend the rights of civil society in Cuba, if the people who can defend them in court are defending the interests of the State. An attorney that

[113] John Carro, 'The Structure of Legal Education and the Practice of Law in Cuba' (1985) 25 Rev Der PR 101.

[114] Michalowski (n 112) 74.

[115] Yanelis Ramírez Cruz, 'The Freedom to Practice Law in Cuba' (Civil Rights Defender, 15 January 2020) <https://crd.org/2020/01/15/the-freedom-to-practice-law-in-cuba> accessed 7 June 2024.

[116] Organización Nacional de Bufetes Colectivos, 'Quiénes Somos' <https://portal.onbc.cu/quienes-somos>.

[117] Resolution No 938 (1978), cited in Clark (n 98) 429.

[118] Clark (n 98) 435.

> cannot or does not want to be part of this organisation [ONBC] will be limited in the exercise of its profession, and in the defence of civil society.[119]

The ONBC, despite its autonomy to deal with its own internal affairs, may operate as the institutional venue for the state to control lawyers to ensure they work for the state and to prevent citizens from using their rights with the support of lawyers to oppose the state.

VII. CONCLUDING ANALYSIS

A. Preservative Intention

Cuban legal reform is a top-down project of the party-state. The legal reform project expresses political intentions to update the legal system while retaining its core socialist features. The project of legal reform is introduced as a part of the broader Updating Socialism policy. The project of legal updating expresses the political elite's intention for systematic and extensive improvement of the formal features and partial change of the substantive features of the socialist legal system. The project of legal updating leads to the rapid enactment of formal law. At the same time, legal updating expresses the commitment to the Revolution, which shapes the limited scope of substantive legal reform. Legal updating does not involve extensive modifications of the socialist legal principles.

B. Legislative Method

Legal updating is undertaken through the formal enactment of legislation. Cuba's NA is the institutional platform for formalizing measures of legal reforms. Reforms of substantive laws were carried out through legislation. Institutional reforms of the administrative and judicial systems also entail legislative enactment. Due to the intention for systematic and extensive reforms of the formal features of the legal system, legal reforms in Cuba involve more new enactments and replacements of legislation than legislative amendments. Constitutional replacement is another factor of legislative replacement and new enactment. New laws are enacted and old laws are replaced to conform with the 2019 Constitution.

[119] Cruz (n 115).

C. Incremental Strategies

From the Special Period to before the enactment of the 2019 Constitution, the Cuban state adopted the classical incremental strategy to introduce some sporadic adjustments to the socialist legal system. Since the 2019 Constitution was adopted, the state has turned to new incrementalism as a strategy for legal reform: the NA adopted systematic plans for legal reforms to be implemented every five years. As the political elites have consensus on basic directions for updating socialism as embodied in the Guidelines and the Conceptualization, they can adopt more systemic plans for legal reforms. In addition, as the 2019 constitutional changes are extensive, legal reforms must be correspondingly systematic. The domination of the Communist Party in the NA enables the legislature to adopt systematic plans for legal reforms. The plans, which anticipate the enactment of many laws, must be implemented incrementally due to the constraints of time and human resources, the unpredictable effects of legal reform, etc.

D. Positive Change

Legal reforms have improved the Cuban socialist legal system. The state is committed to creating a 'socialist state of law'. Cuba has enacted many laws reflecting formal and procedural features of the rule of law. The substantive contents of legislation also reflect human freedom, for example, the protection of vulnerable people in the Family Code. Administrative reforms lead to clearer distribution of the executive power, decentralization to local governments, and consolidation of the supervision of the administrative power. Judicial reforms enhance the institutionalization of the court system, professionalism of judges, judicial independence, and judicial review. The number and professionalism of lawyers increase. Lawyers function as legal professionals providing common legal services.

E. Factors

Cuban legal reform is animated by the internal gap between the existing legal system and the new commitments to updating socialism and building the socialist state of law. Updating socialism requires legal measures. Therefore, legal reforms are carried out to realize the commitments to the Updating Socialism policy. In addition, the new commitment to building the 'socialist state of law' induces legal reforms to institutionalize the state and provide a stable legal framework for the state to manage society. Apart from the internal gap, the external gap between the existing legal system and the changing society and economy triggers legal reform.

For example, when the existing legal framework fails to deal with the expansion of private businesses, reform of business law becomes necessary. Institutional reforms are also animated by societal changes. The social-economic changes as the consequences of the expansion of private businesses generate new social conflicts and legal disputes, which require more effective judiciary to deal with them. The development of lawyers also stems from societal changes. The development of foreign investment, tourism, and the emergence of private businesses create new social demands for legal services, which induces the reforms of the lawyer system. The impact of transnational and comparative law is another factor of Cuban legal reform. This is particularly evident in the Criminal Code and the Family Code, which both draw on transnational legal norms. The adoption of judicial protection of constitutional rights is also in part informed by comparative judicial review. The gap between domestic law and transnational law induces reformers to consult the latter.

F. Continuity of Socialist Law

Due to the preservation of the Revolution, the Cuban legal system remains strongly socialist. The socialist nature of Cuban law is debatable. Some believe that 'Cuba's current legal regime is indeed based on the civil law tradition, but it operates under the broader rubric of a one-party socialist state of workers with a socialist constitution.'[120] Cuba has a long history of civil legal tradition. However, Cuba's current legal system belongs to the socialist legal tradition. The Revolution led to the replacement of the civil legal tradition by the socialist legal tradition in Cuba, and the latter still dominates the country's current legal system. Five key principles of the socialist legal tradition are hegemonic in the Cuban legal system. Law and legal institutions (such as the courts and lawyers) are the instrument for the party-state to pursue socialist development. The law is the expression of the Party's policy, embodying Party vanguardism. Democratic centralism shapes the structures of the bureaucracy and courts. Business law is shaped by domination of the state in the economy, including the state's plan economy, ownership of the means of production, and regulatory power over the economy. Rights are strictly regulated and controlled by the state. The Cuban legal system may have some legal rules and procedures deriving from the civil legal tradition but its ideational foundations are shaped by the socialist legal tradition. Socialist legal principles and ideas provide the normative justifications for the existing Cuban legal system.

[120] Grant and others (n 17) 87

G. Prospects

As Cuba is in the early stage of extensive legal reform, room for future legal reform is spacious. The early stages of legal reforms tend to focus on institutional aspects of the legal system. The future reforms may turn to substantive aspects, especially the enactment of substantive laws to support economic development and deal with social issues arising from economic changes. However, without the transition into a socialist market economy, Cuba would not have comprehensive legal reforms like the cases of China, Vietnam, and Laos.

PART III

COMPARISON AND CONCLUSION

9

Conclusion: Legal Reform, Socialist Law, and Comparative Law

I. INTRODUCTION

The preceding five chapters have explored legal reforms in the five current socialist countries in the last four decades. This chapter generalizes similarities and differences in legal reforms in the five countries. Legal reforms in these countries share common features but their variations are considerable. Five distinctive projects of socialist legal reform are recognizable: exceptional (China), universal (Vietnam), cooperative (Laos), self-reliant (North Korea), and preservative (Cuba). This chapter addresses conceptual implications for understanding the transformative nature of socialist legality and the potential of the rule of law under socialism, and the dynamic of authoritarian law generally, and law and development.

II. COMPARING SOCIALIST LEGAL REFORMS

A. Commonality of Socialist Legal Reforms

1. Top-down Reforms

Legal reform in the five socialist countries (China, Vietnam, Laos, North Korea, and Cuba) over the last four decades is the top-down project of the political elites. The socialist legal reform projects express the political leaders' intentions to improve the existing legal system while retaining its core socialist principles. Although various internal and external actors (domestic jurists, citizens, international experts, and agencies) are involved in the legal reform process, the domestic political elites retain the dominant role in the formation and implementation of legal reform projects. The legal reform projects therefore express the socialist leaders' interests and aspirations. The top-down nature of the socialist legal reforms is determined by the authoritarian nature of the socialist institutional settings in which a single party (the Communist Party) controls key aspects of the legal system, from lawmaking to law enforcement. The socialist legal reform projects are initiated, implemented, and supervised by the Party. The projects therefore express the Party's reformist intention. In some cases, specific aspects of legal

Legal Reform in the Contemporary Socialist World. Ngoc Son Bui, Oxford University Press. © Ngoc Son Bui 2024.
DOI: 10.1093/9780191948053.003.0009

reforms are animated by the bottom-up dynamics of society,[1] but legal reforms generally do not largely reflect the public intention. The rising civil societies in these countries, which occasionally put pressures on legal reforms, do not control but are controlled by the party-state. Therefore, the party-states are not forced to adopt society's reform demands but retain the authoritative power to adopt or reject the demands.

2. *Legislative Method*

Legislation is a powerful method of legal reform in the five socialist countries. Legal reforms involve legislative enactments, amendments, and replacements. The reforms of substantive laws (such as criminal, civil, and business law) involve legislation. Administrative reform, judicial reform, and legal professional reforms are also carried out by legislation. Four socialist countries (namely China, Vietnam, Laos, and North Korea) have even enacted the law on legislation to manage the lawmaking process. Alan Watson writes that 'The course of development of a legal system, I believe, may be influenced to a considerable extent by the nature of the predominant source or sources of the legal rules, whether custom, judicial precedent, juristic doctrine, statute.'[2] Legislation is used as the main method of legal reform because legislation is the predominant source of law in the socialist countries. The prominent role of legislation in the socialist countries is due to jurisprudential and institutional factors. First, socialist jurisprudence is a kind of legal positivism, which underlines the role of codified legal rules in the sources of law. Second, socialist legislature is a supreme power, and hence its statutes play a prominent role in the legal system. Therefore, changes to the socialist legal system must be reflected at a legislative level.

3. *Incremental Strategies*

The socialist leaders adopt incremental strategies in legal forms. Classical incrementalism was a common strategy in the early stages of legal reforms in China, Vietnam, Laos, and Cuba in the 1980s and the 1990s, and in North Korea since the 1980s. Accordingly, these countries adopted sporadic adjustments to the socialist legal system without a coherent plan. At the turn of the twenty-first century, the current socialist countries (except North Korea) turned to the neo-incremental strategy, adopting coherent plans for legal reform to be implemented gradually in five years, a decade, or several decades. The neo-incremental strategy is adopted to consolidate and systematically extend legal reforms. The socialist leaders can adopt a coherent plan for legal reforms thanks to their willingness and institutional

[1] Mark Jia, 'Authoritarian Privacy' (2024) 91 Univ Chic Law Rev (2024) 733 (SSRN) < John Gillespie, 'Localizing Global Competition Law in Vietnam: A Bottom-Up Perspective' (2015) 64 ICLQ 935.

[2] Alan Watson, 'Comparative Law and Legal Change' (1978) 37 Camb Law J 322.

setting. The achievements of sporadic legal reforms render the political elite more willing to move further with bigger but cautious steps. Their willingness to undertake planned reforms is also due to their better understanding of systematic problems of the existing legal system, which cannot be handled by sporadic adjustments. Moreover, systematic reform is shaped by the political elite's intention to integrate the country into the international legal and economic order. The socialist leaders can adopt a systematic plan for legal reform thanks to the institutional setting in which the Communist Party dominates the legislature, which can ensure the political consensus on legal reform.

4. Positive Changes

The implementation of legal reform measures in the last four decades has led to the improvement of the socialist legal systems in the five socialist countries. The socialist legal systems are now basically based on statutory law rather the Party's policy, executive edicts, and personal fiats. Legal structures are more institutionalized with the stable establishment of the bureaucracies, courts, and lawyers. Legal personnel are more professional. Legal institutions and personnel (courts, judges, law firms, and lawyers) perform legal, not merely political, functions. Some administrative laws allow citizens to claim their rights and interests and to constrain administrative actions. The courts can handle legal disputes and lawyers are growing as legal professionals providing common legal services.

5. Factors

Socialist legal reform is animated by the internal gap between the socialist commitments and the existing socialist legal system. Generally, political leaders seek to reform the legal system to realize commitments to building socialism. Specifically, all the five socialist countries attempt to build a socialist rule of law state, which necessarily induces legislative enactments and institutional improvements. Socialist legal reform is also engendered by the discrepancy between the existing socialist legal system and social-economic changes. Particularly, market development creates new social relations, disputes, and problems, which necessitate legal responses. New laws are enacted to deal with new social issues. Existing laws are revised to adjust to the changing economy and society. The administrative system becomes more decentralized to better manage the emerging market relations. The courts become more efficient to deal with legal disputes. Lawyers become more professional to meet the social demands of legal services. Finally, socialist legal reform is driven by the change of the external legal environment. Socialist legal reform is influenced by external legal norms. Particularly, socialist legal reform (except the case of North Korea) is externally influenced by the law and development movement. Socialist elites adjust domestic law to the external legal environment to facilitate better transnational integration and to court foreign investments.

6. *Limited Change*

Legal adaption is an essential factor of the resilience of socialist law and socialist regimes. It involves the adjustment of the socialist legal system to the surrounding environment. Core principles, institutions, and rules of socialist law are maintained but adapted. The socialist states also adopt non-socialist principles, institutions, and rules rooted in comparative law and international law. The consequence is the co-existence of both socialist and non-socialist legal elements in the legal systems of the socialist states. However, the socialist elements remain hegemonic, while the non-socialist elements are peripheral. The socialist legal elements shape the way the non-socialist elements are adopted, understood, and practiced. Therefore, despite reforms leading to the adoption of the non-socialist legal elements, the legal systems in the socialist state remain essentially socialist. At the deep level, socialist legal principles and institutions remain alive.

Instrumentalism continues to dominate the function of law in the five socialist countries. Law and legal institutions remain an instrument for the state to pursue socialist development. The socialist legal system serves the socialist political, social, and economic systems. Law and institutions are used to protect the socialist political regime, to educate citizens to socialist life, and to foster the development of the economy towards socialism.

Party vanguardism continues to shape the legal structure of the five socialist states. The Party leadership penetrates the legal structure through three channels: personnel, institution, and operation. Party leaders hold key posts in the legal structure (leaders of the legislative, executive, and judicial bodies). Party units are set up within legal structural institutions to place the legal institutions under the Party leadership. Finally, the Party issues directions to guide the operation of the legal structural institutions.

Democratic centralism continues to be the constitutional principle for the legal structure. It shapes the external and internal relationship of the legal structural institutions. The legislature, like the Soviets, is located at the top of the legal structure, while the executive and judicial bodies are subordinate to the legislature's supervision. Decisions by the legislature cannot be challenged by the executive and judicial bodies. Within the administrative bodies, decisions by the superiors cannot be challenged by the inferiors. Courts can be functionally independent in some commercial cases but not so in political cases. Structural judicial independence is not accepted. Courts are under the supervision of the representative bodies and do not have the independent power to review the constitutionality of law.

Statist rights continue to shape the substantive contents of public law related to individual rights. Individual rights in the socialist states continue to depend on the state's regulation. Laws related to political and civic rights empower the state to regulate the practice of these rights. Laws related to social, economic, and cultural rights establish the state's positive duties to implement social, economic, and cultural policy.

The statist economy continues to shape substantive contents of private law such as civil, business, and commercial law. The state enacts economic law to regulate the economy. Business and commercial law are shaped by the leading role of the state economic sector in the economy. The state's ownership continues to dominate the property law regime.

The continuity of socialist principles is shaped by both material and intentional factors. First, as there is no fundamental change to the socialist mode of production, there is no fundamental change to the socialist legal identity. When the working class controls means of production through socialist ownership (state ownership and cooperative ownership) and state enterprises, and hence dominates the political power through its Communist Party, the fundamental principles of the socialist legal system remain unchanged.

As the persistence of the socialist mode of production is essential to the persistence of socialist legal principles, the socialist political elites would intentionally use law and legal institutions to consolidate the socialist model of production and prevent the emergence of the capital relations of production. The fundamental law entrenches the socialist state's ownership of means of production and the dominant role of the state economic sectors. Economic law provides the tool for the state to regulate the economy. When private economic sectors become a threat to the socialist model of production, they will be limited or punished.

7. Prospects

Socialist legal reforms are ongoing. Despite reforms, the socialist legal systems retain, to various extents, common shortcomings such as ambiguous and inconsistent legislation, corrupt administration, poor legal enforcement, the deficiency of legal personnels, and the low quality of legal professionals. All five socialist countries are committed to continuing legal reforms to deal with the remaining shortcomings of their legal systems. There is room for continuing legal reform, although it varies between the five countries.

B. Variety of Socialist Legal Reforms

Despite the common features, the political elites in the five countries have different specific intentions for legal reforms, leading to five different socialist legal reform projects: exceptional (China), universal (Vietnam), cooperative (Laos), self-reliant (North Korea), and updating (Cuba). The variety of socialist legal reform projects is shaped by a wide range of internal and external factors: the individual country's historical legal background, culture, religion, level of development, geographic size, population, and international relations.

1. *China's Exceptional Project of Comprehensive Legal Reform*

Legal exceptionalism is the dominant intention shaping the Chinese legal reform project. Chinese political leaders intend to develop a distinctive Chinese legal model as an alternative to Western liberal models. To be sure, the concerns that legal reform must reflect domestic values and local conditions are evident in all five socialist states. However, the exceptional intention is dominant in Chinese legal reform. Among the five countries, China is the biggest country in terms of population and physical size and plays a stronger role in the international order. The size of the country, global power, and extensive experience of legal reforms render Chinese leaders confident to develop China's own legal model.

The Chinese project of legal reform is comprehensive. It seeks to make law to cover all aspects of the society. It also aims to systematically improve structural, functional, and personnel dimensions of the legislature, bureaucracy, courts, law schools, and lawyers. Comprehensive legal reforms involve substantial modifications of fundamental principles of the socialist legal order. The modifications of principles include the distribution of state power, the recognition of market economy (including the institutions of private ownership and private enterprises), and the recognition of human rights. The exceptional intention to create a new distinctive legal model requires comprehensive development of the legal system. In addition, the country's internal openness (the transition from the socialist market economy) and external openness (regional and international integration) enables comprehensive legal reforms in China.

2. *Vietnam's Universal Project of Comprehensive Legal Reform*

In contrast to China's project, the party-state in Vietnam seeks to converge the national legal system with global legal standards, indicating a kind of legal universalism. The country's international integration and the influence of the law and development movement shapes Vietnamese legal universalism. To be sure, legal transplants are the common mechanism for legal reform in other socialist countries, particularly China and Laos. Chinese leaders, however, do not have the attitude to rely on global legal standards for domestic legal reforms. Lao legal reforms rely on external technical assistance but the domestic leaders do not consider universal legal norms as the convergent points.

The Vietnamese project of legal reform is comprehensive. Like that of China, it aims to create a legal framework for all aspects of society and thoroughly improve the legislature, the administrative and the court systems, law schools, and the lawyer system. Comprehensive legal reform in Vietnam also involves significant modifications of socialist legal principles, leading to the adoption of non-socialist institutions, particularly judicial independence, private ownership, private enterprises, and human rights. The comprehensiveness of Vietnamese legal reform stems from universal aspirations. As the party-state attempts to rely on global legal norms as the standards for domestic legal developments, legal reforms must be undertaken systematically in all major aspects of the legal system. Like the case of China, legal reform in Vietnam is comprehensive thanks to the transition from the planned economy into the socialist market economy and the country's deep integration into the regional and international economy.

3. *Laos' Cooperative Project of Comprehensive Legal Reform*

Laos is strongly reliant on external assistance to introduce and implement legal reform measures. Like the case of Vietnam, legal reforms in Laos have been strongly influenced by the law and development movement. However, the political elite intends to cooperate with various sectors of the internal community in technical matters due to cognitive, personal, and financial constraints. Substantively, they do not consider global legal norms as the standards that domestic law must converge with. The prominent role of Buddhism and customary law prevents Laos from legal convergence despite the international cooperation in legal reforms.

Like those of China and Vietnam, Laos' legal reform project is comprehensive. It envisages legislative enactments to all aspects of society and systematically improving the bureaucracy, courts, law schools, and lawyers. The legal reform project also involves modifications of the socialist legal principles, which allows for the adoption of non-socialist institutions such as private ownership, private economic enterprises, and human rights. The fact that Laos has opened up domestically and internationally stipulates its engagement with international agencies to carry out comprehensive legal reforms.

4. *North Korea's Self-Reliant Project of Sporadic Legal Reform*

In contrast to Laos, North Korean leaders intend to rely on internal resources to improve the domestic legal system. The country's isolation and *Juche* ideology shape North Korea's self-reliant intention regarding legal reforms. Consequently, legal reforms in North Korea are mainly sporadic legal innovations without the strong influence of external legal norms. Although there are efforts to promote human rights in North Korea, the country's isolation policy and external sanctions mean the law and development movement almost does not affect North Korea.

Unlike those of China, Vietnam, and Laos, the legal reform project in North Korea is sporadic. It does not attempt to revamp all aspects of the legal system but only occasionally adjust some. The sporadic legal reforms do not involve substantial modifications of the socialist legal principles. As North Korea does not attempt to transit into a socialist market economy and does not open the country internationally, its legal reforms are sporadic.

5. *Cuba's Preservative Project of Extensive Legal Reform*

Cuban legal reform is shaped by the political intention to update socialism while committing to the Revolution. Different from China, Vietnam, and Laos, Cuban political elites do not intend to modify the fundamental principles of the socialist legal system. The principled commitments to socialist values of the Revolution differentiate legal reforms in Cuba from those in other socialist countries. However, to some extent, the legal reform projects in Cuba and North Korea have some common features. Particularly, both countries adhere to the planned economy and deny the transition to a socialist market economy. Therefore, the legal reform projects in Cuba and North Korea only allow for limited development of private economic sectors. Cuba's legal reform project, however, is more extensive and systematic than that of North Korea. Despite extensive legal reform, the denial of systematic change to a socialist market economy prevents Cuba from engaging in comprehensive legal reforms like those in China, Vietnam, and Laos.

III. COMPARATIVE CONCEPTUALIZATIONS

After four decades of legal reforms, the current socialist states are generally not lawless. There are a lot of laws in these states, including North Korea. Legalism therefore remains a useful conceptual model to comprehend the nature and dynamics of legal development in the contemporary socialist world. Some things remain unchanged at the fundamental level of the socialist legal systems: that is, the Marxist-Leninist normative foundations of the socialist legal systems. This indicates the continuity of the socialist legal tradition. Other substantive and institutional aspects of the legal systems change significantly. Socialist legality is transformative: law is used not only to repress but also to support economic and sustainable development, distributive justice, and state building. Beyond the rule *by* law, the rule *of* law is strategically accommodated under socialism to some extent. The experiences of socialist legal reforms have general implications for a dynamic conception of authoritarian law and the distinction of horizontal and vertical law and development.

A. Legal Reform and the Continuity of the Socialist Legal Tradition

In the wake of the fall of socialist regimes in the late 1980s and early 1990s, China, Vietnam, Laos, North Korea, and Cuba have retained their socialist regimes and undertaken legal reforms. In the last four decades, these five countries have continued to reform, not to replace, the socialist legal systems. The normative foundations of the legal systems of these countries are still essentially shaped by Marxist-Leninist principles: the instrumental concept of socialist legality, the vanguard role of the Communist Party, democratic centralism, statist rights, and the state's domination of the economy. Legal reforms in these countries present the adaption rather than replacement of the socialist legal tradition, which remains a living legal tradition and should be re-integrated into mainstream comparative law.

First, the socialist legal tradition rests on a set of Marxist-Leninist legal, political, and economic concepts. Socialist law is underlined by distinctive fundamental ideas and doctrines, which differentiates it from other legal traditions. The ideational foundation of socialist law is rooted in Marxism-Leninism, defined by these distinctive legal, political, and economic concepts: socialist legality, vanguardism, democratic centralism, public ownership of means of productions, and statist rights. These concepts are hegemonic in the socialist legal systems, dominating the lawmaking and legal discourse and practices of politicians, legislators, lawyers, officers, and ordinary citizens.

Second, Marxism-Leninism is embodied in legal institutions, sources of law, and substantive contents of law. A communist party is an integral institution of the socialist legal system. The legislature, the government, and courts are the institutional embodiment of democratic centralism. Legislation and regulation are the main sources of law, embodying the concept of socialist legality. Public ownership shapes substantive contents of civil law and economic law, while citizens' rights regulated by the state inform various aspects of public law.

Third, the legally embodied Marxist-Leninist principles are historically extended. Socialist law was formed in Russia after the Communist Revolution in 1917. Socialist law then diffused to the Soviet Union and East and Central Europe and five other socialist countries: China, Vietnam, Laos, North Korea, and Cuba. Social revolution and diffusion of Soviet law led to legal revolution or the replacement of the preceding civil law tradition by the socialist legal tradition in these five countries. Since the 1980s, these countries have carried out legal reforms but through adaption rather than replacement of the socialist legal tradition, so the core of the socialist legal tradition remains unchanged.

B. Legal Reform and the Transformation of Socialist Legality

The instrumental concept of socialist legality remains dominant in the five socialist states. However, the instrumental nature of socialist legality is transformative. Before legal reform, socialist legality focused on the adherence to law (mainly criminal law) as an instrument to punish enemies of the socialist regimes. The implementation of legal reforms transforms the instrumental nature of socialist legality. In the reform era, law in the socialist countries is used not merely to negatively supress the ruled class, but to positively facilitate social-economic development and state building.[3] Law therefore includes not only public law but also various aspects of private law.

[3] For the case of China, see S Wang, *Law as an Instrument: Sources of Chinese Law for Authoritarian Legality* (CUP 2022).

The transformative concept of socialist legality holds that the instrumental function of law in the socialist states changes from negative repression to positive empowerment. To be sure, the repressive aspect of socialist legality remains. Law such as criminal, criminal procedural, ideology, and administrative punishment law allows violent suppression of opposition. However, many laws in the socialist states seek to pursue positive outcomes. The constitutions and related organic laws consolidate the state power but also facilitate the building of stable state institutions. Civil and business laws aim to support economic development. Laws on natural resources and the environment seek to support sustainable development. Social laws are enacted to distribute welfare to the population, particularly laws protecting and supporting the elderly, women, children, and disabled people.

C. Legal Reform and the Socialist Rule of Law

The rule of law is normally conceived of as an antithesis to communism. For example, Martin Krygier argues that Marxism did not support legal restraints on power but offered 'considerable support to the repressive, ideological and purely instrumental uses of law and the rejection and destruction of the rule of law, which were characteristic of communism'.[4] However, all five socialist countries attempt to create a socialist rule of law state. This poses a conceptual question: how and why is socialist rule of law possible? The adoption of the concept of the rule of law in the five countries is a significant adaption of legal instrumentalism. The socialist rule of law seeks to control the legality of the administrative and judicial agencies. Law is therefore not merely an instrument for the state to control society; it is also a tool for top leaders to control lower authority to ensure the implementation of their developmental laws.

Socialist rule of law does not mean rule by law. In the socialist rule of law framework, law can rule state officials. Yet, the socialist ruling of law has a narrow scope: law rules administrative and judicial agencies. Socialist rule of law does not have space for law to rule lawmakers. There is little room for law to govern legislators. Legislators are not limited by the law made as courts do not have review power. This means legislators can change their law at will, which explains the frequent amendments and replacements of law in the socialist world. In making law, legislators are also not constrained by higher legal principles. Although socialist constitutions lay down principles for lawmaking, these principles are interpreted and applied by the legislators themselves, which means there is little room for higher law to rule top decision-makers.

[4] See eg Martin Krygier, 'Marxism and the Rule of Law: Reflections after the Collapse of Communism' (1990) 15 Law Soc Enq 633.

The socialist rule of law remains instrumentalist. The adherence to law is a means to pursue the state's objectives of social-economic development and ultimately socialism. The instrumental conception of the rule of law is not distinctive to the socialist states.[5] Law and development theories often consider the rule of law the element of social and economic development. However, the distinctive feature of socialist legal instrumentalism is that the rule of law is considered the means for the ultimate goal of socialism.

The socialist states can accommodate the rule of law for strategic reasons. The strategic approach, which has been applied in economics, political science, and more recently legal studies, focuses on rational actors' calculations of costs and benefits of 'potential courses of action'.[6] As David Collier and Deborah L Norden write, 'a strategy is a calculus of behavior adopted to enhance the likelihood of achieving some goal, such as reform or democracy'.[7] Applying the 'strategic-realist approach' in comparative constitutional inquiry, Ran Hirschil argues that 'The quest to increase benefits and lower risks and costs—most notably by enhancing regime legitimacy and stature, promoting centralization and fostering nation-building or locking in a certain set of contested worldviews and policy preferences-is a major determinant of constitutionalization.'[8]

The strategic accounts are particularly relevant to socialist regimes where law and politics are indistinguishable. The socialist regimes that survived the fall of the Berlin Wall are dynamic enough to adjust themselves to the changing world, which explains their resilience.[9] Nowadays, they have been operating under domestic and international milieus substantively different from the Soviet era. Domestically, they have to consolidate the sociological base of legitimacy by their actual performance, and economic development is a key concern. The accommodation of some forms of the rule of law can benefit economic development and enhance the socialist elite's legitimacy. Moreover, the socialist states also need to build state institutions, which is instrumental to their consolidated power and legitimacy, because powers that are institutionalized can become stronger and more legitimate than personalized powers. Some forms of the rule of law can also be used for these institutional purposes. Internationally, the socialist countries (except North Korea) have actively integrated politically and economically into the global order. To acclimatize to the changing world, the socialist states have been compelled to adapt their ideology, institutions, economy, and law by, among other

[5] BZ Tamanaha, *Law as a Means to an End: Threat to the Rule of Law* (CUP 2006).

[6] Ozan O Varol, 'Stealth Authoritarianism' (2015) Iowa Law Rev 1673, 1718.

[7] David Collier and Deborah L Norden, 'Strategic Choice Models of Political Change in Latin America' (1992) 24 Comp Pol, 229, 230.

[8] Ran Hirschl, *Comparative Matters: The Renaissance of Comparative Constitutional Law* (OUP 2014) 175.

[9] For ideological, institutional, and economic adaption in communist regimes, see generally MK Dimitrov (ed), *Why Communism Did Not Collapse: Understanding Authoritarian Regime Resilience in Asia and Europe* (CUP 2013).

things, accommodating some forms of the rule of law familiar with the global community to gain more international legitimacy, which in turn can also consolidate domestic legitimacy.

But the socialist regimes have been confronted with a dilemma. On one hand, the rule of law has the potential to ruin the socialist regimes. On the other hand, these regimes have to be dynamic enough to be resilient by, among other things, accommodating some forms of the rule of law. The solution for this is to adopt some realistic strategies for legal reform. These strategies must guarantee the hegemony of communist rule and the accommodation of the rule of law at the same time. The rule of law is accommodated to the extent that it will not substantively challenge the existing socialist regimes. To achieve this, the socialist regimes adopt differential and partial strategies of legal reform: the rule of law can only be achieved differentially and partially. By this, legality under socialist regimes is transformative, not revolutionary. The comprehensive practice of the rule of law (with the substantive adoption and practice of judicial review, judicial independence, the separation of power, multi-party system, free elections, and civil-political rights) will damage the socialist regime, for which this is impossible. But the 'partial form of the rule of law', as Wang Yuhua argues in the context of China,[10] is a legal reform, not legal revolution, for which this is possible.

The 'differential' strategy means that the socialist regimes have different approaches to different types of and the application of the rule of law in different areas of society. This resonates with Albert Chen's argument.[11] First, the socialist regimes practice different types of the rule of law but would give priority to the types that are more instrumental to their legitimacy and less damaging to the existent regimes. This explains their prioritization of the formalist type of the rule of law. Second, within a single type, the rule of law is applied differently in different realms. As Wang's study suggests, the Chinese government can accommodate the (legal process) rule of law in the commercial realm but not in the political realm.[12] However, this differential approach is not limited to the procedural rule of law. On the substantive rule of law, the socialist governments may have different strategies for different substances of law. For example, they can accommodate more social-economic rights than civil-political rights, as the former can consolidate the sociological foundation of the political legitimacy, while the latter would open the door for the citizens to challenge the existing regime. To illustrate, the freedom to do business is more accommodated than the freedom of speech and expression.

[10] Y Wang, *Tying the Autocrat's Hands: The Rise of The Rule of Law in China* (CUP 2014)18.

[11] Albert Chen, 'China's Long March toward Rule of Law' or China's Turn Against Law?' 4 Chinese J Comp Law 30 (2016).

[12] Wang (n 10) 3.

D. Legal Reform and the Dynamics of Authoritarian Law

Socialist law and its reforms have a broader implication for a dynamic conception of authoritarian law. Comparative authoritarian law is predominantly shaped by instrumentalism, although there are various instrumental conceptions.[13] Legal instrumentalism holds that authoritarian law serves authoritarian leaders' interests (eg regime security, social order, economic development, state capacity, and domestic and international legitimacy).[14] Behind instrumentalism is the rationalist assumption that authoritarian elites are capable of calculating costs and benefits and making choices. Instrumentalism remains a useful approach to authoritarian law, including socialist law. Authoritarian states adhere to legality for the outcomes external to the legal system. The outcomes are therefore not legal but social, political, and economic: regime resilience, social stability, and economic development. This book indicates that law is an instrument for the socialist states to pursue state interests, consistent with the institutional accounts of authoritarian law elsewhere.

However, legal instrumentalism can take a more dynamic approach. Dynamic legal instrumentalism holds that authoritarian law is a means for the external outcomes, but the elite calculation of the outcomes is constrained by the change of authoritarian law, state interests, elites, and society. Dynamic legal instrumentalism perceives authoritarian law as a changing process. Authoritarian legal change includes both negative (legal regress) and positive (legal reform) change. These changes may happen at the same time and compete with each other. Dynamic legal instrumentalism also considers the dynamic interests of the authoritarian states. The state interests in promoting authoritarian law may change overtime. When the achievements of economic development reach a certain level, authoritarian leaders may prioritize regime security and social stability over economic development. Dynamic legal instrumentalism takes into account dynamic authoritarian elites. Authoritarian leaders may be replaced; their interests might be conflicting; they may be challenged by officials. Finally, dynamic instrumentalism considers the dynamics of the society. The emergence of new social classes, their public discourse, and their social activism may challenge the authoritarian elites' instrumental use of law and legal institutions. Once law and legal institutions are available, citizens may give them normative internal values that might compete with the state's external expectations. The dynamics of authoritarian law, state interests, political elites, and society may complicate the instrumental function of authoritarian law. Authoritarian leaders could miscalculate the interests and the consequences. Law

[13] For a survey of various instrumental approaches (eg law and order, law and discipline, rule by law) to authoritarian law (particularly China), see Donald Clarke, 'Order and Law in China' (2022) 2022 U Ill L Rev 555–58.

[14] J Delisle, 'Authoritarian Legality in East Asia: What, Why, and Whither?' in Weitseng Chen and Hualing Fu (eds), *Authoritarian Legality in Asia: Formation, Development and Transition* (CUP 2020) 25.

may not generate the external outcomes they expect: instead, it may generate those they do not expect. Consequently, authoritarian elites' use of law is not always unlimited. The reform dynamics under authoritarian regimes create the space for both systematic rule by law and sporadic rule of law.

E. Legal Reform, Law, and Development

All the five countries seek to reform their laws to support social and economic development. The law and development movement strongly influences legal reforms in China, Vietnam, Laos, and Cuba. The socialist experiences of legal reform have general conceptual implications for law and development.

Marketization and democratization in the developing world have triggered the international movement of law and development.[15] This refers to the movement in which national, transnational, and international agencies undertake a set of practices to promote legal reforms as a tool to foster political and economic reforms in developing countries.[16] The movement rests on the assumption that market regimes and government require legal underpinnings.[17] Law and development normally took the form of diffusing Western legal institutions and codes into developing countries.[18] 'Developing countries' refers to 'countries with, relatively speaking, low per capita incomes, low rates of labor productivity, and large segments of their populations engaged in agriculture',[19] or third-world countries that 'have not yet achieved, but generally aspire to, self-sustaining economic growth'.[20]

How do external actors promote international and comparative law norms in the domestic legal system of a developing country? Drawing on Goodman and Jinks' diffusion theorizing model, three corresponding mechanisms of law and development can be identified: inductive, persuasive, and acculturative.[21]

[15] Amy L Chua, 'Markets, Democracy, and Ethnicity: Toward a New Paradigm for Law and Development' (1998) 108 Yale LJ 1, 4.

[16] ibid 11–13. See also Benjamin van Rooij and Pip Nicholson, 'Inflationary Trends in Law and Development' (2013) 24 Duke J Comp Int'l L 297 Kevin E Davis and Michael J Trebilcock, 'The Relationship between Law and Development: Optimists versus Skeptics' (2008) 56 Am J Comp L 895; Yong-Shik Lee, 'General Theory of Law and Development' (2017) 50 Cornell Int'l LJ 415; John KM Ohnesorge, 'Developing Development Theory: Law and Development Orthodoxies and the Northeast Asian Experience' (2007) 28 U Pa J Int'l Econ L 219.

[17] Brian Z Tamanaha, 'The Primacy of Society and the Failures of Law and Development' (2011) 44 Cornell Int'l LJ 209, 210.

[18] ibid 211. For a recent case study, see Connor Vignali Steelberg, 'Late Development and the Private Sector: A Perspective on Public-Private Partnerships in Vietnam' (2021) 59 Colum J Transnat'l L 726.

[19] Chua (n 15) 10–11.

[20] David M Trubek, 'Toward a Social Theory of Law: An Essay on the Study of Law and Development' (1972) 82 Yale LJ 1, 2.

[21] Ryan Goodman and Derek Jinks, *Socializing States: Promoting Human Rights through International Law* (OUP 2013) 21–25.

Diffusion theories have been developed in various intellectual traditions to explain the global spread of institutions, policy, and legal norms, including norms of international law.[22] In their sophisticated study, Ryan Goodman and Derek Jinks provide a useful distinction of the aforementioned mechanisms of international human rights law diffusion: material inducement, persuasion, and acculturation.[23] *Material inducement* refers to the mechanism 'whereby states and institutions influence the behavior of other states by increasing the benefits of conformity or the costs of nonconformity through material rewards and punishments'.[24] *Persuasion* is the process whereby 'target actors are convinced of the truth, validity, or appropriateness of a norm, belief, or practice', and it occurs when 'the practices of actors are influenced through processes of social "learning" and other forms of information conveyance that occur in exchanges within international organizations and transnational networks'.[25] *Acculturation*, or socialization, 'is the process by which actors adopt the beliefs and behavioral patterns of the surrounding culture, without actively assessing either the merits of those beliefs and behaviors or the material costs and benefits of conforming to them'.[26] Drawing on a range of empirical evidence, Goodman and Jinks argue that acculturation, rather than material inducement and persuasion, accounts for the diffusion of human rights norms.[27]

1. *Inducive Law and Development*

Inductive law and development refers to a mechanism whereby a state or institution impels another state to comply with external legal norms to foster domestic law reform and societal change. The base of this inductive influence is material interests such as the access to development aids or the transnational market. This form of inducive law and development is material conditionality. Material conditionality can be positive or negative.[28] Positive conditionality means the external actor rewards the host country with material benefits for its national law's compliance with the external legal norms.[29] Negative conditionality means the external actors sanction the host country through withdrawal or restrictions of material benefits for its national law's failure to comply with the external legal norms.[30] As

[22] See eg Zachary Elkins, Tom Ginsburg, and Beth Simmons, 'Getting to Rights: Treaty Ratification, Constitutional Convergence, and Human Rights Practice' (2013) 54 Harv Int'l LJ 61, 63, 66 (2013) (discussing authors who have examined the diffusion theory); BA Simmons, F Dobbin, and G Garrett (eds), *The Global Diffusion of Markets and Democracy* (CUP 2008).

[23] Goodman and Jinks (n 21).

[24] ibid 22.

[25] ibid 22–24.

[26] ibid 22.

[27] ibid 28.

[28] F Schimmelfennig, 'A Comparison of the Rule of Law Promotion Policies of Major Western Powers' in Michael Zurn, Andre Nollkaemper, and Randy Peerenboom (eds), *Rule of Law Dynamics: In an Era of International and Transnational Governance* (CUP 2012) 111.

[29] ibid 123.

[30] ibid.

a result, the host country may integrate some external legal norms in some parts of its legal system, leading to the formal convergence between the host county's national law and the external legal norms.

2. Persuasive Law and Development

Persuasive law and development refers to the process whereby a state or institution propels another state to accept external legal norms to foster domestic law reform and societal change. Different from the inducive model, the base for persuasive influence is not the incentives of material interests but the normative appealing of the substantive contents of the external legal norms. Through learning forms—such as 'legal technical assistance',[31] scholarships for overseas study, exchange of legal information, or best legal practices—the external actors try to convince the host country about the normative values and correctness of the external legal norms. If the host country is persuaded by the values of the external legal norms, it may internalize them. The legal internalization driven by persuasion will lead to functional convergence: the external legal norms are not merely adopted in the host country's formal law but are also embedded in its legal practice.

3. Acculturative Law and Development

The process whereby a state or institution compels another state to conform to the surrounding legal culture to foster domestic law reform and societal change is acculturative law and development. The base for this acculturative influence is not material interests or normative values but the social relationship between the host country and the external surrounding community.[32] Through dialogic forms such as transnational human rights or judicial dialogue[33] the external actors propel the host country towards a surrounding legal culture—ways of legal behaviours and attitudes about certain legal norms—adopted by the external actor and the larger international community. This may lead to social convergence: the host country may adopt certain legal behaviours and attitudes in order to be recognized by the surrounding community. This social convergence can boost the international legitimacy of the host country's legal and societal development.

The three models of law and development are drawn on but complicate Goodman and Jinks' diffusion theory. First, this study situates Goodman and Jinks' diffusion theory within the context of law and development. While Goodman and Jinks provide a useful framework, they have not yet substantively accounted for the function of international law diffusion in fostering legal reform and socio-economic development in developing countries. This study suggests a functional

[31] Rooij and Nicholson (n 16), 299.
[32] Goodman and Jinks (n 22), 26.
[33] Anne-Marie Slaughter, 'A Global Community of Courts' (2003) 44 Harv Int'l LJ 191.

connection between international law diffusion and legal and societal change in the developing world.

Second, while Goodman and Jinks' theory focuses on the diffusion of international human rights law, this triple construction of law and development expands to international legal norms generally and is not limited to human rights law. Although human rights normally feature law and development projects, development agencies have broader concerns of legal reforms beyond human rights law, including, for example, reforms of business and labour law. In addition, in the developing country's legal needs, laws for development include not only laws for the protection of human rights but also laws for the promotion of the market (business law), state building (constitutional and administrative law), and social welfare (social law).

Third, while Goodman and Jinks focus on acculturation as the main diffusion mechanism, this triple construction of law and development is more holistic. Acculturation might work prominently in the area of international human rights law where enforcement relies mainly on the state's voluntary acceptance of international norms. However, acculturation alone may not explain why international legal norms can be diffused through trade agreements. Emilie M Hafner-Burton argues in an empirical study that preferential trade agreements, rather than human rights agreements, are more effective in changing the repressive behaviours towards respecting fundamental norms of human rights.[34] As opposed to human rights agreements (a kind of soft law influenced through persuasion), preferential trade agreements (a kind of hard law requiring legally enforceable binding obligations) 'influence through coercion: [preferential trade agreements] provide member governments with a mandate to protect certain human rights, while they supply the material benefits and institutional structures to reward and punish members' behavior'.[35] This coercive mechanism is consistent with Goodman and Jinks' concept of material inducement. Hafner-Burton's account, however, tends to be dichotomous.

From a holistic perspective, I contend that vertical law and development is mainly driven by the inducive mechanism, and the other two mechanisms are supplemental. Inducive law and development can be horizontal and vertical. In the *horizontal model*, the states or institutions directly impose external legal norms into domestic legal systems. The case of Japan's post-war Constitution imposed by General Douglas MacArthur provides a textbook example.[36] In the *vertical model* of inducive law and development, the states or institutions integrate norms of public international law (such as human rights, labour, and environmental

[34] EM Hafner-Burton, 'Trading Human Rights: How Preferential Trade Agreements Influence Government Repression' (2005) 59 Int'l Org 593, 595.
[35] ibid.
[36] For imposed constitutions generally, see Richard Albert, Xenophon Contiades, and Alkmene Fotiadou (eds), *The Law and Legitimacy of Imposed Constitutions* (Routledge 2019).

standards) into international economic law (eg trade agreements), which may lead to their adoption in the national legal system of another state. International economic law mainly induces government's compliance with international law norms through material sanction and reward. However, it may supplement mechanisms to convince the government to accept the validity of international law norms, and to put pressure on the government to adopt the surrounding behavioural legal patterns. Therefore, vertical law and development is principally inducive but partially persuasive and acculturative.

Much of the law and development scholarship has explored the horizontal dimension or the donors' direct involvement in promotion of legal reforms in developing countries.[37] External donors have provided financial supports for legal reforms in China, Vietnam, Laos, and Cuba. Apart from horizontal law and development, the case of EU promotion of legal reforms in Vietnam through the EU–Vietnam free trade agreement provides the experience to theorize about a model of vertical law and development.[38] Vertical law and development is defined as the process whereby a state or institution integrates norms of public international law into international economic law, which may then be adopted in the legal system of another state to facilitate domestic law reform and societal change. The mechanisms to diffuse international legal norms vertically are mainly inducive through material conditionality but partially persuasive and acculturative through learning and dialogue respectively.

The concept of vertical law and development is connected to the rich body of scholarship on transnational law, transnational legal order, and transnational legal process.[39] Particularly, this conceptualization of vertical law and development builds from Yale Law Professor Harold Hongju Koh's concept of transnational legal process, defined as 'the process whereby an international law rule is interpreted through the interaction of transnational actors in a variety of law-declaring fora, then internationalized into a nation's domestic legal system'.[40] Koh distinguishes 'horizontal' or the state-to-state level of the transnational legal process from 'the mechanisms of 'vertical domestication', whereby international law norms 'trickle down' and become incorporated into domestic legal system'.[41] Drawing

[37] S Humphreys, *Theatre of the Rule of Law: Transnational Legal Intervention in Theory and Practice* (CUP 2010); John Gillespie and Pip Nicholson (eds), *Law and Development and the Global Discourses of Legal Transfers* (CUP 2012).

[38] For other experiences, see Matthew S Erie, 'Chinese Law and Development' (2021) 62 Harv Int'l LJ 51; Simon Butt, 'Intellectual Property in Indonesia: A Problematic Legal Transplant' (2002) 24 EIPR 249 (noting that Indonesia reformed intellectual property law in line with the World Trade Organization's [WTO] Trade Related Aspects of Intellectual Property [TRIPs] Agreement).

[39] See generally PC Zumbansen (ed), *Oxford Handbook of Transnational Law* (OUP 2020); TC Halliday and G Shaffer (eds), *Transnational Legal Orders* (CUP 2015); Gregory Shaffer, 'Transnational Legal Process and State Change' (2012) 37 Law Soc Inq 229.

[40] Harold Hongju Koh, 'The 1998 Frankel Lecture: Bringing International Law Home' (1998) 35 Hous L Rev 623, 629.

[41] ibid 626–27.

on the latter, I define vertical law and development as a transnational legal process whereby a state or institution integrates norms of public international law into international economic law, which may then be adopted in the national legal system of another state to facilitate domestic law reform and societal change.

Vertical law and development contain Koh's four features of transnational legal process: non-traditional, non-statist, dynamic, and normative.[42] The following paragraphs elaborate these features but within the context of vertical law and development and with a focus on the conceptual level.

First, as a transnational legal process, vertical law and development is *non-traditional* in the sense that it departs from the binary distinction between international and national law and the distinction of different areas of international law.[43] Vertical law and development prompts international law as a part of national law. In vertical law and development, international economic law is used as a tool to diffuse norms of public international law in domestic legal systems. In other words, public international law is integrated into international economic law. Vertical law and development is also non-traditional in that it departs from the conventional scholarship of law and development, which focuses on horizontal, direct state-to-state legal transplant processes. In addition, the concept of vertical law and development departs from the traditional prescriptive and evaluative accounts of law and development. It does not ask how law should be reformed to facilitate development, or how law and development projects are successful or unsuccessful. Rather, vertical law and development is an exploratory and explanatory concept. It tries to explore and explain how and why international law norms are integrated into international economic law to foster national legal and societal development.

Second, vertical law and development is *non-statist.*[44] To be sure, a state (eg the United States) may integrate international law norms into its trade agreements with developing countries to foster national legal and socio-economic development. However, beyond nation states, transnational actors (such as the European Union) and private actors (eg national and transnational civil societies and enterprises) may engage in mobilizing for the application of international norms in domestic legal systems.

Third, vertical law and development is *dynamic.*[45] This process involves numerous interactions of multiple transnational and national actors. The interactive fora can be formal (such as legislative sessions and negotiation meetings) and informal (such as the mobilization of the transnational and national civil societies, and the exchange of information between the development agencies and the host country). The consequence of vertical law and development is nonlinear.

[42] Harold Hongju Koh, 'Transnational Legal Process' (1996) 75 Neb L Rev 181, 184.
[43] ibid.
[44] ibid.
[45] ibid.

International law norms may not be merely copied but adopted, adapted, and resisted in national legal systems. Even when international law norms are integrated into formal national law, this does not mean they are internalized in domestic legal practice. While a developing country may adopt an international law norm in its national legal system, the actual implementation of the norm depends on a range of contextual, dynamic factors such as the host country's interests, its capacity for law enforcement, local legal culture, and the engagement of the civil societies.

Fourth, vertical law and development is *normative*.[46] It is normative in two senses: legal and developmental. In the first instance, international law norms are diffused into domestic legal systems to facilitate domestic legal reform (eg adopting new laws, revising the existing laws, creating new legal institutions, or adjusting the existing legal institutions). Vertical law and development aspire to modernize the law of the developing world according to international legal standards. In the second aspect, vertical law and development aims to foster domestic societal development (meaning political, social, and economic transformation) in the developing world. The developmental normativity is connected to the preceding legal normativity. Vertical law and development are premised on the assumption that societal development requires national legal development according to international legal standards.

The concept of vertical law and development is built from and can enrich Koh's transnational legal process theory. The concept situates the transnational legal process within the developmental context. Transnational legal processes can occur in both developed and developing countries. Koh's theory focuses more on developed countries (particularly the United States), and therefore the normative feature of the transnational legal process in his theory is predominantly legal. In the context of developing countries, the normative developmental feature of the transnational legal process is particularly prominent. Transnational legal process theory should pay more attention to the developmental normativity of the transnational legal process.

[46] ibid.

Index

For the benefit of digital users, indexed terms that span two pages (e.g., 52–53) may, on occasion, appear on only one of those pages.

Tables are indicated by an italic *t* following the page number.